KEITH RICHARDS

SATISFACTION

KEITH RICHARDS

SATISFACTION

Christopher Sandford

CARROLL & GRAF PUBLISHERS
NEW YORK

Keith Richards
Satisfaction

Carroll & Graf Publishers
An Imprint of Avalon Publishing Group Inc.
245 West 17th Street, 11th Floor
New York, NY 10011

First Carroll & Graf edition 2004

Library of Congress Cataloging-in-Publication Data is available.

ISBN: 0-7867-1368-2

Printed in the United States of America
Distributed by Publishers Group West

To Nicholas

CONTENTS

AUTHOR'S NOTE

Whatever else, my research for this book goes back about thirty-five years. Around 1968 I developed a passion, later tapering into a sort of respect, for Keith Richards, and I've squirrelled away the notes ever since. I interviewed over 200 sources. My own angle, for what it's worth, remains that of a critical fan; as well as his series of narrow escapes, Keith, it seems to me, has also been responsible for some of the most thrilling noises to emerge from rock's first half-century. I met him at his English home in February 1977, and have enjoyed one or two Stones 'VIP' passes in the years since. That said, I should make it crystal clear that the book you're holding isn't authorised by its subject.

For better flow, please note that I've referred to 'Keith Richards' not 'Richard' (his stage name from 1963 to 1978) throughout.

ACKNOWLEDGEMENTS

After handing in *Springsteen*: *Point Blank* a few years ago, I promised never to write another rock biography. This is it.

More than once while researching *Satisfaction*, I was reminded of Keith Richards' quote protesting 'I got nothing to hide. Nothing's a state secret with me.' Open, then, but not necessarily accessible to the jobbing author. Several of Keith's friends I approached for interviews told me that, 'after checking', they'd prefer not to talk. One or two took the opportunity to vent at me. It crossed my mind that this book might well spell the end of my Rolling Stones VIP passes, and so it's proved. For the record, it was written by someone sympathetic, or much more, to its subject; hopefully, some of that came through to the 200 or so people who did speak to me. I'm extremely grateful for their time and their nerve.

For recollections, input or advice I should thank, institutionally: Abacus, the American Clinic (Tarn), ASCAP, *Billboard*, Blue Lena, Book Mail, the British Library, British Newspaper Library, Chapters, Companies House, Dartford Borough Council, Dartford *Chronicle*, FBI, Focus Fine Arts, gimme shelter, the Gulf Beach Motel, Helter Skelter, HM Prison Service, City of Lausanne, *Loaded*, Main Offender, Maltese Falcon, Multimap, Performing Right Society, Public Records Office, Rock and Roll Hall of Fame, Rolling Stone.com, RN Officers Club, Seattle Public Library, *Seattle Times*, the *Spirit* (the Brian Jones fan club), State of California, the *Sunday Times, The Times*, City of Toronto, Toronto *Star*, Tower Records, UK Family Records Centre, US Embassy, London, Vital Records, *Vogue*, www.Keithrichards.com.

Professionally: Dick Allen, Luciano Amore, Jan Andres, the late Walter Annenberg, Jeffrey Archer, the late Hal Ashby, Mike Atwood, Bob Beckwith, Ross Benson, Jonathan Boyd, Ben Brierley, Gary Brooker, the late William Burroughs, Lorna Chapman, Noel Chelberg, Allan Clarke, Andrew Dellow, Mike Dent, the late John Diefenbaker, the late Lonnie Donegan, Alan Edwards, Tony Edwards, Josh Epstein, Alan Etherington, the late Adam Faith, Chris Farlowe, Zach Fjestad, Judy Flanders, Charlie Gillett, Lynn Goldsmith, Nick Gough, Ryan Grice, Jeff Griffin, Bob Harris, Roger Hayes, Dick Heckstall-Smith, Gill Hickman, Peter Holland, Walter Isaacs, David Jacobs, Ronnie Jacobson, the Jaggers, Lorraine Jerram, Norman Jewison, Paul Jones, Lenny Kaye, Edith Keep, Alan Kennington, Joan Keylock, Tom Keylock, the late Alexis Korner, Donovan Leitch, Juliana Lessa, Barbara Levy, Carlo Little, Nick Lowe, Robin Medley, Nick Miles, Hugh O'Neill, Paul Ovenden, Chris Page, Graham Parker, Andy Peebles, Wayne Perkins, Bill Plummer, Terry Reid, Tim Rice, Cliff Richard, Julia Richards, Mike Richards, Clive Robson, Sandie Shaw, Don Short, Ron Simms, David Sinclair, Tony Smith, Gill Snow, Winston Stagers, Walter Stern, Robert Stigwood, Lindsay Symons, Don Taylor, the late Frank Thorogood, Rob Townsend, the Villars, Lisbeth Vogl, Rick Wakeman, David Waldman (formerly Coroner for East Sussex), Carol Ward, Adele Warlow, Mark White, Tony Yeo.

And socially: Ammanuel, Pete Barnes, Ray Bates, Benaroya Hall, Hilary and Robert Bruce, Albert Clinton, *Cricketer International*, Cricketers Club of London, Monty Dennison, the late John Dowdall, the Dungees, Lorraine Esterling, Mary Evans, Fairmont Waterfront Hotel, Malcolm Galfe, the Gay Hussar, James Graham, Griffins, Richard Hill, Amy Hostetter, Jarvis/Lyzcinski, Tom Keylock, Kinko's, LA Frames, Joan Lambert, Terry Lambert, Belinda Lawson, Brooke Little, Richard Lloyd-Roberts, Vince Lorimer, Lee Mattson, Jim Meyersahm, Sheila Mohn, the Morgans, John Murray, National Gallery room 34, Chuck Ogmund, Phil Oppenheim, Robin Parish, Peter Perchard, Chris Pickrell, the Prins family, Amanda Ripley, Malcolm Robinson, Debbie Saks, Alan Samson, Delia Sandford, Karen Sandford, my son Nicholas Sandford, Sefton Sandford, Sue Sandford, Peter Scaramanga, Seattle CC, Fred and Cindy Smith, Sportspages, the Stanleys, Subway 49902, Jack Surendranath, Fred Titmus, Ben and Mary Tyvand, William Underhill, Derek Underwood, Von's, Jim Wheal, Craig Whitworth, the Willis Flemings, Tom Wolfe, Betty Wolstenholme.

Thanks, Fields family.

C.S.
2003

'God's in the star, the stone, the flesh, the soul, and the clod'
Robert Browning

'I don't regret nothin'!'
Keith Richards

1

Connection

TO GET TO THE CENTRE OF LONDON FROM DARTFORD, JUST DOWN THE OLD DOODLEBUG ALLEY, TAKES ABOUT THIRTY MINUTES BY TRAIN; TO FORGET THE DEADLINESS OF THE PLACE HAS TAKEN KEITH RICHARDS MOST OF HIS LIFETIME. A twee little town at heart, it succumbed to several layers of later ugliness. Keith was born there on 18 December 1943. In those days, from the top of Chastilian Road, you could see the northern sky lit up by firebombs and, crossing over Watling Street, the smouldering craters blasted into Slade marshes. In summer the Dartford estuary sent up a thick reek, blitzed-out houses standing beside salt bogs which bubbled and stank. On bad winter nights the river froze solid and the cold seemed to have the pygmy's power of shrinking skin. In short, it was the kind of place that teaches a boy to be practical while it forces him to dream of other, headier options. After 1962, when he stormed out of his parents' council house, Keith didn't return to Dartford officially until Christmas 1983, when he appeared there in a red stretch limo accompanied by his new wife.

That visit seemed to unleash something in Keith. For reasons both pragmatic and sentimental – some part of him clearly missed the joint – he'd drive back more and more often in his forties and fifties. In turn Dartford and various local boroughs took the opportunity to plaster his name, sometimes without him even knowing it, on everything from an allotment to a garage and, the capstone of this phase of his career, a miniature bowling rink. Keith perhaps forgot that he'd once called Dartford the arsehole of Britain.

In 1953, Keith's mother Doris had begun taking him on his first visits to London, which was still flattened by bomb damage. It was that same spring, while the new Queen's coronation was being planned, that people started paying attention to Keith's voice. He had a beautiful soprano, with perfect pitch, and was a born performer whether soloing or leading the school choir. His *Messiah* always hit a wonderfully dramatic climax. Through long hours of practice and competition, Keith and two Dartford friends would be chosen from a field of hundreds to sing in Westminster Abbey. It was his sixth or seventh visit to town, and his first ever without Doris.

The boy sitting in his ruffled surplice in the corner of the third-class rail compartment was thin, pale, with keen brown eyes that gave the face its vitality. His high forehead and amazing jug ears made the whole of his head seem much rounder. From time to time, he glanced out at the wet, nearly colourless scene falling away to reveal Britain's main visual drama, the flash of bunting and of Union Jacks growing ever larger and louder.

The day was Tuesday 2 June 1953. Patriotism burnt in Keith Richards like a blue flame. It was his 'greatest ever gig', one friend insists, the first of more than a thousand to date. 'Keith never forgot the rush', nor improved on his ratings. At the very least, his rendition of *Zadok the Priest* would be heard by an audience of ten million in Britain alone, given the BBC's bold decision to broadcast proceedings.

The parts of the three-hour ceremony – the Anointing, Crowning, Communion and Homage – all went well, though some in the Abbey were in agonies of emotion or cold. There were ermine-clad peers and peeresses, with, here and there, splashes of oriental colour – Pathans from Pakistan in high turbans, the sultan of Zanzibar and various Arab sheikhs and emirs. For them the most poignant scene would come when, with drums pounding, the guest choir sang 'May the Queen live for ever and ever' in lines from *Zadok*. One particular voice rang through the dank air, on which the choir's breath floated out like steam. There was a shameless and lovable melodrama about this noise, which caught the top notes wonderfully well and swooped histrionically down the register. The congregation was riveted by these astonishing closing passages. Winston Churchill later recorded that this singular rendition had moved him to tears. The young chorister in question sounded much like he looked, hammy but striking. A spotlight glinted on his lightly oiled quiff, his full lower lip all but quivering with emotion. Several of the royals would speak of the reprobate-angel – yes, it was Keith – who, all agreed, stole the show that morning. Fifty years later he would still be active, making noise, and happy to rattle cages.

Keith went back to Dartford as something of a star. Doris and her husband bought him a new bicycle. The person known to fame as the Human Riff was still fuelled by an equal mixture of loneliness and shyness, and loved nothing more than to sing along with his mum to the radio. There were no real problems at school, where he excelled at tennis and cricket. Soon, he joined the Boy Scouts.

Twenty years passed.

Hollywood, January 1973. Keith Richards at the height of his 'elegantly wasted' phase. On the 18th, the Rolling Stones played a benefit ostensibly for Nicaraguan earthquake relief, but also to impress on US immigration authorities that, without their help, the band's very survival was at stake. The next morning, Keith apparently found himself wandering the northern end of Griffith Park, he wasn't sure why, where he visited the Great Cat den located in the LA Zoo. As a lark he started serenading the nearest lion with one of his favourite country songs and the beast went mad, roaring at Keith and trying to vault the retaining wall between them. A keeper had to be sent for to restore order.

Six weeks later Keith returned to his new house, Point of View, sitting atop a hill on the north coast of Jamaica. Whenever he was in residence the place teemed with Rastas, rude boys, bodyguards, chauffeurs and overadrenalized flunkeys who dutifully rounded out Keith's clan, one that made Sinatra's look like the Bloomsbury Group. The very first night, one of the entourage forgot himself and there was a dispute about money. Keith's reaction to this misunderstanding was to allegedly seize his .38 revolver, put it in the man's ear and offer to blow his brains all over Ocho Rios. After that there was a loss of interest in cash, or in the man's prolonging the quarrel.

Travel was Keith's inheritance from the flighty Doris's family, but the jet-set role was one he made his own. After a week he was headed for London, leaving behind his partner, and mother of his two children, Anita Pallenberg. Pallenberg was promptly busted for ganja possession and hustled into jail, where she was serially raped and beaten up. According to his friend Tony Sanchez, Keith paid out a bribe of $12,000 and she was deported, 'run[ning] into his arms', we're told, 'sobbing like a lost little girl'.

Meanwhile there were arrest warrants out for Keith and Anita in France, he was banned from Japan and only after protracted hassles allowed to tour Australia. On 7 April a judge in Warwick, Rhode Island, ruled that Richards would have to stand trial the next time he entered the US as a result of a July 1972 punch-up with a photographer.

Keith tolerated the growing strife with notable composure. 'I may need this for my memoirs,' he rasped. Thereafter, he actually sat down for two or three hours a week making notes for a projected book.

Keith also began discussing life with a second German actress, called Uschi Obermeier, if a mumbled 'yep' or 'nope' could be elevated to the level of discussion. There were whole areas, Uschi came to realize, about which you couldn't talk. Richards' closest friend at the time would often drop by and conduct a serious Q&A about this book idea, which had been floated past all the Stones, and Keith was only too happy to discuss. Amid all the chitchat, a core truth emerged. The friend reckoned that, in his more troubled moments, Keith knew something even a Byron (whom he read nonstop) hadn't worked out: there were corners you couldn't write your way out of. You could only escape by living the outward journey, and Keith had long since learned how to do that.

In May, Keith missed a photo shoot for the new Rolling Stones album cover. Having ascertained that David Bailey was in his studio waiting for him, he turned around and drove a girlfriend to Scotland for the week.

This last development, as Anita herself knew, was of a piece with Keith's single-mindedness. He'd told her in 1967 that his job came first; whatever was left starred her. His immersion in his work, his creative life, and himself was total. Remaining loyal to his gift, he'd added that he only felt fully alive when writing or playing music. But by 1973 he only wanted to be fully alive in that way for, at most, a few hours a day; sex and drugs increasingly filled out the time once given to rock and roll. Later that spring Keith and Uschi moved into the cottage at the foot of his friend Ronnie Wood's garden. The two men soon seemed to be turning into each other, and there were rumours that Woody would replace Keith in the Stones. Mutual friends saw Richards coming apart before their eyes. As someone intimately familiar with Section 5(A) of the Dangerous Drugs Act – the one stating that, under British law, a homeowner can be charged with anything illegal found on the premises – Keith considerately buried his massive Diamorphine supply deep under a stable block on Wood's grounds. A few days later he all but tore the building apart looking for the stash, but in all probability it remains there to this day.

For over six years now, various drug squads had shadowed Keith, compiling reports, occasionally meeting their prey, and gradually building up such a grudging respect for him that several actually apologized while in the throes of a raid.

That 26 June, Luigi the caretaker opened the door of Keith's London home to a party of ten policemen. Richards must have had no illusions about what the dawn visit meant. Between them, the narcs carried off armfuls of grass, heroin, methodone, Mandrax tablets, water pipes and brass scales, as well as the .38 Smith & Wesson, a shotgun and boxes of bullets. Keith, characteristically, retained both his dignity and a grim sense of humour throughout. He, Pallenberg and a house guest were arrested and charged.

After that Keith, who became quite plausibly convinced his phone was tapped, began to spend more and more time in the anonymity of Wood's Georgian eyrie, craning out over Richmond Hill like a pop Berghof. In this instance, at least, Keith's self-image as a romantic stood him in good stead. His view of himself as a composite outlaw-gypsy and his talent for constant mobility helped him survive some close scrutiny. He moved about incessantly. Bystanders grew used to the sight of Keith's spiffy yellow Ferrari hurtling up or down Hill Rise, often with the Metropolitan Police right behind him. Richards would later refer cryptically to certain 'things having gone down behind the scenes' with the law. He spent much of 1973 on the fringe of court, jail, or worse. When plans were made for any kind of Stones activity, nobody knew until the band actually hit the stage if Keith would be with them. Miraculously, he always was.

Over the summer, his sense of persecution and self-protection grew. Keith heard clicks on the line and saw the same dark van parked a few yards down the road from Wood's house every day. In late July he took himself off for an infusion of R&R at his legendary weekend home, Redlands.

It lay over the south downs in a village of scattered orchards and small neighbouring farms, a timbered house with a guest cottage, surrounded on three sides by a shallow moat. As with Keith's other lairs, security arrangements were elaborate. The main building was hidden behind a brick wall topped off by a thick screen of bushes. A sign read 'Beware of the Dog'. The thatched roof that was to prove so combustible was, however, fully visible from the road. An aura of quaint country charm belied Redlands' recent history of drugs raids, all-night Rolling Stones sessions and other exotic rites.

The music room was the dark womb of the place, furnished with oriental rugs and chairs apparently made out of antlers, tightly shut in by Moroccan drapes. An indoor forest of metal, bone and wooden masks could have doubled as the clubhouse of a voodoo cult or the set of a rather heavy-handed Stones biopic. Where Redlands had once echoed to madrigals sung here over 300 years earlier there now rose the clang of Keith's guitar. It was said by several visitors who knew these things that the place was haunted, and Keith himself sometimes spoke of it that way when, late at night, he turned off the lights and lay on his back in front of the log fire. Several of his best songs had been written in this posture.

What was meant to be a pleasant summer's rest began, allegedly, with a knock at the door. A well-known musician was there with a friend called Jaws. Did Keith mind if Jaws brought his pet rat in as well, asked the man. All animals were welcome at Redlands, Keith told him.

The three of them sat around on cushions swigging from bottles of French wine, listening to Richards strum his guitar and talking about the mess Ted Heath was making of the country. Whenever Keith played like this, strange things always seemed to happen – a dog would howl, a plate crash to the floor. Bad juju, he called it. The atmosphere would become so heavy, even his loved ones sometimes withdrew from him in fact as well as spirit. Keith's pet deerhound Syph now retired to the garage, where it made the better acquaintance of the rat. Anita went upstairs with the couple's two children, aged three and one. Jaws was later to say that Keith was perhaps drinking and smoking more than was good for him, or anybody who happened to be around when he was doing it. At some stage towards dawn his guests left and Richards evidently fell asleep. The next thing anyone knew Anita was running downstairs with a basin of water yelling, 'Keith! You messer! Wake up! We're on fire!' Not even he could ever remember a worse moment of truth. There was a kind of blinding flash, sparking behind his eyes, that could be achieved only through being bawled at by Anita Pallenberg. A witness to the scene reports Keith's shock as cut short by Pallenberg's hurling the water in his face. Between them they managed to get the children and at least some of the antique furniture and vintage guitars to safety. Redlands, though, was all but gutted. The fire gained ground steadily. It smouldered here, flared there, soon ignited the roof, snatched at beams and got its teeth into trees in the garden, and they in turn set light to the cars. Explosions were heard. By the time help arrived from Chichester, some ten miles away, only a blackened wall or a façade remained of rooms that had stood since Elizabethan times. It was well into the next morning, 1 August, before the emergency services took leave of Redlands, having warned Richards and Pallenberg about the inadvisability of their smoking under a straw roof late at night. The relief felt by Keith, as the police declined a search, can be imagined.

A month later the new album, *Goats Head Soup*, was released. Keith, having rescheduled with David Bailey, was seen on the cover as if spontaneously combusting. 'Charred' was his own word. The photo was probably the most interesting thing about the whole record.

On 6 September the Stones hired Blenheim Palace for the album's launch party. Amid all the beautiful people filling the crowded, bustling room, Keith and Anita started a scene and then ended up yelling across a marble hall, discussing the matter. According to Tony Sanchez, 'all hell broke loose' once back in the limo. 'Keith punched her hard in the face. Anita grabbed him by his hair and jerked him down to the floor ... Every ten minutes or so, throughout the two-hour drive, they attacked each other again.' Sanchez watched the couple's small son stare impassively out the window while his parents fought. At journey's end, when Keith put his arm around Anita and said, 'Sometimes these things piss me off,' all was forgiven and the relationship survived.

Keith's moods also didn't kill the work ethic. He was on the phone to management, once or twice a day in Uschi's presence, checking on gigs. The Stones began a quick tour of Europe that month. Keith still loved playing, and on the very best nights there was a sinewy power there that belied his queasy leer. In between dates in Bern and Munich, he subjected himself to three days of haemodialysis – the filtering-out of waste and toxic substances by a kidney machine – entirely successfully in his case, though followed by common dialysis-related problems such as cramps and passing blood. The Nosferatu legend that Richards had been sluiced out in a Swiss clinic would hit iconographic status in years ahead. Keith himself was well aware of the 'vampire bit' and collective death fantasies swirling round him. When they tried, at first unsuccessfully, to wake him up after his treatment, one of the nurses had finally leant down and started slapping him.

Keith's eyes opened, and then, in a whisper, came his first words.

'I'm still here, darling.'

Somehow Keith made all the remaining dates on the tour, a twitchy figure in black, corpse-pale, hissing his back-up vocals through carious teeth. The drug intake was massive. While waiting to go on one night the horn player Bobby Keys told Keith that their friend Gram Parsons, a baby-faced twenty-six-year-old who pioneered the great country, busted-heart lyric, had died of a tequila and morphine overdose in California. Ten days later, Keys himself collapsed and left the tour. By the time of the last show in Berlin, Keith was quaffing a bottle of Jack Daniel's and snorting lines of coke just to get through the ninety-minute set. Yet his habits, dire as some were, seemed to be not so much vices as the working out of a complementary dark side without which the juices couldn't flow. Keith restored himself with what might have killed him, and almost did. There were great moments on stage, as well as some truly excruciating ones. Real indignity befell the encore in Berlin. While Keith strummed Angie, the Stones played Satisfaction.

At the post-gig party Richards looked on, apparently indifferent, while a blonde waltzed around naked, and other guests performed on each other with champagne bottles. The familiar traits of shyness and embarrassment emerged in Keith even on tour. So did solitariness. At the very climax of the hobnobbing Keith's head dropped and he nodded off, actually snoring. But almost as soon as he was asleep, free of the madness for once, he was up and moving again. A fan watched as his idol, draggled and hollow-eyed, seemingly still hobbled by cramps, shuffled back to his room without a soul around him.

Keith and Uschi Obermeier flew to London together and took up residence in the Ritz. But as the days and weeks passed, and Anita continued to call, Keith would sometimes move back into their house in Chelsea. The children and their long history together apparently made him want to keep one foot over the threshold of the door Anita held open for him. That 15 October, she and Keith were given a one-year suspended sentence for use, supply and traffic in cannabis, and a 5,000 franc fine for heroin possession by the Court of Grand Instance in Nice. The charges dated from the couple's recent year of tax exile on the Riviera, and effectively ended Keith's life as a Frenchman. A week later Richards and Pallenberg were tried at Marlborough Street magistrates' court, found guilty and again emerged with, respectively, a fine and a one-year conditional discharge. Celebrating that night, Keith nodded off in the Londonderry House hotel and burnt his room down. He, Anita and the Rolling Stones were immediately banned from the hotel for life.

Keith's beating the rap and continued survival came as a welcome relief to those of his fans who had been simple enough to believe Sgt Maurey of the Sûreté when, a year earlier, he'd vowed that France would throw the book at their degenerate guest. Many people had thought it possible that he and Anita would do lengthy jail time. Keith himself seemed to cut an ever more gaunt, Byronesque dash in 1973, sinking cases of Jack Daniel's and snorting mountainous lines of coke from off the tip of a switchblade. And yet, deathly as he looked, there was something about him oddly and irrepressibly alive. On peak form, he remained teasable and fun, smart, famously good company, excitable in a boyish way. 'Cool, ain't she?' he'd say of a new guitar. This was the man-child equally in thrall to the Goons and Chuck Berry, who liked nothing more than wolfing his beloved bangers and mash. As Britain plunged into industrial chaos that winter, with train drivers and miners on strike and Heath ordering a three-day week to save energy, Keith would become, in his way, a vital and endearing national asset. His performance of personality – the shark's tooth earring, the smudged eyes and the wack habit – recycled the bohemian pose he'd studied in the Fifties. 'It [was] selling a look, an attitude, an image,' he'd reflect some twenty years later. That dismal time and dreary place, he said, needed to be dazzled. On this reading, Keith wasn't courting death so much as he was courting being alive.

Between October and December, the Rolling Stones were hard at work on a new album. They recorded in Germany, putting in twelve-hour days, six days a week. On 18 December, back in London, Keith Richards quietly celebrated turning thirty.

Twenty-six years, same location. The approach to Wembley is a sump of ticket touts, the ambient stench all burgers and pot. There are randomly scattered Strictly Official Gear stalls alongside the fringe entrepreneurs. The Stones themselves arrive backstage in a fleet of deliberately low-profile transit vans. It's one of the curious dictates of security that the World's Greatest Rock 'n Roll Band choose to report for work much like a team of plumbers. On a wet Friday night, they're giving their first full concert on home soil in four years. For the small, elfin figures who emerge from the convoy, an etiquette of finely tuned call and response immediately rules:

they communicate with their court in nods or grunts, and the slightest touch of the lips means 'Get us a drink.'

Once safely decanted into the stadium, a thin man in black jeans shuffles between a caravan and a tented bar, where a low murmur of VIP recognition is audible: *Keef. Mmm . . . Keef!*

It is indeed Keith Richards. With time, he's become the most recognized rock musician alive and certainly the most physically striking. Up close, Richards' hair, eyes and teeth all look tinted, and his flesh seems made of a lab-developed polymer that's been deeply tanned, like an old football. It's an impressive appearance, and he knows it. Keith, whose work uniform consists of sprayed-on drainpipes, a torn shirt and sneakers, exudes the rude bursting energy of a child combined with an ancient Dean Martin slur, a noise much like a lorry crunching over gravel. Following a red carpet as it curves with the shape of the stadium, he pads about and makes some of his throaty warming-up sounds. 'Hai-ai-ai-ai. Hai-ai-ai-*reeeee*.' Keith does a quick shuffle, his white gym shoes snapping against the felt. Despite or because of the presence of two heavily tattooed, but otherwise expressionless bodyguards, the general vibe is relaxed and friendly. 'Eric and Ernie,' Keith chortles, bumping up against one of the minders. Between laughs, the talk is technical: instructions for the set list, lighting, bits of business. Over to one side of the marquee are a group of people who seem to be standing in line awaiting their turn to try and impress him. Mick Jagger, who walks by in a furry hat and overcoat, rolls his eyes and says, 'Now for something completely different.' The visual effect is of a hip Czar strolling among his troops in the early years of the century.

Keith ignores him.

As Richards in turn paces up to an interviewer, the man flinches and almost draws back. The whole area is brightly lit and heaving with young models, which perhaps makes the contrast more vivid. But *wasted*. In this company, Keith looks like somebody's debauched though good-natured uncle. You expect the teeth, but nothing quite prepares you for the dark, sharp eyes, bluish hair, and the skin of a particularly gnarled lizard. Keith's constitution has always been exemplary: low blood pressure, a liver which resisted the ravages of drink and dope, an iron gut, and even a nose that has taken such a frequent pounding from falls. What's more striking, however, is his sheer, resilient cheerfulness. Many of the same entourage who avoided Keith in the Seventies have since become his beneficiaries and devoted fans.

Even in the lost years, he'd go to extraordinary lengths to help when they faced health problems or financial difficulty. 'He's our Elvis – you know when he's in the house,' one long-term employee recalls.

Once clocked on and changed for action, the Stones are a conspicuous presence in floor-length duster coats, makeup and identical, wraparound shades. This disturbing spectacle appears first on a giant screen, making them look like a chain gang from a Sam Peckinpah film. Long before Keith gets near the stage you can tell that something extraordinary is going to happen. The tilt of his head, the loose swing of his arms and the general air of self-confidence all signify that no mere pop star approaches. Suddenly, the quiet of the marquee is broken by the clatter of boots from down a guarded corridor. Two guitarists merge with a drummer and singer, like a sports team taking the field. The four men trot past, one after the other, in a frisky Cup final procession. Wembley roars.

Keith is immediately on the case, opening proceedings with a spare but shimmering Jumpin' Jack Flash. Hammer hits anvil with an electrifying peal. Likewise, the Stones expertly deliver their inimitable stage shtick, a deft wedding of vaudeville and punk attitude. It's clever, cocky and ultimately ageless. They do a better pastiche of the Sixties than Austin Powers. Clearly, the key ingredient, though, is less of a celebration of wheezing geezers and more of a master class in folk-pop dynamics. After all these years, Keith still strikes at his guitar in tiny, shocked gestures, often snapping his hands away altogether. Playing fast but unhurriedly, he can both smoke a fag *and* make all the right changes, even at the breakneck speed at which Jagger sings. By the time he struts out Satisfaction, admirers are already waving banners with the slogan KEEF RULES.

Although they're treated to some of the most famous guitar bolts in rock, it's quickly borne in on Wembley that Keith Richards is no mere slash 'n burn merchant. One of his strengths is his sentimentality, and in mid-concert he somehow turns the stadium into a nightclub, performing an unlikely set of cowboy ballads which he croons in his dry, sexy drawl. When he slows down, you hear anew how basic and brilliant are Keith's rhythmic innovations, with dramatically placed breaks between the notes. It's an almost perfect example of virtuosity and economy. And passion. Keith has a long public history of troubles and triumphs to take on the road, and his handsomely weathered oldies are seized on by both the audience and him as a kind of autobiography: You Got The Silver – first love for Anita; Beast Of

Burden – trouble ahead; All About You – their public split. Throughout, Keith displays the confident craft of a born storyteller with a panoramic knowledge of American blues. But these are no mere retreads: they're subtler, more autumnal. Thief In The Night, in particular, finds Richards deflating his public don't-fuck-with-me rock persona to take the role of the wistful singer–songwriter. Even in full band knees-ups like Brown Sugar, Keith's accompanists only chase his riffs. While Jagger gyrates, it's Richards whose playing translates emotionally. He's reaching for the audience and they pull for him – they're on his side.

It's the sweetest of ironies. When the Stones first toured America, in 1964, they were treated as village idiots on the *Hollywood Palace Show* by Dean Martin. Voted by Martin and Frank Sinatra 'the band least likely to', the Stones and their detractors have come full circle. Exactly thirty-five years on, those with long memories at Wembley can easily make the connection to four other middle-aged men lurching around stage, tooting their booze and ogling their broads. Any resemblance to the *Ocean's Eleven*-era Rat Pack is purely intentional. The notion, particularly, that Dino's touch of insurrection and tipsy slur might have been handed down from arch-swingers to Jurassic rockers like himself must tickle Keith. There's even the totemic Jack Daniel's in common. Like most of the Rat Pack before them, the Stones have gradually acquired special status as the officially tolerated moral slobs of the middle class. Time has been on their side, after all.

On their first night back in London, the Rolling Stones pack the joint and leave the audience baying for more. Backstage, the interviewer is invited to Keith's recovery room, a small trailer parked off to the side of the VIP enclosure. It's empty. Outside in the cold Wembley streets sirens scream into the night. The Stones, their escort and eventually the press regroup at the band's hotel, where the bar and buffet seem surprisingly modest for rock stars. Keith himself lopes in wearing a white fluffy bathrobe. He works his way along the table with a studious expression, as if back onstage fashioning one of his curly, Chuck Berryish riffs. There are sausages, eggs, beans, chips, peas, shepherd's pie and HP sauce. On a crested silver tray embossed with the Stones logo are placed what are probably cigarettes. 'Ambrosia,' says Keith, taking a plate and flicking the cap off the sauce bottle. For added relaxation, he plugs in a George Formby tape. Even rock and roll may have produced no odder sight than this, the suicidally decadent Human Riff, at ease in a room he calls the Baboon Cage, primly eating shepherd's pie and humming along to the chorus of Grandad's Flannelette Nightshirt. After a Wembley-sized roar of laughter, he allows that, 'I'm just a herbert from Dartford. None of you guys ever gets your shit straight.'

And then Keith does what he's always done, what he's done for so long that quite probably he no longer realizes what he's doing.

He becomes someone else again, a shy, quiet and oddly self-effacing Englishman, the perceptive and unassuming soul who says, 'I can be the guy on stage any time I want.' For Keith, it's taken a lifetime to work out the riddle of whether he owns the legend or the legend owns him.

2

Mannish Boy

IN DECEMBER 1939, THE EVER-FESTIVE GUS DUPREE BOWED TO THE STIFF SUNDAY NIGHT CROWD AT THE HAMMERSMITH PALAIS, BEGAN STRUMMING HIS SPANISH GUITAR AND ADDRESSED THEM WITH HIS USUAL DISREGARD FOR NICETY. He was a tailor's assistant and weekend musician, an assassin of grammar, a lover of fast women and slow horses, and an inveterate tippler whose shiny dinner jacket was generally stained with wine. Although a virtuoso performer, the instrument he really played best was his audience.

Looking round at the depressing spectacle of gas masks and tatty dresses, Gus drew on a lifetime of experience to find the words with most telling effect.

'Shift your arses,' he rumbled. 'That means when the music starts, get up and *move*. When you sing, put some bloody lung into it.'

Gus Dupree had a gentle, piano-playing wife who, although she'd long since despaired of rubbing off his rough edges, was shocked at his use of even mild profanity, 'at Christmas time and in *the Hammersmith Palais*,' as she put it reproachfully. He had seven grown daughters who all played instruments, and who weren't shocked at all. Together, the nine made an amazing family, the girls inheriting strength and crudity from their father, strength and delicacy from their mother, and blending these into a unique combination of talents that would shape Gus's beloved grandson, Keith.

The Duprees were exiles, Protestants who had been driven out of France in the seventeenth century to the Channel Islands. A branch of the family settled in Monmouth (eventually siring the cellist Jacqueline du Pre) and another in Canterbury, Kent, around 1790, just a century before Theodore Augustus – Gus – was born. They were people who earned their daily bread by the work of their hands, farmers who, through the long winters, took whatever other jobs they could. The furnishings Gus grew up with were of the plainest kind: a small cot, a tin bath, a half dozen rickety wooden chairs. There was a piano, possibly a few other musical instruments. Gus enlisted on the outbreak of war in 1914 and eventually saw combat near Ypres. In July 1917 he was partially blinded in a gas attack and survived only by wrapping a bloody shirt round his face and clinging on to a comrade who was slightly less badly afflicted. After evacuation to a field hospital, Gus was treated and invalided out of the army.

In 1922 he and his wife Emily settled in north London with their daughters. The youngest girl, Doris, was just turning seven, a pretty brunette of strong will, quick temper and exceptional energy. Gus was her hero. It was her father's bluntness, independent spirit and love of good music, Doris said, that were her lifelong inspiration. Like him, she wasn't much given to self-doubt.

The period around 1930 when Doris began discovering folk and jazz clubs was one of the happiest of her life. She apparently loved to help Gus carry his equipment in to gigs, and sometimes accompanied his small dance band on the piano. The applause, she noticed, always peaked when Gus stepped forward for a solo, or jigged around wearing his wide, rather salacious grin. Even the sparsest Sunday night audience would, said Doris, 'go mental' when her father bashed out a Chick Webb-style riff on the drums. By now Gus had quit the saxophone because of his damaged lungs, but otherwise would nonchalantly pick up any instrument to hand and bring down the house with it. He was becoming a grand old man who played with a wit, vigour and virtuosity that was the envy of many a younger, professional musician. Years later, Gus would perform accomplished violin duets with Yehudi Menuhin.

But the period, in a different way, was also one of the hardest of Doris's life. With no qualifications she had to take whatever work she could get; there was one month, after she was laid off as a temp, when she reportedly lived on two shillings a day. In the morning, she ate a chocolate bar in her room and, at night, a can of cold spaghetti or beans. Doris's adolescence was further punctuated by violent rows at home. After Emily discovered

Gus *in flagrante*, his enforced separation from his family, interrupted only by a few brief visits, lasted a full year. When Doris found work on the night shift in a factory she's said to have taken the early morning bus, more than an hour's journey across London, in order to bring Gus his breakfast.

In 1933 Doris met Herbert William – Bert – Richards, a trainee electrician and aspirant foreman at first General Electric and then the Osram's lightbulb factory in Hammersmith. She was musical, he was tone deaf. Where the Duprees were apolitical, the Richardses were outspoken Fabians, marchers and organizers who believed that Britain was a poorly run society deep into a mire of frivolity and decadence. Bert's father Ernest, a school caretaker, was a Labour Party worker and later councillor in Walthamstow, where his wife Elizabeth was elected mayor from 1941–2. With a Dupree there was never a doubt about what they felt or meant. With a Richards there was a slight air of ambiguity about everything except politics. In the council chamber, noted *The Times*, Ernest 'dazzled'. He was particularly popular with local children, for whom he organized a municipal Christmas party and who knew him as Uncle Ernie. But at home, like Elizabeth, he scarcely said a word, and if he did it was in a voice so weak as to be almost inaudible. Nobody would ever remember seeing Ernest drink, smoke or listen to music. Even Elizabeth used to say that he was well named. (The 'Richards', too, is made up of Old English elements for serious and strong.) Ernest sometimes invited their son to attend Council meetings, and Bert would later describe his seminal teenage memories, when he watched men in dark suits give speeches and pass composite motions. Unsurprisingly, he grew into a monosyllabically dour young man. By the time Bert met Doris Dupree he was nineteen but prematurely aged, with cultural poverty stamped all over him. She was his first serious girlfriend.

Bert eventually qualified and the couple moved in together at 42 Edinburgh Road, next to Walthamstow cemetery. On 17 December 1938 they were married in nearby St Barnabas church. The bride and groom were then twenty-two and twenty-three, respectively.

The newlyweds didn't see much of each other for the next few years. In fact, it seemed a mismatch from the start. He was uptight, clenched, going through social motions; she was enjoying herself whenever possible, opening herself up to new experiences. One was playing for time, the other was full of life for the moment. The son of an icy man and a fiery mother, it was Keith's lot to be torn evenly down the line: from the male side, he got his intensity and self-containment; from the Dupress the wit that often stunned those who knew him as Bert's son. After a twenty-four-hour honeymoon on the coast, the groom went back to Hammersmith, his pretty bride to a new job at the Co-op. Bert's diaries would show that for the next few years he spent half an hour, at most up to an hour, a day with his wife.

Making their way to a compromise home between Walthamstow and the Duprees in Kent, the couple hit on Dartford. Both their first flat, by a chemical plant, and their second, above a grocer's shop, were far from elegant.

The loftiest rise of land visible from the Richardses' in Chastilian Road was occupied by a smallpox hospital, 'the plague pit' as Keith calls it. 'Built and left there for lepers.' The town planners had also selected this choice spot for a sprawling industrial park, so that the west Dartford residents could look up, as they emerged each morning, and see in the distance the drab brick chimneys of both the munitions works and the crematorium. There was never a bleaker scene, or a worse day than any twenty-four hours of late 1940 in southern England under the Blitz. On 15 September the Luftwaffe destroyed the women's ward at Dartford County Hospital, killing a nurse and twenty-six patients. The refinery that lay just over Watling Street went up the same week, a black oily pall shrouding Chastilian Road. Incendiary bombs hit Dartford on sixty-nine out of a possible ninety nights that autumn. Gas masks were issued and blackout curtains hammered over windows. With merchant ships also coming under heavy attack, food and clothes rationing soon followed. Like every adult, Bert and Doris received just three ounces of meat, three ounces of butter and two ounces of tea apiece each week. When, as happened four times, the Dartford reservoir was bombed, the long-suffering Doris would walk the mile and a half to a communal pump in the town centre. The apparatus was rusted and the water itself a faded cherry colour. Queues were long.

The couple's only child followed ten years after they met and exactly five after they married, a baby boy, Keith or 'Ricky', who arrived on Saturday 18 December 1943. Doris apparently told friends that she'd become pregnant for the sole purpose of avoiding wartime factory work. By then Bert had been called up, and would serve three distinguished years as Private 5955740 with the Beds & Herts regiment. Following his father-in-law's own career trajectory, Bert was later wounded and invalided out to a hospital in the Midlands.

Keith Richards was born in the Marina Wing of Livingstone hospital, then little more than a redbrick cottage dumped down on the corner of

Watling Street. Both the labour and delivery were difficult. Doris's nurse would make much of the fact that Keith was 'a screamer', describing him later as 'beefy' with 'a crop of black hair' and 'Prince Charles ears'. Though Doris was in bed until Christmas, Bert was given only a weekend pass from his unit.

Keith entered the world with a deep horror of sirens and explosions and claims, even today, 'If I'm walking through a hotel and I hear a TV, and it's playing one of those Blitz movies the hair goes up on the back of my head and I get goose bumps. It's a reaction . . . something I picked up from what happened in the first eighteen months of my life.'

Doris remained wary of gas attacks, and found the nighttime incendiary raids even harder to take. The war was characterized by the most brutal outrages against civilians, particularly those unlucky enough to live, like the Richardses, in the middle of a bombing corridor. Although the home front had stabilized somewhat by 1943, Dartford was still targeted, largely because of its north-end refinery and armaments factories. Whether Keith's own house was flattened or not isn't as certain as that he felt himself to be under fire.

As she struggled out through the streets – or what had once been streets – obstructed by blackened bodies, broken glass, crockery, furniture and debris, Doris must have felt that she and the baby had been thrown into a completely new, horrific world. It was as if Dartford had gone to bed in a Constable painting and woken up in a Bosch. In the midst of property that no longer belonged to anyone and was disappearing under the rubble, the difference blurred between right and wrong. 'There was no set rule.' As well as the looting, Dartford suffered from frequent interruptions, if not complete breakdowns, in supply by both road and rail. On the occasions the town was effectively cut off from the world, even the most basic official ration had to be slashed. By late 1943 some 12,000 inhabitants had either left voluntarily or been evacuated out of town to the north and west. Most of those who remained were hardened, some of them unprincipled, but all of them, by now, tough, capable and self-sufficient. The children of these people weren't apt to be weaklings.

Other news that 18 December was of the Pacific, where the US Sixth Army expanded a newly won beachhead on New Guinea; of Berlin, on which RAF Lancasters dropped 1,700 tons of high explosives and incendiaries, and in doing so lost thirty-eight planes; of London, where

Winston Churchill was recovering from a lung infection which, though downplayed at the time, had been close to fatal; and of Dartford itself, where the talk was of queues, protests, and the imposition of judicial birchings on two teenagers caught looting a railwaymen's hut.

Meanwhile, an exotic future loomed: In Chicago, 28-year-old Muddy Waters now began his professional singing career. Fresh out of prison, a delinquent named Chuck Berry was learning the guitar. Albert Hoffman, a Swiss research scientist, discovered the hallucinogenic properties of the drug LSD when, in the same week Keith Richards was born, he accidentally swallowed some.

The deadliness of the time leeched into Keith's childhood, where the accent was on 'making do', a penance bewilderingly mingled with outbursts of singing, dancing and drinking. Bert Richards would appear in Dartford only two or three times a month, and was sent to the front in 1944. Doris and her sisters, kindly and modestly educated women, some with aspirations to respectability, raised the boy through the war years. The Duprees united all the traits alien to the Richardses – zest, impulsiveness, flamboyance, a good disposition and a bad temper, imagination, patience and a wit that made any room they were in rock with laughter. They talked freely to people they liked, and to people they didn't like in order to stop *them* from talking. Bert, by contrast, was self-disciplined, responsible and honest, but also tight-fisted and gruff, with a startling growl that could penetrate across factory floors or into locked bedrooms – 'an injustice collector', one relative calls him. This core conflict between Keith's mother and father would tick away steadily for the next twenty years, at which point it promptly exploded.

All of Keith Richards was there in bud: a funny little boy with a leer who befriended stray dogs. Both parents were shouters.

Keith would make much of his 'sign', too – Sagittarius, often associated with the best and, in every sense, the most curious brains, with eccentricities to match. Sagittarians are said to thrive on independence and freedom, to love change and travel and to be castratingly rude in speaking out. Asked by a journalist if he had any truck with astrology, the adult Keith Richards nodded and replied, 'I'm half-man, half-horse, with a licence to shit in the street.'

From the start, Keith was obviously traumatized by the war and those sirens plunged into his subconscious. But 'Ricky', as his friends and family called him, was also fascinated by the subject, turning the Nazis and Nazi memorabilia into a full-blown obsession in later life. This was a style appreciation and emphatically not a condoning of Hitler; rather, a fetish that existed despite him. Keith would think nothing of walking around Paris or St Tropez dressed in full SS garb, medals clanking, the red swastika armband set off smartly against the black boots.

'My best suit,' he called it.

Even at two, Keith would filch Doris's makeup, sit down and daub on a comic moustache, in premature fulfilment of a popular quote of the Seventies, 'Adolf was the first rock star.'

On the cold moonlit evening of 5 June 1944, 29-year-old Bert Richards embarked on his own part in Hitler's downfall. Bert's regiment was among the first to storm the Normandy coast shortly after the initial assault in the pre-dawn hours of 6 June. The British landings on Gold and Juno beaches, just as feared, met with heavy German resistance; it took twelve hours of horrific blood-letting to secure a beachhead and a week more to consolidate the Allied positions into a single front. Bert Richards was one of those who fell – wounded in the leg – in the prolonged second wave of the fighting. The war was over for him. Bert's first and, for many years, only excursion outside England ended on 2 July when he was shipped home to an orthopaedic hospital in Mansfield, Notts. 'I've done my time in hell,' he told Doris. The irony was that Bert's injury would, in turn, save his wife and child from the carnage.

The date was 15 June, the time shortly before midnight. From somewhere a siren wailed over west Dartford, followed, within seconds, by a flash of blue and yellow flame and an ear-splitting roar. Windows and doors blew out. Clouds of thick smoke billowed up. Parts of the oily Stanham river and the marshland behind Chastilian Road went up in a secondary explosion. The first of Hitler's V1s, the so-called miracle weapons, found their targets with deadly accuracy. For the next two and a half months, London and the southeast were again subjected to unmitigated terror from the skies. The Dartford *Chronicle* for that June and July conveyed the horror: 'Flying Bombs Night and Day ... Parents, Daughter and Cook Killed ... Old Tavern Blasted ... Child Killed Running for Shelter ... Tragedy of Two Sisters.'

Chastilian Road was hit on the night of 5 July, the rocket whistling in over the town centre, cutting its motor and dropping silently out of the sky on to the terraced street. In the explosion two houses, numbers 27 and 29, were destroyed with the loss of five lives. The Richardses, at number 33, lost their front windows and part of their roof, but otherwise escaped miraculously intact while hell raged all around. 'Hitler dumped one of his V1s on the house ... Nothing [was] left,' Keith said, although his imagination seems to have provided more richly furnished accommodations. On the night of 5 July, he and Doris were actually 150 miles away to the north, visiting Bert at the hospital in Mansfield.

The family went back to Dartford, and Bert to the Osram's factory, only in January 1945. Keith Richards was too young to remember the outbreak of peace, and Doris gleefully tearing down the blackout curtains, four months later. On 8 May a victory party was held in Dartford town centre. A group of children was entertained to tea, after which there was music and dancing in the street, with floodlighting. Later, the *Chronicle* intones, 'each child received a bag of sweets and a Savings Stamp'. Curiously, of the sixty young guests present that evening, one, a 12-year-old named Peter Blake, would become a renowned pop artist, and two others went on to be rock stars.

Even apart from their sinister appeal, which was considerable, Keith soon had added reason to remember the Nazis. Back in his old bedroom, he would wake up each morning to the sound of hammers and saws, the shouted orders and grumbles of builders, and all the animation that marked the refurbishment of historic Dartford into the 'Thames Gateway'. Although the bulldozers went to work elsewhere in Chastilian Road, number 33 had only to be patched up. The tiny flat on the hill was cold and smelly, with rancid vegetables heaped up in the shop below, and a narrow back yard. A bright blue tarpaulin stretched over the roof would remain there for months, until it worked all but loose from its moorings, keeping a kind of demented beat as it flapped wildly above Keith's head.

The next few years in Britain were probably the hardest of the twentieth century. For Keith, the post-war decade was one of icy nights in gaslit rooms, of whale fat and tinned beef – the comically vile ingredients of a serious sacrifice he never forgot. Clothing coupons and food queues remained a way of life. Keith would wait until 1953 for the government to lift controls on chocolate and sweets. While rationing continued, so did the Ministry of Food with its raft of regulations enforceable in the courts. For years after the war, 'snoopers' were officially encouraged to report anyone suspected of the Babylonian luxury of enjoying a meal. A woman in Chastilian Road apparently discovered that Bert Richards was smuggling home tea and, worse still, sugar from his plant in London. The neighbour consulted a policeman, who promised to arrest Bert if he were caught, but wouldn't promise to keep the informant's name out of the paper. A day or two later, the policeman came back, knocked on the woman's door, and told her that Bert was a war hero whose trial would be bound to engender local publicity. The matter was dropped. Although Bert's shameless tea consumption continued, there was never any scandal.

One of Keith's earliest memories was of dancing with his numerous aunts, or singing along to the big bands Doris liked to listen to on the radio. It was their only substantial piece of furniture, a vast mock-teak box that could easily have doubled as a coffin. Still a toddler, he sat on the windowsill of the front parlour, his mother beside him, taking in the thrilling sounds of Duke Ellington or Billy Eckstine.

His second memory would be of pure fear. Bert Richards would slam out of the flat every morning at six, leaving Keith to fret about one day having to follow him down the 'shit road' to Osram's. This, too, as a number of Keith's friends would note, was a reaction he carried with him throughout early childhood, unadmitted and unrecognized but with a singular motivational effect: the sense that the world of soul-destroying slog wasn't for him. It was doubtless this same conviction that led the millionaire pop star to sing 'Never want to be like papa/Working for the boss every night and day'. As the years passed, Keith's real distaste for drudge work would take on a quality of obsession.

An only child, with six aunts, Keith 'was a bit spoiled', notes Doris. His first afternoon at infants' school 'he was in a terrible state . . . I had to carry him out. He was frightened that maybe I wasn't coming to get him.' Once safely home in Chastilian Road, Keith balled up in a corner sobbing and panting, and miserably pleading with Doris not to send him back. The terrified four-year-old insisted she mustn't leave him, ever, or she'd be sorry, he'd come over queer and die. This was one of the earliest of Keith's talents, making himself sick. When Doris took his temperature she found, to her amazement, that he was running a high fever. Keith had no close friends at infants' school; nor did he seek any. The happy, playful boy who charmed his dotty aunts would grow into an idle, resentful, nicotine-stained teen.

Keith harboured a love–hate for Chastilian Road, and Dartford, for years to come. Part of him, clearly, loathed the 'shithole' which prided itself on its gaudily modern facelift in the 1940s and 1950s. The town's newer buildings were all concrete slabs; the word was 'clearance', the result acres of dead tramway lines and rubble dumped into the green, still hair-oil of Dartford creek. Bingo at the Gala Club. Eel and mash at Kenroys. Central Dartford's fatigue and chronic scuzziness ('Fresh AND Frozen', 'REAL Imitation Antiques') mingled with the faint tang from the Wellcome chemical works. On the other hand, it was precisely in the normality and 'muck' of the place Keith felt himself grounded, and in that light he interpreted his success. 'I'm outta suburbia,' he'd say, from the far side of fame. 'Dartford's a good place to come from. It's just not a great place to go back to.'

Pop psychiatrists will dismiss the normal, but they'll pay attention to the muck.

Despite, or because of, all the reconstruction, Chastilian Road remained a grim spot. At number 33 there was no phone, no fridge and no radiators. You walked in through the grocery shop and climbed a flight of concrete steps into a dingy and low-lit parlour. A two-bar fire there gave off as much heat as a 60-watt bulb. On bitterly cold winter mornings Keith would enjoy a minute in front of it, his hands chapped raw, before starting, he assured Doris, for school. He often didn't bother, opting instead to sidle down back streets to the Dartford Odeon. Even in the drenching rain which seeped through the roof there, Keith could soak up the lushness and grandeur of the American landscape he loved. By his sixth birthday, he was gripped by cowboys in general and, in particular, by Roy Rogers, whose Saturday matinees enthralled thousands of British youngsters. Most of these youngsters graduated from the simple frontier yarns and campfire fantasies they fostered as they grew up. For Keith Richards, however, the fantasy never ended. As a rock star he still listened to the old cowboy ballads, and would write several in the same vein. Singing them with the bluesy wail of Jimmie Rodgers and a funky swagger inspired by Elvis, Richards added an intimacy of his own.

By the time he was eight Keith already had an ear for a tune. The radio, said Doris, was a kind of shrine. 'He wasn't just musical – he was totally musical.' Keith wouldn't hesitate to correct Doris or any of her sisters if, for example, when belting out Cockney favourites like My Old Dutch, they wandered off key. But his loftiest contempt was reserved for any Establishment types he suspected of 'faking it'. Keith's characteristic argument was that British dance music, as represented by a Billy Cotton, was 'utter wank'.

It probably wasn't true, as Doris had remarked, that given the option, Keith would have chosen to be born, like Johnny Cash, in rural Arkansas. But it probably wasn't entirely false. Keith couldn't keep his hands off the big Motorola in the front room, knew scores of songs by heart, and was already making a name for himself as defiantly 'special'. They saw less and less of him at school. He appeared never to have heard of homework. It was Keith's habit, as soon as he came in the front door, to tune in the American Forces station on the radio at ear-splitting volume, and then to wolf as much of the family food ration as he could. He never bonded with any other children his own age, but made close friends of several mangy looking stray dogs. A pet mouse peered up from a cardboard box in his room. Even more worryingly, to Bert's mind, Keith loved to read and devoured *Ivanhoe* and *Treasure Island* with the same zeal as his food. He could, and did, quote whole pages of the stuff from memory. The adventures became both a dream world and an escape route from Chastilian Road.

Soon things took a further turn for the worse. Both parents were to comment on a world-famous stubborn streak. As one of Keith's later colleagues, Bill Wyman, would say, 'He's obstinate . . . If things don't suit him, he simply won't go along with it. And that's the end of the subject. There's no liaison. No *Should we do that?* It's simply *No*. And when asked *Why not?* Keith would say, *"'Cause I don't want to."'*

April 1951: the path of Dartford's arch punk crossed with that of its hero. Early that spring, Keith became pupil 109 at Wentworth County primary school. His first morning there he was lurking on the back porch, demonstrating a new cowboy gun he'd coaxed out of Doris, when the door opened. A relief teacher called Jack Mills and some colleagues came out, followed by pupil 112, who struck Keith as 'a weed', though actually he was five months older than him. He was a slim though large-headed boy with bushy brown hair and a dazzling grin that lit up like the smile of a model in a toothpaste advertisement. Brandishing a small chemistry kit in one hand, he was busy telling the masters that he intended to build an atom bomb. 'I don't doubt it,' Mills remarked. Chuckling with pleasure at the prospect, the boy turned towards the group huddled around Keith.

'When I grow up,' he announced gravely, 'I'm going to blow things up. I'm gonna blow up the whole world.'

The boy acknowledged the laughs this got and sprinted off down the passage.

'Who was that?' Keith asked Mills.

'Mike Jagger.'

'He looks in a big hurry.'

The other masters and boys shrugged and rolled their eyes upward.

As it turned out, Richards and Jagger were nearly neighbours. Mike and his family lived just three streets away, in Denver Road, where there were smart pebbledash houses of some pretension. Those three suburban streets were worlds exquisitely segregated. Where the Richardses' was hardly better than a slum, the Jaggers' boasted a neat front yard and that zenith of respectability, a doorbell that played Greensleeves. The one major difference between the two households was Mike's mother Eva, a cosmetics demonstrator and dogged social climber who carried a well-thumbed copy of *Mrs Beeton* with her in her handbag. Eva, who'd emigrated from Australia as a small girl, would become an expert on English form. She also danced a mean gavotte, being observed one Friday night in the Glentworth Club leading eight-year-old Mike through such a dance, the latter 'dolled up like Fred Astaire'.

Mike Jagger was a bright, genial boy whose vivacity was already proverbial; he had a pronounced facial likeness to his mother and the wiry frame of his father, a physical-training instructor. Mike was outdoorsy and radiantly well scrubbed. Keith was lean, tense and dark, with vivid shadows around his eyes in a crabby, pinched face his aunts found cute. As to baths, he didn't seem to overdo them. Mike was easing compliantly into adolescence, teasing adults about blowing them up, while actually planning a career in education or the civil service. Keith was learning how to smoke and to swivel a six-shooter. One was focused, the other was virtually dead to the world beyond music and the cinema. Jagger was born on a Monday morning, Richards on a Saturday night. A ginger-beer addict, Keith was constantly knocking over bottles of the stuff that Mike, with his zeal for order, would mop up with scolding, high-minded tuts of disparagement, even in Keith's own house.

Naturally Keith adored the mother who pampered, praised, protected and fussed over him, bringing him both his drink and a steady supply of cakes from the bakery where she worked part-time. 'He wore a little brown hat with little brown boots. He always seemed to have a cold. His nose was always red and his face stark white,' Doris later put it, approvingly. As a toddler he'd insisted on sleeping with her, and was apparently still her bedfellow when he was seven and a half. Keith was 'badly pissed off' when Bert came home and made a fuss. Doris told Keith that when his papa worked late or stayed up in London he could sleep with her again. Keith said, well, he wished he'd get on with it.

Bert's own appraisal of Keith was that he was spoilt rotten. Despite the former's utter professional misery throughout the 1950s, he felt himself a shrewd observer of what it took to succeed, a formula that didn't include playing American Forces radio or dancing the hoochy-koochy. Starchy correctness was all. One of Bert's more penetrating career judgements was that 'You'll never make a penny out of jungle music.'

'Learn a trade,' he continued. 'If I'd had your opportunities in life, my God – you've got it soft, boy.'

That such was true, added Bert, was obvious in the undreamt-of luxury being enjoyed by the younger generation. Radios. Jungle-jive. 'Soft,' he repeated, in a tone that dared Keith to fight.

It was a tempting prospect, and Keith mulled it over. But, on one level, Bert was right. He was actually entering an era of slowly rising prospects. Under the first post-war Labour government, social reform had changed the working man's status for ever. The radical legislation of 1945–51 helped set the political agenda for the next fifty years, and kick-started the economic machinery of the nation. Bert caught the times perhaps better than he knew when he talked about kids having it good, and being about to have it better.

It was a decade when the British high street first met with the slick packaging of Madison Avenue. A glimmer of American consumerism now reached even the Dartford *Chronicle*, where sketches of Frigidaires, Hoovers and huge, boatlike Fords jostled alongside ads for Mazawatte Tea, Beecham's Powders and other remedies for the English winter. In London the South Bank, home of the Festival of Britain, showed 3-D 'Telecinema' films: *The African Queen*, *An American in Paris*, *High Noon*. Rationing ended. The influx of Italian POWs led to the arrival of espresso coffee, sold in cafés that soon turned into *salons* for young men in polo necks. The Beats, Johnnie Ray, TV, Everest and *Playboy*. Even in combination, it never exactly made for a mood of national optimism or freewheeling mobility. There was still a lot of forelock-tugging. England remained the only nation on earth where a self-made businesswoman like Eva Jagger could feel socially uneasy in the presence of the vicar or a seedy schoolmaster. But it did seem there was more choice about. At weekends Keith would sometimes earn pocket money by helping Doris demonstrate fridges and washing machines at her other job, in the Co-op. Or he stayed home all day and listened to the radio, which, as he said, 'paid shit'.

He preferred the radio.

'My mum would be looking for Django Reinhardt, the bop [hour], she knew exactly where on the dial to go,' Keith told his friend Stanley Booth. 'I'd hear Ella, Sarah Vaughan, Nat King Cole, Billy Eckstine, Louis Armstrong. It was a house full of noise.' After jazz ended at noon – a caesura between the hip and the highbrow – everything became more Reithian. Keith also soaked up 'Beethoven and Mozart and Bach ... I know they're great guys but when I was growing up that shit was too heavy for me – still, I listened to it every day.' But the musical border jumping didn't stop there. Keith also had his beloved cowboys. He listened to dixieland as though it had something genuinely of interest to say. Even the chanteuse tradition took hold, leading to Keith naming one of his cars the Blue Lena. Jazz, swing, ragtime, folk, country, classical, all were equal when it came to the Richardses' Motorola. If Keith and Doris never tuned in to the blues, that must have been the sole form of music not to be heard in Chastilian Road.

As time passed and his voice improved, Keith became an outstanding chorister both at school and in Dartford's Holy Trinity church, with occasional gigs as far afield as Westminster Abbey. This was no pilgrimage of faith. Like Bert and Doris, Keith seems to have viewed a church as a venue, rather than as the tangible expression or receptacle of any religion. Another attraction was that he was excused chemistry class (something he caught up on later) because of his choral excursions. At ten Keith also joined the local Boy Scouts, 1st Beaver Patrol unit. One dank morning in May 1954 some thirty Wentworth students and three masters boarded a green Southdown bus for a school outing to tour Wembley Stadium. The group included both Keith and Mike Jagger. A photo was taken showing the party huddled together in their regulation grey macs and tasselled knee-length socks, Jagger characteristically having found a prop – a stray black kitten – to pose with. While every other child looks straight at the camera, Mike, alone, stares impishly over his shoulder. Instinct told one that that boy would go far.

Keith and Mike drifted apart, as they so often would, when, in late 1954,

Bert put down £80 deposit for number 6 Spielman Road, on the new Temple Hill estate in east Dartford. The move was both uphill and downmarket. The sheer desolation and uniformity of the place took the breath away. Coming home late at night, Bert sometimes walked up the wrong driveway. 'How are you supposed to tell these dumps apart?' he asked. Adolescence would prove a stormy period for Keith, who spent the next eight years in a ghetto of identical redbrick semis and daubed graffiti, while Mike and his family moved into Newlands, a four-bedroomed house surrounded by apple trees, in suburban Wilmington. Nothing could better demonstrate how 'everything seemed to come easy' to the Jaggers, whose elder son passed into Dartford grammar school in September 1954. By contrast, 'utter shit' was always there for Richards, who soon began getting into fights around the estate. Never physically strong, Keith became quite adept at the tactical kick to an opponent's groin followed by a swift exit. Had his career in rock 'n roll not worked out, that sort of lifestyle would strike Keith as a 'pretty fair alternative' and, to be honest, not all that different. Early in 1955 he took and failed the 11-plus exam and was sent to Dartford Tech for a desultory four years.

Keith, now shooting up like a weed, remained a striking presence in the choir there. Doris would say that she could always pick out his voice from the others and a kindly master at the Tech, Jake Clair, wrote that 'Keith [had] a naturalness ... not great technique but a wonderful ear.'

People were marvelling at Keith's naturalness right up until the summer of 1956, when his voice broke. For the average boy of twelve-and-a-half, being rudely ejected by the choir and violently berated by his father whenever he dared touch the radio might be the end of any musical ambitions. Keith Richards was no average boy. He'd inherited the Duprees' love of rhythm, and now the ebb and flow of a strange new sound on the Motorola wafted the breath of life to him. Overnight, as Keith put it, everything turned, 'zoom! From black and white to glorious Technicolor.'

The role models came to him, as they did to millions, under the covers, shivering and belted on his long bus journey to the Tech, or hunched over the radio before Bert appeared in the evening. *Rock and roll.* Portly, cheroot-sucking and as phlegmatic as the Wall of China, Bill Haley was the unlikely prophet whose grunted lyrics, set to a slapped double-bass and a brisk backbeat, so vexed British parents and electrified their children. From Haley, Keith would quickly discover Fats Domino, Huey Smith, Elvis, Buddy Holly, Eddie Cochran and his holy of holies, Chuck Berry. The last named was already pushing thirty, with a conviction for armed robbery, when he began writing chugging, four-bar guitar licks that tapered into fast-moving songs about girls, high schools and cars. Keith would later call 1956, the year he first heard Berry's Roll Over Beethoven, a watershed, 'ground zero . . . it hit England like Hiroshima'.

Besides truancy and fighting, Keith's only other teenage relationship was with music. The riffs came through, static-ridden yet somehow intact in their joyous derangement. Keith was, he says, 'shitstruck' by Berry and Elvis, though even that downplays a case bordering on reincarnation. Rock radiated the fragrance of escape. As a solitary latchkey kid, he'd often stolen into the Odeon to watch Roy Rogers head down the lonely trail. Keith found the new landscapes even more appealing. Within a short time he was 'zonked – totally gone', visualizing himself not in the dreary east Dartford streets but sashaying around Memphis or hopping a box car through the Southern cotton fields. As well as the pop licks echoing thinly from the Motorola, Keith embarked on both a self-improvement and fantasy course in the blues: Leadbelly, Howlin' Wolf, Fred McDowell, John Lee Hooker, Willie Dixon, Muddy Waters. A year or two later, he actually saw Sonny Terry perform in London. Using these men's lyrics as ammo, Keith began to strafe Bert, just as Bert, as he always would, strafed him back. Keith already knew he could never live like his dad did. But he knew something else, too. If two archetypal value systems were at odds, the tougher man would win – and he, Keith, was it.

The spotlit side to Keith's life, first switched on with such voltage at the Coronation, resumed when Doris began taking him to visit Gus Dupree in, aptly, London's Seven Sisters Road. 'I guess he caught me at the point where I was transferring my interest from singing to playing. Don't know what he saw in me, but whatever it was, he made it.' Balding and slight, and as compressed as a power coil, Gus bounced around town with his flamenco guitar, still, in his early seventies, playing every chance he got. Keith was invited to tag along and sometimes even to sit onstage and strum. By age fourteen, he was really living two lives. Keith sleepwalked through engineering and carpentry class by day and thrilled to butt-wagging rock by night.

Before long, Keith pitched the idea that he too would be a musician. Some time early that winter, he dragged Doris down to the high street.

There it was in the window of the Co-op, conspicuous against all the Hoovers and Frigidaires, notable for its thin, hollow quality but immediately responsive to Keith's touch: Rosetti's Professional Style Acoustic Guitar. With that and a cheap gramophone, similarly coaxed out of Doris, he now began copying the early 'beat' records like White Sport Coat or Butterfingers as fast as he could get them.

The late Fifties promised newly equipped teens like Keith better if still modest prospects. Now was the era of Woolies 'house' versions of American hits, plaid shirts, Brylcreem, Spam and Players Weights cigarettes. The boxy Austins and Rileys, the boiled cabbage smell ground deep into the worsted suits, the red-eyed girls in overalls with scarves over their hair trudging to the Wellcome factory – those were the madeleines, or stale Hob Nobs, of Keith's adolescence. But like a stagnant pond, motionless to the naked eye, 'youth culture' was already teeming with furious, invisible activity. On 13 April 1958 the Marquee Club opened in Soho, catering first strictly to jazz and then, to the purse-lipped disgust of even the club's owner, the likes of Lonnie Donegan and the strange hybrid, all strummed washboards and banged dustbins, of skiffle. Keith's three fads that year were Donegan, Elvis and the film *Jazz on a Summer's Day*, which he saw fourteen times. Soon the Dartford *Chronicle* began reviewing the new 'long players' alongside its bowls scores and recipes involving powdered egg. The only mention of crime records a sorry fall from grace: on or around Christmas 1958 someone on the Temple Hill estate spray-painted the words SKIF RULES on a brick wall. Although Keith admired skiffle's raw power, there was no suggestion that he was tied up in this scandal.

Keith also loved the British slapstick, end-of-the-pier tradition. Even in the wrecked years, there was always some knock-kneed Crazy Gang skit or Max Miller routine afoot in his hotel suite. At fourteen, he could do a manic Hitler impersonation. Before long the constant refrain in Spielman Road became 'What will the neighbours say?', or Bert's snarled 'Get a job'.

Mike Jagger was to comment on Keith's appearance, and other qualities besides, several times in years to come. But there was never to be a greater shock than his seeing him one wet morning in December 1958. Keith had, not untypically, missed his bus to school, and now, at Bert's insistence, was cycling down Oakfield Lane towards the Tech's wrought-iron gate, not far from the Jaggers' in Wilmington. Mike would refer to the sight frequently: in contrast to his own uniform of starchy white shirt and gold-edged maroon blazer, Keith travelled in dark glasses, a faded denim jacket and, it emerged, not one but two pairs of trousers. Richards arrived at school wearing the regulation grey issue; these were then removed to reveal a pair of stunningly tight black drainpipes. Passers-by couldn't help but notice that Keith liked to ride the bike in a zigzag pattern and that he carried his guitar slung over the back wheel.

Mike gaped, and then he knew. He literally knew. This was it.

By 1958, the year he passed eight O levels, Jagger was a part-time beach peddler of ice cream in summer and street vendor of his mother's cosmetics in winter. He sometimes listened to rock and roll and even sang a bit, in between doing his homework and arranging Avon products. (Contrary to folklore, he was never a member of any organized group, let alone one called Little Boy Blue & the Blue Boys.) It was largely thanks to Eva that Mike both shone at school and earned such extra pocket money. He was the first British teenager anyone had heard of to shun Woolies, and instead write off to Chess Records in Chicago for the latest Chuck Berry release. Jagger began to attract attention at Dartford grammar school when he walked around with *One Dozen Berries* under his arm.

In early 1959 the Tech, irritated by Keith's attendance record, expelled him. After the shouting had died down with Bert, he managed to enrol at art college three stops up the line towards London, in Sidcup. Keith would later say that he left the Tech because of the headmaster's objection to his having jumped on a motorbike and taken off 'in search of chicks'. But he may have forgotten that he also failed or cut his fourth-year exams, indicating a more relaxed posture than *The Great Escape*.

That Keith did, in the end, make it was due, in about equal parts, to talent, luck and others' deep faith in him; that and an underlying self-confidence that he wasn't only in – strangely – the right place, but there at the right time. 'A lot of what I learnt at [Sidcup] came home to roost,' he later said. 'About selling a look, an attitude, an image.' It remains debatable whether art school did any academic good for the likes of Keith, John Lennon, Pete Townshend, Eric Clapton, Jimmy Page, David Bowie and Ray Davies, all of whom enrolled there. But it undeniably rewarded anyone with an ear for a tune and a streak of irreverence. The downwardly mobile path now beckoned.

Just exactly where that might lead, Keith couldn't say. 'Shitty reality' was the daily trip to Sidcup, which adjoins Dartford but lacks any of its neighbour's raw energy, vital nightlife and racy promise.

His new friends soon noticed that Keith was, as Doris always said, special. Here was someone whose sole apparent purpose was to slouch in the school 'bogs', dressed in his drainpipes and fluorescent mauve socks, playing the blues. His posture there was so arthritic, both sitting and standing, a cold butt end permanently clamped in the corner of his mouth, that he seemed to be keeping himself awake only with enormous effort. Keith varied the routine only by haunting the students' kitchen, with its leaky gas-rings and the sharp tang of fatty foods. Everyone was positive that he'd be the first of them to drop dead of a heart attack.

Encouraged and accompanied by Gus, Keith would take an evening train to London, head for Soho and there listen to skiffle with missionary zeal. The bands' quality, if any, made little difference. 'Really crude!' Keith would shout elatedly, as though eyeing a primitive tribe of head-hunters. Or quite incisive stuff like 'Good comping – I dig the turnarounds.' After he went back to Sidcup at dawn, Richards snacked on benzedrine. Keith's friend Dick Taylor recalls the Midnight Rambler fondly. 'He was a real ted, and I used to love him for that . . . We were both on a pretty steady diet of speed and other stuff, sprays, inhalers, anything. Right across the street there was this little wood with an aviary that had a cockatoo in it. Keith used to go over and feed it pep pills. When he was bored he'd bung the bird another leaper and watch it flap around on its perch.'

Another day, Taylor would recall Keith tossing a well-aimed match into a bath of flammable silk-screen wash. 'When I think of him at Sidcup, I think of cockatoos and stuff burning.' In time the drugs and pyromania brought Keith further untold grief from Bert and completed a caricature role as school misfit. When Sidcup's graphic design class went on a field trip to Heal's, the London furniture store, Keith sat down on a leather sofa and dropped hot cigarette ash on it. For half an hour.

Back in the lavs, Keith, having swapped a stack of records for his first electric guitar, was laboriously teaching himself the riffs of Hound Dog and Ramblin' Jack's Cocaine Blues. He slaved over Big Bill Broonzy, Josh White and Woody Guthrie. John Lee Hooker. It was a cause of prolonged vexation to Sidcup's staff that, had he worked as hard in class as he did behind it, he could have been a stellar artist. It was usually after Keith's triumphant emergence with a new song in his repertoire that Bert, too, was apt to mention that Ricky's time, in his opinion, was being wasted, or that he had a bloody screw loose.

Only Doris and Gus seemed to understand who he really was and share the high regard in which he was held by a select few like Dick Taylor. Bert, crabby and often petulant even in the old days, didn't become more chirpy now his juvenile-delinquent son began keeping him awake nights with the din. Soon it was war. When Bert came home after a twelve-hour shift he'd find Keith sitting at the top of the stairs, playing and banging on the wall for percussion. Or (a variant of his Sidcup technique) he'd move into the Spielman Road bathroom for hours on end. The ensuing rows were often low key, though once or twice brutal and frightening, especially when Bert tried to grab back the guitar. One night, when they were really going at it, Doris had to throw herself between them. It was in the very week Keith learnt Tutti Frutti that his father, whom he tactlessly called Adolf, took a shy at him. Asked to turn it down, the teen had replied 'Wop-bom-aloo-*mop.*' In the mini-riot that followed several neighbours pounded on the Richardses' door, and some of them yelled 'Don't kill him, Bert!' and Bert himself vowed the opposite, as Doris tried to shout above the uproar. Bert wasn't generally a man for violence, but he demanded respect. 'I told him to knock it off,' he said later, 'and he laughed at me.'

The first time the Human Riff played before a crowd was at a scout hall – not, as he later told a credulous fanzine, a brothel – in Eltham that winter of 1960. It was the season of *South Pacific*, the then greaseball Cliff Richard's Please Don't Tease and Tony Newley warbling Why?; but there were no show tunes in the repertoire Keith and two friends eked out that Saturday night. Facilities were basic. There was a combined chaperon-MC (the local vicar), a table lamp, and two beaten-up radios serving as amps. The hastily named Sidcup Shaggers performed half a dozen Johnny Cash and Hank Snow hits and made a wild stab at Elvis' Blue Moon Of Kentucky. Country and western was big in England in 1960. Sweating throughout, Keith took deep ironic bows after each rendition. The vicar leapt on stage after the final number to urge everyone to leave quietly, but there was no problem – most of the subdued audience had already shuffled off. (After this inauspicious debut, Keith missed the last train home and 'spent the night freezing in a bus shelter with a local slag. That was my introduction to showbusiness.')

A day or two later, Keith went back to Sidcup and set light to his silk-screen wash to celebrate. Booze. Pep pills. Bert muttered some more about him being a layabout. With a set-up like this, Keith's formative years equipped him for only two things: the stage or prison.

He chose the former, though the latter would still beckon. There were occasional run-ins with the law around the estate, and Keith sometimes complained that they were out to get him. He thought this even before it was actually true. The prevalent view was that he was free-spirited and fast-witted, a pest.

Keith's musical tastes, too, were already sharper than those of even 'with it' peers like Dick Taylor. It wasn't just that his imagination ran wilder, or that his sense of rhythm was deeper. It was more magical; his flashes of inspiration with the guitar seemed to come from out of the blue. Like Gus Dupree, Keith heard the sounds in his head first and learnt how to play them later. 'He wasn't one of us,' the other Shaggers noted constantly.

As the Sixties began, there were three distinct views of Keith. A few visionaries, including Taylor, and certainly all Doris's family, thought he was troubled but gifted, technically brilliant. Bert Richards agreed about the trouble but doubted the brilliance. Most of his peers, in thrall to Lonnie Donegan's My Old Man's A Dustman or the dixieland strains of Kenny Ball, found him disturbingly other-worldly. He was a youthful outcast with the ear of a mature musician. All three parties could make out a reasonable case for Keith's being 'different', and he joined the consensus. Richards later recalled, 'I always felt like my fly was open.'

Even now, Keith had a deep antipathy to what he called 'clever bastard' music. At the same time as he laboriously deconstructed his cherished blues riffs he was in the business to find the best *natural* way to 'go straight for the gut'. Along with a more finely honed guitar sound, he likewise sought to eliminate the 'decorative shit' of devices like grace notes; he believed this symptomatic of British pop and its absurdly fussy nuances and subtleties, which he loathed.

Instead, Keith sought rhythm and tone, what he called 'straight' music: just plain, unadorned notes. Ron Simms was both a grammar school and Hit Parade student when he came to Spielman Road in 1960 in response to Keith's need for someone to lend him records. One day, Simms forgot himself and played Richards the Shads' Apache, then well on its way to selling its first million. 'Fuckin' awful,' Keith said when it finished. 'They're just wanking around.' Keith immediately picked up his guitar and 'played a beautiful blues run, the simplest kind possible'. Right there in the poky council house bedroom Richards began improvising a song, accompanying himself in a reedy but, to Simms, 'spine-tingling' voice. Keith's critique of 'clever' music now came to life. He embodied the blues so hauntingly that it suddenly seemed possible to imagine they were thousands of miles away, riding that lonesome train through the night. As Simms staggered back out onto the street he found he was strangely moved.

'The way Keith played, he could bring tears to your eyes.'

A deep dislike for merely copying – whether at school or, now, with the guitar – was the hallmark of Keith's adolescence. He wanted bustle, activity, trial and error, anything to 'go for the gut'. The disparity between his emotional maturity and musical side wasn't just vast, it was freakishly so. Many of what would become Keith's lifelong fetishes – Chuck Berry syncopation, 4/4 rhythm, the science of acoustics – were already in place. Around his seventeenth birthday his obsession began to take on an urgent quality. Bert was home on disability, and no longer shouted at Keith to turn down the guitar every night. Now he did so all day long. Keith, who didn't deem it vital to immediately take Bert's advice, began staying in London, playing or busking, every chance he got. Now more than ever, he seemed frozen in his strange and dreamlike state; he barely existed without the guitar. When the Commercial Art class at Sidcup put together a yearbook in 1961, its editors wittily noted that 'several Dr Livingstones are exploring the new jungle beat here'. But the book included no biographical sketch of Keith, as it did of every other classmate. His life was missing.

On the raw, autumnal morning of 17 October 1961, Kent and much of the southeast was covered in fog. The trains that Tuesday morning were running late. On the drab northbound platform at Dartford station, a lone passenger, draped in an overcoat and a purple, black and gold scarf, was waiting for the delayed 8.28 to London. Mike Jagger, having passed three A levels and an entrance exam that summer, was on his way to a Politics lecture at the London School of Economics. Clutching his copy of *One Dozen Berries* under his arm, he was jumping up and down, half from cold, half with his usual nervous energy. The time was shortly before nine.

In a career discussion earlier that week with his LSE tutor, Walter Stern, Jagger had repeated his plans to become a school teacher or, failing that, a civil servant. Mike's father, Joe, thought he had it in him to be a top economist. Walter Stern, for his part, already had doubts about Jagger's mathematical ability, but high hopes for him in advertising. 'That boy always had some campaign, you know, some scheme.'

Almost anything, they all agreed, but music.

As Jagger peered down the curve of platform two, that particular option seemed singularly improbable. A minute later it became inevitable. Coming out of the depths of the fog was Keith Richards, lugging his guitar.

Over the next few weeks, Keith and Mike bonded over Chuck Berry and Muddy Waters. They found they had a mutual accompanist in Dick Taylor. By Christmas of 1961 the three of them, and an occasional guest from college, were spending their weekends crouched with guitars and gramophones in one or other of their parents' suburban, pebbledashed houses. After Eva Jagger and, inevitably, Bert Richards complained, the preferred venue became the Taylors'. The early schooling of the Rolling Stones took place among the chintz of 34 Alexander Road, Bexleyheath.

Dick Taylor remembers fondly how 'one day, Mike would become Keith. But then a day or two later, Keith would be like Mike.' Taylor wasn't alone in marvelling how each seemed to find something they admired and envied in the other: the tough but surprisingly tenderhearted punk, and the diligent economics student with a taste for slumming. Within a week of re-meeting Keith, Jagger was using the word 'bourgeois' in tutorials. At a session with Stern on 3 November, in which he appeared dressed in jeans and winklepickers, he announced that he'd no longer answer to the name 'Mike'. From now on it would be Mick.

In the Jaggers' hierarchy, Keith was 'the local ted' – trouble. The social reputation of the Richardses stood low. When Mick brought his new friend to tea at Newlands he promptly dropped a heavy plate to the floor, causing Eva to flinch. Keith, with his pet mouse, fag ash and spots, must have been among the very last house guests she would have chosen. Nonetheless, when Bert and Doris took a rare family holiday that winter, to Devon, Keith and Mick accompanied them. The two teens played together one night in the local pub, crooning Everly Brothers hits on stools in front of a mike.

'We're gonna be famous,' Mick explained.

Keith turned eighteen that same week. He and Jagger were the first postwar generation not to do National Service, while the media now spoke the excited rhetoric of consumer demand. There were just two million cars in Britain in 1950; by 1962 there were over seven million. Television became commonplace – in fact Mick and his father had sometimes appeared on an ATV programme called *Seeing Sport*. An election had just been fought and won on the slogan 'You never had it so good'.

Keith, too, became more ambitious as an adult. 'I wish,' he told Doris, 'me and Mick had a manager.'

It was inevitable that Keith would leave Sidcup unqualified. With a few rare exceptions, staff and students had long since learnt to give him a wide berth rather than stop to chat. Hardened educators declined to enter into the briar patch of teaching him, and classmates blanched when they saw him coming down the corridor dragging his new Hofner guitar. Keith left art school for the last time in spring 1962. By now he was a dab hand at life drawing, and could doodle a cartoon in four or five sweeping lines, but those were his only feats in the studio. At Bert's insistence, Keith took his portfolio to the top London designers – including the man soon to do the titles for *Goldfinger*, Robert Brownjohn – but all declined his services. (In 1969, Keith would commission the same Brownjohn, one of the few to be civil to him, to design the cover of *Let It Bleed*.) Apart from one or two friendly hipsters who talked to him about music, most couldn't wait to get the pill-chewing young punk out of their offices, at least until four or five years later, when some of them began remembering him and ringing him back. As Keith said, 'a kick in the nuts from those guys – that counted as a warm hello by their standards'.

Keith was often in London, but this seems to have been more to visit Gus or to trawl the speciality record shops like Dobell's than to job hunt. As Bert had rightly feared, he wasn't career minded. Besides the Duprees, Keith's one love was of the guitar, and for him happiness – 'ducking the shitstorm' – came out of a finely tuned call-and-response with the Hofner, the channelling of some potent gut-level force that called for the union of man and instrument. It was better than sex. 'The shape of the guitar is really feminine. There's many times I've slept with that fucker.'

The Shagger who made this observation was busy honing his craft, playing all over town, on the bus, in Tube carriages, for this was an obsessed case. Keith constantly badgered Doris to buy him guitar strings, records and, first thing every Thursday, without fail, the trade press. On 15

March 1962 he was browsing through the interminable jazz reviews in *New Musical Express*, when out of the dross a small ad brought him awake:

Alexis Korner Blues Incorporated
The Most Exciting Event of the Year
Ealing Broadway Station
Turn left, cross the zebra and go down steps
between ABC teashop and jewellers.
Saturday at 7.30 p.m.

Keith, Jagger and assorted Shaggers would make it to west London – there'd been trouble raising the fare – on Saturday 7 April. The Ealing club had no pretension to elegance. An iron gate gave on to sixteen foul-smelling steps, the stone worn to the thinness of paper, leading down to a sort of crypt. This stygian pit shook whenever a train passed by, and rainwater frequently seeped through the brickwork. A canvas tarp was strung up under the skylight to prevent the musicians from electrocuting themselves.

Nine o'clock on Easter Saturday and six or seven middle-aged men were milling about playing instrumental blues, along with a smattering of 'trad' standards. Korner himself was sitting on an office chair strumming a Spanish guitar. He looked arresting, with his aura of black fuzz, sweat rag and Rupert the Bear trousers, a thirty-three-year-old exotic whose enthusiasm exceeded his, frankly, meagre ability. Keith had just turned to Mick with the verdict 'This is a wank', when his attention was drawn to something happening on stage. Korner came forward. 'This' – he indicated a blond bouffant in the shadows – 'is Elmo Lewis. He's come from Cheltenham to play for you.' For the next ten minutes, Korner's group performed like a Porsche swiftly being run-in. An Elmore James medley of I Believe and Dust My Broom, with stinging bar slide guitar, ended to wild applause.

A kick in the groin couldn't have affected Keith more. When Richards and Jagger beheld Elmo Lewis – in reality a twenty-year-old named Lewis Brian Jones – they knew what it was to, quite literally, feel the earth move. Backed by a Tube train percussion, Jones's guitar slithered and swooped, slicing through any last vestige of dixieland.

'Fucking hell,' Keith whispered to his companions, 'that guy's a *star*.'

And Jagger, vowing he'd never forgive Richards for saying that, went up to introduce himself.

*   *   *

Brian Jones, who related the episode often, would look back on that first meeting like Crusoe finding Man Friday's footsteps. Silent and uptight as a teenager, an affront to Cheltenham's blue-rinse image, he'd been effectively run out of town for theft, multiple impregnations and playing blues guitar. Jones would have a number of casual addresses over the next two or three years, before taking up full-time residence in his fame. Once in London, he made to Ealing at a brisk trot. Brian was a short man, with stubby legs and squat shoulders (a 'little Welsh bull', Keith thought), and a face that photographers dream about: massive head, immaculate blond fringe, shaggy-dog eyes, button nose and a wide, expressive mouth that, on a girl, would have been gorgeous.

Personally, too, Brian was that rare mixture, a Botticelli angel with a cruel streak. During the next seven years he'd display a remarkable talent for charming people, like Korner, before savagely mauling them. Jones's pockets were already always stuffed with unfinished but twisted song lyrics and poems vowing revenge on those who had ignored him, abused him or doubted his genius. Other writings of Brian's dealt with fauns and hobbits. Even Keith would call him 'a weird bunch of guys' and a 'contradiction in blond'. Jones was the former choirboy who spoke in a lilting, effete voice that, sooner or later, gave way to an exquisitely calibrated fuck-you snarl. Five years after that first night in Ealing, a court-appointed psychiatrist would tell a judge, deciding whether or not to send Brian to prison, that he was intelligent but 'emotionally unstable, with neurotic tendencies'. The shrink concluded, 'This individual vacillates between a passive, pathetically weak child on the one hand, and a pop idol on the other.'

As Jones climbed down from the stage for his historic meeting with Keith and Mick, Korner's bass player toppled drunkenly into the drum kit. It went over with a molten crash.

'There goes yer fuckin' rhythm,' said Brian to Korner. He had Mick's own gift of tongues; when he turned to Richards and Jagger, he was his old fruity self. 'A new band?' he said. 'Let's chat upstairs. The air here gives me the croup.'

After 1962, Jones would never quite share in the group ethic. 'There was always this incredible conflict between Brian, Mick and me,' said Keith. Richards and Jagger would have to soar into ecstasies at Jones's embryonic songwriting, for example, or risk moving Brian to tears, and to the reiterated charge that others were out to 'fuck' him. Sexually, too, the three-way friendship soon curdled. Within six months of meeting him, Mick had managed to screw Brian's steady girlfriend. With heroic self-restraint Jones limited his retaliation to spending most of that winter huddled together in bed, for warmth, with Keith, creating the Rolling Stones.

For six years, Richards had wanted to be famous, to be recognized as a 'real musician', sometimes turning up the volume to the point where his voice warped. 'Slowly getting my shit together, ANY DAY NOW!' he'd written to a Tech mate when he was fourteen. He was now nearly twenty, and those early try-outs with Jagger and Jones were proof of how far he'd come. Keith had long since learnt Waters' song Honey Bee with its distinctive buzzing tone, could churn out Jimmy Reed hits like Honest I Do and virtually channelled Chuck Berry. In those days his playing had a lazy, almost drunken quality, and even on the faster numbers he seemed to be chugging not soaring, while the famous open-tuning was nowhere to be heard. Yet Keith also employed a light right hand and enough innate 'feel' to point the way ahead. His version of Berry's Sweet Little Sixteen included a brisk two-bar lick of three notes, E, F-sharp and A, that spun heads whenever he let it rip. That particular bolt would be incorporated six years later into Jumpin' Jack Flash. The barre chords of Down The Road Apiece foretold Brown Sugar, while an off-beat, syncopated riff would resurface in Honky Tonk Women.

The key ingredient, though, was Keith's willingness to do whatever it took, along with the stamina to carry off his hard-won gains. 'He always looked like the unhealthiest cat in the group,' said Korner. 'But we knew he was the strongest physically. Keith was always the first to look really devastated. And once he looked devastated, he was still working. Meanwhile, [Brian and Mick] would slowly collapse . . . The guy had a heart of gold and balls of steel.'

Keith, with his peerless sense of rhythm and talent for style-hopping, was now a name to be reckoned with; men like Jones admired him, while some of the goateed swingers who ran proceedings at Ealing were appalled by this vision of teen delinquency, all tight jeans and acne, whom Korner invited up 'for a blow'. Cyril Davies, for one, a north London panel beater by day and Korner's harp player by night, audibly muttered 'fucking greaser' whenever Richards took the stage. Davies' fellow blues traveller Dick Heckstall-Smith thought Keith had the 'allure of a charging rhino'. One or two of the older jazz diehards refused to play with him. In short, apart from a few seers like Korner himself, Keith was generally regarded not as a musical genius but as a purveyor of odd looks, uncomfortable noises and proto-punk attitude.

The Ealing crowd much preferred Jagger, who proved just the ticket needed to sell old men's music to a young audience – tossing his head around like a hair fetishist. 'Mick hadn't developed his grand aura yet,' said Korner, 'and without it he was actually rather sweet.' Whenever Jagger sang at Ealing, he insisted that Keith accompany him.

Within months the subterranean club, with its grubby stage and rotational cast of 'guest artistes', would become a lab for such edgy interactions between the music of one era and that coming up behind it, fast. As well as Richards, Jagger and Jones, Rod Stewart, Eric Clapton, Jeff Beck, Jack Bruce and Eric Burdon were some of those regularly sitting in, to varying degrees of acclaim, on Saturday nights. What gave many of these nights their spark was a cool-looking drummer who played in a relaxed, jazzy style yet whose backbeat could make the stage jump up and down the street. Charlie Watts.

By May 1962, Brian Jones was squatting in a room in London's Powis Square. (Years later, Jagger would go on to imitate Jones and Keith in the film *Performance* – set in 25 Powis Square.) While the Dartford camp bided their time, Brian began scheming to get the best of the Ealing crew rehearsing separately under his baton. Most of the early try-outs took place in dusty rooms above Soho pubs like the White Bear or (after the Bear's landlord caught Jones pilfering) the Bricklayer's Arms. This was where musicians drifted in, sat around and played a few Muddy Waters songs, and where Brian, in keeping with his longstanding policy, insisted that each pay him a 'session fee' for their trouble. The first to audition was a twenty-three-year-old shipping clerk named Ian Stewart. 'Stu' arrived at the Bricklayer's in leather cycling shorts, carrying a pork pie which he proceeded to eat from one hand while playing piano in a loping, barrelhouse style with the other.

Stu, a breezy, no-bullshit Scot with a vast Cro-Magnon jaw and generous beer-gut, would always remember Keith that first day in the pub. Previously, Richards had endured a brief and unsatisfying 'blow' with several Ealing pianists in their formal, churchy style; for them, even jazz was a sort of worship. Keith's job, which he found insufficiently stimulating ('a total wank'), was to accompany their renditions of In The Mood or Don't Sit Under The Apple Tree with discreet guitar arpeggios. With Stu, a chance arose to jam on *'real* whorehouse blues' – boogie-woogie and ragtime sixteens – and Keith grabbed it. The room, dreary and dark most of the time, suddenly began to rock. That rehearsal would be the last time Jones, or anyone else in the band, would recall the unflappable Stewart ever looking at another musician and saying, 'Fuck, you're *good.'*

Stu was in. He joined Jones, Richards, Jagger, Dick Taylor and anyone they could find on drums. Brian was after Charlie Watts, but he was too expensive for them.

This would be the line-up, Jones had decided, that would 'change the face of British music'. After the laughter had died down, Brian also insisted they join the Jazz Federation to boost their – Jones admitted – only fair prospects of work. He brought the papers in to the Bricklayer's on 2 July 1962. At the line marked 'title of artiste' Brian, in Keith's words, 'looked down: there's a Muddy Waters record, and the first song on it was Rollin' Stone Blues'. Later, Keith thought the name made them sound like a bunch of Irish acrobats.

The big break came when Korner was summoned from a gig at the Marquee to play, instead, on the BBC Light Programme's *Jazz Club.* A hurried relief group of Elmore James fanatics, blues freaks and the *ne plus ultra* of rock 'n rollers duly took the stage as 'Mick Jagger and the Rollin' Stones'. Stu, presciently, thought that 'Brian [would] resent that to the grave'. The date was Thursday 12 July 1962.

The fifty-minute show was paced at the speed of booze – the tempo of scotches and brandies they all downed throughout to calm their nerves. This tight, gamut-running band took its sense of urgency from the chap-faced guitarist, dressed completely in black, who called out each title and encouraged the drummer by both hammering one spindly leg up and down and yelling 'Fuck you! Faster!'

Not coincidentally, the Stones had great rhythm.

It was six o'clock in the morning when Keith went back to Dartford for the last time and started packing.

'What's going on?' his father demanded.

'I'm leaving.'

Bert saw the light moodily. 'You won't last ten minutes on your own, you bloody layabout.'

Halfway through the ensuing scene, Doris came out on the landing. Bert remarked to her that their son was a complete lout, and good riddance to him. And if Keith thought he could ever come waltzing back, there was no reason in the world for him to expect any sympathy.

Bert and Doris had just reached this point in their exchange when the front door slammed shut.

Keith announced himself at Powis Square by pounding on the basement window with his guitar case. Brian, scratching himself vigorously and torching the first of the day's sixty cigarettes, opened the door and welcomed Richards to the squat and to London. Jones led his bandmate, carrying only the Hofner, a few records and a spare pair of boots as his worldly possessions, into the bedsitter-cum-kitchen/WC and made them a breakfast of cold beans from the tin. Graciously, he allowed Keith to move in with him for only nominal rent, which Brian would deduct from Keith's future earnings with the Rollin' Stones.

This arrangement lasted until – as they always did at Brian's, sooner or later – the bailiffs called. Richards and Jones then made an undignified retreat to a shared room in Brackley Road, Beckenham, a neighbourhood of sturdily built but decaying Edwardian villas choked with weeds, and not known for rock 'n roll – although David Bowie would live only a few doors away in his Ziggy Stardust phase. There the two Stones used to 'lay around, listen to sounds and play all day and always read *Billboard*, just to see what was goin' on . . . used to read every page, even jukebox profits. Used to know everything about what was happening [in the charts], absolutely everything.' When that, too, ended in eviction, Keith, Brian and Mick moved back to London and a slum located in, aptly enough, World's End, Chelsea.

Number 102 Edith Grove was a place which Keith would say made even Spielman Road 'look like fucking Balmoral' by contrast. It was a two-room dive with a gas meter, naked light bulbs and a few sticks of utility furniture. Mostly this was cardboard boxes, beer crates and soiled bin liners. The one armchair was reserved for visiting dignitaries like Korner, under whom it repeatedly collapsed, dumping him onto the cement floor.

'The first time I walked in,' said Ian Stewart, 'the stink almost knocked me over. There was mouldy food and old cigarette butts all over the place, dirty clothes flung around and that disgusting smell, like rotting cabbages.'

When she heard about Edith Grove, Doris Richards came up to visit. It affected her, too, 'like a punch to the face'.

While Jagger still dutifully took the bus in to college every morning, Keith and Brian holed up at World's End, listening to records whose raw, fast paced riffs they accompanied on guitar. It was their favourite hobby, playing Muddy or Howlin' Wolf and tracing licks put down in Chicago twenty years ago. At night Jagger would sit with gritted teeth for as long as he could and then excuse himself with the explanation he had work to prepare. Decades later he told *Rolling Stone*, 'I wasn't totally committed; music was a good, fun thing to do, but Keith and Brian were beyond that. They wanted to rehearse all the time.'

The two emotional misfits in Edith Grove were capable of both surprising dedication and acts of kindness. At a legal hearing years later an older musician of no prominence or obvious professional clout told the judge that when he'd been cold and hungry in the autumn of 1962, Keith had helped feed him from his own meagre supplies. A girl named Eileen Giles, with the thankless job of cleaning Edith Grove, 'was up in the flat ironing one afternoon and somehow I got distracted, and when I turned back Keith's prize purple shirt had a big hole in it. He only had two shirts. There I was trembling and apologizing, and Keith was totally sweet.' One night that winter, which happened to be the worst in over 200 years, Richards gave another young visitor to Edith Grove the coat off his back. 'And then he said, "Come listen to this".' Within five minutes, the teenage girl was 'absolutely spellbound ... Keith played me the most beautiful song. The way [he and Jones] worked together was incredible.'

What she was hearing, amid all the scorched clothes and festering dishes, was the birth of the Rolling Stones. The whole alchemy, as Keith says, 'is the way we work two guitars'. The sound he and Brian were chasing turned out to be equal parts R&B, with a rich lode of Broonzy, Leadbelly and Champion Jack Dupree (no relation), and trace elements of Elvis and Buddy Holly. The two roommates wrote at least one song together in Edith Grove, but this turned out to be mannered and trite – 'utter shit' in Keith's bleak assessment. 'It sounded like a 1920s musical ... Brian was utterly impossible to work with. He would dominate anything he was into – there was no way you could suggest anything.' A key problem with Jones's songwriting was that it tended to be derivative, and mainly derivative, unfortunately, of himself. Brian's 'smash hit single', a breakthrough he'd predicted, on and off, for about five years, he finally abandoned after three notes. The tune was aped from a song Jones had first whistled at Cheltenham grammar school, which was itself lifted from Tommy Steele's imitation of Guy Mitchell's cover of Marty Robbins' Singin' The Blues, which Brian wished he'd thought of himself.

With Keith and Jones there was an added layer of poignancy, in that even then Richards had the pop sensibility Brian sadly lacked. Jones took out his frustration by playing Keith off against Mick, as part of his campaign to divide and conquer. He almost succeeded.

Stu, who saw more of this static than most, was driving the three of them home one night from a party. Brian had insisted on squashing down in the back seat, between Keith and Mick, and was murmuring intrigue in both their ears. Suddenly, Stu said, 'they all started shouting at each other ... Brian flung a punch at Keith, and Keith hit him back. I stopped the car and told them to piss off and fight it out between them. They did!'

In October the Stones had four gigs, in November six. On all too many days, Keith would remember, 'We didn't bother getting out of bed. Nothing to do.' Nor were prospects improved when, at a 'hippy happy yule' show, Harold Pendleton, owner of the Marquee club, muttered the word 'tossers' as the band climbed on stage. Keith retaliated by trying to brain Pendleton with his guitar. After that it would be eight years before the Stones returned to the Marquee. Keith took a swing at Pendleton on that occasion, too.

Thick fog soon descended on London, followed by snow. The Edith Grove pipes froze solid, and Keith survived on a few food and clothing parcels from Doris. Jones kept his own end up by shoplifting from their friendly local grocer. Jagger was still at college. At this sorry nadir, the Rollin' Stones entered a studio for the first time. Keith, Mick and Brian paid to cut a three-song demo, which Jones sent to a contact named Neville Skrimshire at EMI. Skrimshire took all of a minute to reject it. Thoroughly demoralized, Dick Taylor left the band. His replacement, who auditioned one snowy night in the Wetherby Arms, a pub near Edith Grove, was a Brylcreemed ex-bookie called Bill Perks, a name he'd recently changed to Wyman. The impression he made on the band could hardly have been worse. Wyman arrived neatly dressed, as always, and stood fiddling with his pearl cuff-links while Keith and Brian studiously ignored him. Stu would always marvel at the cool phlegmatic strength with which Bill handled the mass rejection. The ice was broken only by Wyman's wheeling in two massive Vox amps and the sensational discovery, shortly thereafter, that he could really play.

After that, Bill bought everyone a round of drinks and offered cigarettes. 'These were jumped on as if I were delivering famine relief.' Wyman was in, albeit with reservations. To Bill's prim sensibility, the Stones, with their sullen faces, jumping Negroid music and unheated, fetid shithole of a flat, were 'disgusting . . . squalid beatniks'. Even so, Bill would recognize that there was 'something between' Keith, Mick and Brian, a spark and a tension that transcended their surroundings.

According to Anita Pallenberg, it was that same month that allegedly 'Brian broke up a lot of things by actually going to bed with Mick. And I think Mick always resented him for having fallen for it.'

Doris came up to World's End several times that winter. After twenty-nine years together, twenty-four as man and wife, she and Bert had separated shortly after Keith left Spielman Road. Doris found conditions in Edith Grove strangely reminiscent of their wartime digs. 'It was an incredible place, mould everywhere and broken crockery . . . like a bomb had gone off.' Late one night graffiti appeared on the slimy wall of the communal bog, one floor up: FUCK OFF MICK YOU TWAT. By morning the last two words had been erased by an unknown tenant who still agreed with the main thesis. 'All very weird,' said Stu. 'I think Jagger was beginning to feel left out. Mick didn't have much to contribute, but he had a lot of ambition and vanity and he was damn smart, and I could see him looking at Brian in a way that was a little menacing. I could sense back then the beginning of Mick's desire to distance Keith from Brian . . . I used to think they were all fucking insane at times.'

Richards and the Rollin' Stones came of age that winter of 1962. Whatever abuse Keith would later heap on himself, nothing could compare to those eight months framed, on a wider canvas, by the Cuban missile crisis and the Profumo scandal. To Keith, Friday 21 December was probably the low point: the band arrived at the Piccadilly Jazz Club 'Rave of the Year' to find six people waiting. Helped by a bottle of Hirondelle wine, Richards managed to fall off the stage. The next morning he signed on as a relief carrier at St Stephen's sorting office, but was caught sleeping on the job – thus ending his career as a postman. Keith spent much of January in bed, huddled against the coldest snap in living memory. In fact, it was the worst winter in London since 1740. By day thick fog descended, leaving spectacular rime deposits on streets and houses. At night the sea froze solid. One of the house drummers at Ealing, Carlo Little, visited the Stones' flat: 'I took to Keith right away. He was so tough but funny. A rocker, dead keen on Chuck Berry, but very endearing and very, very British. He was like a character from a Dickens novel.'

Alexis Korner, while thinking no more highly of the Stones than Harold Pendleton did, always felt 'Keith was the one ... Brian was interested in portraying himself as any of the fantasies he had of himself. Mick was always very deliberate about the way he held himself. Keith was the least interested in portraying himself as something other than he was. Keith is a man of belief, Mick a man of fear.'

Momentously, Keith and Brian did finally co-opt Charlie Watts into the fold. The Stones' new recruit was a small, glum-looking man, head characteristically cocked to the right, a dresser, who drummed for Korner at night and worked as a trainee artist at Gray's ad agency by day. He wasn't like the other Stones, preferring jazz and forties hipster-style suits. He had a career. The draft board, the desk and the £200 p.a. contract all promised job security, and the money to spend on Charlie's beloved Bix Beiderbecke records; on the other hand, Watts, too, took to Keith, 'hilarious, the classic naughty schoolboy'. Gray's told him not to worry about it. He could always come back. The new line-up – Richards, Jones, Jagger, Stewart, Wyman, Watts – gave its first performance at the Flamingo Club on 14 January 1963.

Unless you were a hepcat and closet bohemian like Charlie, it would be hard to fully appreciate the scene at Edith Grove, where Keith and Brian existed on a diet of pilfered spuds and everyone communicated by daubing the walls in a solution of snot and chewing gum. On the other hand, if you had any sort of ear for either rhythm or comedy, it would be hard to top the experience of listening to the nineteen-year-old Richards playing his guitar. During these ad hoc concerts, Keith, whose spoken free associations were a show in themselves, connected the dots between seemingly unrelated subjects. While performing Cry To Me, dripping with soul, he'd give a running five-minute seminar on the Goons which included side-splitting impersonations of Bloodnok and Eccles. Keith also made some spirited announcements in regard to Charlie, 'the coolest honky alive'; the Rollin' Stones were 'the best beat group in Britain'.

Late in February, Brian met another well-heeled blues fanatic and father-figure, this one a Russian émigré called Giorgio Gomelski, and wheedled him into booking the Stones into the back room of Richmond's Station Hotel – which Gomelski quaintly dubbed the Crawdaddy Club. Stewart: 'It was a hip gig.' Stu's first impression as he entered – a man in his mid-twenties – was that in doing so he'd raised the average age in the place to nineteen. It was like falling into a river of heat, noise and sweat. The jostling-room-only club soon became a weekly date for the Stones. By mid-March Keith had become a hero there and, for the first time in his life, found himself surrounded by people who looked at the world more or less as he did. Within a month of Sundays, a new cult ratcheted into high gear. It would spread. Fast. From the first bars of Talkin' 'Bout You, Keith would be off and chugging and pacing everything, working the gruff low end of the guitar, and the jam-packed crowd would look at each other – they'd heard nothing remotely like it – and start to yell. Community chanting inside suburban pubs was still a novelty in 1963. Word soon got around and crowds began to form outside on Kew Road early every Sunday afternoon.

Big crowds. Those loud, teeming nights in Richmond, where the steam rose, girls rushed the stage and Jagger learnt how to dance, were like the mob scenes in *Strange Days*, half heaven, half hell, and no one who survived ever forgot them. Inside the Crawdaddy, Keith felt truly at home.

The pale, emaciated guitarist stage right was no beauty, some would sniff, with his pinched, borstal-boy face and spider crouch. Keith's rougher edges, however, only served to emphasize the tribal stomp of a Mona, and the other Richmond showstoppers. The set's Berry and Bo Diddley climax rocked harder than the Stones ever had in the past. Clever, cocky and not over-burdened by technique, Keith gave classic black R&B a face lift without smoothing the wrinkles.

Everything now went overboard. To a generation starved of its own music, and force fed trad, the Stones were manna. On 7 April 1963, the first anniversary of Keith and Mick meeting 'Elmo Lewis' in Ealing, the band played to an overflow audience of 400 fans. While Jagger took the bus to college the next morning, Richards, Jones and Gomelski, now the group's de facto manager, plastered fly-posters – 'R&B with the Inimitable, Incomparable, Exhilarating Rollin' Stones' – over west London, mixing up the paste in the bath at Edith Grove (its only known function). On 13 April the band were noticed, sensationally, in the *Richmond and Twickenham Times*. Next night, the Beatles came to pay homage at the Crawdaddy.

They stood right at the front, in matching leather overcoats, with just a few feet between them and the Stones. Then John Lennon and Paul McCartney leapt up on a table and started dancing.

Several hours later, Brian arrived back at Edith Grove with his new friends John and Paul, still high on adrenaline. He felt his poise crumble as he opened the door. Keith and Mick were huddled in bed together, for warmth, writing a song.

The Stones' life as a band began to come together on 28 April, when they got a call from a semi-obscure record plugger and failed pop singer (trading under the name Sandy Beach) called Andrew Loog Oldham. Oldham came to Richmond that night. Keith found him an 'incredible hustler', younger even than the Stones – born, illegitimate, in January 1944 to an English mother and a Dutch-American father who was killed in the war. Oldham was that rare mixture of a slightly foppish, Edwardian Jekyll and beatnik, upper-fuelled Hyde, swaying around Soho in hip-hugging black as though on some permanent audition for the Laurence Harvey role in *Expresso Bongo*. (He saw the film sixteen times.) Oldham had already achieved two-thirds of his burning ambition to become a 'teenage tycoon shit'. Now opportunity met with motive. Andrew related to the Stones in much the same way, Brian Jones would sneer, a train does to rails. Keith and Mick, Oldham rapidly concluded, were the ones prepared to slog. Brian was a 'talented chancer'.

'What'll become of the guy?' he asked Richards and Jagger.

No reply.

Oldham's own entrepreneurial juices were quickly flowing. He seemed but vaguely interested in the day-to-day business of managing a band – this would be left to his much older partner, Eric Easton – but Andrew's 'front', worth more than any office graft, was soon to reap undreamt-of goodies; the man's *chutzpah* knew no bounds. A pageboy cap was pushed rakishly back on Andy's sandy hair, and he projected the manic assurance and panache of a hip Colonel Parker. Before him, British showbiz was still dominated by middle-aged men in bad wigs who tended to play things by the book. Oldham tore it up. He, Keith and Mick became another triangle.

Night after night, Andrew stood watching the boy with the tyre-tread lips and the glowering blond and brunet guitarists, quaking with a whole new mutant kind of energy. He didn't even speak. He just knew.

Oldham was in. The Stones waited for Gomelski to come back from his father's funeral and then fired him.

Andrew promptly put the band in tight black jeans, black sweaters and Beatle boots, and ordered everyone to grow their hair. Next, in the subtlest name change in pop, Keith Richards became Keith Richard. (The shorter version sounded 'more *Clockwork Orange*', Oldham would say, even if it raised the dire threat of Keith being confused with Cliff Richard, then still basking in the popular acclaim of *Summer Holiday*.) The question of whether they were the Rollin' or Rolling Stones was settled for good. On 1 May Oldham then dropped a bombshell when he told Keith and Brian that Stewart would have to go. The others had always admired Stu not only for his ability but because he was the only member of the group who was normal and uncompetitive. But it was precisely his normality that was the cause of his downfall. Looking straight, said Andrew, was dead wrong for the band.

Twelve months earlier, Stu had boggled everyone's minds with his virtuoso piano playing. Now he was out. Although he loyally stayed on as their roadie, his fondness for the Stones would always run more to their music than their image.

The band were still making only £30 a night from their sold-out shows at Richmond. Moreover, their creditors included several loan sharks, the Edith Grove landlord and now IBC studios, where the Stones had just cut another vanity 'demo' for a princely £106. But when Oldham offered to pay Jones an 8 per cent royalty, split six ways, on future record sales, Brian said that he 'wouldn't insult the boys with peanuts'. The eventual deal was a 6 per cent royalty, split five ways. Despite Brian's promises, Stu was never cut in on the action.

The Stones signed papers with Oldham and Eric Easton on 6 May 1963. They were all talking about making their first million. Andy's mother had to act as his attorney, since he was still legally under age. Brian did the negotiating for the Stones (giving away a full 25 per cent of the band's gross earnings) and relayed the details to Keith and Mick, who waited for him in a Wimpy Bar round the corner. Andrew was now playing tough, so tough that he sold the band to Decca's Dick Rowe, the A&R man who had famously refused a group of mumbling and – it then seemed – deeply uncommercial Liverpudlians crooning My Feet's Too Big and Besame Mucho. Forever stigmatized as The Man Who Turned Down The Beatles, Rowe responded to the Stones with a rapid nod, an excited and spluttering puff of cigar smoke, and the high-pitched word 'Fabulous'. The band signed with Decca on 16 May.

Mick Jagger now arranged to take a term off from his studies at the LSE.

Keith thought the Rolling Stones might last two years. That was the 'average lifetime of anybody except Elvis. Nobody got longer than that, and then you [were] dead as a dodo.' It didn't, meanwhile, escape Jones's bitter attention that now the Stones had an office, a reporting structure and the like, he was being outflanked by 'the unholy trinity'. Brian responded by trying to bed Oldham, but Andrew backed off, provoking unfounded rumours that he and Mick, rather, were having an affair. In a memorable duet some two years later, Jagger and his manager would croon I Got You, Babe on Ready Steady Go! while stroking each other's hair.

Keith had never had a steady girlfriend, and lived in a climate of comparative monasticism. Full of amazing noise on stage, he struck Easton as 'quiet and shy, the runt of the pack' in private. He took a few uppers, liked a beer and a smoke, but his only real addiction was to music. It particularly pissed Brian off to see Keith composing a song. Whereas Jones would take seven days to write a three-minute tune, it actually took Richards three minutes to write a three-minute tune. Keith had already worked out his major creative strategy: to weld fury to melody. Within a year, he was blasting the parochial shackles off British pop in a way not even the Beatles would top.

Perhaps earlier than most, Oldham spotted Keith's strong and weak sides. Taking Brian's natural flair into account, Andrew had at first tried to establish if not intimate, then at least stable relations with him. Jones sabotaged that by insisting that, as the band's founder, he be paid more than the so-called droogs. These were brave words. And, spoken at a time when Keith's musicianship had begun to shine, they were virtually a suicide note by Brian. Things between Richards, Jagger, Jones and Oldham were always ticklish. The central issue was that Brian and Mick both aimed at leadership of the band, and both realized that Keith's was the swing vote. Oldham quickly showed himself to be a surprisingly good manager. As he carried out his tasks, he paid special attention to the long-term advantage of the band furnishing their own material. Stu would say, 'Whereas we hadn't a clue, Loog could see ... zap, the bucks. That meant songwriting, and songwriting meant Keith.'

Even after the Decca contract, the Stones were working on a shoestring. When they played a gig, as they still did at Richmond or Twickenham or as far afield as the Ricky Tick Club, Windsor, the stage was bare, they plugged in hire-purchase gear and went home in Stu's van with £20 or £30 between them. A poverty format became the Stones as it did few others. Some nights found them in the midst of a full-scale riot – Beatlearama, they called it – a fiver each for fifty minutes' mayhem. Live performance would always be the band's forte. To make it more interesting, there were gigs when the Stones began to fight among themselves, loudly accusing each other of fucking up tempos by 'wanking off'. Even Cliff and the Shadows never said that.

Now, as he proudly wrote Doris, 'an ARTISTE!', Keith could still raise the roof with his wild, free-association Goon skits or an outlandish 'Nanker' face pulled from behind Brian's back. He'd try anything, even the impossible, injecting music-hall themes into rock, slinging off Swing melodies, and romping through George Formby riffs when the spirit moved him. What Keith could do with a Chuck Berry lick wasn't to be believed. Above all, he knew how to turn technique and ideas into genuine music – a notion lost on most Sixties guitar manglers. The Stones were never boring when Keith was on the job: it was on-the-edge stuff, fun and life affirming.

The inevitable comparisons to the Moptops were becoming more flattering, which delighted Brian. Elmore James died on 24 May and Jones had no more use for any of 'that sharecropper shit'. The way Korner remembered it, 'Keith was a compulsive who had to play, regardless, and Brian was only really interested in becoming a pop star.'

Bright lights, big city. That spring, Keith worked all hours, before, after and frequently during gigs, on his songwriting. 'He was quiet, but he wasn't half as laid-back as you'd think,' Stu would say while discussing how, with no experience, no formal credentials, the ex-Shagger had been able to manoeuvre himself into pole position as the band's composer. 'His silences were brilliant . . . the flitting between Mick and Brian stood Keith in good stead. Nobody quite knew what he was thinking, and that kept the pretty boys off balance.'

That Keith seemed a tad on the remote side was all part of his charm. Nowadays he dressed mainly in black, avoided eye contact and hid behind silence as behind a bomb-proof door. Although it was taken for granted by mid-1963 that he was straight, Keith was still held in a kind of baffled awe by various older, gay showbiz types, who were fond of remarking that he was obviously 'rough'.

Even later, in the Human Riff years, people would speak of the quiet, shy man behind the legend. 'Keith's basic gentleness was unique in a profession where most people are like Hitler,' Korner said.

It wasn't just that fame struck in 1963. There was a complete U-turn in Keith's life.

If Andrew Oldham hadn't kick-started the Stones, nobody could possibly have guessed how Richards' later years would pan out. He'd be remembered as a somewhat toothy suburban dreamer, whose pet phobias included excessive drink and drug use, as well as the 'commercialization' of music. Given these prejudices, you could have gotten long odds against Keith becoming a junkie, a boozer and a millionaire pop star.

With Decca now calling for product, Keith began pondering the band's first single. The Stones rehearsed several blues standards, sung by Brian and Mick, with Richards adding both guitar and a queasy descant. Keith's energy and determination were astonishing enough, but he had the added gift of brilliant mimicry and improvisation; all this noise – from the melodic precision of Crossroads to the hysterical squall of Tutti Frutti – jostled together, spin drier fashion, in Keith's repertoire. The problem lay in covering just one white-hot song, instead of the waterfront.

Richards and Oldham eventually chose an obscure Chuck Berry ditty to introduce the Stones. Come On was shorn of its distinctive rumba beat and instead given a punk tempo; the finished product broke the two-minute barrier. Jagger insisted on singing the words 'stupid guy' instead of, as Berry had, 'stupid jerk'. In a further lapse, he trilled the chorus in falsetto.

Representing the barest of investments, Come On was released by Decca on 7 June 1963. It and its B-side (I Want To Be Loved) weren't much, but between them they did form a hyphen linking Little Ricky to the Human

Riff. A few days later, *NME* gave him his first national notice: 'A song performance aimed straight at the current market for groups. Good guitar sound.' Several friends remember Keith running back to Edith Grove waving a copy of Come On. He put it on the Dansette turntable and shouted 'It's here!' and 'We're pros now!' That meant a lot to him.

That summer Brian launched his last major offensive to control the band. Stu heard Jones gripe to Eric Easton that 'Mick had always had a weak voice . . . They'd just get rid of him if necessary.' Another reservation about Jagger, in Easton's view, was that 'the BBC' – here his own voice fell to a reverential murmur – 'wouldn't like him'. After Oldham balked, Brian used a trademark combination of charm and coercion to persuade Easton that five in a group was one too many – look at the Beatles. The 'other guitar guy' would have to go. When Decca heard of this they called Brian into the office. 'Do you want to tear up your contract,' he was asked, 'or grovel to Keith?'

Grovel to Keith.

3

'So Ugly, They're Attractive'

OLDHAM GOT THE STONES £143 AND MATCHING CARNABY STREET GEAR FOR THEIR TV DEBUT ON *THANK YOUR LUCKY STARS*. Even when they were dolled up in their prissy hound's-tooth jackets, black pants and shiny new Beatle boots, the compère, Pete Murray, treated them like a disease. Around the Stones in '63 there was always the sound of fans braying and squealing, MCs sternly asking for order and police chiefs rumbling 'Disgraceful!' The headlines followed suit: THUGS ... CAVEMEN ... APES was the consensus, thus sadly undermining Andrew's PR campaign with the teen magazines. For every rave issuing from *Jackie* or *Valentine* there was a matching rant like the *Mirror*'s 'Horrendous – none of them smiled or *tried* to entertain.' When Murray introduced the Stones, they just stood there and played! In a very short time, Keith was rediscovering the power of music to shock people.

And be rewarded for it. When they began a first British tour, the Stones also started getting weekly accounts from Easton. Keith was handed a cheque for £193, or roughly what Bert brought home from Osram's in three months.

Those gigs in far-off Wisbech and Prestatyn exasperated many. Brilliantined club managers, on hand as a Greek chorus of disapproval, watched in shock as the Stones ditched their cutesy uniforms and wandered on in mufti. But they thrilled many more. Most kids would never go for indifference, the band believed, but outright contempt would charm them. Allan Clarke and the Hollies topped the bill on some of the northern dates. 'Keith was this incredibly sleazy, anaemic-looking kid. He had the complexion of a vampire. You've never seen someone as haggard and washed out. But, God, the minute he strapped on a guitar . . .'; it was like the metamorphosis scene in *The Nutty Professor*. Keith was, if possible, even more devoted to the job now he was getting paid for it. A part of his life was ending; he couldn't say what would happen, but he'd never again be anyone's little Ricky.

The Stones bit Britain and it went mad. On 28 September they played what Stu called 'World War 3' in Walthamstow town hall. When a Saturday night crowd met the Stones, mayhem was inevitable and violence the rule. The council chamber had seen nothing like it when Liz Richards was mayor there.

Those hopped-up forty-minute gigs taught Keith and Mick how to 'put over' not only a song, but themselves. The trick involved more sleight of hand than either let on, and left Brian (already badly zonked, and suffering from a whole raft of mysterious allergies) struggling for a role. There was the little harlequinade of lip-pursing and arse-wiggling that Mick strutted out when not busy appraising the floor. The comically deadpan rhythm section. Keith was fascinating precisely because he stood stock still, right up against Charlie's kit in order to hear the beat over all the screams. Occasionally he crouched down with the guitar, combat-style, also for better acoustics. The eye tracked to him, pasty-faced and intense, as it somehow didn't to Jones, crotch-thrusting and stoned. One was play acting, the other working out an obsession.

On 3 October, Keith ordered a takeaway chicken dinner backstage at the Southend Odeon. When he returned from a few minutes off in a side room, 'with a well-known groupie,' he says, the meal was but skin and bones.

'Who ate me chicken?' Keith asked.

'Brian ate it,' said Bill.

'And just at that moment,' Keith remarked, 'the stage manager sticks his head in the door and yells "You're on!" So we're picking up guitars and heading for the stage, and as we're walking downstairs Brian passes me and I say, "You *cunt*, you ate me chicken!", and bopped him in the eye. We went onstage, and as we're playing Brian's face starts to swell up and change colours.'

Richards and Jagger moved out of Edith Grove that month into a flat at 33 Mapesbury Road, Kilburn, where they were joined by Oldham. Not surprisingly, Jones made other arrangements. When on the road Brian quite seriously insisted that, as 'leader', he stay in a better class of hotel than the band. (Stu often selected this not on the basis of its proximity to the gig, but to one of his beloved golf courses.) The rest of them laughed it off, but then they discovered that Jones was also pocketing a regular weekly bonus for being head Stone. A friend asked Richards how he'd felt about that.

Keith: 'Freaked out. That was the beginning of the end with Brian.'

Let it bleed. More flying tomahawks and fuck-you's all round. Bill took regular flak for being not only a family man but a 'London Ernie', prone to a dab of Brylcreem and – as if there could be anything worse – listening to Cliff at top volume. It was possible, too, to see just how Mick's new stage act could provoke scorn. Alluding to Oldham, the genial Stu announced, 'I wouldn't piss on him if he was on fire.' Jones fared worst of all. Keith and Jagger both did a wicked impersonation of him, hunching down like Toulouse-Lautrec in reference to Brian's stocky legs.

The Stones first broadcast for the BBC that 26 October on the old Light Programme. Easton's worst fears about the Corporation were fully realized: the music went well, but the show's compère, Brian Matthew, found their attitude 'extremely truculent'. Matthew was a venerable figure, used to gently riveting the bolts between the Beeb and the Establishment. Left alone with Keith, he sounded as if he'd been trapped with a wild dog. It was one of the most unintentionally funny things ever heard on the wireless. Matthew asked Keith whether he voted, read, watched TV or had a hobby. The one-word answer, repeated four times, was 'no'.

The Stones gave sixty-one shows that autumn, as part of a package cobbled together by Easton – night in, night out, the same frantic R&B pastiche, fourth on the bill to, incredibly, Little Richard, the Everlys and Bo Diddley; a sound sculpture of the whole history of pop. For their five bob, the fans packed into Gaumonts and Odeons got twenty minutes of unprecedented support-act frenzy, complete with Mick's Tiller-girl hoofing, a feral beat and lusty swings of Keith's guitar – one of the birth cries of Sixties rock – all amped to the pain threshold. Their reaction was, understandably, a trifle demonstrative. Keith would call the tour his 'higher education', learning how to perform amid a mob orgy. Musically, the Stones were coming into their own. Visually, they already beat the traffic out of the heavy punchers, including their lamé-suited headliner. The band's jiggly front trio and studiously bored back line quickly became a pop archetype, one which in turn would help nurture new entries into this exciting growth field. You could almost see their hopeful little heads poking out of the soil.

On 3 November the Stones brought down the house at Hammersmith Odeon, where the audience included an electrician's mate from Bromley called Jones, later relaunched as Bowie. Five days later the band performed in Newcastle, making a lifelong fan of the twelve-year-old Gordon Sumner (aka Sting). In Freehold, New Jersey, an enterprising teenager had bought a mail order copy of Come On and was now badgering his father, named Doug Springsteen, for a guitar. Meanwhile, the young Pete Townshend, backstage at St Mary's Hall, Putney, watched Keith windmilling his right arm over his head just as the curtain went up, ready to twang the first chord of Poison Ivy. Townshend nicked the gesture as his own.

This kind of patronage cut both ways: the Stones' second single was hustled on them by the Beatles, a Jurassic rocker (with a topical lilt of Bo Diddley) called I Wanna Be Your Man. Brian's slide guitar rendered the song vertebrate. Released on 1 November, it hit number twelve in the chart.

Lennon and McCartney's easy gift to the Stones was a sign of the way the pop zeitgeist was going. Now Oldham, too, decided his band's greatest potential was for in-house writing. When he came to fix on a Beatlesque duo there weren't many contenders, and the verdict was quickly reached. Keith had already been honing this particular side of his craft for more than a year. Brian, who all agreed could make a guitar ring like a bell, was away with the pixies creatively. Jagger, perhaps, was more of a stretch, but had the virtue of living under the same roof as Keith and Oldham at Mapesbury Road.

On 11 September 1963 Andrew formed company number 00821988, otherwise known as Nanker-Phelge. It aimed for breadth: 'to carry on the business of writers, composers, licensers, distributors, publishers and dealers in radio and television shows, cinematographic film, plays, dramas, opera, pantomimes, revues, song, sketches and entertainments and productions of all kinds'. (The debut work, a Stax ripoff in which Jagger barked 'Stoned . . . Stoned . . . Stoned outta mah mind' gave due warning that the main product would be something other than all-round family entertainment.) Oldham now famously 'locked [Keith and Mick] in the kitchen for a day and a night, and said, "I'm not letting you out until you've got a song".' The first fruits were an uncategorizable mishmash, swiftly followed by tear-jerkers with titles like My Only Girl and It Should Be You, foisted on to Easton's protégé, the crooner George Bean. The second result was the further demotion of Brian Jones, who proved sadly unsuited to the gerbil existence the daily slog of writing can be. When it came to the contract between a star and his public, it seemed Keith and Mick had read the fine print and Brian hadn't. One whiff of success and he went nuts. While Jones was becoming the Sixties prototype of a debauched pop idol, Keith and Mick limbered up by penning a half-dozen increasingly assured and lucrative ballads. Soon they cut through all the old Tin Pan Alley convention. Inside just over a year, Keith had completely rewritten the rules of what a hit rock song should sound like.

But first there was the troubling matter of the contract Easton had just signed with the Kellogg's company. The two young turks came up with a jingle and a lyric that went:

> Wake up in the morning,
> There's a pop that really says
> 'Rice Krispies for you and you and *you*!'

It's hard to say exactly when the Stones arrived at the dangerously combustible centre of the pop universe. How they got there, however, is no mystery.

There was the tour that began on 3 January 1964, an intoxicating mix of showmanship and musicianship. There were wild concerts, full of smoke, chrome and slashed cinema seats which gave way to reveal the main visual drama – tiffs and, in not a few cases, 'spankings' in the adjoining alleys dealt out by rival gangs of Mods and Rockers. There were riotous appearances on *Ready Steady Go!* and *Top of the Pops*. There was the band's first EP, which went to number one and stayed there for thirteen weeks. There were headlines like the *Sketch*'s 'Who would have thought Britain would fall for five toughs with hairy pudding-basins for heads?' (Not the *Sketch*, obviously. They seemed genuinely puzzled.) Finally, in March, there was *Melody Maker*'s classic WOULD YOU LET YOUR SISTER GO WITH A ROLLING STONE?, which eclipsed even the fuss over the Beatles conquering New York.

Most of all, though, the impact was musical. Keith rescued pop from terminal triteness.

Many fumed at his success. Any day of the week, at any time – he was already doing speed, staying up all hours – Keith knew he could expect to have his cage rattled 'like some fucking pet ape'. On 7 January the Stones were enjoying a late-night meal at Heathrow airport when a party of three or four middle-aged Americans started yelling insults. *Fags. Fucking fairies.* Keith knocked down one of them, scared off another and cocked back his red-knuckled fist at a third. He made his own first plane journey later that month. To Glasgow, where the Stones provoked a shower of bras and girdles. Back to Cheltenham, where Brian came under a barrage of home-town abuse. To Liverpool, where banners proclaimed Liz & Julie's Luv for 'Keef' and the arresting 'BETTER THAN BEATLES'.

When Keith revamped Not Fade Away into a stylistic pileup between Buddy Holly and Bo Diddley, he virtually invented the Stones sound for the next forty years. This pivotal moment came from sheer hard slog: Keith and the band worked their way through eighteen takes of the song before they emerged with something that felt raw and completely spontaneous. Allan Clarke was at the Fade Away session held late one night in a studio at the far end – a nice touch, this – of Tin Pan Alley. 'Keith's energy level was off the chart. Even the rehearsal was a blast.' Beset by 'difficult new single' syndrome, Keith went forward by going back, refurbishing an oldie into a rollicking but deft hit. Oldham would later call this 'the first classic [Richards] wrote'. That Keith was still just twenty with a Chuck Berry yen and no musical training didn't seem to bother anyone. The prevailing view of him was that he was a rough gem unburdened by the rules of formal composition. Adding insult to injury, Brian could only feebly approximate – churning out hackneyed tunes with sub-Tolkien lyrics about elves tiptoing through the daisies. Unamazingly, they were never recorded.

The journalist Keith Altham remembers accompanying Keith, Mick, Charlie and Bill driving through thick fog to a gig in Aylesbury, while Brian travelled in alone.

> I got aboard the Stones bandwagon, and my illusions of the sweet life were shattered . . . After only fifteen minutes on the road, Keith keeled over in the front seat and slumped into Mick's lap. Bill said, 'You can't keep 'im awake. He just flakes clean out and dozes off for a couple of hours.' A one-hour trip had already taken three hours and we were on the outskirts of town when Mick shouted

as Brian's car loomed out of the fog and began to pass us. Brian was obviously totally lost and heading in the opposite direction. We all yelled out of the window, but were unheard. Brian disappeared into the night.

Some of those primitive gigs looked like an Hieronymus Bosch painting of hell. Fans swarmed across the footlights and dragged Keith or Mick head-first into the pit. Guitars and drums would be smashed, the stage all but destroyed and even the band drowned out by an ungodly roar. It was the sound of youth in full, giddy swing, of a generation embarked on a new golden era: brash, exuberant and unfeasibly flush with cash. All the old rules went.

Keith: 'It was like they had the Battle of the Crimea going on . . . People gasping, tits hanging out . . . You took your life in your hands just to walk out there. I was strangled twice . . . It was climbing over rooftops, getaways down fire escapes, through laundry chutes, into bakery vans. It was all mad. We ended up like [a cartoon] without even realizing it.'

But all that was just Keith's day job. He was also something of a style plate with his Cecil Gee jacket, corduroy cap and burgeoning sideline in Nazi accessories. It was said that he was better read than other pop stars, which might not be difficult. Keith enjoyed snooker, darts and Dunhill cigarettes, which he smoked in three or four monster drags before immediately lighting another. He looked impressively unhealthy. For Keith, dinner in those days often consisted of five or six pints and a tobacco chaser. He was extremely generous to Doris. Andrew would inform the world (thirty-eight years after the event) that he and Mick were found around now allegedly 'cuddled up' in bed together by his mum, who was none too pleased: Mrs Oldham preferred Keith, 'because she'd seen him be kind to her dogs'. There were also some darkly revelatory moments around town, frequently after Keith had overdone his beloved 'bennies' or Peruvian flake. There was the day he kicked a tactless heckler in the face. And the time Keith sashayed down Oxford Street with a new cine camera, zooming in on anyone looking sick, frail or otherwise vulnerable. Then there was the priceless moment when, bereft of licence, he tried to start Jagger's prized Ford Consul and promptly got the car stuck in a ditch, rear pointing to the heavens, front sinking in the mud.

Keith failed his driving test several times.

Unlettered as he was, Keith was, however, that much better thing – natively shrewd. A wit once claimed that Richards' vocabulary contained no more than 300 words, but the remarkable thing about them was that he always used them in the right way, at the right time, and in the right place. On 26 April Keith was invited to 11 Downing Street by the Chancellor's daughter Caroline Maudling. 'People expected this raving loony.'

Instead, Keith discussed economics.

Despite the usual fumblings up against walls or backstage with a groupie, Richards had had no sex life to talk of. On the industrial scale on which the Stones later slept, the band's few knee-tremblers in 1964 barely broke the national average. We're indebted to Bill for the information that Keith, Mick and he had six, thirty and 278 women, respectively, in the first two years after fame struck. 'People made a dead [wrong] assumption about who was active sexually.' This the bassist himself would note with considerable pride. Yet Keith was already moving up in the world that spring, into a more fan-resistant flat at 10a Holly Hill, Hampstead. And he fell in love.

Her name was Linda Keith, and when he met her she was working at *Vogue* and about to become a successful model. Dark-eyed, hip and as thin as a cigarette, Linda was in exile from her well-heeled Jewish family and in search of the bright lights. In particular, she was passionate about both music and musicians.

Linda, too, thought Keith 'shy, introverted, very appealing'. As an admiring friend says, 'They needed each other. I doubt they'd have won the Nobel prize for Chemistry.' Where Keith was still fighting childhood wars, Linda seemed a more straightforward type, the seventeen-year-old free spirit who 'dug people'. Her inner life, while rebellious, found its outlet on the runway.

They set up home together in Hampstead, where they were soon joined by Mick and his girlfriend Chrissie Shrimpton. But the old 'unholy trinity' was broken up. Andrew, in that remarkably fecund period, was now reportedly diagnosed as a manic depressive. Mired in bad business deals, quarrels with Easton and pills, he would come to question his own sanity. Occasionally Oldham even disappeared into voluntary seclusion in a monastery.

As for Jones, the downward spiral continued. At a fancy dress ball that March, most of the Stones went as Chicago gangsters. Tripping, Brian dressed up in a sheet, an unforgettable and fragile image. 'I feel dead,' he was able to mutter to friends.

The next day, Keith thought that a good meal might help Brian. Mick was griping about the cuisine as well. So Richards went out through a blizzard to the shops, and spent the rest of the morning cooking on a gas ring he found in their hotel. Lunch consisted of fried eggs, chips and dripping, which he served to the band. Jones took one look and ran to the lavatory, whose door he left open for them to survey him during his retchings. Between times he managed to gasp out his qualms about playing that night's gig.

The Stones, in turn, already had their doubts about Brian. Oldham was talking of firing him.

In the midst of this emotionally charged situation Keith was leading the Stones, as arranger and de facto producer, through their first album. Everything was terse and direct. Keith pushed the band from one song to another with no fuss, no bullshit – even as Brian begged off from sessions with the 'shakes' – and no waste, no mistakes. One of Keith's great charms was the sense that he came at whatever he found in life, savoured it, and moved on. One minute he could be doing Goon Show skits, the next he could suddenly cut off to flail the power chords of Carol, and then soar away in playful homage to Chuck Berry, before once more returning to an animated chat about the Wehrmacht.

Sitting around one night, Keith began playing a child's keyboard and doodled a riff, which he gave to Mick. Several hours later, Jagger had managed to come up with the title Shang A Doo Lang. On 27 March they sold it to the singer Adrienne Posta at her sixteenth birthday party. Also present was Paul McCartney, McCartney's friend John Dunbar and Dunbar's 'chick', a slim, tooth-white girl who looked like something out of a Scott Fitzgerald novel: Marianne Faithfull. Appraising Faithfull's blonde hair and stunning face, modestly turned, Oldham had a vision of 'an angel with big tits', and duly signed her. Keith was summoned and promptly wrote the melody of As Tears Go By, which went Top 10 that summer. It was a career high for Faithfull, who spent much of the rest of the Sixties as a celebrity without portfolio.

17 April 1964: the Stones' first album released in Britain. The seeds of Keith's all-night sessions start to bear fruit, and contain a revelation: the school dropout has the focus of a bullet in flight when it comes to music. Even Brian would acknowledge his unerring knack of zooming in on a

song's weaknesses – ones Jones might sense as he sat in the control-room but rarely bothered with. Keith always did.

The LP is a sensation. First, the cover – instead of the Beatles' corporate smiles, five skulking profiles, no words or title. On the back Oldham's immortal quip, 'The Rolling Stones aren't just a group; they're a way of life.' There's only one original song, the warbling Tell Me, but the Stones bring enough raw power to the party to raise the event above a mere retro theme night. Time and again, the clipped quality of Keith's guitar soars to the occasion, making even Route 66 fresh again. Other highlights include Willie Dixon's I Just Wanna Make Love To You and Slim Harpo's King Bee. All interpretations, maybe, but with energy to burn. These twelve 'crying songs' offer living proof that white kids from Dartford and Cheltenham can cross over to a vast, multiracial audience. *The Rolling Stones* not only kick-starts a career, it breathes new life into an urban blues tradition hijacked by the likes of Cliff Richard.

In all, it's one of the two or three truly great debut LPs in rock. And what's so remarkable about Keith's crying songs is just how good they make people feel. *The Rolling Stones* sells 100,000 copies overnight.

Inside a week the album would hit number one, dethroning the Beatles.

Tuesday night, 21 April, Keith flew back from Geneva and got royally mobbed at Heathrow. When Richards and Jagger set to saying 'piss off' when asked for autographs, the two schoolmates triggered the kind of shock/horror the press hadn't enjoyed since the Profumo scandal. It was one great tabloid headline after another. Bert Richards, still bitterly clocking in every morning at Osram's, began to get some knowing looks from his colleagues.

On 9 May Keith finally got to meet Chuck Berry, who was playing as part of a package tour in London. Berry told him to fuck off.

Keith's feet first touched American soil on 1 June 1964. The Stones took BOAC flight 505 to New York, made their way through a mob of two or three hundred screaming girls (bussed in for the event by management) and checked into the Astor hotel. Keith would remember how Oldham had watched the first-phase British Invasion as keenly as a fakir watches a snake – 'the Beatles kicked the doors open; we zoomed in behind 'em'. In private Andrew worried, with some reason, that the Stones would be laughed off as a novelty, little more than a freak act, but the band proved 'tougher little fuckers' than he'd thought.

If 1963 was the year a mass market discovered the Stones, then '64 would go down as the year the Stones discovered mass marketing. As well as management's cheerleader campaign, there would be press kits, photos, badges, buttons, posters, programmes and exclusive accessories – everything from socks to pageboy caps. If a teenager could wear it, Keith and the boys were on it. Decca's US subsidiary, London Records, had also hired Murray 'the K' Kaufman, a hyperactive Manhattan DJ and the so-called Fifth Beatle, to squire the Stones around town. Their chaperon did a good job of plugging both the band and himself; as well as hosting the Stones on his show (where Kaufman sold them on recording the Valentinos' It's All Over Now), he bullied them into wearing Radio WINS T-shirts. Keith would call Murray the K 'Murray the Kunt'.

In June 1964, nobody in New York was talking about peace, love and flowers. When the Stones arrived on a cool, drizzly evening, they saw a city inhabited by funereally clad men with Eisenhower burr-cuts, by the peculiar musty stench of horse-meat burgers being sold from carts, by fire-and-brimstone street preachers, interminable ghettoes and a few facilities still marked White and Colored. American politics were a sorry spectacle, most attitudes pre-Lincolnian, race relations tense. The major news item that week was the controversial passage by the US Senate, 73 votes to 27, of the Civil Rights Bill. To the Stones, everything appeared strangely uptight. For all its size and diversity, there was nothing that hip about a society whose choice of presidency lay between Lyndon Johnson and Barry Goldwater.

The Stones' first clash with middle America, later that week, came as a mutual shock. New York was one thing, Minneapolis (where the film Dr Strangelove had just been banned by court order as 'subversive') quite another. The band's itinerary passed from sea to shining sea, starting in LA and winding up back in Manhattan. Their first TV appearance was on the old Hollywood Palace Show, compered by Dean Martin. Martin and the Stones loathed one another. The generational clash started the moment they arrived, and continued through the band's brisk performance of I Just Wanna Make Love To You. (This reintroduced America to its own heritage.) Lurching towards the old-fashioned stand mike, Dino then delivered his monologue about 'smaller foreheads and higher eyebrows' before introducing a trampolinist as 'the father of the Rolling Stones – he's been trying to kill himself ever since'.

Keith was the only one who laughed. He would grasp immediately what the others missed. Dino was yesterday's papers.

Having flunked their screen test, the Stones played their first live concert at the Swing Auditorium, San Bernadino. Thanks in large part to Keith's endless pop ingenuity, the band went down a storm. Not only were there screams and stage invasions, the local paper presciently called the gig 'tooth-rattling but musical ... Keith Richard was mesmerizing, roughing up the tone, keeping tempo, and allowing the group's surprisingly good taste to come to the fore.'

Other critics went for the jugular. On 6 June the Stones appeared to a backdrop of straw bales and horse shit at the San Antonio State Fair. Coming out of the shed that served as their dressing room, Keith bumped into the great country singer George Jones. Jones affably showed him a few Nashville tunings on his guitar. From this point, things began to deteriorate rapidly. Cowboys gaped, then wolf-whistled, when Mick went into his funky-butt routine. Not untypical was the scathing *World Herald* review, calling the band 'gum-chewing, undisciplined, skinny, ugly and a menace'.

After Keith got into a shoving match with an irate customer backstage, he and Wyman went downtown and, for $35 apiece, bought themselves Browning Automatics. Richards would never again be without a gun when touring America.

2120 South Michigan Avenue, Chicago. The lanky, plucked-chicken look that sustained the Stones in London drew only jeers and catcalls in the Windy City. For years, they'd all revered the place like an American Mecca. Now reality struck as the band pulled to a stop at the kerb in front of a drab bunker marked Chess Studios. 'That boy'll help you,' their driver told them. 'He works here.'

Keith glanced across the forecourt and saw a rumpled-looking black man of about fifty, dressed in overalls, shuffling through the studio door ahead of them. It was Muddy Waters.

Keith: 'He was painting the ceiling. He wasn't selling records at the time, and this is the way he got treated. My first meeting with Muddy Waters is over the paintbrush, dripping, covered in crap. I'm *dying*, right? I get to meet The Man – he's my fucking god – and he's out of work.'

The only way the Stones themselves could avoid this fate was to establish an act for the long haul.

Keith plugged in and, take one, nailed the ferocious riff of It's All Over Now. His foot bashed the floor in tempo. In the space of three hours, the Stones then cut I Can't Be Satisfied, Around And Around, Time Is On My Side and an instrumental jam they called Stewed & Keefed. As they were leaving, Muddy Waters put down his paintbrush and shook Keith's hand.

Like most of their midwestern concerts, the next gig, in Omaha, began quite sedately. After doing a local TV show the Stones played to 1,200 generally subdued fans, only 'a few of whom *sang and danced*', as the *World Herald* put it reprovingly. Backstage, everyone sat down for the customary junk-food buffet accompanied by Cokes and a bottle of scotch.

The affair might have ended quietly, too, had one of Omaha's finest not wandered into the dressing room, seen the whisky and made the Stones pour it, together with all their other drinks, down a sink. 'The thing was,' said Keith, 'I was only drinking Coke. I refused to pour mine away thinking, why the fuck was an American cop telling me to pour the national drink down the bog? The cop pulled a gun on me. A very strange scene, a cop ordering me at gunpoint to pour a Coke down the john.'

Back in New York, the law found an even less appreciative audience for their talents, in the hundreds of teenagers who disrupted the Stones' show at Carnegie Hall. Forty-seven arrests were made. As the curtain came down there was a full-scale riot in progress, suddenly ended, as if by a thrown switch, by everyone freezing in place for the National Anthem.

For Keith, the riot and the flag would become the twin images of America, and he never quite got over the jolt of his first visit there. More than thirty years later he was still describing the scene: How, one night in New York, he'd torn between the Peppermint Lounge, the Apollo Theater and finally the Basin Street playhouse, where, to his delight, Ella Fitzgerald was singing. How the cops had stomped around with semi-automatic guns in their hands, threatening to blow people's brains out if they misbehaved. How some days the Stones had driven 400 miles, and others they flew for fifteen minutes. How Keith had been stopped from entering Canada because he'd lost his passport, the exact opposite of the problem thirteen years later, when leaving would be the big deal. How, above all, meeting the king of the blues working as a housepainter in Chicago had 'straightened me out'.

'I thought, "Oh, this is the record business, right? Mmmmm. The highs and the lows . . ."'

While Keith and the Stones were flying back from New York, Linda Keith was driving home from a Midsummer Solstice rave at Stonehenge. Her car was in a collision and Linda hit her head, hard, on the windscreen. As soon as Keith landed in London and heard the news, he split off from the other Stones, who all went home to recover from the most gruelling three weeks of their lives.

The last man standing was the one who had already stayed up two straight nights drinking and listening to soul records.

Linda Keith says, 'My face was messed up so badly my family had been and couldn't recognize me. I wasn't allowed mirrors and I was frightened about what had actually happened to me. Keith came to the hospital and saw me, and he leant down and kissed me on my face, and at that moment – I'll never forget – showed me that I wasn't a monster and I wasn't revolting. And *that* was Keith.'

The hundred or so days from 22 June 1964, when a jet-lagged band honoured a commitment to play the Magdalen, Oxford, ball until they re-toured America, this time triumphantly, were the headiest of their career: the start of both superstardom and 'the Sixties'. Keith was in perpetual motion. In one four-week period he flew the Atlantic, played a half-dozen shows in London and the southeast, drank champagne with the Beatles, flew to Paris and back, caught a connection to Blackpool, started a riot, left another gig by shinning up a ladder and running over moonlit rooftops, saw It's All Over Now hit number one, casually wrote several new songs, missed his plane to Belfast, caught the next flight that evening, met up with the Stones, brought the house down at Ulster Hall (400 fainting cases), flew back to London for more gigs, played to a screaming crowd of 25,000 at Longleat House, outraged a TV audience of ten million on *Juke Box Jury* and finally, on 3 August, went home.

Once, when Keith was at the cinema with Linda, she noticed him digging into the side of his chair and asked what he was doing; he realized that he was looking for a seat belt. Another time, Keith woke up in an anonymous hotel room and asked Jagger how much time they had before that night's gig. Mick told him that they'd already played it.

On 1 July 1964, Keith Richards, describing himself as a 'theatrical artist', became a director of The Rolling Stones Ltd. The most startling image of the year, and the first that Middle Britain had seen of the band, was that Saturday's edition of *Juke Box Jury*. Having voted all but one of the proffered selections a 'miss', the Stones' ill-mannered guffaws and catarrhal grunts were themselves panned in the Sunday press. 'Ugly', 'rude', 'moronic' and 'neanderthal' came round like stops on the Circle Line. A few days later a clerk at the Ritz hotel, unimpressed with Keith's appearance, hinted that his presence there be more sparingly required.

'Perhaps Sir might wish to consider his position.'

Sir might. Keith gave it a second, then told the Ritz to go fuck themselves.

24 July, the Empress Ballroom, Blackpool. It was a Scots holiday weekend and the place was packed with day-tripping Glaswegians ('many of them,' Wyman intones, 'drunk'.) First up was twenty-four-year-old Tom Jones, belting out his brand new hit Chills And Fever. The crowd started to shout, then to pogo up and down, as Jones writhed and thrust his crotch at them, launching a tradition of sorts: amid the screams, the first pairs of lingerie came sailing over the footlights on to the stage.

Next, the Rolling Stones. Excited by the obvious potential for chaos, Brian immediately began taunting the male members of the audience while mouthing lewd endearments to their women. The Stones in turn came under a barrage not of bras and knickers but of insults and shaken fists. Characteristically, Keith moved over to the centre of the action and gave the ringleader some verbal between songs. Minutes later, the intro to Not Fade Away was cut short by Richards taking a gob of spittle to the face.

Those who witnessed Keith's fury would long marvel at the scene, speaking of it like old salts recalling a historic hurricane. 'You Scotch *cunt*,' he shouted. At that Keith took one step forward, looked down, and plunged a steel-toed boot into his assailant's teeth.

In the ensuing riot amplifiers, drums and an entire Steinway piano were demolished. The theatre's red and gold velvet curtains, embossed with the municipal crest, were torn to shreds. A teenager climbed the safety rope and swung, apelike, from a chandelier. Brian Jones was evidently confused for one of the audience, and had his collar felt by an usher. He wriggled free and made a run for it, shrieking high-pitched abuse over his shoulder. Unluckily for him, however, the man set on preventing his general circulation in society soon outpaced him, and a nasty to-do ensued. The other Stones were smuggled out of the building over a roof and into a police van, which dropped them twenty miles away. They left behind some £10,000 worth of damage, forty-five arrests, sixty injuries. The Deputy Chief Constable wrote to the Home Office that 'such scenes cannot be tolerated'.

A week later the Stones played Longleat, where Keith discussed literature with the Marquess of Bath before sparking the mass orgy. Twenty-two stretcher cases. Brian told Stu he wanted a bigger amp than Keith's. On 8 August a crowd in Scheveningen, Holland, went berserk the moment the band appeared. Stu, standing in the wings, was hit on the head by a bottle. Keith and Mick managed to run offstage, Charlie was mobbed and Bill stood playing the bass, his face deadpan. From the back of the speeding getaway car, Brian cackled, 'Fuck me! I'll be in the *Daily Mail* again!'

Late in August, someone acquainted with the band's tour itinerary broke into Holly Hill while Keith was 200 miles away, on stage in Guernsey, and stole most of his clothes and guitars. Not surprisingly, the atmosphere around the Stones' hotel turned distinctly chilly. Early the next morning, a shaken Keith managed to fall off a go-kart he was racing and flayed most of the skin from his back. The headlines that greeted even this double misfortune were the time-honoured ROLLED and STONED. The band then had a rare weekend off, allowing Keith to fly home and buy a replacement wardrobe. An excited fan took a photo of him trying on a dramatic, zippered shell-suit, to which Keith added red 'bug-eye' sunglasses and a long black scarf. Less publicly, he also took the opportunity to step up his collection of Nazi regalia.

Not long after moving in together, and only days after her release from hospital, Keith and Linda were talking marriage. Much of their off-duty time was spent shopping around Hampstead, where they made a striking couple. What he-Keith had in cash, she-Keith more than matched in class. When Richards felt like going for a walk, he'd take a taxi to a quiet part of Hampstead Heath, where he and Linda could stroll around without being swarmed by fans. Although Keith was now notorious for having unleashed riots and frowned throughout *Juke Box Jury*, he'd always feel that his 'bad-boy bit' was only a business asset.

In fact, they both thought him an incurable romantic.

Keith: 'It boils down to the fact that I've never just been interested in a lay ... I've never started a relationship just for the purpose of wham-bam-thank-you-ma'am. Chicks are too precious for that. I mean, I love chicks. I love them too much to just roll over and stick it in.'

Hence, too, the huge relief you sensed in people who had read or heard about Keith and then actually met him. Many of the stories swirling around him were dodgy, at best, variations on 'Would You Let Your Sister Go With a Rolling Stone?' The promoter Robert Stigwood, for instance, was alleged to have short-changed the band by £12,000 during their seventy-two-show British tour that autumn. At the height of the dispute, Keith was rather fancifully said to have met Stigwood in a London nightclub and, according to the journalist (and later Stones PR man) Keith Altham, 'started to beat the crap out of him. Every time Stigwood tried to get up, Keith would belt him again. "Keith," I said. "Why do you keep hitting him?" "Because he keeps getting up," he said.'

Total bullshit, notes Stigwood.

'It didn't happen. There was no beating, whatever [the] legend. Violence didn't come into it.' What did was a well-oiled PR machine that was busy turning out 'Brute!' and 'Moron!' headlines as fast as the *Mail* could publish them.

As Keith said, he and Mick had woken up and found themselves in a cartoon. A riot or two and hey, hey, they were the Monkees.

The reality, as usual with the Stones, was different. Keith actually put the highest premium on loyalty, friendship and trust when it came to outsiders, even if colleagues weren't necessarily eligible for the same courtesy. He sniggered, for example, at the groundless rumours linking Jagger (who with makeup looked disturbingly like Hayley Mills) and Oldham. For his part, Brian Jones was becoming known, not affectionately, as 'Mr Shampoo', or plain 'Shithead'. Insecurity, never far from the surface with him, now ripened into paranoia. Jones was already doing pills and drinking heavily, frequently muttering in his cups about 'the fuckers'. He took his first overdose that summer. When Brian, whose aptitude for searing guitar was limited by his inability to pluck the strings, reported to Regent Sound to record Little Red Rooster, he found a note from Keith telling him the track was complete and to 'just do a dub'. Meanwhile, the middle-aged Wyman remained a running joke. Even Charlie was briefly transformed into 'Dimwatts' when, on 14 October, he sheepishly admitted to having married.

Later that same week the Stones were in France, peeling off the kilometres to the tune of Maybellene, sizzling down the rue de Flandre to the Paris Olympia. Backstage there they met an Old Etonian army officer-turned-art dealer-cum-junkie, Robert Fraser. Fraser in turn introduced Keith and Mick to the film-maker Donald Cammell and the designer Christopher Gibbs; through Gibbs Keith met Cecil Beaton, who brought along 'Prince' Stanislas Klossowski de Rola, aka Stash, beginning a long-running if troubled friendship. It became a kind of chain-letter to the more raffish elements of the aristocracy; bewilderingly, these people began actually hanging out with the Stones, not denouncing them in the press.

The band's return to New York, on 23 October, prompted a pitched battle between pro- and anti-Stones groups at the airport. The twenty-five-day tour, Keith quickly discovered, would be the perfect backdrop for a series of such 'us v them' generational clashes. An elderly reporter, watching aghast as the band sprinted across the JFK tarmac pursued by seven or eight hundred screaming girls, gleaned the following:

'Who do you prefer, the Beatles or the Rolling Stones?'

'I think that the Rolling Stones have a lot more sex appeal than the Beatles ... When the Stones are performing on stage, there's a lot more excitement coming through.'

'Er ... How about you?'

'I think they're the greatest, they dress different and they're the best thing that's ever happened in the United States.'

'Why do *you* like the Rolling Stones?'

'Because ... Keith is beautiful ... and they're so ugly, they're attractive.'

On the evening of 25 October, sixty million Americans tuned in, as they had every Sunday for seventeen years, to the *Ed Sullivan Show*. But this was something special. Sullivan milked the occasion, savouring the buildup, spinning on his heels and, finally, bawling the peak-decibel intro. *'Lezz 'n gennlemun, here are five fine young men who overnight have become England's newest hitmakers. Let's really hear it for the fantastic, fabulous Rolling Stones.'* Amid ear-splitting screams in the studio audience, the band did Around And Around, then returned for Time Is On My Side. The switchboard at CBS (the very company that would later buy the rights to four Stones albums at $6 million apiece) was jammed with complaints from parents.

As some of them had just realized, the last vestige of adult control of the culture vanished at that moment. When society had degenerated into an uncouth strain of kids who had no idea how to behave, walked about in goddamn beads all day and shrieked abuse at anyone who frustrated them for five seconds – why, then Uncle Ed would be sorry, always provided he was around to see it. That kind of thing. Next morning, a rattled Sullivan promised the press, 'They'll never be on again. Never. Never. We won't book any more rock and roll groups and we'll ban teenagers from the theatre.' Six months later, Ed would beg the Stones to headline his show.

Keith went up to the roof of his hotel that night with Mick, Tom Jones and assorted Herman's Hermits. Hundreds of kids were down in the street screaming for them. The musicians, who a year or so earlier had all been broke and living with their mums, smiled at each other.

The Stones then topped a bill at The Teen-Age Music International (TAMI) festival that boasted Chuck Berry, Smokey Robinson, Marvin Gaye and the Supremes. Sessions at RCA studios, Hollywood, including Keith's new Heart Of Stone. The familiar riots: Cleveland, Fort Wayne, Dayton . . . after a while the names tended to blur and mingle. Throughout there was a carefully orchestrated image of the Stones as filthy, shaggy-haired bums who wanted to burn your town and steal your women; only half true, but it polarized opinion. America's idea of a pop group was fast tumbling forward, and the Stones captured the moment. Amid the orgy of upside down faces mouthing tributes through his car windscreen, Keith would calmly turn to Wyman in New York and say, 'Bit different this time, isn't it?'

While Richards and Jagger stopped off to drink champagne with James Brown, Jones was admitted to Chicago's Passavant hospital suffering from 'stress' and 'extreme exhaustion'. When his condition deteriorated he became delirious and had to be fed intravenously. The Stones duly played four sold-out shows as a quartet. On 16 November, a pale Brian flew back to London to find that Little Red Rooster, the song largely recorded behind his back, had shot straight to the top of the charts.

Brian had always been prone to hurt things, whether pets or his girlfriends' feelings, but only recently had he got round to self-destruction. There had been bitter disappointment, both inside and outside the band, when he missed those four midwestern gigs. After the MC left the stage in Dayton, having announced the Stones were a man short, several hundred teenage girls had also made their way out. Respectful applause greeted the four musicians (discreetly backed by Stu) who toned down their act a notch in favour of more melodic arrangements and less adventurous riffing. 'You can't cover what you want from the Stones with one guitar,' Keith told Stanley Booth.

Some industry insiders say that there's a hard streak to Keith, an occasional coldness. And every so often a chill wind did blow through Richards country. Long stretches of flowing Keith-laughter and startling kindness would be followed by bouts of impenetrability and dark rage. He and the Stones were all down on Brian for his having committed the one unpardonable crime, 'screwing the band'.

Stu summed up a mood when he said, 'Brian's sin was being so fucking stupid about himself. There was no need for him to get in that out-of-it state he used to. He did it because he thought that was the way rock 'n roll stars should behave.'

In the five days and nights he was in hospital, Wyman and Watts were the only two who troubled to visit their bandmate.

The day he flew back from New York Keith went straight to the *Ready Steady Go!* studios, performed Little Red Rooster, then fought his way through a mob orgy at the stage door before being driven across town at wild speed to play the Empire Pool, Wembley. Immediately after the show, he collapsed. A doctor was called, who prescribed rest – which was not available. For one reason or another, Keith had now been up for five nights.

The results of Keith's exertions were staggeringly impressive. A second British EP, called *Five by Five*, stayed at the top of the charts for nine weeks; the Stones were also on top of the singles and LP charts in America. They were actually outselling the Beatles in many markets. A statement from London Records in New York shows that in 1964 each band member received a cheque for $16,000 (now worth roughly ten times as much). Stewart would say that Keith 'encouraged thousands of kids to pick up a guitar' by, knowingly or not, proving its commercial possibilities. Richards 'definitely played a role in merging rock with the entertainment industry and turning it into really big business', Stu added.

Another colleague remembers, 'Keith watched the market like a hawk, then went for it. Other musicians would stop caring, but not him. All his records aimed at hammering [the] blues to a pop audience.' One obvious example was the way he sat around in Hampstead riffing on his new Epiphone guitar, deconstructing Top 10 hits like the Four Seasons' Rag Doll. Another was the session at RCA in Hollywood, where Keith worked for eighteen straight hours, from 11 a.m. to 5 a.m., steering Heart Of Stone through twenty-five or thirty takes; the idea was to capture the perfect, spontaneous feel. There was always a canny gleam in Keith's eye as well as a sharp tongue in his head. He could be witheringly blunt. As he said, 'Brian was great. It was only when you had to work with him ... The harder the work got, the more awkward he got, and the more fucked up he'd get himself ... Mick and I were merciless on him.'

On the morning after he collapsed, Richards was back in Holly Hill strumming his guitar. Sitting knee to knee, Keith would play old Chess or Stax riffs and Jagger would mumble, over and over, moving words and music against each other to find new songs forged in the process. Richards had only just kicked off his training wheels a few months earlier. Now he had the tunes, and his first masterpiece. Cramming its man-size wallop into the comparatively snug confines of his Hampstead sitting room, Keith hit on the stinging four-note phrase of The Last Time. That one riff immediately left you spoilt for any other guitarist.

In the same week, Keith, Mick and Andy Oldham formed a publishing company outside the Stones called Mirage Limited. The Last Time was released in February 1965 – the opening salvo in Mirage's campaign to grab hold of American dance music, rough it up and send it back whence it came. Richards then threw in a second new song, the incongruously smoochy but snide Play With Fire.

Keith had no clear idea yet what rewards pop would bring him. But he knew he could do the stuff better than anybody else.

In many ways, Keith was exactly what people expected a Sixties rock star to be – black clad, shaggy and pale, with limbs like rubber bands. Hair-triggered. But he offset the stereotype with a ready smile and a whooping laugh that brought to mind someone going down the first hill on a big dipper. The more successful he became, the more his fickleness threw people off. Keith would flip so suddenly, with so many rapidly mimicked voices thrown in, that it was sometimes hard to figure out who he was or what he was driving at. To Linda, obviously, he could be 'the most charming guy'. Doris, too, as well as her father and sisters, were showered with gifts and letters that were droll, uninhibited and crisply phrased, with sudden and surprising jolts of insight. The private Keith was a sweet but shy Dartford boy who feared becoming yesterday's man – not quite getting it, losing his touch, growing old and stale, flailing around like Bert. In keeping with others in the business, he swung helplessly back and forth between moods in which it seemed to him that music was his life blood, and others in which it was a bloody nuisance.

Catching him between these cycles could be a risky business. Keith and Jagger were enjoying a quiet drink in a Paris bar that 20 October when a heckler tactlessly asked, 'Are you the Supremes?' Before the laughter had died down, Keith vaulted the counter and punched the man in the face.

The headlines kept coming, and he was fast getting a name. The Stones had done four British tours, two European tours and two American tours in 1964. They'd had hit singles and albums, been described as 'scum' by Ed Sullivan and 'lewd' by the *News of the World*. While other pop groups might rate a dig from their local vicar, the Stones were panned by the Archbishop of Canterbury. On 18 December Keith was doing his Christmas shopping when, right there in the street, a shrill, Dame Edna-type woman went berserk, lashing out at him for 'singing trash'.

Four more shoppers quickly came by in a rowdy group, and joined the consensus. Three were yelling, and one swung at Keith with her handbag. A final pedestrian appeared, bellowing querulously about 'filth', bringing the total congregating there in just a few moments to six, all but one of them screaming at the top of their lungs. It had been a dramatic year for Keith, but even he must have been struck at how it ended: making smartly up his local high street, fleeing the jeers, howls and catcalls of a posse.

He was twenty-one.

Keith's first adult experiences were only slightly less violent. He'd later describe some of his massive drug use as simply a way of coping – 'We worked our asses off, non-stop, every day for three years.' On many of those days Keith would have to write or record new songs, do interviews, play a show and then sprint away from fans through the kitchens of hotels and down dark alleys. It was amazing that he could still combine such stress with a relentlessly full social life. By now he was using coke as well as speed to stay awake for two or three nights on the trot.

Like most Stones occasions, their first tour of Australia and New

Zealand dragged everyone to the edges of lunacy. The reporter Judy Wade remembers a siege atmosphere at the band's Sydney hotel, where 'Keith was busy dropping whisky glasses from the balcony into the [empty] car park five storeys below'. He looked tired at the start, before the gigs began, and he was hassled throughout; Keith was even chased and rammed when he put out one afternoon in a rowing boat. The same qualities that made Richards effective in interviews came into play here, as he searched for the words with most telling effect. 'Fuck off,' he snarled, at length.

Keith's pose of reserve broke, under extreme pressure, on one or two other occasions Down Under. Sydney's *Morning Herald* didn't much care for it, and declared the Stones to be a 'blatantly wild bunch' who ought to be banned. 'They're shockers. Ugly Looks, Ugly Speech, Ugly Manners' the paper noted.

To his credit, Keith usually managed to reach down for the much needed reserves of humour and patience. On the other hand, certain vulgar critics got as good as they gave.

Driving through New York's Central Park one night that spring, Richards and Jagger were saluted by four or five men who yelled the word 'Faggots!' from a passing convertible. Keith immediately ran after the car, caught up with it at a light, dragged the driver from his seat, took a glancing blow and, in return, booted the man hard in the mouth.

Far from disturbing his creativity, the madness of life on the road only served to spur Keith on. That 17 January he flew to LA, went straight to RCA studios and stayed up all night buffing The Last Time to a gloss. The single reached number one in Britain, number nine in America. Sporting ferocious guitar and a livid hook, Keith's knife-sharpening hit announced the arrival of a major talent.

The first thing you noticed about the Stones' second LP, once past the disturbing close-up of Keith's acne-pocked face on the cover, was how the titles sounded angry: Grown Up Wrong, I Can't Be Satisfied, Pain In My Heart. So did the music. Almost every cut opened with a snarl of Keith guitar, then chugged into an R&B groove with offhand vocal interjections and Brian's curly little flourishes. A highlight was Off The Hook, which set the sound of misogyny over a snappy Motown beat. When Keith was doing the locomotion, even the seriously played-out covers like Suzie-Q came to life. He and Mick also slowed it down once or twice into a discount-Dylan strum. *The Rolling Stones No. 2* was less manic but more assured than its predecessor – against the prevailing wisdom of musical typecasting, Keith straddled everything from gospel to pop to down-home Memphis soul. The album spent thirty-seven weeks on the UK chart.

The Stones were neither the first nor the biggest of the British Invasion groups, but by now they enjoyed the worst image, one that Al Goldman memorably called 'sado-homosexual-junkie-diabolic-sarcastic-nigger-evil'. Keith was fast establishing himself as both a hard nut and custodian of his art. 'I suppose the Stones somehow reverberate to some universal vibrational mode,' he allowed. 'Music's always been streaks ahead of any other gig. After air, food, water and fucking, I think maybe music is the next human necessity. It is for me.'

The Stones were built on the bond between the two songwriters, which was often a mute one, since Keith frequently communicated only by guitar and Jagger muttered or flared his nose as soon as spoke. The old schoolmates stayed alert to each other's moods like animals grunting in the woods. Brian, meanwhile, was already swinging from pop star excess to a spokesman-for-a-generation role that was perhaps a touch overdone. 'Every era brings a fresh wave of ideas, and if this were to be stifled society and culture would be doomed ... I'd like the government to spend more on neuro-research. When man can understand the human brain, he'll understand everything.'

'Jones was an arsehole. A nonstop whiner and victim,' one Stones insider put it harshly. At twenty-three, Brian was already burning out. It now seems quite probable that, as well as being an alcoholic and a junkie, he was an undiagnosed depressive and, so Wyman believes, an epileptic. Brian thought Dylan's Like A Rolling Stone, recorded that spring, was a send-up of himself.

As the band's price rose, Eric Easton revealed that he'd rejected a $2 million offer for all Richards–Jagger songs written over the next five years. Keith himself was essentially living on pocket money, just £50 a week throughout 1965. He soon began to conquer his shyness with the help of a lawyer, and from there it was a relatively short step to the Bentley and the country estate. He also hired a thirty-nine-year-old ex-paratrooper and legendary fixer, one Tom Keylock, who rarely strayed from Keith's side over the next six years. Keylock, no pushover when it comes to character judgement, calls Richards 'a hard man with a heart of gold. If I'd had a son, I would have liked him to be like Keith.'

18 March 1965: a two-week, twenty-eight-date tour of old Art Deco British fleapits wound up at the ABC, Romford. At about eleven that night, Ian Stewart was driving the Stones in Jagger's black Daimler up the A118 into central London. Stu turned the car into the Francis service station where, according to the attendant, forty-one-year-old Charles Keeley, 'a shaggy-haired monster wearing dark glasses' enquired, 'Where can we have a leak here?'

'Sensing trouble', as he later put it in court, Mr Keeley asked the Stones to move on. The forecourt wrangling then became noticeably bitter. Mick Jagger remarked, 'We piss anywhere, man', a phrase that was taken up by Keith and Brian, who repeated it in 'a kind of chant'. Wyman took the opportunity to urinate against a nearby wall. A small crowd began to gather, and some of them yelled encouragement to Bill, and Keeley himself yelled the opposite, as Brian jumped up and down like an enraged ape in a monkey house. This went on until Wyman returned to the car, which accelerated away, one occupant – Keith – making 'a parting gesture with two fingers'.

Summoned for insulting behaviour, Jagger, Jones and Wyman were each fined £5, with costs, when the case reached East Ham magistrates court on 22 July. Keith, in his first ever appearance in the box, was called as a witness. He testified that he saw 'nothing happen' at the service station.

That same month, a Glasgow magistrate named James Longmuir publicly called the Stones 'long-haired morons' when sentencing a youth who happened to be a fan. 'They wear their filthy clothes, play their banjos and act like clowns', was the judge's scathing review. The Establishment's galumphing backlash served only to shift even more records for the Stones, who were now turning them out as fast as Decca could press them.

For Jones and Oldham, the band's warring image makers, there'd been good reason for cutting through the old 'showbiz shit – all that brushing your teeth and grinning into the lights'. But the real star had sprung from other quarters, and before they knew it, both had been left behind. Back on tour of America that May, Keith casually wrote the riff to quite probably the best rock song ever. As soon as he got home he bought Doris her first car, and left Holly Hill for a suite at the London Hilton and a flat in St John's Wood. Keith had exactly £942 on deposit at the Bradford & Bingley, but from now on his credit would always be good.

In July Oldham produced a thirty-three-year-old 'neighbourhood guy' from New Jersey, once and future Hollywood mogul and bookkeeper of genius, Allen Klein. Klein was incredible. Squat, beady eyed and built like a bag of spanners – invariably dressed in ill-fitting jeans and greasy sweaters – he and his wardrobe were so brazen that both defied ridicule. Klein made his name with an aggressive business style punctuated by catchphrases – 'Bada-boom, bada-bing!'; 'Gedouttahere!' – from the Jewish-Italian streets of Newark, and his choice of white tube socks indicated that he was still keeping it real. 'Al's negotiating [technique] would have raised eyebrows on a pirate brig,' one friend says admiringly.

Klein had qualified at Uppsala College, specializing in the new field of showbiz audits. His image as a 'fat little kid from Jersey' belied the enormous care with which he served his clients. Klein was famous for having nosed out unpaid royalties, sometimes in the hundreds of thousands, on behalf of artists like Bobby Darin and Sam Cooke. He once handed the teen crooner Bobby (Blue Velvet) Vinton a cheque well into six figures in 'recovered fees'. Klein did his first British deal in 1964, and was now managing the folk singer Donovan. Meanwhile, Oldham had tired of Eric Easton, and was looking for someone to act as the Stones' business manager while he, Andy, handled the 'creative thing'.

It was an historic moment. Although there were major bumps in the road ahead, Klein would eventually help turn Keith's 'little kid's fantasy' into a global enterprise that landed the Stones on Times Square billboards, the cover of *Fortune* magazine, and in boxed-set CDs in households everywhere.

When Oldham first introduced him to the Stones, Klein promised to make them millionaires inside a year.

'Who writes the music?' he asked.

'That one,' said Oldham, pointing to Keith.

Keith in turn thought Klein (with whom he shared a birthday) 'fantastic', the Stones' ticket 'out of cheapo-dom', while Mick worried that 'Fatso' might, on the contrary, end up costing them. As it turned out, both men would be proved right. On 26 July, Klein was hired as the band's business manager. Oldham would retain control both of the records and the 'We piss anywhere'-type publicity. Easton was fired.

Klein's first act was breathtaking. The Stones were ordered to dress in black, with sunglasses, and accompany him to a showdown at Decca House. There they met Sir Edward Lewis, the florid and supremely dignified company chairman.

'Ed, you've been fucking us over!' Klein shouted. 'Haven't you?'

The next few moments were exciting. The Stones averted their eyes, and Lewis, who abhorred bad language in the boardroom, reddened further, as though keeping his temper in check.

'I can assure—'

Klein smoothly cut in on him with a sudden flip of tone. 'No. Listen to me. You want the Rolling Stones. The feeling is mutual. Let's talk turkey.'

The band left an hour later a million pounds richer. Klein also got them a better royalty rate, 9.25 per cent, than even the Beatles enjoyed. Perhaps it was too dark behind the shades for the Stones to read the fine print, which made everything payable to Nanker-Phelge Music USA, a company controlled by Allen Klein.

Keith's golden phase began that spring, at exactly the same time he'd originally predicted the Stones would break up. The band were back in America for their third tour inside a year, opening 29 April in Albany. Once in New York they taped their second *Sullivan* show, sought out James Brown and, in turn, got death threats from the Ku Klux Klan for consorting with 'niggers'. The Klan nearly had their wish when, a week later, the Stones flew into Atlanta. The brakes on the band's plane failed and they had to slide down emergency chutes through clouds of smoke and fire.

6 May, the Jack Russell baseball stadium, Clearwater, Florida. The Stones got through four numbers before the fans rushed the stage. It was the south's first real rock concert: the words entered the language, alongside RIOT and ANIMALS, in the next day's Miami *Herald*.

Back to the plywood Gulf motel. A suddenly quiet Thursday night, with Charlie sitting alone by the small pool and Jagger, Jones and Wyman all *in delicto*. Brian beat his girl up and Mike Dorsey, one of the roadies, thumped him, breaking two of Brian's ribs. Bill notes that Dorsey's initiative was well received by the group. Keith went up alone to room 3 (there were only seventeen in the place), watched the *Tonight Show* and nodded off. Towards dawn he woke up with a riff – three notes rising a minor third from B to D, or phonetically, *dunt dunt, da-da-da* – ringing in his head. Keith, who was in the habit of keeping a tape recorder by his bed to capture such moments, grabbed his new Gibson Firebird, taped the lick, then fell asleep again. In the morning, he forgot about the incident, stuffed the cassette in his back pocket, where it narrowly avoided being washed along with his jeans, and was later about to record over it when he stumbled on the riff. Keith listened to it once and then played the famous eight-bar intro to Jagger, whom he told, 'The name of this song is Satisfaction.'

It took several days to figure out in the studio, until Stu casually produced a distortion unit, or fuzzbox, for Keith's guitar. That did it. The eventual track cut at RCA, Hollywood, on 12–13 May boasted some emotionally pent-up lyrics and, courtesy of Watts, a bullet-train momentum that fairly screamed 'rock anthem'. The basic riff had echoes of Dancing In The Street; while Jagger married Wilson Pickett barking to a sly, pissed-off delivery of lines like 'When I'm watching my TV/And a man comes on and tells me/How white my shirts can be'. Throw in Charlie's punishing 4/4 beat, Bill's rubbery bassline and the most famous riff in rock, and you had musical history.

Released in June 1965, (I Can't Get No) Satisfaction doubled pop's specific gravity overnight. It also became one of those standards that works its way under the skin, shedding spin-offs and a slew of re-releases and covers, until it stopped being a hit and turned into an industry. In chronological order, it topped both the American and British charts, survived being cut by everyone from Otis Redding to Joe Loss, got itself re-tooled into a jingle for candy bars and voted the 'greatest song ever' – nosing out Stairway To Heaven and Respect – by a VH1 poll of music-biz insiders before being rediscovered by the likes of Britney Spears. Along the way, Satisfaction became a vivid presence in the world's imagination. Keith's dream was responsible for the most commercial slice of teen angst until Kurt Cobain wrought his unique brand of rock havoc on *Nevermind*, a quarter of a century later.

The transformation of the man who wrote Shang A Doo Lang in 1964 into the man who wrote Satisfaction in '65 was revolutionary. There was a complete overhaul: compositional ideas grounded in Memphis and Harlem, a totally fresh guitar sound, and a richly rendered public image. Released from the low horizons of his 'shit years' into American optimism, Keith began to kit himself out in gaudy Ivy League shirts and chinos. Money was being poured into Nanker Phelge. Klein handed each of the band a cheque for £2,500 that August, along with the kind of assurance rock managers love, 'You want it – you got it.' The Stones were no longer the London competition for the Beatles: thanks to Keith, they were the environment.

18 December 1943.

School outing to Wembley, May 1954. KR is in the front row, fourth from left. Mike Jagger is at centre right, holding a black cat.

The flat above the shop at 33 Chastilian Road, Dartford, where Keith spent his first ten years.

The northbound platform at Dartford station, where Keith loomed out of the fog at Jagger on the morning of 17 October 1961.

Four men who helped turn Keith's 'little kid's fantasy' into a global enterprise that eventually landed the Rolling Stones on the cover of *Fortune* magazine:

Alexis Korner

Allen Klein

Andrew Oldham

Tom Keylock (seen here with Betty Keylock and Jack Dyer, the inspiration for Jumpin' Jack Flash)

KR, Brian Jones, Mick Jagger, Bill Wyman and Charlie Watts celebrate as The Last Time hits number one, March 1965.

With his first serious songwriting money, Keith bought himself a Bentley and began to trawl London's 'with it' shops. Although he enjoyed the military look, he wasn't above the occasional silly hat.

Marianne Faithfull, who described going to bed with Keith as 'the best night of my life'. A few days later, she began a long relationship with Mick Jagger.

Jagger and Richard will appeal

Daily Record

BID TO FREE TWO JAILED STONES

MAN SHOT DEAD IN BANK RAID
—Back Page

HIGHLAND ROW FLARES
—Page 3

RAILMEN SAY NO TO STRIKE
—Centre Pages

FAREWELL TO JAYNE MANSFIELD
—Centre Pages

Why girl was wearing only a rug

PETROL PRICES GO UP BY 2d.

Keith and Mick's drugs trial in June 1967 ended with the judge telling the jury to put out of their minds any prejudice they might have about Keith's looks, clothes, lifestyle or his views on 'petty morals'. They were also to ignore everything they had read and heard about a nude girl who had been lying in front of the fire when the police arrived, and not to let her rum behaviour in any way influence their verdict. The jury found Keith and Mick guilty.

Keith's legendary country home Redlands – a mixture of Olde England and Sixties crash pad – before and after it caught fire.

The Rock 'n Roll Circus, including, back row (l–r), John Lennon, Yoko Ono, KR, Mick Jagger, Brian Jones. Twenty-eight years later, the Stones got around to releasing it on film.

After Brian Jones flipped out in Morocco, his girlfriend Anita Pallenberg took up with Keith. The exotic Anita spoke six languages and was a major part of the Stones story for the next twelve years.

Keith and Anita leave hospital with their son Marlon, August 1969.

Keith and Marlon at Nellcôte, the villa perched on a clifftop overlooking Cap Ferrat, where the Stones recorded *Exile on Main Street*. Two weeks after the family left, French police raided the house and charged Keith with having used drugs there.

Altamont.

The *Exile*-era Stones on stage with Mick Taylor (far left).

The rest of the third American tour afforded the perfect testing ground. There were riots in Chicago and San Francisco. In Long Beach, fans danced on the Stones' car, nearly crushing their heroes like sardines in a can. The cloaca-tongued Jones, heavily taped up, was muttering about chicks. While Richards and Jagger were busy songwriting, Brian's main priority was getting his nuts off. On 20 May, Keith debuted Satisfaction on TV's *Shindig* where, at his request, fifty-five-year-old Howlin' Wolf, making his television debut, closed the show. A mark of Keith's respect for the Wolf was the removal of the butt-end he otherwise kept clamped to his lip when not actually singing.

Back in England, Doris was proudly keeping a scrapbook of her Ricky's achievements. On the mantelpiece there were snaps of Keith as a boy, as well as pop fan magazines neatly displayed on the coffee table. Nobody had heard from Bert for three years now.

Keith sometimes kept a photograph of Dartford in his wallet for inspiration.

At tour's end, Richards and Jagger headed off on a motoring holiday through the Arizona desert. The conversation turned to Brian Jones.

'He's class but he's impossible,' said Keith. 'All that rock 'n roll superstar bullshit. It's incredible. Beating up hookers and everything. As far as I'm concerned he walks the plank if he doesn't shape up.'

'Better if we could hold out. You may have noticed the chicks love him.'

'Mr Jagger, the voice of reason.'

Snappy guitar had existed before Keith – largely thanks to Chuck Berry – but not quite like that in Satisfaction, which was about much more than technique. There were plenty of better axemen around, like Eric Clapton, whose tasteful chops would never quite conjure the same menacing brew of thrift and swagger. Keith was the anti-Eric: a touch player with a stylistic range as vast as his output, who was also totally unique. The best rock composer of his generation also happened to be the best rhythm guitarist of his generation, and managed to be both creative and practical at the same time. Keith wrote not only the music but often (as with Satisfaction) the title and chorus, leaving Jagger only the elegant filler. Richards' sound was, and is, physical – doing for noise what John Cage did for silence – while also connected to the mysteries of soul. It's both earthy and tasteful, going at full tilt and yet capable of restraint, if not quite teen-idol schmalz. 'Working the field,' he calls it. Keith's cauldron of pop, R&B, country and jazz had been stirred at Doris's knee. Each early Stones hit was the bruised but marketable fruit of a Dartford adolescence.

Steeped in the glories of Fifties rock 'n roll, Keith was fully alive to the feel and precision of great songwriting. Wyman recalls how Keith thought The Last Time was 'weak ... he tried for a long period to improve it', before turning it in. Keith's ear for melody was also evident in the twenty-five or thirty outtakes of Satisfaction. (He kept calling the early versions of the song 'utter crap'.) Behind Keith's lash lay a broad streak of professionalism, even perfectionism. He wanted every note and every bar to count and he wanted to grow as a writer. Richards was never too proud to ask an acknowledged master like Muddy Waters for advice. Keith 'had only to be shown, and he never forgot ... The man absorbed knowledge like a blotter.'

Keith flew home, bought Doris her Austin 1100 and took Linda on holiday to Greece. They got back just in time for yet another tour, this one of northern Europe. Early on 24 June the Stones and their women were walking across a roped-off stretch of tarmac at Oslo airport. Several thousand screaming girls were there to greet them. Without warning, the band and their fans found themselves in a novel situation – being subjected to water cannon fired by Norwegian riot police, led by an officer on horseback waving a sabre. The charge didn't rout the fans but it impressed the Stones, who briefly debated which one of them should lodge a protest. Keith volunteered.

In his speech Richards told the cops a hard truth: They were wankers.

In the bright midsummer nights that followed, it seemed as if all Scandinavia went mad for the band. On 25 June they played an open-air show to 20,000 on a Finnish beach. Flying, Brian performed Popeye The Sailor Man while the Stones played Satisfaction, and there was renewed talk of axing him. Back in London (where the new single, already platinum in America, was about to ship), Klein handed Keith a letter.

> Because of your phenomenal success in the recording business, which we gratefully appreciate, we have decided to increase your royalty on all record sales so that all royalties received on gramophone sales will be divided equally – fifty per cent for the Rolling Stones and fifty per cent on behalf of the producer.

The Stones soon had to beg Klein, and his remote New York office, for cash.

This was irksome, but Keith's life was too manic to let him do much about it. Oldham and his booking agents still had the day-to-day say of things. 'There was no time to sit back and think about what we were doing,' Keith recalled. 'Things just happened.'

He was doing better than any Richards ever had, better than Gus Dupree ever dreamt of doing. Keith couldn't grow as a guitar player – that would wait until the Stones came off the road in '67 – but two years of breakneck gigging had taught him how to 'sell' a song. Here, plainly, was a born rock 'n roller who combined bluesy grit with an instinctive gift of melody. Similarly instinctive was the acknowledgement of Keith's virtues by the fans. It was the tempo and balance that made for his trademark rhythm, and that rhythm which the kids were saluting when they punched the air in time to Satisfaction. Keith didn't play long fluid runs, although the Stones could move like a train when they wanted to; it was more a question of his strategically placed guitar bolts, which continued to squeeze more mileage out of the whiplash four-bar riff than anything since Maybellene.

Locating a middle ground between Berry and *Top of the Pops* fare, the Stones' new singles all pointed to a man whose mastery of his craft said Satisfaction was just the start. Keith began his invention of the future by going back to the past, specifically the soul grooves of James Brown, Wilson Pickett and the Staple Singers (whom he shamelessly copped for The Last Time). But within a year, thanks to Keith, the Stones' signature sound had a swagger all its own. Then, it had been a formulaic channelling of Stax and Chess. Now, it toyed with the familiar genre of crunching blues licks while skilfully avoiding almost all cliché. Daringly, Keith followed up Satisfaction with the spacey, Isley Brothers-on-speed Get Off Of My Cloud. A long way, that, from As Tears Go By.

For someone who wrote songs in his sleep, Keith recorded agonizingly slowly. The studio, for him, was a lab for fiddly experimentation often at odds with the available time and budget. Keith's protracted fine-tunings typically made for sessions in which nothing seemed to happen, but which, through countless five-second takes and smart engineering, moved forward to the climax. The result, as often as not, was a pop crown jewel.

Unlike his Seventies image, Keith didn't yet look the slightest bit wasted, crazed, gnarled or vampiric. He looked tired, though. Anyone thinking the Stones' fame was an accident, a kind of listless fluke – or that it was all lashings of sex 'n dope – should have been there in late summer of 1965. On 14 August Keith flew to New York, where he was backstage for the Beatles show at Shea Stadium; then it was all-night sessions with Klein, to cut record and movie deals; more raveups in the north of England and Ireland, TV and radio appearances to plug Satisfaction; forty-eight hours in LA to record Cloud, I'm Free and Lookin' Tired; a chance encounter with Frank Sinatra, who called Keith (to his delight) Ringo; back to London and straight to the band's last ever ballroom gig, on the Isle of Man, and finally to Germany, where Jagger goosestepped around stage and Keith met the mother of his first three kids. That would be for starters. Most days, Richards would also have to write songs, read scripts, sign contracts and generally schmooze with Klein and Oldham. Things went well enough on the road but, not surprisingly, Keith's relationship with Linda was strained.

Many mornings, he'd come home from a club at dawn, take some uppers, and then drive off to the next gig.

One visitor to the St John's Wood flat remembers it as a sump of Edith Grove-cum-Bombay proportions. The two Keiths 'lived [among] crapulous laundry, stale fag smoke and dirty dishes. The whole place stank like a litter box.'

Thanks to Satisfaction, Keith was now able to run up awesome bills that he waved away airily on presentation. Whether all were settled even after 'Fatso' completed his shrewd and brilliantly executed raid on Decca, is moot. Klein's *chutzpah*, however, was indisputable, for – according to Bill – if one of the band needed cash, management would loan him back his own money at interest. Quite often even this proved impractical, and the Stones resorted to firing off cables along the lines of 'What the fuck's happening?' and 'The phones and electricity will be cut off tomorrow'. Keith's down-payment on his new house would be extracted from Klein only by deep surgery.

Management hassles aside, Keith was now well-off. Armed with the first royalty statement for Satisfaction ('a quasi-Marxist blitz on consumerism': pop critic Bob Palmer), Richards bought a Bentley S3 Continental, which he painted blue and adorned with external speakers to blast thunderous rock down the streets of London. He began to trawl certain 'with it' shops for batik scarves, floppy-brimmed hats and, more furtively, his military tunics. Keith seemed to have been born without brakes. He drank extensively, smoked heavily and had to be forced to relax. He was, however, unabashedly fond of the Queen, *Carry On* films, cricket and horse riding; Tom Keylock calls him a 'very English rebel. Fucking brilliant career mover.'

Keith was famously good, too, at courting danger. Most pop stars wouldn't have been willing to take the risks he did in order to escape 'cheapo-dom'. Certainly not the other Stones. When the band originally met at Oldham's office to discuss hiring Klein, Wyman and one or two others had suggested they have a lawyer read the various contracts. Perhaps research Fatso. 'Don't be so fucking mercenary,' Keith had yelled. 'We've got to trust *someone*.'

Just about that same time, the US Attorney in Manhattan was charging Klein with ten tax violations, for failing to file some small sums in payroll deductions. He was the starring figure, often as plaintiff, in more than a dozen other lawsuits. Two years later, the US Securities and Exchange Commission briefly suspended over-the-counter trading in Klein's Cameo-Parkway Inc, based on three years of reported losses. Spurious rumours of stock rigging and double dealing surfaced from time to time, as did tales of Klein's fabled negotiating techniques. 'THE TOUGHEST WHEELER-DEALER IN THE POP JUNGLE' was one frequently seen headline.

Was the guy for real? Keith thought so. He admired the deals Klein did for the band, but getting their hands on the stuff was 'a wank'.

The Stones were in for another blow on tour in Germany, where Brian was again nodding off at inappropriate moments, such as on stage. When Jones did manage to get in tune, it was to gleefully reprise his Popeye countermelody to Satisfaction, a song he loathed. Not surprisingly, Keith and Jagger went nuts, expressing their views with a zeal that struck Bill, Charlie and Stu as much as the challenge: did any of them know what to do about Brian?

They didn't.

Keith enjoyed drinking and toking, as well as a discreet coke habit, but never – or not yet – to the extent of hurting the Stones. He found Brian's nonstop debauchery beneath contempt. When the band drove to Munich early on 14 September, they were laughing about an incident backstage in Hamburg, where Keith had taken a half-filled whisky bottle, peed in it, shaken it up and offered it to the riot police busy cracking the fans' heads. The Stones, particularly Keith, were all in fits when the cops had proceeded to swig away, happily toasting the boys' health.

But on that warm Tuesday night, as the band checked into the notoriously haunted Lilienhof hotel, they also muttered about Brian's flaky behaviour, about how he'd slept (one of his great talents) through whole recording sessions, including the one for Satisfaction. The consensus was that he'd fucked up royally, deserting his various kids – even the Stones drew the line – and doing nothing for the band except looking elegantly wasted. Oldham was again planning to fire him.

And then, to everyone's amazement, Jones himself sauntered in with the most ravishing, drop-dead girl on his arm anyone had ever seen. But *gorgeous*. Bone-thin yet built, with a shock of cropped blonde hair and clad in a shiny black nano-skirt; her face corpse white but for two droopy, coal-black eyes that gave her an air of boozy languor. Yet, as the Stones were about to learn, she had already starred in films and been on the cover of fashion magazines all over Europe. At twenty-two, she was a veteran of Warhol's Factory, through which she knew 'everyone' in New York. She spoke six languages. And, most surprising of all, she didn't give a toss about the Stones, whom she considered 'little schoolkids' and who went mad for her as a result. She was some piece of work.

Anita Pallenberg.

Keith was staggered. Ho-ly shit. What did a chick like that see in *him*?

For weeks after that the gossip columns in *Nova* and *Queen* kept up a breathless drumbeat. Brian Jones was going to marry his beautiful fraulein! Anita was spotted at a bridal salon! Bob Dylan would be the best man!

None of it happened, but for the first time in two years Brian was smiling again. The next day the Stones brought down the house in Berlin (later trooping up Potsdamer Strasse, in the lee of Hitler's bunker), blitzed Austria and then home to England. Jones had almost abandoned the guitar by now; onstage he only rarely played any sort of musical instrument, and when he did it was filler. On his better nights, he added an inspired piano to Keith's rhythm assaults. Brian's organ solo on Time Is On My Side was a rare treat. Jones told everyone that he thought the new batch of Keith songs a drag, but that he, Brian, was prepared to wait the short time necessary before being commissioned to write music for 'Anita's movies'.

Jones didn't, however, disdain the business of entertaining the Stones' fans. He still loved to bait an audience, and effortlessly worked up the crowd on 16 October at the ABC, Northampton, into a gale of rowdy chants. During the second number someone threw a metal chair leg, which knocked Richards out cold. He collapsed flat at Jagger's feet. While Mick dropped the mike and saw to him, Brian threw his head back in the spotlight and, it seemed to many, chortled. After a few minutes backstage, Keith recovered and continued the show.

The fourth North American tour opened a week later, just as Cloud topped the chart. Concert promotion may have been a new calling for Klein, but his latest coup was fully on a par with his success in bludgeoning Decca. In Times Square, Keith's very face loomed down from a hundred-foot-high billboard.

Opening night in Montreal was a battle between the Stones, their fans and the law. One cause of disquiet was the discovery that Keith had once again lost his passport; the band moved through Immigration so fast, jumping in front of one another like a shell game, that nobody noticed. The next day's flight into Toronto was nerve-racking, through clouds most of the way, with sudden terrifying jolts into burning sunlight. Safely ensconced in the Maple Leaf Garden, Brian sat down at the electric organ. As to his proficiency, not even the most gnarled pop critic could hazard a guess – the dominant noise was one of frenzied screaming.

Meanwhile, the *Out Of Our Heads* album was released in America and Britain, on different dates and in different format. An oddity, there were a few clunkers: Gotta Get Away was folk meets the blues, but not in a good way; and most of the Stax covers suffered from satirically duff vocals. *Heads* was, on the face of it, little more than a collection of tacky, would-be soulful ballads. But closer inspection would reveal a pop sensibility as savvy as *Beatles For Sale*, with rather more guitar chug; Heart Of Stone mined grittier seams than most British Invasion fare, and contributed to an LP that ranks, after several listens, at the top of the Stones' second division. *Out Of Our Heads* was on the American chart for sixty-five weeks. Christmas saw yet another US release, *December's Children*, a grab-bag of rejects, outtakes and Jagger's deliriously woozy calling over Keith's helium-voiced response. On the upside, there was both Cloud and the definitive treatment of Route 66. *Children* ended with Blue Turns To Grey, whose mild dullness could be traced to the fact that it sounded a bit like Yesterday without the string quartet.

That album shifted a million, too.

Once onstage in Boston or Newark or Tulsa the Stones would typically do a nine-song, $30,000 set, climaxing in a snarled Satisfaction. Unlike all the other male English singers, Jagger no longer uses the bottom half of his body simply to stand on: whipping up what a critic calls 'wet panty hysteria', his rooster-on-acid gyrations mesh perfectly with the laconic guitarist stage right, apparently indifferent, who cuffs the riffs. There's no holding the Stones now. The 'love 'em or leave 'em' headlines scroll across a nation already tearing itself apart over Vietnam: HEY! YOU! GET OFFA MY CLOUD! ... MONSTERS ... ROLLING STONES CONCERT A HOWLING SUCCESS ... KIDS GET SATISFACTION ... CRUDE AND RUDE STONES WHIP 20,000 INTO FRENZY ... applause brawls riots gladiatorial sex drugs filthy filthy filthy!

A young photographer, Gered Mankowitz, went along on the tour at Oldham's invitation.

'Keith was the sweetest guy. He was always up, really enthusiastic for whatever was going on. There was a high level of fun ... and he was writing the whole time. You'd hear odd lines and a bit of a tune and realize that it was a new song taking shape.'

Winging her way on Learjets and cruising on 200-foot yachts, Anita had spent the autumn scene-hopping around the Riviera. On 19 November she flew in from Paris to join Brian in Miami. Bill notes that the couple 'spent most of the time in their room', while Stu remembered that, on emerging, they fought 'like kids', trading pushes and slaps. Another party claims that Brian liked to 'ponce around' with Anita dressed in outrageous, frilly clothes. Hers.

Keith continued to eye up Miss Pallenberg, and the other Stones all exchanged grunted asides in which Brian was contrasted to his disadvantage to the noble and classy example of his stacked chick. The press were waiting when the lovebirds waved goodbye in Detroit, duly mangling Anita's name on the 6 o'clock news. From the perfectly fluted lips of Annie Pallenberd, America heard it officially: 'Brian and I are going steady. If we're going to get married it will be soon. Otherwise, it won't be at all.'

Jones was on top form at that night's gig in Cobo Hall, playing a lusty Popeye throughout.

3 December, Memorial Auditorium, Sacramento. Three lines into the first verse of The Last Time, Richards ran up to sing harmonies on the chorus, nudging the ungrounded mike stand with his electric guitar. There

was a bolt of blue flame, an unearthly screech and Keith collapsed to the floor. Then a ghastly burning smell. The Stones, Brian included, dropped their own gear and ran to their stricken comrade. Keith stayed down so long, seven minutes in some estimates, that people began to panic – there were a few screams, then deathly silence from the audience. Police and medical attendants were swarming all round him. Then, suddenly, Richards opened his eyes, absentmindedly scratched his chin and said, 'Hiya'. The little jokes Keith cracked, through grotesquely charred lips, before staggering back to his feet became part of Stones legend: 'What do I do for an encore?' and, to a worried knot of theatre management figures, 'I won't sue, guys.' The sound of Richards' voice, at once reedy and totally calm, settled the band down. They recognized in him the true rock 'n roller. Compared to Keith, everyone else was just a musician.

When the Stones looked at Keith's guitar they found that three of the strings had gone up in flames. The doctors told him that his rubber-soled shoes had saved his life.

Against orders Keith played the rest of the tour, which ended up with an LSD party thrown by the writer Ken Kesey. Richards, Gered Mankowitz and some of the minders then disappeared for a riding holiday in the McDowell mountains of Arizona. Mankowitz remembers that 'Keith invited us, paid all our expenses . . . First thing we did – at his insistence – was to get kitted out from top to bottom in cowboy gear.' It was the old Dartford Odeon fantasy brought to life.

On paper, Klein and his men had certainly done the Stones proud. The band commanded an unheard-of $30,000-plus a night, and made a profit of $214,152.65 after all expenses for the tour. (Klein, in accordance with the contract, quite legally held the cash and doled it out to them on demand.) Back to RCA Studios, with its windowless, Vegas-casino atmosphere, where Keith first strummed the chords of 19th Nervous Breakdown and the Stones cut half of what became *Aftermath*.

Keith was starting to look permanently jet-lagged, having played 244 gigs in a year. Also, he was getting in the habit, Linda noticed, of travelling with an entourage, devoted PAs who did literally everything for him it wasn't vital he do himself. When he got home, would there be withdrawal symptoms?

In fact Keith's career and Linda's drug intake had begun to skyrocket in unison, as if the two of them were in unconscious competition to see who could burn out first. Linda won and, by winning, lost. By now Keith was doing pot, uppers and a little coke, but – other than letting him stay up all hours, playing meltdown guitar – the stuff didn't faze him.

Linda Keith: 'I was crazy and I became a bit hard and nasty, probably, and I think I was less likeable by then than I had been. I suppose that was part of the problem we had. He wasn't happy with the stoned Linda . . . I think Keith maintained his way and I turned, but I think both Keith and I behaved horribly . . . I just couldn't go on – our relationship wasn't going anywhere.'

Paranoia and concealment became the Keiths' norm. Leaving Oldham to explain he was rehearsing, Richards began to disappear for days on end. With immaculate timing, just as Keith's home life went south, Anita arrived in town to be Brian's official, live-in girlfriend. The two of them cut a swathe in blond, swaggering around in matching fur coats and virtually inventing the notion of Swinging London. Jones and Pallenberg were part, or head, of the liberation movement linked by its scorn for the Britain of *Dad's Army* and Old Etonian judges. The couple's new soundproofed pad in Elm Park Lane, Chelsea, became a Xanadu of sex, drugs and, some whispered, more exotic rites. (Jones claimed he saw ghosts there.) A good friend of Brian's, Dave Thomson, was soon made aware of the cyclical nature of the relationship: Jones would use his fists on Anita, whom 'I actually saw going into their room with a bloody great whip. I could hear her whipping Brian.'

In his euphoria Jones told people he'd broken through to a higher plane, but it proved to be a trampoline, his manic highs followed by suicidal lows.

Brian's broad leer was always in place in public. But in the morning, after a heavy session in Blases or some recording studio, he'd fall into his silver Rolls-Royce and start off to his haunted mews pad. And, driving home, he would cry: Brian Jones, the Cheltenham Shagger; the first, and perhaps the best slide guitar player in Britain; Brian Jones, who had brought crowds to their feet; Brian Jones, driving up King's Road with tears running down his face.

Keith, too, was falling for Anita, but he bided his time. Apart from the questions of Linda and Brian, whose musicianship he still admired, there was always a fresh crisis on hand with the Stones. The Tech dropout was now a company director and the creative force behind an organization turning over $20 million annually.

Even so, it was impossible to leave a boardroom with the feeling that you'd been brought into the intimate presence of the real Keith. Sometimes he'd nod off, right there in the office, only to suddenly hear his name, smile broadly and then go back to the waxworks. Keith simply didn't care for 'reading shit on cash flow and logistics'.

There was already a lot of apparatus involved. On tour, a chartered jet took the Stones from city to city, streets got roped off, police were everywhere outside and Klein's men everywhere inside. This had the effect of raising the ante on Keith, wherever he went – but back home he could still be engagingly normal. On 20 December 1965 Richards queued up at a busy licensing centre in Neasden to take his driving test. He failed.

Keith was back in Australia with the Stones ('Whatever they have, it's indefinable' hazarded a report; 'cultivated arrogance', said another) in the new year. By now they were happening like war happens – twenty-minute blitzkrieg concerts, take the money and run, twenty-four hours in New York for the *Sullivan* show – the first ever colour broadcast on US television – where, in an awkward scene, Keith threw a dustbin at a Sullivan flunkey who failed to recognize him. 19th Nervous Breakdown was going gold, and the band turned out the first of many hits collections, *High Tide & Green Grass*. Richards put his name to one of the weirdest classical LPs of all time, *Today's Pop Symphony*, which proved, if nothing else, that Keith and the London Philharmonic were strangers to each other's time scales. On 6 March the Stones flew back to Hollywood and RCA. In seventy-two hours there they cut eighteen songs, including the rest of *Aftermath* and three future hit singles. Nothing could stop them now.

Meanwhile, *Disc* had had the novel idea of asking each Stone to describe another. Jagger on Richards:

> We've had arguments. In fact we disagree quite a lot, but we usually come to a compromise. There's never any hard feeling . . . He's very good about the group. Very optimistic. This cheers me up when I'm feeling low. We're well matched.

In fact, the two men sat on opposite sides of the fault line that runs through pop. Keith no longer saw much of Jagger socially, but he did manage to hang around Jones's flat a good deal, strumming guitars, mutually fuelled on drugs. Along with friends like Christopher Gibbs and 'Strawberry Bob' Fraser, the Stones were at ground zero of what *Time* now dubbed the 'swingy city'. There was square and there was hip, and then there was the world in which Keith and co. lived. Within weeks a triangle had formed, Richards again becoming thick with Jones, visiting Anita and him at home in Chelsea, and then consoling Pallenberg when Brian beat her up.

There was probably an equation that defined the rate at which Jones's potency as a musician declined while his sex life soared. It was a sorry trend. The recent spate of albums offered a good chance to study Brian's ups and downs: already marginalized on *December's Children*, by the time *Aftermath* came round he was the Stones' in-house exotic, trading in his blues guitar for marimbas, dulcimer and sitar; an intriguing sideline, not main-feature stuff. The liner photos of *High Tide*, meanwhile, made Brian look like a village idiot.

Jones may have done the randy shagging, but he wasn't the only member of the principal cast to swing. Keith was developing a taste for clubs like the Scotch of St James and the 'happening' Soho bistro La Terrazza, as well as a wack pot habit. The Dunhills were now joined by Beirut Flake and Congolese Bush. When he was going strong, really out there, off the road, a binge could last three days, three nights sometimes, without sleep, without a wake-up call and without Linda, though, unlike Brian, Keith was never a tabloid Romeo. Or flameout. Tom Keylock remarks admiringly how Richards, even half-loaded, was 'always together', well tasty, a real character and no mistake.

Keylock was fully on the scene now, a wiry, bespectacled cockney with a passing resemblance to a swarthy Michael Caine. He was in good shape; needed some dental work, but that was about it. Keylock had thick black hair like steel wool and a face that seemed to have been built in a foundry. More importantly, he was as straight as the day was long, and the Stones all loved him. Among Tom's chief duties was ferrying Keith around in the Blue Lena. The car had recently been resprayed, and then set off by a vast Confederate flag. When that proved an insufficient deterrent to traffic cops, Keith replaced it with first Turkish and then Chinese government insignia. The intended note of mandarin formality was rather spoilt by the sound of Satisfaction booming out of the Bentley's speakers, which at least got a few good look-at-that-bugger-jump laughs from behind the tinted glass.

Tom picked Keith up at the Scotch most mornings, then took him home in the Lena, top speed, Soho going past like a streak of mercury, while both continuously told jokes, cracking each other up.

'Keith had a great sense of humour. He saw the funny side of being a pop star,' Keylock would say. 'Unlike Brian and Mick, he really wasn't interested in poncing around like Liberace.'

Maybe that was why Richards and Keylock got along. The two of them could sit there together, backstage after a Stones concert in Paris, watching the Beautiful People, savouring the daftness of it all. 'There's that bloody Brigitte Bardot,' Keith would banter. 'I had to fight 'er off last night. "Piss off, Brigitte," I said to her. All over me she was, that girl. Shameless.'

Richards was jarred from his routine by the sight of Anita crossing the room. Tom noticed how Keith had reacted to Brian's ascendant love life. 'He couldn't fucking believe it.'

A surprisingly warm, witty man, but also a hard one. Early in 1966, Sir Edward Lewis had a passing word with Richards about his, Keith's, interest in plugging As Tears Go By. He had none. 'I don't want the aggro and I don't need it.' When the label grovelled, he told them – nothing unsatisfactorily vague here – to sod off. Despite or perhaps because of all the drugs Keith was writing every spare minute, and remained 'laser focused', on the move – 'a very tomorrow guy'.

Anything could happen, it seemed, when he was on form. Keith had it all, the talent, the charm *and* the cool calculation. There were other stars in whom two of these were evident but no one else in whom all three applied, and royally. Shoehorned between Australian and European tours, Keith had come up with a dazzling new set of songs, which he steered through his usual twenty or so takes. *Aftermath* was staggeringly eclectic, and thus not exactly the 'cohesive tone experience' Decca wanted, but those who like to hear the envelope being pushed would be amply rewarded by Lady Jane. Sir Edward and a few cynics had wondered, in a flurry of inter-office memos, whether there was 'more to [the Stones] than migraine guitar?' The doubt was decided in the band's favour when, on the first album consisting solely of Keith originals, they transcended all their influences.

Richards kept up a siege of Klein's New York office in the spring of 1966, eventually scrounging $40,000 (£16,090) to make up the purchase price of a new home. He moved in on Saturday 16 April. The place wasn't a typical rock star Taj Mahal, with its low ceilings, cramped bedrooms and relatively modest grounds. But Redlands was, nonetheless, a stunning house. The setting couldn't have been more pleasing: a timbered cottage over three hundred years old, near the sea in West Wittering, Sussex, surrounded by a shallow moat and trees 'that were here when Shakespeare was jiving around'. Keith shipped in a copper garden fountain, exotic Moroccan drapes and a dog of uncertain pedigree named Ratbag. Redlands also came to feature a small but well stocked greenhouse.

Over the years Keith built up an impressive collection of records and books, which he enjoyed while sprawled in front of the house's baronial log fire. There was little furniture in the usual sense, Keith preferring slabs of stone, wolfskin rugs and brightly coloured bean-bags to the sordidly conventional world of tables, chairs and beds. Inside the lid of the downstairs lavatory was a collage of photos of Brian and the band. The overall impression was of a Sixties crash pad with submerged Olde English charm. Having bought the adjacent staff cottage at auction Keith declared the Redlands estate 'a work of art', and remains there to this day.

Out the week he took possession, *Aftermath*. A seminal album, Mick's barrow-boy grunting lending credence to the idea of 'classlessness' – then all the rage – and booting Richards–Jagger on to level creative terms with Lennon–McCartney. Keith had never had trouble locating the perfect riff, but here that ability ran riot. The best tracks were so deftly done that *Aftermath*'s trippy mood never palled. Highlights included (on the album's two different versions) Mother's Little Helper, another of Mick's social critiques, performed with an ironic curl of the lip; Paint It, Black, more psychodrama in shake-your-arse 4/4 time, which Leonard Bernstein would call genius, and which put death on *Top of the Pops* thirty years before Marilyn Manson; I Am Waiting, a dulcimer workout pretty enough to be a Mantovani Christmas single; the Beatlesque Out Of Time; and an eccentric drum and marimba groover (and later target of feminist ire) Under My Thumb. While unlikely to keep the neighbours awake, Lady Jane boasted a tumbling vocal line and Brian's characteristic, seemingly casual endorsement of the novelty item – again, a dulcimer. All intoxicating stuff, with plenty of highly evocative, fuzzy guitar.

On the downside, the extended piano intro to Flight 505 suggested a drunken pub rehearsal included in error; Stupid Girl flaunted cheesy lyrics and no discernible tune; while a decent three-minute track signalled wildly to be let out of the neverending Goin' Home. There was also the problem of the Decca punctuation man. The album (initially called *Could* You *Walk on the Water?*) was spelt *After-Math*, *AfterMath* or *Aftermath* in various pressings, while the rogue comma in Paint It, Black aroused the sort of fanzine debate later enjoyed by the 'Paul is dead' jape.

While decay and loss were recurring themes on *Aftermath*, one old friend, missing presumed dead since Chuck Berry's day, turned up safe and well: the commercial blues. It took Keith, famous within the Stones for judging a room's acoustics by merely snapping his fingers, to prove that there was Top 10 life in the genre, moving the focus back on to exquisitely crafted, rootsy fare that appealed to more than a cult audience. 'Pow! What a stormer!' was *NME*'s verdict. *Aftermath* was an instant hit in both Britain and America.

25 May, Dolly's Club, Mayfair. Keith and Brian met up with Bob Dylan, who was touring Britain and being 'minded', with Keith's blessing, by Tom Keylock. The two Stones had already enjoyed a toke and several cocktails while in their car. 'Everyone overdid it,' notes Keylock. Another trip or two to Dolly's bar and one to the gents and Keith was flying. Somehow a discussion began about Like A Rolling Stone. Keith accused Dylan of taking the piss and Bob retorted that 'I could've written Satisfaction, but no way you fuckers could've written Tambourine Man'.

Keith's response to Dylan was that same challenging look of insolent reserve that had been the bane of schoolteachers and other authority figures since the day he walked. Clearly, it wasn't going to be one of those Sixties outpourings of peace and love.

'Fuck you, man.'

'Fuck *you*, man.'

At that Keylock intervened. 'I told Keith to piss off, that that night I was working for Dylan and if [Richards] wanted a fight he'd have to come through me. With that I grabbed Bob, pushed him into the car and took off back to the hotel. Then I look in the rear view mirror and right behind me are Keith and Brian, in Brian's Rolls-Royce. They're out of their brains, the car's doing about eighty, weaving in and out of traffic. I get to the hotel and hustle Dylan in, just as I see the Rolls jump the kerb and fucking nearly ram the front door.'

By the time Keith came to in the morning, only one disquieting thought survived. He'd paid for all Brian's drinks.

On 1 June, for the first time, US planes bombed Hanoi. Race riots broke out in Chicago, Detroit and Los Angeles. Mick Jagger was briefly hospitalized suffering from exhaustion. Jones was fighting nonstop with Anita. Fourteen of New York's top hotels made it known that the Rolling Stones' welcome would be less warm there. Klein protested to the state's attorney general, and Oldham issued a $5 million writ on the boys' behalf, claiming the ban subjected them to 'insufferable humiliation, ridicule and shame'.

Now Keith was ready to tour the States again.

By 1966 the Stones were the match to the blue touch-paper of some of America's biggest riots. On opening night in Lynn, Massachusetts, hundreds of fans broke through police cordons and stormed the stage. It was an authentic mob orgy from which the band escaped as fists flailed on the roof of their car (a write-off) and tear gas canisters exploded in the crowd. There would be no more rock concerts in Lynn until 1985.

On 2 July the Stones played Forest Hills, Queens, under the steely gaze of the *New York Times* arts critic:

> During the combo's last number, Satisfaction, several girls appeared to be crying uncontrollably. About a dozen youngsters wilfully broke through the police lines ... The combo withdrew immediately and within seconds the park lights were up and the Rolling Stones' helicopter took off into the night.

Keith then made straight for the Café Wha? in Greenwich Village to see the week's resident act, a hip young guitarist called Jimmy James. Outside, some 4,000 fans queued for admission – rather a lot for a club seating two hundred. To Richards' chagrin, James immediately performed a Dylan medley including Rolling Stone, at peak volume, adding washes of screeching feedback. Linda Keith had flown to New York and she, too, gaped at the psychedelic-clad gypsy who bounced around stage as freely as a pinball. Afterwards, she drove back to the hotel and returned with one of Keith's custom-built Stratocasters, which she offered to James. Unsurprisingly the two Keiths had a spirited debate about her casual gift to a fellow, if not rival, player. The couple formally broke up after that, and Linda found solace in James's arms. A month later, Richards would phone a 'horrifying report' – mentioning drugs, for starters – to Linda's parents, who made her a ward of court and flew to New York to rescue her. Once home in London she had a final showdown with Keith, and effectively told him she felt 'very betrayed' and didn't want to see him again. Jimmy James became Jimi Hendrix.

Meanwhile, one of Bill's groupies broached Keith's famous reserve. She would describe him as a 'shy, lovable guy', but one of the great sack artists of all time as well. 'That tongue!' The whole thing, alas, turned out badly, and both Stones ended up on a nasty penicillin course.

No less an authority than the Seattle *Times* called the Stones 'unsafe and lewd' when the tour then went west. In Sacramento the band played for the first time in almost total silence: instead of pubescent girls, the audience was made up of half-naked, superbly hirsute boys smoking hash pipes – this being the year the first wave of Baby Boomers hit college, men and women for whom heavy rock became the aural equivalent, and frequent companion, of a drug trip. On 25 July the Stones performed to 17,500 in LA, then jagged between San Francisco and Hawaii, winding up at the International Sports Centre, Honolulu. By now they all knew it was the end of something, the last of the anarchic 'Battle of the Crimea' tours and, as it turned out, the last American concert for three years. The only person deeply affected by the historic occasion was Andrew Oldham, who'd always loved the frenzy of the road. As if in celebration, Anita flew in to join Brian. The couple rowed throughout, and then split for Morocco, where Jones threw a punch, hit a wall instead of Anita, and walked around with his fist in plaster for a month.

Despite the disappointments with Linda, Keith did enjoy some unforgettable experiences that fifth tour of America. One of the best scenes came in LA, where, as dusk fell, the band's helicopter had headed off between crags and hills which suddenly dissolved in a startling close-up of the Hollywood Bowl. The craft swooped over the top, then hovered above the brightly tented backstage area. Gazing down on fans whose own heads strained upwards, Keith said, 'This is the business.'

Back at RCA, the Stones cut a dozen new songs including the big 'n brassy Have You Seen Your Mother Baby? Manic was the word. The new single was badly recorded, badly mixed and sold (comparatively) badly, hitting only number nine in Britain – but it did feature the most talked-about sleeve art in pop history. The Stones first met the New York photographer-cum-director Jerry Schatzberg in late 1964. Schatzberg, a small man with a pointed goatee, sweeping around in an opera cloak, was enthralled. 'These guys would look great in drag,' he'd confided to

Oldham. Two years later he found out. By means of razor, rouge, resin and no little uplift Mick, Brian, Charlie and Bill were converted into Sarah, Flossie, Millicent and Peppy; 'Molly' Richards, meanwhile, pouted from under her ratty wig, like a rock Miss Havisham. After the shoot the band calmly strolled into a bar still gussied up, had a beer and a smoke, and, this being Lower Manhattan, no one said a word.

Next night they were back on the *Sullivan* show. Keith played the piano on Mother while wearing a khaki Panzerkorps tunic, then mimed to Lady Jane and Paint It, Black. It seemed the whole country heard these songs, but nobody actually listened to them. The Stones were inundated by a tidal wave of screams, closely followed by Sullivan himself hurling out his hand and hollering, 'I love 'em ... yessir ... *Love* 'em!' Immediately after the show the band went to a party at Schatzberg's, where they declined to reprise their drag act. They dressed as Nazis instead.

4

An Inspector Calls

Once upon a time, The Royal Albert Hall was strictly off limits for any of these strange 'beat music' happenings. On 23 September 1966 it hosted the Rolling Stones. Long before the warm-up Terry Reid performed, the joint was rocking to a lusty chant of 'Mick! Keef!!' which soared up to the pain threshold as showtime approached, and then went on from there to get rowdy. Soon Reid found himself eyeing up the room, hoping to locate an emergency exit he could reach in the event of trouble, and periodically appealing for 'calm'. It wouldn't have mattered if he'd been reciting the Black Panther Party manifesto, because nobody could hear him. Finally the Stones slouched on, five tiny stick-figures caught in a jet blast of nonstop screaming. The place exploded.

Reid's breathless account gives a good flavour. 'It was fucking chaos. The band appeared, Keith hits Paint It, Black, goodnight. There must have been five hundred kids on the charge. The stage was like D-Day.' The Stones themselves came under heavy fire, with Brian ducking down the orchestra tunnel chortling, 'Fuck me! I'll be on the news again!' Abandoning their instruments, Mick, Charlie and Bill exited similarly hastily. Peeking out from behind the velvet curtain, Reid and four of the band then watched the bizarre scene of Keith, last off, apparently being torn to shreds by the audience. 'He finally staggered, surrounded by a flying wedge of commissionaires, backstage. "You fucking bastards! Thanks for leaving me!" Keith's strategy had been to save his prize guitar from being trashed, at all costs, which I rather admired. I mean, the rest of them just *ran*.'

Keith was fast becoming a being apart from the other Stones. Reid recalled his normal attire when out in society: he wore field jackets (bought from a shop called Hollywood Military Hobbies), and once 'a full-length leather number with a dangling Iron Cross and jackboots'. Later Keith went in for shaggy Afghan garb, patched, multicoloured jeans and granny glasses with purple lenses. Friends also remember Richards' absentmindedness and extravagant, generous nature, all traits that made life endlessly complicated, not only for Keith himself but for Keylock, who was forced to run a permanent lost and found agency for him – though he was royally compensated.

> Brian and Mick, frankly, could be cocky little bastards. Keith, too, but he was also a softie – a real family man. I used to see him playing on his hands and knees with my kids down at Redlands. Forever on the phone to Doris. I always wanted a son like Keith. Not that he couldn't drive you mad. He was so scatterbrained he'd ask me, 'Tom, where's the bleeding gig tonight?', so I'd push him in the Bentley and he'd give it all this 'You're fantastic, man, Mr Get-it-Together, I couldn't do it without you' etc, etc. I know he was still bitter about [Bert] and that whole scene in Dartford. Looking back on it, I was sort of Keith's dad.

Now Richards told Keylock that he wanted to see this Swinging London. He finally had the time and money to do so.

Keith had recently left his St John's Wood flat only after a sulphurous row with the landlord. The distressing inventory check revealed numerous cracked or missing items, messages daubed in smoke on the walls and cigarette burns throughout. Someone appeared to have been conducting a disastrous biological experiment in the kitchen and bathroom. The whole place stank.

From autumn of 1966 Brian and Anita moved from Elm Park Lane to a new eyrie at 1 Courtfield Road, South Kensington. While Redlands was being decorated, Keith joined them there. With its split-level living room, minstrel's gallery and specially installed 'trippy' lighting, Courtfield Road quickly became a band hangout. The proximity of high-quality hash and Dylan's *Blonde on Blonde* blasting constantly from the record player both rounded out this Sixties prototype of a rock-star pad. Pallenberg evidently overcame Keith's doubts about cohabiting with Brian. Also on the scene was Oldham's 'angel with big tits', now a twenty-year-old wife and mother whose pop career, after As Tears Go By, remained frustratingly stalled. Marianne Faithfull was secretly in love with Keith, and he with Anita. Mick Jagger was in the throes of splitting from his girlfriend of four years, Chrissie Shrimpton. As is the case of so many who find their partners incompatible but still deserving of fondness and respect, Jagger and Shrimpton hoped for an amicable break, but it became a bitter one. That Christmas Eve she was reported to be in the Greenway Nursing Home after attempting suicide; the hospital bill was sent to Mick, who returned it.

From the first, the new Rolling Stones ménage spelt trouble. On a wet Tuesday night that winter, Keith, Mick and Brian attended a party given for the American crooner Bobby Darin. Darin might have seemed hip in any company but this, but his tux and cuff-links jarred badly against the Stones' mouldy tribal gear. They left at a clip. Across town, Jimi Hendrix was playing his first ever British gig. Somehow Keith and Brian got into a row backstage, just like the old days, and had to be parted. Jagger's own normality and ambition set him on the opposite end of a see-saw with his two often moody guitarists. Keylock characterizes the Stones' new sessions at south London's Olympic studios as 'heavy', even by their standards. 'Brian was something else. A complete shit-stirrer. Basically, the guy would lie to Keith about Mick, then lie to Mick about Keith. That would piss everyone off . . . By then [Jones] was mental – a really complicated bunch of blokes. It was like, how's Brian, Brian and Brian?'

Keith and Marianne Faithfull soon tumbled into bed in Courtfield Road, an experience she describes as 'the best night of my life'. Faithfull fell in love with Keith as she rejected Jagger's blundering sexual advances. Which he repeated with astonishing resilience. Only a day or two later Keith unselfishly confirmed what Marianne already knew.

'Mick's really stuck on you. Go on, luv, give him a bell. He's not so bad.'

Marianne would, after that, phone Jagger, 'this powerful guy promising me the moon', and in so doing become stigmatized as 'rock totty' throughout the late Sixties. Jones and Andrew Oldham were also smitten by the voluptuous Miss F. But when she split formally from her husband and took up instead with their lippy colleague, the spell was broken. She and Richards, at least, lusted vaguely after each other for years. 'The whole time I was with Mick,' Faithfull says, 'I fancied Keith.'

Richards' love life wouldn't fully come into its own until 1967, and even then never became public property like Jagger's. The central idea was thoroughly romantic. A London journalist named Judy Flanders met Keith at Blases club one night that winter. 'Forget what you read. He wasn't macho at all . . . he *courted* me. Keith was a very, very sweet guy. You'd laugh all night with him, sleep on silk cushions and in the morning he'd serenade you with his guitar. What's not to love about a man like that?'

In the weeks that followed, the Stones virtually lived at Olympic, a large, cluttered room, sub-divided by baffle boards, where the band kept their usual vampire's hours. Any lingering daylight was barred by the heavy wooden shutters and strips of sheeting that sealed off Barnes High Street. Tom Keylock soon grew accustomed to the twilight world of recording with the Stones and their house engineer Glyn Johns. Without the constant cigarette glow and the coloured flickering from the control room, they might as well have been in a tomb.

In Olympic, Keith continued his transformation from pop geek to composer of twentieth-century standards when he casually played the band two new songs. The Stones listened to these in rapt silence. Title 8, which became Ruby Tuesday, was all Keith's, an exquisitely turned ballad about Linda; Jagger meanwhile knocked off the lyrics to the jumpy, piano-pop Let's Spend The Night Together. If Tuesday sounded like healing music, Mick's cunnilingual rap on Night – 'I'm goin' red/and my tongue's getting tired' – marked the moment when Jagger-the-priapic-stud was born. This expertly curated image, which initially owed everything to Keith and Marianne, remains proverbial some forty years later.

On 10 December 1966 the Stones released *Got Live If You Want It*, a frantic hits party padded with spurious 'rarities'. Keith, Brian and Anita then went to Paris together for Christmas. Jones would later remember, and ruefully, Richards playing Ruby Tuesday to Pallenberg in their George V hotel suite. Few rock stars could voice broken-hearted resilience, rancour and regret quite like Keith, who also lent a tenderness and melancholy to his portrait of faded love.

Brian felt 'fucking uneasy' about it all.

There were two things you could reliably say about Stones albums. They ran about thirty-five minutes, and the band would be glowering furiously on the front cover. Keith's latest effort, however, was longer and lighter. *Between the Buttons*, with its nursery-rhyme lyrics and fuzzy psychedelia, made Richards sound alarmingly like Ray Davies' long-lost big brother. As varied in quality as in range, *Buttons* at its best was speedy and camp, hopped up on the same nifty chassis of trippy tunes and Edwardian music-hall whimsy as *Kinks Kontroversy*. Connection, co-sung by Keith, was perfect pop; elsewhere tracks ranged from the mundane (Please Go Home, Cool, Calm And Collected) to the mawkish (She Smiled Sweetly). There was even a waltz called Back Street Girl, which was augmented by Brian on accordion. For much of *Buttons*, the Stones seemed uneasily like shot-putting champions who'd strayed inadvertently on to the badminton court. The album was a number two hit on both sides of the Atlantic.

Included on the American version, Ruby Tuesday came complete with Keith and Bill on cello, Brian on recorder and sweet – yes, sweet – harmonies; Night made the great pop leap forward, incendiary at the time and, even today, well-made music to Stairmaster to. Released as a double A-side, the two songs rounded out a cycle of ten classic singles inside three years.

15 January 1967. Back to New York to plug Night, which was being bleeped or banned by DJs. Keith had another fight with security at the Sullivan theatre, then a misunderstanding with Ed himself about the latter's policy on toking backstage. But the main issue was again the song title. 'Either it goes,' Sullivan boomed, 'or you go.' It was close; in the end Jagger compromised, altering 'the night' to 'some time', while rolling his eyes around to register protest.

A week later, *Sunday Night at the London Palladium*. The show was a much loved British ritual, with its bill consisting of choice, family-oriented acts, from Nureyev and Fontaine to Sooty and Sweep. Tradition demanded that, at the climax of proceedings, the entire cast mount a revolving stage to blow kisses and bid cheery farewells to the viewing audience. The Rolling Stones! No way, they hastily agreed: they wouldn't rotate. The show's producer, Albert Locke, told the band that they were insulting everything the Palladium and 'centuries of showbusiness' stood for. Keith told Locke to fuck off. Andrew Oldham, whose own showbiz blood perhaps ran deeper than anyone supposed, sided with the producer and called the Stones' behaviour 'atrocious'. Richards and Jagger in turn yelled at Oldham, who walked out.

The Stones then mimed to four songs and sidled away from the Palladium with a cheque for £1,500. Their refusal to truckle soon netted them far more than that – the press outrage lasted for weeks. Both *The Times* and the *Daily Express* told their readers that the band had become incorrigible, and the Archbishop of Canterbury called them decadent. As if in celebration, Let's Spend The Night Together went gold.

Since wandering into the Station hotel four years earlier, Oldham had long since fulfilled his ambition of becoming a 'teenage tycoon shit'. He'd also worked slavishly for his favourite clients. By 1967 Keith was a wealthy man; he needed to be, and never felt himself flush, but by the standards of most twenty-three-year-olds, even pop gods, he'd little to complain of. He was shrewd, well managed, sensational copy, and often got the best advice. Minor doubts did creep into Keith's mind, but Andrew, he allowed, played a starring role in the band's early career. The result was a true and time-tested partnership. Yet, by the time he flounced out of the Palladium, Oldham's days were numbered. According to Keylock, 'Andy was a clever bugger, but when the Stones needed him around '67 he was in a state, sidelined by Allen, thoroughly knackered and demoralized.' Also very stoned. As Ian Stewart remembered, 'The band were pissed off that Loog didn't step up and relieve them of a burden. He stepped up and created a new one.' Stu, whose own feud with Oldham was of Dunsinane Wood proportions, never quite got over the manner of his sacking. 'I was basically hurt by it. I'm sure Andrew couldn't give a toss.'

The Stones made a quantum leap early in '67 when they snubbed first Sullivan and then the Palladium's 'centuries of showbusiness'. Their double V-sign gave the band a chance to reposition themselves as 'well-heeled slobs' (the *Mirror*) who'd gone far beyond mere Beatle cheekiness. The first major backlash would come much sooner than anybody knew.

Keith: 'They don't like young kids with a lot of money [in Britain]. As long as you don't bother them, that's cool. But we bothered them.'

Swinging London lacked serious outlaws. There was no Che, no 'Red Rudi' Dutschke. The main cultural figurehead, in 1967, was one John 'Hoppy' Hopkins, who enjoyed a brief moment of fame by being arrested on pot charges. The more we know about the rest of the loon-panted icons, the more it's clear they were mere English worthies – solidly earthbound. Even the best of them were conventional, not to say shockingly normal, types, happy to rub along amid the bells, beads, festivals, love-ins and herbally scented 'head' shops in the pantheon of the Sixties. The Stones weren't. Thanks to the riots, Keith and Mick were the most brazen symbol of the swinging decade. By now, the whole world had read the headlines – 'MONSTERS', 'THUGS', 'SHAGGY NEANDERTHALS' who pissed anywhere, man. Nobody who actually knew the band thought of them as anything but talented musicians with a matching flair for trouble. Likewise, it was hard to believe Keith really had a 'heart of stone' or couldn't get no 'satisfaction'. But the image had long since become lore. It was part of the whole process by which 'straight' Britain – the Establishment – adopted the Stones as its very own public enemy.

Back in Dartford, Doris found her son's name in the *Chronicle* almost every afternoon and called it to Keith's attention with a throaty chuckle. She, at least, knew it was 'all a lark'.

They saw a lot of Keith at Redlands that winter. The place was fully furnished by now, the heavy Moroccan drapes shutting out the scenes of wanton debauchery – inappropriate here in West Wittering. Keith spent hours in front of the fire or out on the back terrace, shirt splayed open as if for heart surgery. Generally he was fun and hip, good company, a tad forgetful, passive except when – as happened rarely off the road – in full rant; even Keylock steered clear during major eruptions. Smart. Laid-back. That's what people said of Keith as he clanked around wearing his beads and Berber jewellery, crammed with pot. He had very few close friends. Aside from Keylock, there was an ancient gardener called Jack Dyer, and 'Spanish Tony' Sanchez, a Keith lookalike, who regaled him with tough-guy patter and drugs. Sanchez remembers remarking to Richards that he and Jagger hardly ever spoke to Jones any more.

'Well, he's burnt out,' said Keith. 'Isn't he?'

Just as the Establishment failed to grasp the true nature of the Stones, so even the most devoted fan had failed to listen to the band on stage. As Keith says, 'We never actually *played*. We went to a gig and then a riot started and the kids hit, and the only big deal was how the hell are we getting *out* ... When we finally took time off I went back to blues, back to the beginning. I started to research and found out a lot more about the stuff, which I hadn't had a chance to do since we started working like maniacs ... I progressed as a player.'

Eighteen months later, *Beggars Banquet* would be the first great Stones album in which Keith's characteristic urgency and pace were yoked to real technique. Until then every hook and chorus had seemed larger than life. From *Banquet* onwards the LPs would have all the verve, but wrapped the riffs in some insinuating music. For all the band's ironic veneer, they communicated very real emotions.

Ian Stewart remembered the first person to tell him Keith was a truly creative artist, who hated pigeonholing, and had great new ideas. It was Brian Jones.

Meanwhile, there were ructions ahead with women that made *Dallas* look like *Playschool*. Faithfull rang Allen Klein to tell him she was involved with Jagger but still fancied Richards. There came from Klein a sonic roar of protest. 'Marianne! Please! If you go with Keith, it'll destroy Mick.'

Keith himself phoned the next afternoon while Marianne was making breakfast to invite her to Munich, where Brian and Anita were working on Volker Schlöndorff's film *A Degree of Murder*. Faithfull couldn't go, so Richards, Jones and Pallenberg again travelled as a trio. That same month Marianne told the BBC, 'Marijuana's perfectly safe. Drugs are really the doors of perception. LSD is as important as Christianity – *more* important.' On Sunday 5 February the *News of the World* libellously outed Jagger as a pill popper. Mick claimed the story was a pack of lies and that he intended to 'put down a marker', not just for himself but for others in the public eye. On 7 February his solicitor started proceedings. Keith and Brian then came back from Germany, flying on acid.

Three nights later, Richards and Jagger were in Abbey Road's Studio 1 to witness the climax of the Beatles' A Day In The Life. The Sixties were swinging faster now. The next afternoon, at Olympic, the Stones first worked on the track that became Sympathy For The Devil. Late on 11 February Keith, Mick and Marianne drove to Redlands. Also present were Christopher Gibbs, the photographer Michael Cooper, 'Strawberry Bob' Fraser, Fraser's Moroccan houseboy Ali Mohammed, George and Pattie Harrison and two hangers-on of dubious aspect, David Schneidermann and Nicky Kramer.

Liverish ITV executives, the *News of the World*, a hyper-ambitious drugs squad – and possibly a disgruntled Stones employee. That was the unlikely 'Establishment' coalition now mustering, in turn, against Keith's house party. At midnight on Saturday Ali served dinner, at which very moment a voice was informing Chichester police that an orgy of dope, sex and pop, possibly all three simultaneously, was about to engulf West Wittering.

12 February 1967. Everyone was tripping on Schneidermann's high quality LSD. Sunday was gorgeous, exquisitely balanced between the olde scenery and this giddy sign of the times, people stumbling around

on drugs. Most of them made it over Keith's moat, through the fields and on to the shingle beach south of Redlands. It was a characteristic Rolling Stones party – large, loud, happy, with satiric laughs and dazed, sheepskin-clad guests. Only Nicky Kramer departed from the prevailing mood. Instead of his usual hippy banter about living for the moment, he gave the impression of being bored or distracted. Seven o'clock found Richards and Jagger together, scampering over the moonlit grass, uncontrollably giggly like two schoolkids grown old. It may have been among the best days of Keith's life. As he got back inside, someone began ringing the house's 'secure' number, Birdham 513508. Each time Keith picked up the phone, the caller hung up.

An hour later a convoy of police cars turned up Redlands Lane. Four vans, nineteen officers in all. After a preliminary reconnoitre (the front door being located, helpfully, at the back) they knocked. Keith, suspecting nothing more than curious fans, opened up. 'I have a warrant,' intoned Chief Inspector Gordon Dineley, 'pursuant to the Dangerous Drugs Act.'

A kind of grimace had crossed Keith's face when he saw the law. Apart from this brief, scarcely perceptible contraction of nose and lips he expressed no further welcome. However, he stood aside.

Keith then turned to Jagger and the others, calmly announced, 'We're being busted,' and flicked on a strobe light for dramatic effect.

The events that followed can be quickly recalled: the police fanning through the galleried living room, hung with ornate tapestries and silks, wheezing in the incense and smoke; Marianne, later described under oath as 'in a merry mood and one of vague unconcern' being led upstairs to be searched, or – since she was wearing only a fur rug which she promptly dropped to the floor – ogled; the remaining eight (the Harrisons having left) being frisked; the instant acceptance of Schneidermann's acid collection as 'unexposed film'; the discovery of twenty-four heroin jacks ('for diabetes', he explained) on Fraser, and of four pep pills in a velvet jacket belonging to Jagger; the removal of these and sundry tins, pipes, bowls and even soap and ketchup satchets; the surreal dazzle of the strobe; the cautioning of Keith that, if dangerous drugs were identified without specific proof of ownership he, as householder, would be held responsible. Did he understand?

It was hard to tell where exactly the legalese hovered between a threat and a promise. Typically, Keith stood firm.

'Yeah,' he deadpanned. 'You pin it all on me.'

Keith looked around at the heavy silence that fell, and saw from the inspector's face that he'd blundered on to the truth. The law withdrew. As the convoy moved off Keith serenaded it into the night with Dylan's Rainy Day Women and its insistent wail,

'*Every*body must get stoned!'

The raid on Redlands turned out to be one of those events whose actual success – four pills on Jagger, nothing on Richards – was the least important factor in its public reception. From now on the Stones would be as polarizing in their way as the Great Train Robbers: either heinous thugs or plucky scapegoats. In Britain in 1967 you loved Mick 'n Keef or you hated them. What few people did was to ignore them. Keith himself blamed 'the Bill' for turning a private vice into a public debate and, in consequence, greatly accelerating his own habit.

'If you're gonna kick society in the teeth, you may as well use both feet.'*

A night or two after the raid, Keith sat down and wrote Bert Richards a long letter of explanation. He noted that he was getting a lot of publicity which, Keith admitted, was pretty colourful stuff. But he said that a lot of it was made up. He added that he was working incredible hours, racked with pressure. He concluded that he'd sweated his arse off for four years, non-stop, and that he sincerely hoped he and his father might get together for a discussion of those issues which lay between them.

Bert declined the offer.

'Have received your telex and am resolving bread situation. In respect of the other matter under no circumstances do anything at all until I see you.

---

* For the rest of that fateful winter and early spring Richards and Jagger were busy being pilloried by half the country and fêted by the rest. News of the raid quickly became a rumour and then a fixture in the press – splashed by the *News of the World* on 19 February and most of the broadsheets the following week. A month later the *Mirror* announced that Keith, Mick, Robert Fraser and Schneidermann (who left the country, never to be seen again) were to be charged and tried. Tony Sanchez always claims that the Stones attempted to bribe the police with £7,000, but that the money went to the wrong man. In years ahead the Redlands bust hit almost iconographic status, a Sixties 'scene' which legend demanded – and the law never denied – had taken place amidst an orgy of diabolism, voodoo or worse. The story of Jagger having been found bridging that gap with Faithfull and a Mars bar only surfaced later. 'It never happened,' says Keylock. 'Keith had a sweet tooth – there was a virtual chocolate factory at Redlands. That's all there was to it, dozens of candy bars and some copper's vivid imagination.'

Repeat *do nothing* until I show.' Predictably, the 'bread situation' went unresolved, but Klein did provide unstinting and vital support in the weeks ahead. His bustling arrival in London did wonders for morale: the much derided Klein promptly hired his clients the best available criminal lawyers, including Michael Havers, QC, a future Attorney General. Also engaged was the PR man Les Perrin, admittedly from the prehistory of British showbiz, but a loyal ally over the next decade. The high-priced defence team first met in Klein's suite at the London Hilton on 20 February. Keith and Mick expressed the view that parts of the press were out to 'get' the Stones and Perrin hastened to join the consensus. Richards reported being followed. Such was the paranoia that Klein advised his two star assets – now sullen, like errant schoolboys under threat of punishment – to 'cool it', and preferably abroad. They settled on Morocco.

Tom Keylock ferried the Blue Lena to Paris, where he was joined by Keith, Brian, Anita and a traffic-stopping beauty named Deborah Dixon. There was a misunderstanding at the George V hotel about the party's bill. Keylock's French proved just barely adequate to the challenge and, in the end, there were hissed 'Sod you, froggy's as everyone made for the car. Richards tolerated the administrative lapse with composure. He was in festive mood. Keith eyeing Dixon, Brian eyeing Pallenberg and Keylock surveying his four shag-haired passengers 'like fucking Johnny Morris', the Bentley turned on to the Quai d'Austerlitz, heading south.

It was an unseasonably warm day, and the car was furnished with a cocktail cabinet, fresh flowers, the best food and drugs and a tape deck blasting out the Beatles' Strawberry Fields. No trip with Brian Jones could be entirely tranquil, even so, and by Limoges, after a full day of drinking brandy and toking in the back seat, he was complaining of a 'funny turn'. By Bordeaux, Jones was turning blue. At the American clinic in Tarn, near Toulouse, Brian was told he had an enlarged heart, advanced fatty degeneration and blood in the lungs. No problem, he said: the four of them should carry on to Tangier, and he'd catch up with them there. Jones spent his twenty-fifth birthday alone in the hospital.

Deborah Dixon left the next morning, muttering her premonition of 'bad vibes' ahead to Keylock. 'This is getting weird,' she told him. 'God knows where it'll end.'

For the next twenty-four hours, Keylock spent his time either looking straight ahead at the snow-capped mountains and winding rivers of

Catalonia, or glancing in his rear view mirror at Keith and Anita making love. In a Valencia bar, there was yet another to-do involving a credit card. Soon the management started yelling at Keith, who turned to Keylock and told him to 'sort it'; the dagos'd respect a big guy like him, with an English accent. 'Oi dowtit,' Tom said, and a merry row then ensued at the police station. When everyone got out a telegram was waiting, ordering Pallenberg to return to Toulouse for Brian. Anita tore it up. By the time they made Marbella, on 3 March, it was obvious that the Scott-and-Zelda love affair of its time had begun.

Late that evening in the hotel lobby, Keith said to Keylock, 'That bastard's been beating her up. She's had enough.'

Keylock answered, 'No argument.'

Keith and Anita slept in separate rooms, with a small garden in between. He moved into hers.

Finally crossing on the *Mons Calpe*, they reached Tangier on 5 March; Richards and Keylock made for the tenth floor of the Hotel Minzah where, according to the latter, 'Mick was already installed like a young lord, lying on a huge bed and complaining.' Also present were 'Strawberry Bob' Fraser and Michael Cooper. Anita belatedly returned to Toulouse to collect Brian.

Keylock scored everyone some hash.

On 8 March, Keith, Mick and their entourage drove to Marrakesh, where they met the painter Brion Gysin, Paul Getty and Cecil Beaton, photographer of royalty, who found Richards 'in eighteenth century suit, long black velvet coat and the tightest pants ... Keith himself had sewn the trousers, lavender and dull rose, with a band of badly stitched leather dividing the two colours. But with such a marvellously flat, tight, compact figure, with no buttocks or stomach, almost anything looks well [on him].' For years afterward Keith kept a faded cutting of one of Beaton's photos of himself, over the caption, 'Wonderful Head and Torso'.

As the week progressed, at least at first, the local hospitality flowed. It was a scene to make the Sixties swing.

Tom Keylock: 'We took over the top floor of the best hotel, Keith's lounging around with his guitar, Mick doing little dances. Lots of toking in the moonlight. The first I knew of Brian's arrival was the sound of his voice coming from a room along the corridor. He was screaming at Anita. The little bugger obviously knew something had gone on ... Brian started drinking, getting himself into a state. Next thing anyone knew he'd picked up this pair of dodgy looking Berber whores, tattooed all over, and made for Anita's room. Brian had the idea that he was going to get her to perform with these two birds. That was typical of the guy.'

A lot of rock and rollers enjoy combinations, but most manage a better pitch than Jones, a stickler for decorum in other circumstances, but happy to proposition his girlfriend with 'Suck 'em off!' Anita declined the offer and Brian went berserk, smashing up both the room and herself.

That was enough for Keith. He and Keylock made up a story about a plane load of *News of the World* reporters landing in Marrakesh, hustling Jones off with Brion Gysin to the local souk. No sooner had he gone, Keith and Anita were packing her fourteen pieces of luggage into the Bentley. 'What about Brian?' asked Keylock. 'Fuck 'im,' said Keith. 'We're leaving the bastard here and you're driving.' Jagger and Faithfull, the former still grousing about his hotel bill, flew out. The Spanish police gave the Lena and its three passengers a thorough going-over at the ferry terminal. Tom again saved everyone's skin, hiding the hash under the car's petrol cap. When Brian got back from the souk he found only a few of Pallenberg's things, forgotten in the rush, and a note telling him what had happened. 'Judas,' he hissed at Gysin. Brian began sobbing, then throwing streamers of Anita's clothes into the street. A doctor gave him a shot, and someone from the hotel arranged for a driver with a small, run-down car to pick him up in the morning.

The rest was the ride home.

Jones launched an ill-advised counterattack the moment he got back to London.

Brian insisted that Anita leave Keith, who was 'going to jail' and give him, instead, another chance. It was a spectacularly ambitious proposal to a woman still black and blue from Brian's fists. When Anita turned him down, he flipped. Rejection was the signal for one of those sudden reversals in behaviour that constituted the basic pattern of Jones's life. 'Fuck you!' he growled. 'I'm a rock star! I can have any chick I want.'

Brian immediately started dating Linda Keith.

On 25 March the Stones began a European tour. The mayhem onstage, where banshee audiences fought nonstop with riot police, was paralleled now by open warfare in the dressing room. In certain towns Brian even made separate travel arrangements. He was more comfortable on his own than at the band hotel, where the great music from Keith's guitar came through the walls nightly as though the partitions were made of tissue.

Sometimes the absurdity of Brian's desperation seemed to stir Anita. There may even have been a brief reconciliation of sorts. Even after March 1967, Pallenberg went nowhere without Brian's photograph in a silver frame. A few embers smouldered behind the scenes. In Munich, meanwhile, Richards met a beautiful German model, this one called Uschi Obermeier, and began a brief affair with her that would reignite six years later. Much to some people's surprise, Keith was proving himself a romantic. Uschi would later remark how he offered the promise of warm friendship, witty discourse, male strength and masculine attentiveness without all the 'rock star bullshit'. Yet within a week Keith was back with Anita in Paris. Keylock remembers Brian, stuffed with acid, then 'play[ing] the next two gigs without even knowing he'd done them'. A small but cruel twist of the knife followed when the Stones office sent a chauffeured car to Heathrow to collect Keith and Anita. Due to a bookkeeping error, the bill for the journey was charged to Jones.

By mid tour the Stones had reached a new low. According to Keylock, the band's reception throughout Europe was 'wicked'. They were constantly hassled, their planes subject to mysterious delays. Hotels bizarrely lost track of everyone's reservations. At airports they were greeted by snarling dogs and the snapping of rubber gloves. A French customs official punched Keith, when on his way out of Le Bourget, in yet another row about passports. In Warsaw, their first visit behind the Iron Curtain, the Stones played to 2,000 Party members who sat with their fingers in their ears throughout The Last Time and the first verse of Paint It, Black. Pointing furiously across his guitar, Keith shouted to Charlie to stop drumming. Jagger tried to continue the song, but Keith kept pointing and yelling. 'You fuckers, get out and let those bastards in the back down front . . .'

'Er – *I see a red door* . . .' Jagger began again.

'Leave those kids alone,' Keith shouted, now holding the guitar aloft. The audience kept chanting *Icantgetno! Icantgetno!*, for Satisfaction, and Keith kept yelling at the police, who were bouncing billy-clubs on the audience's heads. The next day's press: EASTERN BLOC PLANNING COMPLETE BAN OF 'UNACCEPTABLE' STONES.

The tour wound up in Athens. Having recently undergone a violent coup,

Greece, too, was in no particularly good mood to host a riot by the Rolling Stones. The emphasis throughout was on the vast and menacing army presence rather than on the music. At the end of the performance Jagger handed Keylock a bouquet of carnations, with the instruction to hurl them at 'the cats'. As Tom did so he became uneasily aware that he was alone on stage; the band themselves had dropped their instruments and run. It was 17 April 1967, the Stones' last public concert for two years and the last ever by the original band. Keith flew to Rome, where Anita was auditioning for her role as the vampire-lesbian Black Queen in *Barbarella*.

Two weeks later, Keith and Pallenberg were in Cannes for the première of *A Degree of Murder*. While they were there Brian unexpectedly appeared in the hotel and begged Anita for an hour with her alone. Whatever he said in the allotted time, it was enough to persuade Anita that she wanted to marry Keith.

Jones took a calculated risk. '*I'll* marry you.'

Words failed him when Anita strolled back to her room after vowing she'd care for him always, but that that was all. Brian flew home that night.

On 9 May 1967 Keith, Mick and Robert Fraser lunched at a London gentlemen's club, then drove to Chichester to face charges of menacing society.

At the hearing the next morning Keith wore a sober navy-blue suit and an expression of mild amusement; he expected a fine. Accused of permitting '[Redlands] to be used for the purpose of smoking controlled substances', Keith nodded affably to his name and legal address (Les Perrin's office in Oxford Street) before pleading not guilty. All three defendants elected trial by jury in a higher court. They were bailed to appear at West Sussex Quarter Sessions on 27 June.

At the very moment of Keith's committal, a pilled-up Brian Jones was answering the doorbell at Courtfield Road. It was the drugs squad. The scene that greeted them was like a life-slice exhibit of junkie degeneracy: the fourteen officers took away water pipes, hookahs, bongs, spoons, ashtrays, cigarette ends and a phial bearing traces of white powder. Brian himself happened to be in the throes of one of his familiar acid nightmares about snakes. He was charged with possession and spent the next six months on remand. Jones's lawyers told him not to have any contact with Keith and Mick during this period.

Seven weeks later Keith came up before sixty-one-year-old Judge Leslie Block, a Tory landowner of naval mien who, by his own cheerful admission, 'hate[d] jungle music'. While the trial took many ducks and turns, one image dominated the proceedings from both sides. This was the Crown's prompt reference to 'the young lady wearing only a fur rug which, from time to time, she allowed to fall, exposing her bare body'. At the last two words there was a collective squeal from the packed press gallery. The 'nude girl' headlines duly proved irresistible and ran for days, along with shrill, though unprintable rumours about Mars bars. One juror would later tell *International Times* that the case rotated on this axis – 'We were really trying [people's] morals, weren't we?' To the stench of drugs and rock 'n roll was added an intoxicating whiff of sex. According to the testimony of Sergeant John Challon, 'The lady in question was taken upstairs and, when she got to the bedroom door, she let the rug fall. She had nothing on. The woman giggled and I heard a laugh from two men in the bedroom.'

The jury took six minutes to find Jagger and Fraser guilty.

Next afternoon, 28 June, Keith stood in the dock wearing a suit of funereal darkness. He heard Michael Havers describe the now proverbial 'Miss X' as 'an alleged drug-taking nymphomaniac with no chance of saying anything in her defence . . . Do you expect me to force that girl to go into the witness box? I am not going to tear the blanket aside and subject her to laughter and scorn. If I can't call the girl, and Mr Richards is in agreement with this, I will not call anyone else.' Marianne Faithfull herself sat demurely in the public gallery.

On the third day of the trial Keith gave evidence in his own defence. He told Malcolm Morris, the prosecuting counsel, that none of his friends smoked hemp, and that if drugs had been found at Redlands they must have been planted there. The Crown then asked Keith about the woman in the fur rug.

MM: Would you agree that in the ordinary course of events you would expect a young lady to be embarrassed if she had nothing on in front of several men?
KR: Not at all. We are not old men and we're not worried about petty morals. [loud cheering from the gallery]
MM: Did it not come as a great surprise to you that she was prepared

to go back downstairs still only wearing a rug in front of twenty police officers?

KR: I thought the rug was big enough to cover three women. There was nothing improper in the way she was wearing it.

MM: I wasn't talking about impropriety, but embarrassment.

KR: She doesn't embarrass easily. Nor do I.

In his summing up, Judge Block told the jury to put out of their minds any prejudice about Keith's looks, clothes, habits, lifestyle, or his views on 'petty morals'. They were to ignore everything they had read and heard about the nude girl who had been lying in front of the Redlands fire in full view of eight men, and not to let her rum behaviour in any way influence their verdict. The jury found Keith guilty. Jagger and Fraser were brought up from the cells and given three and six months respectively. The judge sentenced Keith to a solid year, and ordered him to pay £500 costs. There were high-pitched cries of 'No!' from the gallery, which was packed with young Stones fans. Richards shrugged, raised his eyes to the ceiling, and said nothing.

All three defendants were marched out in handcuffs, an unimprovable snapshot of that Summer of Love.

Later that night the full horror of events was borne in on Keith, when he became Prisoner 7855 in London's notorious Wormwood Scrubs. It was among the very bleakest outposts of a penal system known for its bleakness. While fans demonstrated in Piccadilly Circus and, more pertinently, at the *News of the World*, Keith was photographed and deloused, and exchanged his frock coat for a blue donkey jacket and regulation black shoes. There was no haircut, though that was the one humiliation spared him. The clang of the cell door and the barked order of 'Lights Out!' followed sharp at 10 o'clock. After a sleepless night Richards was frogmarched to the prison factory and taught how to sew mailbags and make Christmas ornaments. Lunch was taken with a dirty spoon. Keith was then supplied with a pencil and paper, with which he wrote Doris a 'don't worry' letter. The other inmates seemed sympathetic, and several offered him great drugs, priced to move.

Michael Havers, meanwhile, worked overnight to obtain leave for Keith and Mick to appeal. On 30 June, three High Court judges granted them bail in their own recognizance of £5,000 each, and at five o'clock that same afternoon Keylock edged the Blue Lena to the Scrubs' gates. Keith emerged wearing a composite of jail and Carnaby Street gear: blue velvet jacket, 'PROPERTY OF HM PRISON SERVICE' shirt, black lace-up boots. He'd been incarcerated for just under twenty-four hours.

There had been hopes in police circles that locking up the Stones might do the band's reputation some harm: it didn't. Most public opinion was generally angry with the sentences and, more particularly, with the indignity of the handcuffs. In the revised view of Keith's fate in which the word 'flash' was tempered by 'hard done by', many newspapers struggled with their souls. By the time Richards and Jagger were bailed, even the *Daily Mail's* tent was pitched on the ground Les Perrin would have chosen. 'Teenagers ask why there is no stigma in being a heavy drinker, while smoking pot, which they consider less harmful, is banned.'

Something very curious was going on in Fleet Street. A truly populist paper like the *News of the World*, with its pictures of footballers and pouting models on the masthead, was calling for the Stones to be jailed. The old bulletin-boards of the Establishment were preaching forgiveness. New lines were being drawn, most famously by *The Times* in its 'Who Breaks a Butterfly' editorial of 1 July:

> It is no offence to be in the same building or the same company as people possessing or even using drugs, nor could it reasonably be made so ... One has to ask, therefore, how it is that this technical offence, divorced as it must be from other people's offences, was thought to deserve the penalty of imprisonment.

In more staccato terms, both the *Express* and *Mirror* leads that weekend became versions of SCAPEGOAT, full of peace, love and triple exclamation marks. For more than four years, the Stones' headlines had dazzled. Now, they blinded.

From that moment on this shy, modest, hard-working and creatively restless man transcended the label of mere 'pop star' and became, once and for all, *Keith Richards*, the lead in a lurid saga of sex, drugs and multiple court appearances that practically amounted to a season ticket. Over the next decade Keith would be involved in four major possession trials, the charges ranging from hash to Chinese heroin.

Between 7 and 22 July the Stones cut half a dozen druggy tracks at Olympic. Brian and the rest of the band weren't speaking.

On 31 July Richards and Jagger came up before the Lord Chief Justice of England. A red-eyed Mick went into the dock. The court, he was told, upheld his conviction but would reduce his sentence to one of twelve months' probation, without costs. Keith had caught a dose of chickenpox, and was kept in a cell downstairs for fear of infecting the nation's top judge. Two hours later an official went to tell him that he'd won his appeal on all counts. The Chief Justice ruled that the whole 'nude girl' section of the original trial should never have been allowed. There were whoops of congratulation outside the court, and a celebratory 'be-in' that night in Hyde Park. Jagger himself appeared – to use an earlier phrase – in a state of mild unconcern when he debated the trial on television, the first of dozens of such appearances. Keith, by contrast, seemed to take the somewhat surreal events of the last month as the kind of temporary setback bound to occur in showbiz, and would admit only to feeling 'spotty'. That same afternoon he sent flowers to Doris and then flew to Rome to join Anita, now heavily into the lesbian shtick of *Barbarella*.

Keith's lurch towards icon status that summer was at once astonishing, exhilarating and deeply odd. He went through a change, almost a rein-carnation, in Rome. Inspired by Anita and the finest Afghan hash, Keith hid his natural shyness with pranks that took him out of himself and into whole new worlds. A close colleague says, 'That's when the Human Riff we know began . . . in about four weeks Keith got into the evil eyeliner and the chunky jewellery.' But for the music, the prevailing vibe that summer was of a 1920s *salon* infested by absinthe drinkers. Before long the Living Theater and a whole slew of experimental filmmakers, artists and writers were gravitating around Keith and Anita's incense-filled hotel suite. So astir was the scene by mid August that Richards seriously talked about moving to Rome full time. It didn't happen, but the place changed him inside and out. 'A Swinging makeover,' his friend calls it. Keith wasn't exactly sold down the *soigné* river, but he didn't hit on his trademark style by accident. For instance, when he wanted to go shopping for shirts he'd insist that Anita accompany him and stay with him until he chose just the right fabric and cut, at which point he'd buy a dozen along with strings of beads and necklaces. The same thing with boots, coats, sunglasses. Keith also got his signature shag haircut, at once hideous and perfect. His gaunt cheekbones were like a period rock-star detail in themselves. Perhaps the greatest change, though, was in Keith's self-confidence. He'd always been surprisingly shy, a shrugging, life-goes-on stoic with a dry wit. By late 1967, Keith tended to yell back when yelled at; sometimes he even yelled first. He was fast and funny and contentious and – openly, publicly – vulnerable. On every front, he'd now overtaken Brian.

The makeover was odd, too, because Keith gave it a twist that was all his own. He was uniquely relaxed about himself, and where he'd come from. Even in megastardom, he had his 'straight' side. He loved visiting Doris, for example, and gossiping about Dartford; a pie, a pint and an old war film – preferably Kenneth More in *Reach for the Sky* – were better than any dope. More and more, Keith's hectic public life was shadowed by this deep need for roots and domesticity. 'A heart the size of Wembley', as Tom Keylock puts it. 'I snapped at my missus once on the phone at Redlands. He overheard me and was well pissed off. I got a bollocking – it was all about "she's your lady" and "show some respect", incredible stuff. I admired Keith for that.'

One part of him was permanently wound up, spending his time gobbling acid and crashing motorbikes – very much the legend. The other was a sentimental man who loved his mum. The two halves would try to control one another; both were Keith.

To capitalize on all the flak, London Records put out a Stones anthology called *Flowers*, the latest in corporate cynicism. The new hits still came on schedule: We Love You, Dandelion and Bill's In Another Land, all evidence that truckloads of hash were being smoked in the studio.

Olympic, Friday 8 September. The Stones' moron–genius Brian Jones, as famous for erratic behaviour as for his exceptional talent, asks 'Where's that pipe?' They find it, after a while, in his pocket, and the session starts. But it stops almost immediately because Brian reels backwards into his amplifier. Blond hair flies. Then, after an absurdly long pause, someone politely asks, 'Is it the snakes again, man?' On the next song Brian drops his guitar pick, takes a toss on a guitar lead underfoot and sprints head first into a pillar. There are, in all, seventeen takes before Keith says 'Fuck it' and troops off to the Bentley. Bill yawns and Charlie sits tapping his drums, his face impassive. The Stones are finishing their psychedelic folly, *Satanic Majesties*.

Mick Jagger: 'The whole thing, we were on acid. Just getting carried away ... We were out of our minds.'

On 13 September Keith flew to New York to join the band for a business meeting and to shoot the new album cover. He was welcomed by US Immigration with a full cavity search. Naturally, Keith wasn't carrying any drugs into America; he got them locally. Richards spent much of the 14th at Michael Cooper's studio in Mount Vernon, blasted out of his mind on acid. When his cue came, however, he was ready. Walking out on to the set with a couple of recent hits under his belt, Keith looked the part of a stoned troubadour. Over the next four hours he and the band posed in a variety of attitudes, adding decorative touches of their own with spray cans, while the room filled with the enticing aroma of Afghan flake. The photo was then processed into multi-coloured 3D and given a special 'trippy' backdrop of mountains and revolving planets. In all £17,000 was spent on this effect. The whole was a pretty representative slice of Sixties pop art and, not coincidentally, a ripoff of Cooper's own *Sergeant Pepper* cover.

There were a lot of other great bands out there, but, as Cooper saw, they weren't all as edgy to be around as the Stones. Listening to the two guitarists dicker all day was like something out of Neil Simon – then in his *After the Fox/Odd Couple* phase, as film scholars refer to it. It was unexpected, too. You went up to suburban New York on a wet Thursday afternoon and there were people on LSD, babbling about cobras.

Keith and Brian weren't overburdened with repartee when it came to slagging each other, but they weren't coy, either. Keith was perhaps still too young to be able to treat either friends or enemies naturally; much of his act was of the flip, couldn't-give-a-shit variety. One visitor at Redlands noted, 'he's nervous and jittery with a loping, disjointed walk ... obviously uptight around strangers and rarely makes eye contact'. Keith had a sarky side and used it to air the aggressions his shyness created. Between the squabbling and the various busts, the Stones came perilously close to disbanding that winter. They'd already lasted long enough to survive the low-radius cycle of trendiness that did for most of the British Invasion. More and more, however, it seemed 'interminable shit' (Stu) was taking the place of creativity. By now Brian was on the outs with Keith, and wasn't speaking to Jagger, Stewart and Anita. Anita shunned Keylock, who couldn't take her or 'Spanish Tony' Sanchez. Sanchez fell out with Keith and Mick over Brian. Bill was uptight about money and more particularly about Klein, who retained his distaste for signing cheques. Charlie just played the drums.

Almost everyone was agreed on a parting with Oldham, who'd been conspicuously absent from Keith and Mick's trials. A formal announcement came on 29 September. The ever-smooth Perrin put it about that the band had 'split from our recording manager, because the Stones are taking over more and more of their own music ... Andrew himself has expressed a wish to get involved in film and theatrical production.' (This came as news to Oldham.) From late 1967 the day-to-day business of the Stones continued from an attic office at 46 Maddox Street, Mayfair, run by a young Californian named Jo Bergman who took her orders from Keith and Mick. The final blow to the already prostrate Jones came that October, when he went on trial for possession. Brian immediately pleaded guilty, and heard himself described in court by his therapist, Anthony Flood, as 'a very sick man', 'deeply distressed' and 'paranoic'.

The judge asked, 'A potential suicide?'

Dr Flood: 'Certainly.'

Brian got nine months. Like Richards, he did a day and a night in Wormwood Scrubs, while the lawyers worked on his appeal. On Keith's orders, Keylock was sent to collect him the next afternoon. 'After waiting an hour, I saw Brian being escorted across the yard ... He had the two biggest coppers I'd seen in my life, manacled to him either side, tugging him along. Brian looked a very sad sight. He could drive you mad, the bastard, but I felt desperately sorry for him that day.'*

Although Keith mistrusted Brian every bit as much as Keylock did, he was also touchingly loyal. Both Richards and Jagger denied in print that the band would ever play live as a four-piece. Nobody faulted them for that. As Keith often said, the Stones owed everything to 'the way we work two guitars'. Even at his nadir, Jones had ridden the songs' melodies with gaudy and often deft flourishes. His fills on *Satanic Majesties* were a work of genius next to the stuff, say, George Harrison produced on *Magical Mystery Tour*. Keith seems to have been genuinely saddened by events, and told Keylock to arrange a delivery of roses from Chivers the Florist 'whenever Brian seems

---

* At Jones's appeal on 12 December, an independently appointed psychiatrist swore to his 'extremely precarious state of emotional adjustment' and 'fragile grasp of reality'. The Lord Chief Justice, noting that 'this is a degree of mercy ... not a let-off', again quashed a prison sentence and substituted probation. Brian promptly celebrated his release with a spree of drugs and drink that landed him in St George's Hospital for 'exhaustion'.

down'. Over the next eighteen months, Keylock would run up a heavy bill with Chivers.

In November Keith flew back to Rome, where Anita was now making *Candy* with Marlon Brando. Brando put it about that he was 'banging every chick' on the set. That same week, Judge Block entertained the guests at the annual Horsham Ploughing & Agricultural Society dinner with a droll take on *Julius Caesar*: 'You blocks, you stones, you worse than senseless things . . . We did our best, your fellow countrymen, to cut those Stones down to size. Alas, the Court of Appeal let them roll free.'

Keylock was astonished by the difference the trials had made in Keith and Brian's appearances. 'Jones had shrunk, and Keith had grown. Richards had been the quiet one when I first met them. Now he was wearing makeup and becoming the total rock star.'

By late '67 it was beginning to look as if Anita's defection had ushered in something more than a mere case of mate swapping. Brian was in total freefall. Linda Keith would soon take a nearly fatal overdose. She recovered, but left him. After that, Brian's landlord evicted him by the expedient of throwing all his belongings onto the street. There were trips to the Priory clinic. Jones began seeing a fashion model and Anita lookalike named Suki Potier, while living on a diet of brandy, hog tranquillizers and LSD. Friends had to remind him to eat. Brian was a familiar figure on the King's Road, wobbling to the off-licence on platform heels for his cigarettes and booze, his lithe figure now potbellied, his fingers nicotine-stained, his eyes pouchy and glazed. He'd all but stopped lobbing his little jolts of joy and fury at the Stones, and instead took more and more overseas holidays – nine in 1967, including the ill-starred tour of Morocco. Keith phoned the band's mentor Alexis Korner to say he was worried about Jones, and Brian himself put through late night calls to Korner sobbing that the Stones were about to fire him.

Several times that winter Keith took the opportunity, according to Keylock, 'to help Brian behind the scenes – lending him Redlands, for instance'. He adds, 'Anita wanted to stir the shit between them, and now and again she did.'

Pallenberg continued to bewitch the Stones. She was amazingly hip and freewheeling: no 'rock chick' ever seized her moment or embodied her times with more cool assurance. Even before Anita herself was a public figure, she was legendary in the pop business. Fame there requires not just looks but presence, and Anita was extravagantly endowed with both. She had the swagger of a star, too. 'There was something about that bird,' Keylock notes. 'She could say "Fuck you" in six languages.'

Anita herself felt 'the Stones looked at me like I was some kind of threat. Jagger really tried to put me down, but there was no way some crude, lippy guy was going to do a number on me. I was always able to squelch him – I found out, you stand up to Mick, he crumbles.'

Over the years, Keith's affair with Anita became catnip to the press and riveted their friends, who were never quite sure when it was going to spin out of control, once or twice violently so. The luckless Stu was in charge of most of the Stones' travel arrangements. As part of his duties he kept a list of airlines willing or unwilling to fly them. By 1967 there were already two or three major carriers where Richards' business wasn't actively sought. He was banned from Alitalia, for one, 'for stayin' in the restroom from Rome to London punchin' that crazy Anita'.

The day before *Satanic Majesties* was released, Keith took a walk outside Decca House, and down on the Embankment, which was grey and drab in the best pre-Swinging tradition, he seemed like something out of a Regency costume drama. Just across the road from Waterloo station, a homeless man asked for some change. Keith handed over a £5 note and, flipping open a leather case, one of his specially rolled cigarettes. ('I love you, man,' the bum groaned, embracing him.) Another time, Keith himself, who seemed to have aged more than two years since 1965, was stopped by a kindly pedestrian and asked if he were all right, or needed a hot meal. Richards told the BBC producer Jeff Griffin, 'There was this incredible hassle, this continual confrontation in '67. I got down a bit. It was a painful year, a year of change for everybody.'

Soon after the bust, Keith had sensibly decided to improve security at Redlands. 'Get it sorted,' he told Keylock. Tom in turn hired a north London neighbour and schoolmate, Frank Thorogood, who over the next year built a 10-foot-high part fence, part wall, 'like the bloody Alamo', around the property. Keith added two new guard dogs, and from time to time even spoke about holding a dope drill, to practise flushing away substances. This last scheme collapsed under the pressure of supply and demand. Keith would never again understand how anyone could trust in British justice, and in fact he knew few who did. Apart from the £7,000 he, Jagger and Fraser apparently paid the law, there'd been the warder's voice as Keith left prison, hissing, 'You'll be back, you bastard!'

When Richards was warned about driving without a licence, he had Keylock arrange for a ringer to take the test on his behalf. 'It's just a fuckin' bit of paper.' The spiral of logic wrapping pragmatism and rule-bending round an aversion to most 'suits' was a Keith speciality. It seemed he loved doing things the hard way, if it meant he got to do what he wanted, and had the bonus of 'kicking society in the teeth'.

Meanwhile, *Satanic Majesties*, an LP that supposedly drove a psychedelic stake through the heart of the band's blues career. No one who had access to a stereo and a bong in the late Sixties will ever forget it. *Majesties* loomed just behind *Sergeant Pepper*, which it shamelessly aped: both albums featured opening numbers later reprised; both included background chat, static and tape loops in the normally sacrosanct silence between grooves; both had a trippy cover by Michael Cooper.

There were a few departures. Keith and Brian meshed, guitar and Mellotron, on the dreamlike ramble of 2,000 Light Years. She's A Rainbow was a smoochy, reflective affair which made hay with some Mozart piano; it also hinted that *Majesties* just might have been influenced by Anita and Marianne. Keith dusted off the Gibson fuzzbox to good effect on Citadel. But most of the rest was a retro, Beatles-lite confection that sounded closer to a pot party than an album.

Residual loyalty meant the LP 'shipped gold', hitting the *Billboard* chart on the day it was released. London Records sent an overexcited cable to Sir Edward Lewis at Decca: 'It's not a hit, it's an epidemic!' *Satanic Majesties* would earn the Stones the biggest royalties and worst reviews of their career.

On Keith's twenty-fourth birthday he and Anita arrived late as usual at Heathrow, flew to Paris and joined 'Strawberry Bob' Fraser, just out of jail, for Christmas in Morocco. As soon as they arrived Keith went across the street and scored from their old friend Achmed the hash dealer. Achmed would grade his kif 10-, 12- or – for discerning customers – 18-denier, according to purity. Over the next fortnight everyone smoked a lot of 18-denier. As an extra thrill, Keith rolled his joints in HM Prison issue papers, a souvenir of the Scrubs. 'Satanic *shit*,' he announced one night by the pool, then angrily jabbed his fag-end at the *Teen* review before setting it on fire. Keith swallowed a couple of tabs, got out his guitar and started to play traditional Robert Johnson blues. He played for twenty-five or thirty minutes without stopping, and the rich dense music echoed off the water and swirled in the air as he segued from one intricate lick to another, his fingers never missing a note. Fraser would remember thinking that what he heard was better than the new album.

Everyone drove back to Paris, where Keith decided to buy a flat in the rue du Faubourg St Honoré. He started to renovate it in classic Richards style – Moroccan tapestries, lots of wolfskin – but spent only a few nights there over the next five years.

Keith was mostly, instead, at Redlands, with Anita and even, after his appeal, with Brian and Suki: a there'll-always-be-an-England arrangement that lasted six months, until Jones was busted again. West Wittering had seen nothing like it. Up until 1966, the place had been a quiet birdwatchers' haven with two churches, a campsite and a pub. After Keith moved in, and particularly after February 1967, it was like the setting for one of those Roger Corman films where the decent folk are suddenly invaded by Hell's Angels. To the neighbours who exchanged ever more scandalized gossip, Redlands might as well have been renamed Sodom and Gomorrah. If rumour was to be believed, the Mars bar legend was the least of it. Sex, guns, knives, mini-hovercraft, ugly dogs, visiting fuzzy-wuzzies in full tribal gear: that would have been for starters. Redlands' decadent squalor was the backdrop, too, to Richards' best work. Sitting cross-legged on the cottage floor strumming his acoustic guitar, Keith wrote Street Fighting Man and You Can't Always Get What You Want. An early morning jam after a night drinking and singing cockney knees-ups became Jumpin' Jack Flash.

The Stones threw every radio-friendly beat they had into these new anthems, and got some great performances – notably from Jimmy Miller, a moustachioed twenty-five-year-old New York session drummer and, more to the point, record mixer of genius. The fruits of this new partnership would be heard on the band's next five albums. Keith played competently on *Satanic Majesties*, but in '67 music as a whole had gone sour for him. He wrote only a handful of songs, and on stage rarely tried more than an awkward-looking sidearm swipe: now and then you could see him watching his *hand* while he played. Keith had grown steadily more versatile since coming off the road. Now the 'Beatlearama' days were over, he was toying with new tunings and would soon perfect his trademark five-string, open-G: *G, D, G, B, D*, low to high, the classic fist-shaking assault of Honky Tonk

Women and the rest. Richards also taught himself slide and bottleneck. The Stones had long since stopped depending on Brian for anything.

The first result was Primo Grande, a driving acoustic strum accompanied by Charlie's toy drum kit (small enough to fold into a suitcase) and Keith himself overdubbing bass. After wandering through an anti-war march in London, Jagger added the title Street Fighting Man. The track was one of Richards' first and greatest forays outside his normal safety blanket of roaring electric guitar. Released in the US, the single was promptly banned amid the riots, murders and political carnage of the long hot summer of 1968.

Keith himself 'didn't give a stuff' about reaching anyone's mind, only their gut. The energy he put into Street Fighting could have powered a small town, let alone a song.

Back at Olympic, the Stones' sessions soon took on the brisk, down-to-business tone that attends a major comeback – or did so, rather, once Wyman carelessly picked out the riff of a lifetime on a dusty piano. For Keith, this was the dinger of the year, given his excruciating struggles to write a smash single since Night and Ruby Tuesday sixteen months earlier. He did no more – and never would, throughout his career – than accept the help freely given, but he also had the ears to hear a hit-in-waiting. Richards listened to Bill's casual gift, grunted an acknowledgement and drove back to Redlands.

Keith: 'It was about six in the morning and we'd been up all night. The sky was beginning to go grey and it was pissing down rain. I started to fool around, singing, and Mick [comes] in. And suddenly we had this wonderful phrase. So we woke up and knocked it together.'

Working from Bill's lick, Keith hit first on a 11-V-1 chord run and then a taut, three-note hook, E, F-sharp and A, that paid savvy and perhaps opportunistic homage to the past. Buried within was the timeless Satisfaction riff, played backwards. Jagger hurriedly added lyrics 'about having a hard time and getting out ... a metaphor for all the acid things'. The title was an in-joke twitting Keith's size-14-footed gardener, Jack Dyer, whom they could just make out through the rain padding mournfully around the Redlands moat.

Jumpin' Jack Flash.

Flash was actually a relaunch for Keith. It was also the beginning of his great stretch, the first of his mature singles and a riff sane critics compare to Beethoven's Fifth. Richards would call it 'my fucking favourite of all Stones songs'. Flash went to number one on both sides of the Atlantic and quite probably saved the band's career. By early June it was selling steadily at the rate of 15,000 a day in Britain, 40,000 a day worldwide, and would eventually add a seven-figure sum to Keith's accounts.

Total Flash songwriting royalties banked by Wyman: nil.

The sessions went on that spring in an atmosphere remarkably like that of a siege. Keith and Mick were being doorstepped by the press, Brian was on the skids and there were problems behind the scenes agreeing terms with Oldham. Bitter money hassles with Klein had come to seem normal. Crowds of hippies, a rare sight in Barnes, lined the street hoping to glimpse the Stones' dawn departures, coats draped over their bowed heads, and 700 people would wait in line for twenty-five seats at Brian's next trial. Keith was writing throughout – No Expectations, Parachute Woman and Child Of The Moon in one two-day burst. Between takes the band's cure for their acid-induced hangover was to jam, all night if necessary, on their favourite Muddy Waters blues.

The familiar STONES BANNED headlines were back in mid-May. Warpaint, tight pants, low slung guitars, not to mention Jagger's mike used as suggestively as in a Cadbury's Flake commercial: the rude shocks never stopped coming in Michael Lindsay-Hogg's dark but juicily entertaining video for Flash. Keith, with jungle-green shades and matching complexion, a shark's tooth dangling, turned into the Human Riff at that instant. Who says television doesn't innovate?

Like a shocking number of relatively young men in rock, Keith had made so much cash, at least on paper, that continuing to work was essentially optional. Yet he rarely stopped. When not in the studio his only real alternative was to lock himself up behind the Redlands wall with Anita, his new wolfhound Syph and a guitar. He had a motorbike and the Bentley. A local man named Nick Gough who saw the Lena making off towards London remembers watching with great interest, not least because the car happened to be exactly the same make and model as the one used by the Lord Lieutenant of Sussex. Gough was peering as best he could through the tinted glass, when Anita leant out of the window and bellowed at him, 'Get out of our fuckin' way! Peese off!' before adding what Charles Keeley would have called 'a parting gesture with two fingers'. It suddenly occurred to Gough that perhaps the Bentley wasn't on official business, after all, but he bears Keith no grudge. 'We've had that Mick Jagger down here because of him' – in his view, a selling point for West Wittering.

Keith went back to Rome in May when he heard more gossip about Anita and Brando on the *Candy* set. Despite the unpromising start, the two men got on well. Brando offered, more or less on a whim, to be godfather to Keith's first child. It didn't happen, but Richards and Pallenberg did name their elder son Marlon.

One reason Keith could mingle so easily with actors and artists while still defining rock attitude was the quality that most appealed to Brando: his humour. The funny voices were disarming. It seemed that he never took himself, or the business, half as seriously as others did. While money rained down from London Records in New York ($32,000 in 'guarantee payments' alone that May) Keith let it be known he was 'fucking skint' – in fact £3,720 overdrawn – at his high street bank. Because it was impossible to listen to Richards for long without wanting to impart financial advice, Brando said something responsible about how he had $32,000 to last him a quarter. 'I don't know whether it's going to last me until Monday,' Keith said.

It had been days now, even weeks, since the Stones last caused a riot, so it was only fitting that they raise the roof at the *NME* Poll-Winners' gig on 12 May. The band made a ten-minute cameo amid almost nostalgic chaos: commissionaires fought with fans as Keith ground out the power chords of Flash. Mick tossed his silver ballet shoes into the crowd. It was Brian Jones's last public performance.

Nine days later the narcs came for Brian in a dawn raid on his new flat in Royal Avenue House, King's Road. They took him away along with a ball of twine with a chunk of hash hidden inside. He told them it wasn't his, that he 'never took the stuff [because] it makes me so paranoid'. Jo Bergman bailed him out and Brian was remanded for trial.

Over the next eight weeks, the Stones moved forward with their masterpiece. Keith wrote the lushly textured You Got The Silver for Anita. Tom Keylock drove everyone to a ruined castle, where they pretended to play cricket for the press. The French *auteur* Jean-Luc Godard arrived at Olympic to film the sessions, and caught Keith providing a shuffling, hypnotic groove to Sympathy For The Devil. That night Godard's kleig lights set the studio ceiling on fire. Brian's bail was renewed. Richards and Jagger flew to Hollywood to mix the album and came back with a photo of a scuzzy toilet wall to put on the cover. The Stones had never been shy about shivering the timbers at Decca House, but this was too much. Over the next four months the band and their label engaged in a heated public debate about censorship. The LP's release date was moved back from July to early December. Keith told everyone that the Stones would be leaving Decca the second their contract allowed. There were a few thumped fists when all parties met for a summit at Maddox Street, a motion that never disturbed Brian, sleeping face down on the boardroom table.

On 26 June the Stones were at Redlands rehearsing a new song, Sister Morphine, which Marianne was talking about recording. The tune took time to grow, and somewhere towards dawn the band's arranger Jack Nitzsche introduced his friend Ry Cooder into the proceedings. Cooder had just turned twenty and was building a reputation as a hot young guitar-for-hire around Los Angeles. Before long he was jamming away, and Keith leant over and said, 'That's a gas, what you're playing; how'd you do it? You tune the E strings down to a D, right, and you can get a drone going, yeah, that's very cool,' and Cooder showed him the lot. By this time, the room was already resounding to the buzz of open-tune riffing and a chunky chord sequence very much like the intro to Honky Tonk Women. There was absolutely no piracy involved on Keith's part but, like many a songwriter before him, he knew when he was on to a good thing. Soon enough, he'd be mingling his deft Chuck Berry homages with a sure, sculpted sound that rocked the paint off arena walls.

Richards also heard the Byrds on their first British tour that summer – 'a straight gas'. While other bands were busy experimenting with Moogs and wah-wah pedals, the Byrds retreated through the swing doors of a western saloon-bar with their twangy steel guitars, bluegrass fiddles and upright pianos. They brought the house down: various Stones and Beatles pummelled the railings of the upper boxes and jaded critics broke into wide grins after their triumphant gig at the Albert Hall. Country rock was born. Keith soon befriended the Byrds' presiding genius Gram Parsons, twenty-two, a musician of brain-teasing agility, trust-fund millionaire and connoisseur of the finest drugs. When his band flew to South Africa, Parsons stayed behind to play cowboy songs and smoke hash with Keith and Anita. They drove him down to Stonehenge in the Lena, and later in the summer Gram would take Keith up into the California desert at sunrise, looking for UFOs. In the course of checking out the blue Mojave skies, the two men soon began riffing on their guitars around a campfire. A number of these dawn jamborees would be worked up on to classic Stones albums like *Sticky Fingers*.

In the late Sixties, before teaching every punk guitarist how to lurch the right way, Keith was busy creating a unique mix of country, rock and blues – a truly integrated style. He didn't give a boot in the knackers for mere one-dimensional 'wank'. Keith's draughtsmanship bound everything together into a fierce wallop. With time on his hands he was blueprinting a whole new line of attack: open tunings, often with a distinct Nashville flavour, and the self-confidence to play *less*. There wasn't a note wasted, and yet Keith could shake up a room with just the sound of his rumbling bottom string, the fattest single noise pop had produced since Phil Spector. His Jumpin' Jack Flash riff deserved its own STD code. Everything would change for Keith after that long weekend at Redlands jamming on Morphine and the rest. As he sometimes joked about himself, 'Five strings, three notes, two fingers, one arsehole and you've got it.'

Cooder went ballistic a year or so later and publicly charged the Stones with stealing his best licks. 'They're *bloodsuckers*, man.'

Keith: 'I heard those things he said and I was amazed. He taught me the tuning and I got behind it. I mean, he was a gas to play with . . . but I learnt a lot of things off a lot of people. In a way, all musicians do is pass it on. Guys come up and say, "This guy is copying you." So what?'

With Brian fading fast, Cooder came back to England ten months after the Redlands jam, apparently believing he might be asked to join the band. 'There were a lot of very weird people hanging around', and Keith paced the sessions more slowly than a state funeral. 'When there'd be a lull in the so-called rehearsals, I'd start to play my guitar. [Keith] would leave the room immediately and never return . . . But as I found out later, the tapes would keep rolling. They got it all down. *Everything*.'

Cooder went back to Los Angeles in June 1969. Six months later he experienced the weird sensation of hearing himself play prominently on *Let It Bleed*. There would be no third collaboration.

While Keith had been busy promoting Flash, as well as sucking up culture from the London stage and cinema, Anita was finishing *Candy* in Rome. No sooner was she home than she was auditioning for a new film, *Performance*, in which she was hopelessly miscast as a drug-snorting vamp who also did women. Her co-star would be Mick Jagger.

Richards was deeply uneasy about her taking the part, which called for much tumbling around in bed and the annoying, to Keith, discovery that she and Mick were really 'doing it'. Meantime, Marianne Faithfull was expecting Jagger's child. Finding that she, too, was pregnant just before shooting *Performance*, Anita reportedly had an abortion. Tony Sanchez claims that Pallenberg, whose knowledge of the black arts extended, famously, to pentagrams and voodoo dolls, then proposed a pagan marriage ritual with Keith. Their friend the filmmaker and diabolist Kenneth Anger agreed to officiate. Anita danced with impatience while their magus went about West Sussex finding the necessary druidical clothes and a sacrificial long-horned ram. When Anger also insisted on daubing everyone with a magickal gold paint, Keith bridled.

'Fucking heavy,' he kept muttering. '*Fucking* heavy.'

In the end Redlands would never be privileged to see Anger at work, and the general feeling was that, while Keith could flip from one persona to another, his preferred form was 'a guy from Dartford' – too innocuous for Beelzebub.

Keith's admirers liked to talk about how grounded he was, and how unfazed, and to contrast his ability to 'handle shit' with Jones's tendency to crack up. (Brian was snoring his way through sessions.) And in the abstract Keith's professionalism was, sure enough, the dynamo behind the Stones' best work. But the devil, as Anger always said, lay in the detail.

If charm and resilience were Dupree and Richards bloodlines, Keith's childhood also contributed to occasional bouts of deep misery and inertia. At times an aide 'had to lift him off the floor and pump his arms up and down to jump-start him'. These were the days Redlands 'could be like a house out of the *Twilight Zone*'. Where rows of stone Buddhas held silent vigil beneath a canopy emblazoned with shrieking gorgons' heads. Where violet candles dripped and flowed across lead-lined table tops inlaid with crimson glass stars. Where water rats capered under the appraising eye of Syph the dog. Keith's own rural pursuits included tinkering with guns and knives, lying prone in a hammock, drawing on a bubble pipe and noting the strange preponderance of UFOs hovering over the South Downs. No wonder, perhaps, Les Perrin stopped arranging visits from the likes of *Teen* and *Valentine*. Later that year Perrin and Ian Stewart would help get Richards into the Lena, up the A3, through Immigration at Heathrow, on to a jet, and, seven hours later, safely down the ramp in New York. Keith remained asleep throughout.

The nearly epic devotion to the razor and the mirror, as well as to the demands of nonstop toking, may have explained Keith's less than total attention elsewhere. But at a time when he was coming to define the wasted myth, Richards could and did function – well. His radar was famously quick to pick up a phony, and his quips about showbiz were a treat to listen to. At no point in his rarefied Sixties existence did Keith ever lose touch with Doris, Gus Dupree, or the pleasures of sitting in the back room of a pub playing cards. He soon became a regular at the blackjack table in Tony Sanchez's Vesuvio club, which went up in smoke a year or two later. Keith made no claim to having any grand views on life, other than that it was a private matter. At one interview, he said that 95 per cent of the stories about him were untrue; later, perhaps thinking this sounded a bit low, he upped the figure to 99. Another time, someone asked him if he recommended taking drugs.

'No,' he said.

Just as Keith's guitar style hardened, something similar went on in the way he handled himself commercially, notably in dealing with Klein. The gist of the Stones' complaint was that he was sweating them, making them beg for their own money. (Although Klein was being probed by the Securities and Exchange Commission, the few infractions were due to ineptitude rather than sharp practice and there was no hint of any illegal activity, either on Wall Street or with the Stones.) Later that summer Richards and Jagger put their names to a telex to New York ending, 'The phones and electricity will be cut off tomorrow. Also the rent is due. We're having to run the office despite your wishes. If you would like to remedy this, please do so.' Jo Bergman, in a memo to the band, added: 'The Klein problem is more than a drag. We're puppets. How can you work, or the office, if we have to spend so much time pleading for bread? It's never going to be different till that's straightened out.'

For months, Keith couldn't get Klein's office to wire him even the down-payment to buy a new London flat. Instead, he and Anita would flop out at Robert Fraser's place in Mount Street, Mayfair. Sitting there one rainy night among Fraser's voodoo fetishes and Tibetan skull collection, Keith wrote the words and music of Gimme Shelter.

Performance began shooting on 2 September, a sardonic epitaph on the Sixties with Jagger strangely impressive as Turner, a reclusive pop star holed up in Notting Hill, where he shares his bed and his ample drug stash with two beautiful women. Marianne Faithfull freaked out the second she read the script. The plot called for Mick and Anita to resolve their love–hate relationship by simulating sex, or, failing that, by doing what came naturally. Such was the zeal of the resulting scenes that a ten-minute snippet was entered in a Dutch blue movie festival, where it won the Golden Dong. Keen-eyed observers didn't miss the point that this meant Pallenberg had now been involved with three of the five Stones.

'We're all one big family,' Jagger said.

Keith, Robert Fraser saw, was 'quietly but deeply pissed' that the band was being upstaged, and his own home life rocked, by his two closest partners. This sly sense of betrayal shaped almost all the new songs Keith was writing for *Let It Bleed*. Most clipped along with the curtness of a telegram, rollicking tunes about midnight ramblers and the like with seriously catchy riffs. He refused to have anything to do with the *Performance* soundtrack, which Jagger and Jack Nitzsche had to record using American session men.

Performance horrified Warner Brothers no less than it did Keith, and the movie 'died in the can'; it was shelved for more than two years and finally opened at New York's Public Theatre, an orphanage for lost films, in January 1971. It has never had a general release. *Performance*'s collage of fast cuts, swirling camerawork, drugs, S&M and disturbing close-ups of James Fox in drag would make it a cult classic. Midnight screenings of it were raided once or twice. The whole controversy dragged on for years, with some tragic results. Fox would suffer a form of post-traumatic breakdown and take a twenty-year break from acting to join a religious order called the Navigators. *Performance*'s co-director Donald Cammell and its writer David Litvinoff both committed suicide. Pallenberg's lesbian interest in the film, Michelle Breton, became a heroin pusher and disappeared, presumed dead, into the Marseilles underworld. A co-star named John Bindon was charged with murder, acquited, and then died. Mick Jagger has never acted as well since.

'*Fucking* heavy' Keith repeated, when he saw *Performance*, and reportedly did something he'd never done before, at least not with Linda. He talked about wanting a child. Something about *Performance* had moved him. Inside a month, Anita was pregnant again.

While most of the Stones had been in Olympic working on Keith's new songs, Brian Jones, at his own insistence, was 1,200 miles away in the Caves of Hercules, outside Tangier, recording the Master Musicians of Jajouka. On 26 September Brian was back in London, on trial for unlawful possession. Richards, Jagger and Keylock sat in the public gallery to hear the judge remind the jury that the burden of proof rested not on Jones but the police, 'whose case is circumstantial. No evidence of his using cannabis was found . . . If you think the prosecution has proved without a doubt that the defendant knew the drug was in his flat, you must find him guilty. Otherwise, he is innocent.'

'Groovy,' said Keith.

Outside in the hall he and Jagger signed autographs. A beaming Keylock timed the jury: forty-seven minutes. As the foreman announced 'guilty' Brian slumped to his seat, head in hands. Richards was visibly shaken by the verdict. The judge said: 'I think this was a lapse and I don't want to interfere with the probation order that already applies to this man. I am going to fine you according to your means. [Fifty pounds with a hundred guineas costs.] You must keep clear of this stuff. For goodness' sake, don't get into trouble again.'

Outside, Keith, Mick and Brian danced for the cameras.

Six weeks later, the Stones recorded You Can't Always Get What You Want while Jones lay sprawled in a corner, toking and reading a magazine. The next evening on Radio One, Mick revealed that the band 'definitely want to tour America [but] there are major hassles with visas'. Two days later, Marianne Faithfull miscarried her child. That weekend Brian took possession of Cotchford Farm, the mid-Sussex estate where A. A. Milne wrote *Winnie-the-Pooh*. Jones particularly liked to sit on the back terrace that overlooked Milne's swimming pool and, beyond it, a grand lawn decorated with bear-shaped topiary. Keylock arranged for Frank Thorogood to drive over from Redlands and help Brian refurbish the place.

On 5 December, the Stones finally launched *Beggars Banquet* at the Elizabethan Room of the Gore hotel, where guests enjoyed a seven-course feast of boar's head and dumplings with an extensive wine list. Later in the proceedings serving wenches handed round cream pies. Les Perrin finally snapped and smashed two on either side of Jones's head, which hung there like fluffy earmuffs. Brian wiped them off slowly. He was familiar with practical jokes. This wasn't one. Keith himself got lost and spent most of the evening driving around London in the Lena, but later told a reporter he was 'chuffed' at the album, which he had no doubt would annoy Decca and get itself banned by the BBC. The future looked rosy.

In fact *Banquet* was a brilliant weave of bluesy simplicity and right-on lyrics, and a big hit both on radio and most university campuses. Punchy, midtempo guitar, singalong choruses and crafty background effects were the main ingredients, and nearly every song was prepared like fast food – cooked up, packaged and delivered in around three minutes. Keith was on peak form throughout.

The kickoff, Sympathy For The Devil, was a perfect showcase for Jagger's fey retelling of Bulgakov's *The Master and Margarita* over Keith's samba beat; Charlie kicked in with the voodoo percussion. Prodigal Son was a throwback to the days when Keith and Brian had jammed in Edith Grove, had a bratty swagger, and didn't need electricity to be heard. Elsewhere, *Banquet*'s songs flowed naturally on classic blues licks instead of 'clever' inside musical jokes like *Satanic Majesties*. The requisitely trippy lyrics and nods to country rock were in the tradition of Dylan and Gram Parsons, respectively. Stray Cat Blues, which sounded like something Keith had hashed out with Lou Reed, managed to be dark and catchy at the same time. Standing above it all, Street Fighting balanced lo-fi technology and acoustic guitars against a riff that left powder burns.

Beggars Banquet was released a year to the day after *Satanic Majesties*. In rock a 'roots' album has often served as a prop rather than a springboard for artistic growth. By risking everything, the Stones had performed the ultimate rescue act on their career.

As Richards drew out a meat cleaver and sent it wheeling towards a tree, the better to stab the photograph of Klein fixed there, Stu arrived at the mature conclusion that, all things considered, Keith was 'uptight about management'. By Christmas 1968 the Stones were being regularly threatened with eviction from their office and rehearsal studio, and there were problems even cashing their cheques. Incredibly enough, most of the band's business was conducted in this atmosphere. While *Beggars Banquet* was going multi-platinum and changing the whole face of album rock, its authors were trudging up the stairs at Maddox Street worrying about gas, phones and electricity.

Klein had already infuriated Jagger when, a year or two earlier, he'd failed to wire Mick's younger brother funds when the latter was trekking in the Himalayas, thus stranding him in Katmandu. That was Al, a tough man to get hold of. Klein's stand on Keith's London pad now led him to explode in rage. Tom Keylock was told to 'get your fuckin' arse over to Fats and get it sorted'. Weighing up the situation, Keylock realized that direct action was called for. He flew to New York, hurried to 1700 Broadway, vaulted over a secretary's desk and into Klein's inner sanctum, before announcing, 'I'm not leaving without Keef's twenty-five grand.' He got the money.

Richards and Jagger saw no way out of the crisis with Brian Jones. The Stones had a great album as well as some unrecorded songs like Midnight Rambler, and they wanted to tour America; 22 March 1969 had been pencilled in for a comeback gig at Madison Square Garden. The US Bureau of Immigration was in no mood to admit a twice-convicted drug felon. Keith and Mick decided to approach Eric Clapton as a substitute, with all five Stones chipping in for his fee. Brian, meantime, would officially remain in the band.

Clapton eventually passed on this arrangement.

Everyone made it up to the old *Ready Steady Go!* studios in Wembley on 10–12 December for *The Rock 'n' Roll Circus*, a Christmas revue noted tartly by Wyman as 'conceived by Mick and financed by the band'. (Klein didn't bother answering their telegrams begging for seed money.) A cowboy on horseback announced the Stones, whose dawn set climaxed with six separate takes of Sympathy, in the final stages of which the audience was barely conscious. As a side-show attraction the band then paraded around the big top: Jagger dressed as a ringmaster, Keith looking like one of the *Sergeant Pepper* dandies after a hard night, and Brian retreating into his wispy, stoned, soft-featured self. Later Keith elbowed Bill aside to play bass in a hastily assembled 'supergroup' with Clapton, Lennon and Mitch Mitchell. The Stones hated their performance, and the film of *Rock 'n' Roll Circus* wouldn't be seen for twenty-eight years.

On Keith's twenty-fifth birthday, he, Jagger, Pallenberg and Faithfull flew to Lisbon and from there set sail for Peru.* Both couples were squabbling. Anita teased Keith about the paternity of the baby she was carrying. She apparently suffered at least one violent haemorrhage – alluded to in Faithfull's new lyrics to Sister Morphine – but kept the child. All along Keith was writing. At the Hotel Bolivar, Lima, he took out a guitar and

---

* This festive cruise included the famous night when an elderly American passenger squinted at Keith and Mick and said, 'You're *someone*, aren't you? Give me a glimmer.' The word stuck, and they billed themselves as the Glimmer Twins on and off for the next thirty-five years.

played Jagger the chord changes and melody of Let It Bleed. A few days later Richards was fooling around with the open-G tuning and hit on the Honky Tonk Women riff again.

Mick was at the minibar, yawning and absentmindedly tapping a foot. And in a flash Keith was knocking out the song, which was both complex and utterly simple.

'Yeah,' said Mick, as the music rumbled and rolled around the room. 'I could sing that.'

Keith finished off the intro, chorus, solo and both verses inside the hour.

That March, Richards finally took possession of 3 Cheyne Walk, a Queen Anne mansion in the same row as Jagger's. The vendor was a former Tory cabinet minister, Anthony Nutting. While the house was being refurbished, Keith and Anita made a London base of the Ritz hotel. They cut a slick dash there, she in hotpants and high heels, he in a shiny black greatcoat and boots. Keith was beginning to do heroin, snorting it through a tube on a gold chain he wore round his neck. He blamed both himself and the law – 'they went public on me' – for this latest development. What Richards seemed to be saying was 'This is, more or less, what you wanted, and you can have a piece any time.' The offer was so generous that several narcs took him up on it. Keith's nightly visits to the studio met with keen police interest. Round-the-clock surveillance, illegal stops, searches, threats: Olympic brought new meaning to the words 'hostile working environment'.

Yet Keith made some of his best music there. As well as the new songs there were retreads of Robert Johnson's Love In Vain and Fred McDowell's You Gotta Move. As a copyist, Keith was an amateur in the best sense of the word. His covers dignified the originals. Much of *Bleed*, in fact, pulled off the trick of appealing to both the Stones fan and the musicologist. The album made hay with Johnson, in particular, and revealed a blazing ambition. Keith's goals weren't specific, but his mission was huge. 'Governments are really out to make that rhythm illegal. I'm here to stop 'em.'

While the Stones worked, Brian Jones was tinkering with his Moroccan tapes and writing lyrics to a morbid song he called My Death. On 18 March he checked into the Priory, suffering from depression. Brian then split up with Suki Potier and began to see a twenty-two-year-old Swedish model, Anna Wohlin, who also looked just like Anita.

Ry Cooder came back to Olympic in early May. This being the Stones, nobody actually spoke to him, though, as he noted later, 'the tapes kept rolling'. Everyone always seemed to be off in side rooms, holding secret meetings. Klein had just announced he was assuming control of the Beatles. By the end of the month, Cooder was depressed and broke, and wondering why Keith would leave the studio whenever he, Ry, showed up. Stu had a word with Mick, who wandered over to the back booth where Cooder was playing on Love In Vain. 'What's the matter, man? Is it bread? A chick?' Mick nodded affably towards several women lounging in the control room. 'Is that it?'

It wasn't.

'I just don't see the point,' said Cooder.

'What do you mean, "point"?'

'Of my being here.'

Ry left then and Keith immediately returned, sending waves of energy through the remaining sessions. The Stones cut the basic track of Midnight Rambler in one take. Keith's guitar gave up the fight and fell in half on the climactic meltdown note of Gimme Shelter. The rest of the music went well, though production hassles and personnel changes kept the band at Olympic till mid June. On the last night, a Cinderella moment in the empty studio after the album was finished and the gear was being stowed, Keith turned to Stu as the latter balanced an amp on his broad shoulders.

'That was a gas, man,' he laughed, and teased, 'I'm glad I made the party.'

Meanwhile, Brian Jones was enjoying the early spring with his new girlfriend at Cotchford Farm. Frank Thorogood was busy restoring the house's antique beams and levelling its stone floors, as well as joining his employer for a bottle of wine most evenings. Brian's parents came down to visit for a weekend in mid May. A muted effort was afoot to persuade them to move into a staff flat on the premises, in the hope they could stitch back together the family life torn apart years before. Brian particularly wanted them to know that he was 'doing well' and could 'afford to keep them'. Lewis and Louisa Jones declined his offer. Thorogood would always remember how Brian stared after the taxi taking them back to the station that Sunday evening, and murmuring hoarsely, 'Mum ... Dad ...' A few days later, Jones made his final recorded contribution to the Stones. Sitting in a corner by himself, he laid down a few haunting grace notes on You Got The Silver, Keith's great love song to Anita.

On 18 May, for the first time, man orbited the moon. Major anti-war protests closed down several American campuses. And the original Stones made their last appearance together, a photo shoot at St Katharine's Dock, near Tower Bridge. Everyone posed behind a sheet of glass covered with fracture blooms, which made it look as though they were back where they began, being stoned by a mob. Keith then took some of the *Let It Bleed* artwork to his friend Robert Brownjohn, the man behind the *Goldfinger* titles. Jagger announced that he and Marianne Faithfull were to star in Tony Richardson's new film *Ned Kelly*, which would be shot in Australia. Some time that week he and Keith talked recruitment with the blues bandleader John Mayall.

On 28 May Jagger and Faithfull were arrested for possession in a raid led by Detective Sergeant Robin Constable. Constable happened to be the very officer who had last busted Brian. Mayall's protégé Mick Taylor, just twenty-one and never been stoned, was startled to get a call that night from Keith Richards. He was invited to Olympic to play on a song the Stones were kicking around called Live With Me. Taylor was painfully shy, peering up at Keith from bulging blue eyes out of an aura of blond fuzz. Many of his guitar fills were sublime. Later Stu handed round bottles of beer, and the band made small talk. As Keith and Bill idly swapped cricket scores, whole careers were actually beginning and ending. Even Mick made a few jokes. His was the air of riding out a good franchise. After a brief consultation, Keith and Jagger casually offered Taylor a salary of £150 a week, he assumed just for a few sessions. The strange evening was laced with a delightful, Pythonesque humour, and Taylor went away thinking how funny and charming 'the big, bad Stones' were.

Three nights later, same venue. The Stones finally cut Honky Tonk Women. Mick Jagger was in a side room doing an interview. Keith lurched in hours late, looking heavy lidded, grabbed his Fender, exhaled a cloud of smoke, and, take one, nailed the riff. Charlie started a drum pattern and Jimmy Miller picked up the beat on a cowbell. Jagger's slurped vocals, then horns and more crackling guitar. Like all true originals, Honky Tonk had a past to which it simultaneously paid tribute and waved goodbye. Its roots lay in a reworking of I Heard It Through The Grapevine, wrapped round a James Brown groove. Keith brought the deft syncopation and an equally smart ear for a killer hook. Mick Taylor was there and thought he was listening to the greatest single ever recorded. Honky Tonk Women was radio heaven, a collage of classic pop ideas wedged into exactly three minutes.

Next day, Keith and Mick offered Taylor a job.

Brian Jones had written the intro and first line of My Death sitting on the terrace overlooking his pool, and was idly thinking of putting together a blues band. Alexis Korner, John Mayall and the drummer Micky Waller all visited him on the farm. Old friends were surprised when they saw what the famous dandy now looked like: Brian had grown plump, and Thorogood would remember him spreading beyond the narrow confines of his dining room chair 'like a ripe cheese'. Jones talked about the Stones rarely, about Anita constantly.

7 June 1969. Saturday night: Keith wrecked his new Mercedes (a remodelled Nazi staff car) taking a narrow corner outside Redlands at 70 mph. Anita broke her collarbone but otherwise she, and her baby, were fine. Spanish Tony helped Keith empty the car of 'bags of heroin, cocaine, grass and opium' which they hid in the branches of a nearby tree. Then, in a Robin Constable moment, the first policeman on the scene, after squinting at Keith and Anita, both of them covered in blood, said, 'I know you – I raided your gaff.' Three disposable syringes and a dozen phials were found on Pallenberg, but she successfully persuaded the rozzer they all contained 'vitamins'.

Next day, Keith mixed Honky Tonk Women from 2 p.m. to 7 p.m., then he, Mick and Charlie drove to Cotchford Farm. Brian had been drinking steadily all evening and was waiting for them. The subsequent interview lasted twenty minutes. Keith: 'We had to go down and virtually tell him, "Hey, old cock, you're fired." Because there was no serious way we could go on the road with Brian. The fact that he was expecting it made it easier. He wasn't surprised. I don't think he even took it all in. He was already up in the stratosphere. He was like, "Yeah, man, OK".' Asked if he wanted to put out a statement, Brian said, 'Whatever you guys do is fine by me.' He declined, however, to share a no-hard-feelings joint with them, insisting he wanted to 'stay clean'. Thorogood would remember Jones standing by the front door, bidding the Stones a cheery farewell, smiling and waving until their car disappeared round a bend, before walking slowly back to the pool. For a long time he sat watching the water fade in the gathering night. Then Brian's lips moved, though just barely, and he spoke in a voice so soft Thorogood had to strain to hear it from three feet away.

'Bastards,' he said.

On Friday 13 June, the first of 200 journalists pulled up behind a small, roped-off enclosure in the south-east corner of Hyde Park. There they met Richards and Jagger, who announced both the name of their new guitarist, and the date – Saturday 5 July – of their biggest ever concert. The Stones were back: official.

In phone calls over the next several days, Keith expressed concern about Brian's state of mind. He asked Alexis Korner to act as an intermediary between Jones and the band, to 'make sure the guy doesn't do anything crazy'. Korner agreed, and drove down to Cotchford three or four times before the end of June. He was always struck by how Richards managed to be 'the nicest of them to Brian'. Keith also shared his concern with Tom Keylock, who dropped by to find Jones 'uptight about all the bills [Thorogood] was running up. It seemed like he always wanted Frank around, but didn't want to pay him.'

Wednesday 2 July. Brian spent that afternoon wheezing with asthma, medicating himself with his inhaler and several bottles of wine. Thorogood and his girlfriend Janet Lawson were spending the night in the staff flat at the top of the house. Around 9 o'clock, Brian knocked on the door and asked if they'd care to join Anna and him for a nightcap. Thorogood looked at Lawson. They would. Everyone drank some more wine, then switched to brandy, until Brian – 'seeming anxious to be occupied', Janet later told the law – suggested a swim.

Jones staggered a bit on the diving board, and hit the water like a depth charge. His two spaniels, Emily and Luther, immediately began barking in alarm. But when Brian came up for air he was laughing, and, in the police report, 'started swimming quite merrily'. Frank joined him and the two women walked back to the house, taking the dogs with them. Thorogood would remember Brian murmuring softly 'I love this place', and then settling back to float silently around the deep end. By now the garden was quite still, head-high in mist, the clouds seeping in the pool like fluid, the surface of the water acting as a filter. All around, the Pooh effigies were fading fast. The two men drifted about, without speaking further, for twenty minutes. Thorogood remembered that the scene gradually took on a sinister hue as everything around them disappeared, leaving only a patch of brilliantly tiled, floodlit water. When Frank announced he was going in, Brian merely grunted. It was midnight.

By the time Thorogood walked the forty yards to the house, dried and lit a cigarette, five minutes may have passed. Lawson was startled by the way Frank looked, and asked him where Brian was. Still in the pool. In Wohlin's recollection, everyone stared at each other and then quickly started back to the terrace, overlooking the deep end. Brian was lying face down there, his arms and legs spread out in a cross formation. Thorogood and Lawson got him out of the water and on to his back in the warm grass. Years later Wohlin would recall how Brian seemed to squeeze her hand when she felt for a pulse, yet he never actually regained consciousness. Half an hour later, the police pronounced him dead at the scene.*

The Stones were back at Olympic, tinkering with a Stevie Wonder song called I Don't Know Why, when the call came.

Keith: 'We were at a session and someone rang us up at midnight and said, "Brian's dead." Well, what the fuck's going on? I don't know, man, I just don't know what happened to Brian that night. If anybody was going to kill Brian, it was going to be me. There was no one there that'd want to murder him. Someone just didn't take care of him.' It says much for the band's spirit that, just a few hours later, they were strutting out Honky Tonk Women on *Top of the Pops*. Backstage, a BBC reporter with a film crew in tow introduced himself with the provocative remark: 'Excuse me, Mr Richards. How do you carry on, under the circumstances?'

* For all the rumours about Brian's death, still regularly exercising the press and conspiracy mongers today, the most plausible verdict remains the official one: Misadventure, specifically, 'Drowning whilst swimming under the influence of Alcohol and Drugs'. By the time Jones flopped into the pool that night he was, by any clinical definition, roaringly drunk. He'd taken several downers. The water temperature was over 90°. Significantly, when Wohlin, Lawson and the dogs went back into the house, Thorogood had the impression that 'Brian was almost nodding off'. A few minutes later, he probably did so. What's certain is that, thirty years after the event, some of the parties involved, though not Janet Lawson, decided to hawk their stories to various journalists, TV shows, and, for that matter, this author. By way of full disclosure, I should say that I knew and liked Frank Thorogood, who was guilty of some poor judgement that night. He was also one of Jones's more loyal friends. Personally, I prefer to believe that Brian died of tragic neglect, not murder.

Keith allegedly grabbed the man by the tie, lifted him up and told him to fuck off.

The new single was out the next day. Keith's serrated riff and Charlie's classic drum groove made Women the Stones' biggest hit yet. On the 5th, they played to 300,000 in Hyde Park. Jagger showed up in a white dress and declaimed Shelley's *Adonais* for Brian. Keith got off some snaky, Nashville-style guitar fills, but the anti-climax came on fast; halfway through the opening number, everybody was out of tune. The stage was dominated by a huge blow-up of Jones, a drunken leer on his pasty face.

Over the next few days, there was intense jockeying between Klein and Jagger's new favourite, Prince Rupert Loewenstein, for future control of the Stones' wealth. Mick had been powerfully impressed by the Austrian dandy who, at weekends, liked to exchange his Savile Row suit for tweeds and a Tyrolean hat with an eagle feather stuck in the band. Loewenstein, suave and self-effacing where Klein was gruff and entrepreneurial, sat down for several 'handover' meetings at the City offices of the bankers Leopold Joseph. He struck one witness there as 'more of a Crufts champion than a pit-bull'. The prince soon began to take responsibility for the band's finances, though Klein nominally remained the boss. Jagger himself wasn't around to help much. He and Faithfull had already flown to Sydney, leaving Keith to gripe, not for the last time, that Mick was 'piss[ing] off to be a film star'. His voice rising with incredulity, Richards would tell anyone who listened that Jagger was 'insecure just singing'.

Brian Jones was buried in Cheltenham on Thursday 10 July. Keylock made all the arrangements. More than 600 mourners gathered outside the parish church where Brian had sung as a choirboy. Among those who attended were Charlie, Bill, Stu, Frank Thorogood and several former lovers clutching Brian's children. Among those who didn't were Keith and Anita. Canon Hugh Hopkins told the congregation, 'Brian had little patience with authority, convention and tradition. In this he was typical of many of his generation who have come to see in the Stones an expression of their whole attitude to life. Much that this ancient church has stood for in 900 years seems irrelevant to them.' The Canon then quoted from Luke 15, the Prodigal Son, and from a telegram Brian had sent his parents: 'Please don't judge me too harshly.'

Outside, at the gravesite, there was a wreath of red roses 'with love from Keith and Anita'.

The couple spent the rest of the summer at Cheyne Walk, now decorated so as to make even a Tory minister feel queasy. When Anthony Nutting casually dropped by to collect his post, he took one look at the front hallway and had to sit down. The house where Nutting had once entertained Winston Churchill to dinner was done to rock-star perfection, from the glittering mirror ball hanging from the ceiling to the black candlesticks and the stars daubed in the upstairs reception room. Keith and Anita shared the bed on which she'd done her sex scenes in *Performance*.

On 10 August 1969 Marlon Richards was born in King's College Hospital. Scarred by his own boyhood poverty, Keith was to give his son almost everything he wanted.

Keylock remembers being astonished at the way Richards bonded with his child. 'I never saw anyone more knocked-out.' Shot through all Keith's conversations were the comings and goings of Marlon. Everyone was based in London while Richards touched up *Let It Bleed*, but escaped to the country in late August. A nanny came to help at Redlands, closely followed by Doris. Keith worked in his small home studio while Mrs Richards sat in uneasy silence with Anita, appraising her smudged mascara and snug mini-skirt. Pallenberg: 'Keith's mum always saw me as a foreigner. Everything I did was strange – "Isn't that strange?" – even the milk bottle I had for Marlon. Everything was weird.'

It was hard to know, meanwhile, what qualified as weird among Keith's paid entourage. Keylock and 'Spanish Tony' fought like ferrets in a sack. One hated dope ('I saw what it did to Brian'), while the other pushed it. Their debates on the subject were legendary, and frequently rattled the Cheyne Walk roof. Sanchez happened to come down with laryngitis late that summer. It was a change: a few days of brooding silence instead of shouted fuck-you's.

All sides had reason to be interested in the outcome of this power struggle. Keylock clearly wanted to spare Keith from going the way of Brian, 'to get him away from all the bullshit'. Spanish Tony wasn't having any of it. In his own recollection, he 'always knew exactly what to do, where to get anything from grass to a submachine gun'. It seemed to some that Sanchez was daring Keith to sink to the sewer with him.

Things were going badly, meanwhile, in the Australian outback. Marianne Faithfull had taken an overdose in her hotel room, and only survived thanks to Jagger's quick thinking. Tony Richardson dropped her from the cast of *Ned Kelly*, which would go on to grace all the 'Worst Movies in History' lists. On 18 August Mick was badly injured when a prop pistol exploded in his hand. The studio nurse stitched him up and told him to keep his right arm immobile. Preferring to doctor himself, Jagger instead picked up a guitar one afternoon and strummed a two-bar phrase around the C, G and F chords, then threw in some bondage fantasy lyrics. This happy collision between boredom and physical therapy would be the best thing to come out of *Ned Kelly*. Once back in London, Mick and Keith swiftly worked up the riff into Brown Sugar.

The Stones put out another hits package, *Through the Past, Darkly*, in September. The LP included the last-ever shot of the original band, and was dedicated with the words: 'Brian Jones (1943–1969), When this you see, remember me/and bear me in your mind/Let all the world say what they may/Speak of me as you find.' The date given for Brian's birth was wrong.

As it happened, the US Bureau of Immigration finally agreed to admit the Stones just three weeks after Jones died. The government officially said that Keith and Mick remained 'undesirable', but that after posting a $10,000 bond, to cover expenses, they could enter the States for sixty days. While Jagger finished *Ned Kelly*, Keith quickly put together both *Bleed* and the band's comeback tour.

Just before flying out on 17 October, Richards took a parting photo of Anita and Marlon. He tacked it to the wall of his study, where he wrote a bittersweet song called Wild Horses. With the possible exception of Parsons', this was the most sublime Nashville-style music around.

Keith's leisurely, ruminative blues was the public face of a very private commitment to Pallenberg. One day at Redlands he'd promised in Keylock's hearing that he'd take Anita to be his old lady, to live together, hold her, comfort her, honour her and, forsaking all others, keep him only unto her. Played her the riff right there in front of the open fire, told her he'd love her, for better for worse, for richer for poorer. The implication was that 'Keith wanted to share his whole life with her', reverently, exclusively, eternally, to 'do things just right'.

It lasted about three weeks. Once back in Los Angeles, Keith took up with a black woman called Emeretta Marks, having left Anita and Marlon in England. Meanwhile the Stones began ten days of intensive recording and rehearsals. Richards was hours late every night, a pattern he'd repeat throughout the month-long tour. Gram Parsons was on hand again, and he and Keith fell into the habit of 'getting royally zonked [and] singing cowboy songs around a piano' before driving up to the Warners lot in Hollywood for the formal session. Gram excitedly told everyone that Keith was going to produce his next record. However, perhaps he misunderstood the arrangements because it would be he, instead, who contributed to the next two Stones albums. Some felt that what Keith was offering Parsons wasn't so much friendship, as friendliness.

The band now toured with an entourage of twenty, including Stu, Jo Bergman, the MC Sam Cutler and sundry writers, filmmakers and photographers. Klein himself joined them on certain dates, where he oversaw security by beating back over-eager fans with a broom handle. The tour's unofficial sponsor, Dodge, was singularly appropriate to both its mad geography and sense of being one step ahead of the law. The giant car manufacturer sent one Jon Jaymes to help organize Keith, and it was always a volatile combination – the company geek travelling with the man whose ritual lateness lowered several shows into their graves. The pixie-faced Jaymes made for a stark contrast with Richards, who had the kind of pasty hue and gaunt physique one critic described as a 'sick weasel's'.

At the end of the tour, Jaymes approached Keith with a Dodge catalogue and asked him to pick out any car he liked, with extras, as a thank-you from the company. Keith smiled and ordered a production-model Charger, which he wanted in purple.

The first sight that most towns had of the Stones was Richards tooling up the power chords of Jumpin' Jack Flash, and it set the tone for what followed. Keith kept firmly astride most shows, bent over his guitar and dressed with his usual elegance: scuffed snakeskin boots, hip-hugging gaucho pants studded with silver beads, spangly red shirt splayed open to the waist. He'd recently added a wolf's-tooth earring. Keith's hair was teased as high as a guardsman's busby, and his own front teeth were rotting out of his head. Physically, he was in peak condition. Musically, Keith got better as the tour progressed: after a shaky start, both he and Taylor played with hellhound fury, and the result was a blast of blues, rock and joist-shaking riffs.

From the shattering bolt of Flash – half music, half siren – at the start of each gig, it seemed Keith was the first ever white guitarist to combine volume, melody, rhythm and a death-wish in one seamless package. He looked classically wasted, and indeed was adding more heroin to his toxic mix. (At trial in 1978, Keith's lawyer would tell the Bench that his client had begun snorting the drug nine years earlier because he was 'exhausted', and was soon doing 2½ grams a day 'just to keep normal'.) He liked to chug Jack Daniel's and beer, quite often in the same glass. Keith was also building up a fearsome arsenal of guns and knives, projecting his most appealing stance – as a 'total fuckin' yobbo' who just happened to make exquisite music.

Mick Jagger also surpassed himself on tour: prancing on in a tall hat and a long scarf, he was a lithe, rippling sinew of a frontman who camped his way through most numbers. He also minced, swayed, frisked and primped, and there were long stretches in many songs when he did little else. When he chose to, of course, he could also be an extremely astute wheeler-dealer behind the scenes. 'That's when the Mick Jagger we know began,' notes a friend. 'After Brian died and Keith started getting tanked, Mick really took care of business.'

On 3 November, for the first time, Richard Nixon appealed publicly to the 'great silent majority of Americans' to support escalation in Vietnam. Riots promptly broke out in Washington and elsewhere. Four days later the Stones opened their tour at the State University in Fort Collins, Colorado. When, that same week, news broke of the massacre of South Vietnamese civilians in My Lai – Nixon maintaining that protesters had 'remained noticeably uncritical of Vietcong atrocities' – a virtual state of civil war existed. In Oakland the Stones were greeted with manifestos flung down from the rafters: 'We play your music in rock 'n roll marching bands as we tear down the jails and free the prisoners, as we tattoo BURN BABY BURN! on the bellies of the wardens and generals and create a new society from the ashes of our fires.'

Some of the protesters were later invited backstage. Keith hung on as long as he could, then excused himself by filling a pint mug of bourbon and chugging it in three or four monster gulps.

Jon Jaymes came in, dapper in his elastic-waist 'weekender' pants and loud shirt. He and a friend got Keith downstairs and safely into a car.

The Stones did twenty-three shows in all, not only setting a standard for power-rock hysteria but virtually introducing middle America to the blues. Their friend Terry Reid would be followed out by a rotating cast of B.B. King, Chuck Berry and the Ike & Tina Turner Revue. After a delay – milked, some felt, to build tension – Cutler's voice would boom over the p.a.: 'Now ... The greatest rock 'n roll band in the world ... the ROLLING STONES!' It was as if P.T. Barnum stalked the hall. Keith himself admitted being 'fucking embarrassed' by all the hype. The Stones were, however, the greatest track-jumpers in the world, swiftly adapting to their new audience. In 1966, many of Keith's fans had been delirious 11- and 12-year-olds, for whom pop music was a kind of hormonal gym. They worshipped the Stones, and wrote impassioned letters to the managers of hotels where the band had stayed. The height of their ambition was to be allowed to gaze reverently on their heroes' bed linen. By 1969, at least half of those venturing their $7.50 ticket money wanted to burn down the White House.

Keith: 'It had changed while we'd been off the road for three years. Now there's an audience who's listening to you instead of screaming chicks ... Instead of playing full blast to try and penetrate the audience, now we gotta learn to play onstage again. So for us it was like a school, that '69 tour.'

They got rave reviews in LA, particularly for the violent head show of Midnight Rambler. The song was so heavy, and wildly performed, several of the critics forgot themselves and the whole audience roared when Keith slashed out the riff. He was right: 'fucking wicked', that tune.

As the Stones crossed California by limo, the small towns' signs and clapped-out neon wheeled and fell away to reveal America's main visual drama, their own name, alongside a daubed 'NUKE HANOI' or 'PEACE'. There were two things you could safely say about the band by mid November. They'd be hours late on stage and, once there, they'd belt out red-hot versions of their last two albums. On the 18th they taped their sixth and final appearance on the *Ed Sullivan Show*. Sullivan moved his entire production to LA for the week, just to accommodate them. The Stones arrived wearing black leather and makeup, with, in Mick's case, a smudge of puce-red lipstick. Ed came out to the door in his undertaker's suit to greet them. Just then a car swerved across the street and there was a loud crunch of glass, a stuck horn.

'They're playing our song,' Keith told Sullivan, not missing a beat.

Whether in San Diego, Dallas or Chicago, Keith, said Stu, 'would traipse into a dumpy motel room and inside of ten minutes fix it'. The preferred look honoured distant roots in Dartford, crossed with a Moorish hash den: a world of ashtrays, bottles and darts boards, all shut in by velvet shawls and batik scarves flung over lamps. Terry Reid thought Keith 'the nicest guy on the tour. I mean, he used to worry about whether your laundry was getting done, or your room was OK.' Late one night Richards slipped on a wet pool surround and crashed to the ground, badly gashing his riff hand, turning his thumbnail blue, drawing horrified gasps from the entourage. 'I thought I'd do that,' Keith said calmly. A friend remembers him 'ringing home for hours every night . . . Anita would put Marlon by the phone and Keith would just *beam*.' The red-eyed junkie with a nose for coke, the proud family man enjoying his son: both were him.

Ninety thousand dollars for the tour struck Keith as 'a shitload of bread' for doing what came naturally.

New York, 27 November, Thanksgiving Day. The Stones held the stage at Madison Square Garden for three sold-out shows. Keith, in particularly high swagger, starts proceedings with Flash and Chuck Berry's Carol, and goes on from there to get raunchy. Swooping solos over a voodoo beat in Sympathy. Better yet, Rambler, with its multiple fake climaxes, Jagger whipping the deck with his studded belt. Everything ends in a gale of Keith chords, hoarse final shout – I'll stick my knife right down your *throat*! – and a whooping crash of cymbals. Mick: 'Charlie's good tonight, inne?' The whole joint threatens to come apart. Keith opens up the amps on Honky Tonk, everyone joining in the chorus, even Klein boogying out with his mop handle. Grown men gone, dancing on chairs. Keith's intro to Street Fighting acts as a sudden klaxon. The first twenty rows rise as one and beat time with raised arms and clenched fists, making the studio version seem almost polite. Jagger tosses a bowl of rose petals into the crowd, most of whom appear fit to riot. Backstage, the band's five steel-armoured black limos, the sound truck and the Garden's concrete walkways all bounce up and down. Keith: 'You could see the place actually rocking. That's the real turn-on. When the audience decides to *join*. That's when it really knocks you out.'

On their last night in New York, the Stones went uptown to help Jimi Hendrix celebrate his twenty-seventh and final birthday. Jagger snubbed Hendrix but stole his girlfriend, Devon Wilson. (At home in London, the black author–actress Marsha Hunt was pregnant with Mick's baby, and Marianne had bolted with one of Anita's exes Mario Schifano.) Keith left early and spent most of the night jamming with Charlie in a jazz club.

Playing to over 300,000 paying fans and grossing $2.2 million in a month, the Stones were now the biggest money-makers in the history of pop. They raked in more on their best nights than the Beatles had in a week. The income from two shows in LA alone was said to be $275,000. Intense and often heated meetings went on throughout the tour about where the Stones should shelter their take, a debate in which Keith took no part. Flying into the very last gig in Florida hopelessly late, the tour manager Ronnie Schneider allowed that 'maybe we should cancel – except we made the guy who's promoting it pay everything in front; we've already got the bread.' Keith looked at him straight-faced and said, 'Well, let's fly over and drop the money on the crowd.'

A day or two later, Keith found himself engaged in conversation with a middle-aged sales executive called Hank Fields on a flight to Atlanta.

Keith: 'I really think it's true that you can't do what you want to do. So many people aren't doing what they should.'

'Most of us do both,' Fields said. 'We do what we do, but we have to make money. It's a compromise.'

'But that's so sort of sad.'

'Well, the world isn't perfect.'

'No,' Keith said. 'The world *is* perfect.'

On 3–4 December the Stones moved into Muscle Shoals studio, a former coffin factory just off Highway 43 in northern Alabama. There they re-recorded You Gotta Move, Keith insisting the ailing Fred McDowell, living in poverty in Memphis, enjoy his full cut. As McDowell gratefully put it, 'Keith, he my boy.'

Next, Brown Sugar. The basic track sounded like a stock-car race involving Elvis, Bo Diddley and Marc Bolan, with a touch of Fred Cannon's hit Tallahassee Lassie, as channelled by Mick in the Australian bush. Keith added the acoustic sub-riff, then turned the whole thing back to front. A simple ruse; but by being played off, not on the beat, the song's hook would grab even tighter, irresistibly danceable. Keith's big raver would soon get its debut amid the blood and muck of a murder scene.

Lastly, Wild Horses, which Keith wrote 'because I was doing good at home with my old lady . . . and I gave it to Mick, and Marianne just ran off with this guy and he changed it all round.' (Keith knocked out a new chorus while in the bathroom at Muscle Shoals.) Faithfull would leave Schifano and fly back to Jagger as soon as she heard the song. Meanwhile, the Stones and their lawyers made plans, of a sort, for a free concert to be held at the Altamont Speedway, outside San Francisco.

5 December, *Let It Bleed*. The band's latest masterpiece began with a song about fear. Keith's open-G drone on Gimme Shelter set the tone for an album balancing ragged guitars against powerhouse melodies and apocalypse-now lyrics. Country Honk was the original, slide-and-fiddle workup of Honky Tonk Women, sandwiched between Dylan and Gram Parsons; Live With Me a shot of roadhouse blues, goosed by Bobby Keys' rasping sax. On the woozily laid-back You Got The Silver, Brian's posthumous riff lent ballast to Keith's engagingly nasal voice. Monkey Man, by contrast, started off smooth and silky and ended in a sound distressingly like Captain Beefheart being sick. The whole thing ratcheted up to a climax on You Can't Always Get What You Want, which proved Keith was still able to toss off terse pop hooks in the presence of a choir and an orchestra.

Let It Bleed was out a year to the day after *Beggars Banquet*, which followed a year after *Satanic Majesties*. But where *Banquet* seemed motivated less by adventure than by a canny retreat, *Bleed* was the great leap forward. Keith's music and Jagger's lyrics would be so widely studied, reinterpreted, sampled and stolen by so many artists, in so many different styles, that those forty-two minutes truly revolutionized pop.

6 December, Altamont. Stung by their right-on critics' complaints about 'exploiting black music' and 'ripping off kids', the Stones decided to say thank you with a free concert. Various locations around San Francisco were scouted out and rejected. At the last possible moment a businessman named Dick Carter offered his derelict stock-car circuit fifty miles east of town, in the dusty foothills of the Diablo mountains. In the rush to erect basic facilities such as a stage, no one gave much thought to the issues of sanitation, food, drink, parking, medical backup or security. Most of the parties involved would later agree that the show should never have gone on. But these were the Sixties, and this was Frisco, where anti-war protesters had gathered peacefully in their tens of thousands just the previous summer. The Stones agreed to appear.

What happened at Altamont that Saturday is history. When Keith flew in on inspection at three in the morning, he took one look and declared the scene 'groovy'. All the Stones later spoke of the sight. A single grey road wound across a high plateau, then up and down through scrub-covered hills, around a slope of forest to a dip where you could suddenly see the crowd, the queues, and, backstage, the red 'staff' T-shirts that darted like a shoal of tropical fish. Less visible, though all too obvious at ground level, were the fights. Officially, the crowd would eventually be put at 200,000. Thanks to gate-crashing and a complete breakdown in security, there were probably twice that many on site by the time the Stones performed sixteen hours later. The two-lane highway leading out of San Francisco up to the hills where the gig was looked like Dunkirk. All around, Altamont was littered with tents, trailers, fires, bin-liners and the wreckage of drugs. Stoned Hell's Angels wheeled their 'hogs' through nude hippies. The convoy of bikes churned up thick dust clouds as an eerie, crescent-shaped moon rose behind the mountains. Shadowy looking parties could be seen foraging for mushrooms. There was a powerful reek of pot in the air. Keith immediately took in this astonishing scene and decided to abandon his suite at the fancy Huntington hotel downtown. Instead he spent the night wandering about Altamont, where several fans affably shared their joints, and Keith in turn happily signed hundreds of autographs while crouched around desert campfires.

Now all that remained was the show, which did not go well.

The Stones had used the sensational success of their New York run as bargaining power in booking the best support-acts for Altamont. In the event, many of these would be no more than a sacrificial warm-up. Throughout the afternoon the Angels began abusing fans and musicians alike, spitting on and finally clubbing any nearby 'longhairs' who happened to cross them. Stage centre, a teenage girl was stabbed repeatedly with a sharpened pool cue. The Jefferson Airplane gave half their scheduled performance, their set truncated when Angels bludgeoned the singer Marty Balin unconscious. Parsons' new group, the Burritos, were followed out by Crosby, Stills and Nash, who scrubbed furiously at their guitars as if late for an engagement. The Angels themselves, some of them riding the tools of their trade through the crowd, were the next act. For an hour they flailed, fought, belched, spewed and spat. Heated debates erupted between bikers and fans. Soon scores of them had clambered up on stage, fists swinging, until, lest anybody out there still be wondering, Cutler explained: 'The reason we can't start is that nobody can fuckin' move ... I've done all I can.' More muttering, then the nuclear deterrent: 'The Stones won't come out until everybody gets off. *Everybody*.'

Darkness fell. Bill Wyman appeared from his hotel in San Francisco.

When the band eventually ran on, in a zap of blood-red light, they were accompanied by twenty-five to thirty Angels and at least one large, unleashed Alsatian sniffing menacingly at Keith's legs. 'Fellows,' Jagger kept muttering. 'Will you gimme some room? Will you move back, *please?*' Both the p.a. and the stage lights kept cutting in and out, the sky stabbed with green, mauve, red. Somehow they got through two numbers. 'Whoo, whoo! Ah, yeah!' Jagger swigged from a bottle of Jack Daniel's on the amp. The whole place was churning, Mick swinging his stripper's belt, and Keith let rip with Sympathy. As Jagger sang about Jesus and His moment of doubt and pain there was an explosion and a hole opened in the crowd. 'He-e-e-e-ey ... Keith – Keith – *Keith!*' Jagger's voice rose in counterpoint to the music, proving that Keith wasn't easily deterred from a good riff. 'Will you cool it and I'll try and stop it.' Keith unstrapped his guitar. 'Sisters,' said Jagger. 'Brothers and sisters ... Come *on*, now ... That means everybody cool *out*. Just be cool now, come on ...'

'Somebody's bike blew up, man.'

'I know. I'm hip. Everybody be cool now, come on ... Can everybody just ... I don't know what happened, I couldn't see ... Everyone just cool down ... Is there anyone who's hurt? ... Good ... We can groove ... Something very funny happens when we start that number.'

Next a 200-pound naked girl, pinned in the red and green spots, lumbered on to the stage. 'Fellows,' Jagger enquired, 'surely *one* of you can handle her?' An Angel duly rendered the girl senseless. Keith got the guitar going and Mick again sang about being Lucifer, in need of some restraint. This roused an Angel to try and physically cut a switch sending 500,000 watts of power to the stage, while jostling a fan with his free hand; at one point he actually flicked the lever for a second, causing Jagger's orgasmic howl to end in a drone. 'Who ... who ... I mean, like people, who's fighting and what for? Hey, people ... I mean, who's fighting and what for? Why are we fighting? I mean, like ... every other scene has been cool ... Like we're—'

'Either those cats cool it,' Richards snapped. 'Or we don't play.'

Everybody looked at Keith, fell silent. Seizing his moment, Stu, as ever the voice of reason, took the mike and appealed for help. 'Can you let the doctor go through, please? ... We have also ... lost in the front here a little girl who's five years old.' 'Play cool-out music,' Keith told the Stones.

Jagger started clicking his fingers, his feet tapping with them, teeth blazing in a wide grin. No one in the crowd seemed to smile back. Keith stretched the notes and slowed the tempo, keeping everyone focused on

Love In Vain. 'Aw yeah,' Mick said as the song ended. 'Hey, I think . . . there was one good idea came out of that number . . . which was . . . I really think the only way you're gonna keep yourself cool is to *sit down*. If everybody, ah . . . we gonna do, we gonna do, uh . . . *what* we gonna do?'

Keith kicked back in, playing the riff of Under My Thumb as the audience suddenly seemed to start, heads turning, bug-eyed, right in front of him. They froze thus for several seconds, then a black man in a green suit went down under a swarm of Angels. Someone let out a wild scream. People began waving bloodstained hands at the Stones, whose song ended in a high-pitched whistle. Jagger cupped an ear, shielded his eyes in the lights, pleading: 'Now there's one thing we need . . . Sam, an ambulance . . . a doctor by that scaffold there, if there's a doctor can he go there. OK, we gonna, we gonna do . . . I don't know what the fuck we gonna do. Everybody just sit down. Keep cool. Let's just relax . . . get into a groove . . . Come on . . . We can get it together. Come *on*.'

The man in the green suit, Meredith Hunter, died later of multiple stab wounds. According to an eye-witness, Paul Cox, 'An Angel kept looking over at me and I tried to ignore him, because . . . he kept trying to cause a fight . . . Next thing I know, he's hassling this Negro boy . . . The boy yanked away, and when he yanked away, next thing I know he was flying in the air, right on the ground . . . He scrambled to his feet, backing up and trying to run from the Angels . . . and his girlfriend was screaming at him not to shoot, because he pulled out a gun . . . And then some Angel snuck up from right out of the crowd and leapt up and brought this knife down in his back.'

According to Paul Cox, Hunter's last audible words were, 'I wasn't going to shoot you.'

The Stones finished Under My Thumb, then blithely debuted their new stomper about drugs 'n pussy, Brown Sugar. The rest of the show passed without event. By Honky Tonk Women Jagger was up and jiving again. 'Well, there's been a few hangups . . . yes . . . but generally . . . I mean, you've been beautiful . . . groovy.' He started Street Fighting Man with his back to the crowd, then wheeled to face it, yelling, '*Everywhere I hear the sound of marching, charging feeeet, boy* . . .' Half a mile away the kids on the hill were dancing, and Jagger was setting the pace, pelvis swivelling, arms flapping, strutting back and forth in time with the beat. 'We're gonna kiss you goodbye,' Mick trilled. 'Bye bye. Bye-by-y-y-y-e-bye.' The drums crashed, the rose petals fell, the Stones fled.

* * *

This is the tidy version of events – the rock critic's summary, trying to make order out of chaos. But elsewhere at Altamont, for both the Stones and their fans, the reality of the 'peace-in' was equally dire, mainly due to the bungled advance work.

The overall setup was a fiasco, with the stage built too low and a sound system that cut in and out. Keith wisely lowered the volume for the 'cool-out music', and everything worked perfectly for ten minutes. He then fired up the amps on Under My Thumb, and the result was the same squawk a plastic toy makes when somebody steps on it.

Stu, ever the thoughtful core of the Stones party, was the nearest thing to an authority figure at Altamont. Having never trusted suits, never liked officialdom and having never believed a cop since February 1967, Keith was if anything a passive anarchist who wanted all law, bar tribal, out of his life. He was a party to the disastrous decision to self-police the show – although, contrary to legend, the Stones never 'hired' the Hell's Angels as muscle in exchange for $500-worth of beer. Altamont had no organized security at all; just roadies shouting to 'get off the fucking stage', and the bikers, with the pool cues, up there braining fans.

There were over 300 injuries and serious ODs on the day, with four deaths: one lynched, two run over by a car as they dozed in sleeping bags, one drowned in a sewer. (Contrary to another myth, nobody gave birth.) The lawsuits began almost immediately, and would rumble on for years. When the Stones next toured America in 1972 there were ugly backstage scenes as bailiffs tried to serve writs at the door of the band's dressing room. The whole sorry performance was filmed, and later released as *Gimme Shelter*. Co-directors David and Al Maysles gave their picture a stylishly dark and moody look, and the effect was more reflective and dreamlike than stark and gory. Some of the best footage was shot by George Lucas, later of *Star Wars* fame.

When the Stones' set ended that night they and their crew ran for their helicopter like fugitives from an invasion. There were fifteen crammed into a passenger cabin built for eight. With a puff of smoke the craft limped off eastward between crags and hills, then slowly doubled back towards San Francisco. It tilted over the concert site, passing immediately above the stage, now bathed in a sulphurous glow. Gazing down on the whole folly, Keith turned away, livid, and started cursing.

'They're sick, man, sick. Some people just aren't ready.'

'I'd rather have had cops,' Jagger said.

The Stones would soon take severe flak for their role at Altamont. Much of the press was hostile and, in a book-length feature, *Rolling Stone* placed the blame squarely on its namesakes. David Crosby: 'the big mistake was taking what was essentially a party and turning it into a star game ... [the Stones] are on a grotesque, negative ego trip, especially the two leaders.'

Jagger would go on to stress his own helplessness in the teeth of the giant forces that overwhelmed him. 'You expected everyone in San Francisco ... because they were so mellow and nice and organized, that it was going to be all those things ... But of course it wasn't.' It also, he notes, 'taught [the Stones] never to do anything we're not on top of. Ever.'

While Jagger flew to Switzerland to bank the swag, Keith went straight home to London. Anita, Marlon and several journalists were waiting for him at Heathrow. The tabloids were saying that the Home Office might deport Pallenberg, as an Italian citizen, unless she and Keith got married. Anita played the occasion to the hilt, holding the baby up for the photographers and crying, 'Keith! Keith! They're throwing me out of the country!'

The Stones gave four, hassle-free concerts at London theatres, then split up for the Christmas holiday. Ten years earlier, 'Ricky' Richards had rung in the Sixties slumped on the stairs at Spielman Road with his cheap Rosetti's guitar. Now the Human Riff went back to his Chelsea mansion. That he'd enriched the decade with the melodic snarl of his music – purer than any of his leaden imitators could manage – was beyond debate. But, for him, money and power were balanced by the realization that it was 'fucking heavy' being Keith Richards.

'What are you gonna do?' the reporters had bawled at Heathrow, as Anita sobbed loudly on his shoulder.

'We'll get it sorted,' Keith said, hugging Marlon, 'but first I've got to get some rest.'

5

Tropical Disease

'ALTAMONT KILLED THE SIXTIES. It killed the Stones. It turned them into a circus act and Keith into a freak' was, more or less, a consensus. Not surprisingly, Keith had little time for it. To him, Altamont was 'just another gig where I had to leave fast'. Maybe nobody saw rock music as a tool of the revolution any more; no one expected it to change the world – but then, Keith never had.

The new decade did, however, ring in a whole series of changes and departures for the Stones. They tore up the blueprint and went for a sound that was raw and rootsy, but also evinced a campy irreverence. Many of their Seventies gigs were like looking through the pinhole of a scenic souvenir charm at some pink-suited Apollo revue, Keith trotting out the funk while the star, the James Brown, prowled the stage, barking, 'I can't git. No! Hey, hey, hey.' Closer to home, Keith parted with Tom Keylock but retained the services of 'Spanish Tony' Sanchez. This wasn't conducive to a sense of stability or order. When Keith's emotions flared, he occasionally lobbed things at Sanchez, who at first picked them up quietly. Over the next five years, however, the balance of power shifted. By the mid-Seventies, Spanish Tony would get tetchy, shout at his boss, 'You buy your own dope' then take off in his Alfa Romeo until both he and Keith cooled down.

With the exception of Marlon, Sanchez would be the closest thing Richards had to a best friend. Like Keith, members of his clan typically had a sturdy humanity that was the result of having weathered hard times. They understood and overlooked Keith's flashes of belligerence because they knew that, if necessary, he'd defend them with the same zeal with which he attacked. Even so, Keylock would be sorely missed. Without him, Richards was well on his way to becoming the sort of rock 'n roll burnout he'd always despised.

Tom Keylock: 'Keith turned into Brian, and Mick took over the Stones.'

In early January 1970, Tom handed back his master key to Redlands and Cheyne Walk, which Keith passed to Spanish Tony. There couldn't have been a greater contrast between the old and new guards. Keylock, thickset, middle aged and cheerful, was fanatically loyal and well liked by both Keith and the band. Sanchez was gnarled, swarthy, malnourished and powerfully fixed in the drug world. Stu would say that Spanish Tony was 'an outstanding hustler, no great brain'. This was a mild criticism. Another visitor to Redlands at the time found Keith 'like a corpse only being kept alive by maggots'.

Mick Jagger says that to the degree he considered Keith's drug problem, it was as a hassle – 'he was still creative but it took a long time'. Richards and Bill Wyman stopped talking to each other for the next ten years. Charlie was friendly but passive, and Mick Taylor never said much to anyone.

One early morning at Redlands, 'Jumpin' Jack' Dyer appeared at the french window to confer with Keith. Richards chatted affably to his elderly gardener while a friend hovered behind, in the living room, with a smirk plastered on his face. Keith was holding a huge horse syringe concealed behind his back. After Dyer padded off towards the moat, Richards turned and plunged the needle into his forearm. Then he injected the contents slowly, with a slight sigh. 'Shoot it right into the muscle,' he said, then burped. 'No tracks, y'know.' The young woman with Keith's friend turned pale and had to lie down on some cushions.

That spring, the Stones began editing their New York concert tapes and cutting tracks at Stargroves, Jagger's crumbling Elizabethan pile outside Newbury, Berkshire. Stu parked the new mobile unit in the gravel forecourt, threaded dozens of cables into the front hall, and everyone plugged in against a backdrop of musty chandeliers and coats of arms. Keith's amp was set up inside an antique bay window. Bitch and Sway were the first two songs cut in these ducal surroundings. Late one night Keith strummed the moody chords to The Japanese Thing, which became Moonlight Mile. Six months later, he was too stoned to make it to the actual Mile session, which the two Micks put together at Olympic.

On 30 July the Stones formally announced that they'd terminated their contract with Allen Klein, who therefore had 'no authority to negotiate' on their behalf. Two years of bitter litigation followed. In 1971 the band sued for $30 million back pay, alleging Klein had used his position for 'his own personal profit and advantage'. Eventually they dropped this part of their claim, and Klein wound up with the rights to all Richards–Jagger songs through *Let It Bleed*. On 9 May 1972, the Stones confirmed 'settlement of all outstanding difficulties' after thirty-six hours of continuous haggling in a New York lawyer's office. The bottom-line, Jagger told the press, 'is that Allen Klein never has anything else to do with us'.

Those five years together evidently cured the Stones of the need for full-time management. Rupert Loewenstein would smoothly assume control of the band's investments, which by 1973–4 were seriously in the money. But the good-natured prince was there to make the Stones millionaires, not to run the albums and tours. He was Gerald Ford during that first impeachment summer, declaring that 'our long national nightmare is over'.

Keith positively loathed business meetings, whether with Prince Rupert or anyone else. He solved the problem by rarely turning up to them, and even then falling asleep. Keith's hard-won signature on a contract, when it came to that, would induce paroxysms of gratitude in Jagger. He'd repeatedly try to express how much 'Rupe' meant to them all, but Mick tripped over his words in a profound embarrassment that masked another, related point – his bewilderment at Richards 'not giving a toss'.

Keith: 'I'm only forced to become [a] suit for short periods of time. Once a year I go through the little folder. This has come in, this has gone out, this is a projection of next year. And then I wonder why the fuck I read it anyway, because it hasn't made the slightest bit of difference to my day, or the next day. What's important is that I keep on doing what I do, not how much money it's making ... As long as there's enough bread to pay for guitar strings and food and a roof over the head, you can keep going and that's all that counts.'

The Stones' hated contract with Decca also came to term in 1970. For six months every major label courted the band, who nearly joined Elvis at RCA. At the last moment a sinister parking lot- and mortuary-based concern called Kinney Group, parent company of Atlantic, came through with a $5.7 million distribution deal. (The albums would actually be released on a vanity label called Rolling Stones Records.) Keith did sprinkle around some words of praise for Atlantic. He credited them with discovering Ray Charles, referred to their boss Ahmet Ertegün as hep and agreed they were way, way better than the wankers at Decca. But the friendly sound bites were often preludes to old gripes about selling out.

'The job of the record company is to distribute. All they've got to do is put [the] fucker in the shops, not dictate to anyone what to do.'

The new deal got under way when the Stones hired Marshall Chess, the man who'd sent Mike Jagger his prize Chuck Berry albums from Chicago ten years before, as their label's president. Keith and Mick came up with the famous trademark, inspired by the Thug goddess Kali and actually drawn by one John Pasche. Pasche was paid his standard design fee, fifty guineas. That tongue logo, slavering in a cunnilingual leer, would quickly become as well known and well nigh as universal as the Nike tick. Jagger also decided to give all the band's albums the serial letters COC, until 1978, at which point he opted for CUN.

The writer Stanley Booth, who travelled with the Stones in America and published a classic book about the experience, spent much of 1970 living at Redlands. Along the way Booth would acquire a nearly full set of Keith-satellite accessories, including a long-term drug habit. Richards generously shared with his guest the fruits of doing business with legally registered addicts. 'My thing with dope,' Keith explained, '[is] like on the connoisseur level. When I found coke and heroin, it was pure shit handed out by the government. I'd buy it from junkies that they gave it to.'

By common agreement, Keith never pushed the stuff on Booth or anyone else.

Richards occasionally roused himself to drive the now Purple Lena around town, once ramming the car at speed into his garden shed. He made it to most, though not all, of the *Sticky Fingers* sessions. There was always, even at Keith's nadir, what the critics would call the creative imperative. He was strumming his guitar throughout, and a tape recorder was always rolling. His daily routine took place amid a welter of cables, amps, effects boxes, microphones and gigantic feedback.

Nonetheless, the essence of the act involved Keith taking drugs and then nodding off, quite often in his bathroom. He could pursue several interests there at once. Like so many rock stars, Keith was both a voracious reader of Russian and French literature, which he consumed in cabinet, and a natural recluse. 'I felt I had to protect Keith,' Anita says. 'He was flying so high in the music world. He couldn't recognize a face or anything. He sat for hours and hours in the bog. And then when evening came he just got very nervous and didn't know what to do with himself, basically, because he had this routine of being on stage. It was very hard for him.'

Anita herself was progressing from kittenish beauty to a kohl-ringed blur, already badly hooked. The Richards family became a strange, late-night crew, hermetically sealed off from the world, yet like many others of their kind: passionate about dope, casual about everything else. Not much intruded on Keith's reserve. Brian Jones's cat Valentino and a large framed picture of Brian himself were both moved into Redlands. Anita seemed unperturbed, and even proud of Keith's reaction to these souvenirs. 'There's something very sweet about him,' she insisted.

Perhaps twice a year Keith would fly to LA, call Gram Parsons and then take off into the Mojave desert. They'd make camp, squat around a fire and, as Keith said, 'fry a few brain cells – Gram [got] better coke than the Mafia'. It was one of the perks of the job, to just tool off and watch the light changing in the valley below, when the smoke from the fire slowly blotted out the horizon. There was always a moment when all that was left was the faint smudge of Hollywood and a dull glow from the throb of distant TV transmitters. The buildings themselves were no longer there, and eventually even the mountains went. That was when Keith might light one of his special fat cigarettes, stretch out and start telling stories about Dartford. More especially, about Bert.

Then silence.

Marshall Chess, who moved into Keith's house on Cheyne Walk, always felt Richards was the one who didn't take his image seriously. 'If the Stones finish tomorrow, Keith would still be Keith. He'll always be the way he was; he'll never change. He may have more money, more drugs, more whatever, but he'll always be Keith and his favourite meal will be bacon and eggs with brown sauce. He's the constant factor.' Keith knew what he knew. He knew who he was. And that doubtless was what kept him sane.

What truly shocked people about him wasn't so much the dope as the sheer, unaffected normality that somehow survived. Keith remained 'a solidly English guy'. He really did like brown sauce. None of Doris's middle-aged friends in Dartford ever had a bad word for him. Several travelling companions of Keith's say they found him 'shy' and 'polite' around older blues musicians. The first thing Richards did after Altamont was to write to Stu telling him that the Reverend Robert Wilkins (whose Prodigal Son he covered on *Banquet*) needed a new guitar, and that if Stu could order one he, Keith, would pay for it.

From 2 September the Stones toured Europe. Keith took Anita and Marlon along, and bonded with the rollicking, good ol' Texan boy Bobby Keys. Keys' tenor sax would hop up many a Keith composition, most famously Brown Sugar. It's probably going too far to call them, as one Keith watcher has, drug brothers – going too far, but not going in totally the wrong direction. Apart from the fact that Richards and Keys were born on the same day, there was their shared love of the razor and the mirror. A certain 007 ingenuity, a hollowed-out pen concealing two grams of coke, would be as much a part of the tour as a certain musical genius of a time gone by. There was also the fake shaving-cream can, and the false bottom built into Keith's amp. When the dope ran low, the Stones had the local promoter go out and hustle some more.

Paris, 22 September 1970. Marianne Faithfull had left Jagger, and he met an olive-skinned beauty with high cheekbones, named Bianca. She was twenty-six, calling herself twenty-one, not that big on rock and roll. Bianca was given a warm cocaine welcome to the tour, and Mick soon flew her back with him to London. At Heathrow she assured reporters that the couple were 'just good friends', adding 'I 'ave no name. I speak no English.' In a semi-daze, Jagger wandered around telling everyone that, this time, he'd 'really fallen'.

Anita hated her on sight. Keith was civil, but even he soon felt the chill: 'I think Bianca had a bigger negative influence on Mick than anyone would have thought possible. She stopped certain possibilities of us writing together because it happens in bursts; it's not a steady thing. It made it a lot more difficult to write together, and a lot more difficult to hang out.'

Back at the studio, meanwhile, Jimmy Miller was doing his best to patch together *Sticky Fingers*.

None of the sessions ever seemed to go as planned, and, without Jagger's driving focus and ambition, the album would probably have been scrapped. As it was, it came close. For long stretches, back at Stargroves, the Stones were forced to live on 'junkie time'. If a session was called for midnight, Keith would typically stroll in around three in the morning. Several colleagues noted that even Jagger would down tools, if the phrase weren't so inappropriate, when Bianca showed. 'Suddenly,' said Stu, 'there were days when Mick disappeared upstairs.'

Meantime, Keith and Glyn Johns had edited the New York concert tapes, reluctantly – in a final row with Decca – doing without the B.B. King and Chuck Berry contributions. Such was the promise and letdown of *Get Yer Ya-Ya's Out!* Even as a single album, it was a glorious throwback to the days when the Stones were a two-fisted band, Keith and Mick Taylor playing solos like bolts of static. Midnight Rambler swaggered with funky guitar accompanied by Jagger's harp breaks. The retooled Love In Vain was equally snappy, yet out-bluesed Robert Johnson. Little Queenie strutted along with its good-time riffs and licks as tight as Keith's gaucho pants. Caught in its campy prime was Jagger's inimitable stage shtick and the band's deft wedding of arena rock and punk attitude.

Whatever 'ya-ya's' actually meant (a voodoo chant, apparently) wasn't explained, but the music steamed like summer asphalt. It went straight to number one.

Sticky Fingers was now about halfway finished, and the band could hardly bring themselves to speak to one another. Keith was paying Spanish Tony a steady £100 a week for doing little more than getting stoned with him and supplying the word *Right!* to his various complaints. Anita's own gripes about Keith – that he largely ignored her, body and soul – were an open secret among friends. To general dismay, Jagger was already planning to marry Bianca. Mick Taylor's own honeymoon with the Stones was well and truly over. Though no longer a salaried flunkey, none of his guitar embellishments on *Fingers* would earn him a writing credit. His help was freely given, but he was naive enough to have apparently hoped for some formal recognition. 'I don't get paid for some of the biggest selling records of all time,' he'd say years later. 'Frankly, I was ripped off.' Taylor, who went into the Stones a macrobiotic health nut, would leave them as a heroin user. Watts and Wyman chugged along, in Bill's case bitterly resentful about money. The various Klein lawsuits flew between London and New York. In San Francisco, both the Hell's Angels and the local press made it known that they, too, blamed the Stones. One last thing: Rupert Loewenstein was telling everybody that the Inland Revenue was after them, and they had to emigrate.

'I ain't going.' So said Keith from the start, when the prince explained it all. The Stones had to leave Britain by 5 April 1971 in order to escape a crippling tax bill for the year 1969–70. Keith dug his heels in, livid at being 'kicked out', and at the grim report Loewenstein gave him. So much of the band's money had gone astray, there was a serious risk of their being forced to declare bankruptcy.

Eventually, though, Keith's tone changed. He began to envision life beyond England: his own gaff on the Riviera – that was his dream. But the nearer his departure came, the more contemptuous he grew of the suits and 'fuckwits' of HM Government.

Keith: 'I think the reason we got forced out was they realized it was pointless. They were showing their own weakness, a country that's been running a thousand years worried about two herberts with guitars and a singer. Do me a favour! They started to look bad. Specially when they hit John Lennon. After they'd given him an MBE, they tried to bust him! That's when you realize how fragile our little society is. But the government allowed that fragility to show. They let us look under their skirts – ooh, just another pussy. To me there was no choice. I'd rather fuck off.'

On 18 December, his twenty-seventh birthday, Keith finished *Sticky Fingers*, gathered up his copy of *Physician's Desk Reference* and walked down the hall to the party room. George Harrison and Eric Clapton came, everyone got high and, soon enough, while the tapes rolled, Clapton hit the riff of Brown Sugar. Keith was zinging along playing breaks and fills nobody had ever heard before. When Bobby Keys nailed the sax solo, the whole joint was rocking. Stu later said it 'blew us away', but, for 'political reasons', the original version of the song would be the one released.

By now Jagger was sufficiently worried about Keith to consult the London-based author William Burroughs, an expert on junk. Burroughs recommended a no-nonsense Scottish nurse known as Smitty, who used the drug Apomorphine to bring about a painful but relatively quick withdrawal. After three days locked in Redlands retching and seeing bats, Keith pronounced himself cured. The very next afternoon Gram Parsons arrived from LA, introducing Richards to the heroin–cocaine speedball. This sorry lapse from Smitty's regime was followed by Keith's nodding off at the wheel of the Bentley, plunging the Lena through an iron fence and into the middle of a traffic island. The front of the car was completely crushed, with steam pouring out of the burst radiator – though, even as Richards legged it over a nearby wall, the sound system continued to blast out Brown Sugar. Keith had Spanish Tony pick up a fluorescent red E-type Jag as a replacement.

On 4 March the Stones began a short, pre-exile tour of Britain. It went ahead in a strange, often ugly atmosphere. The *Telegraph* chided the band for whom 'personal taxation advantage' appeared to be the sole factor. Several papers claimed the Stones' songs had grossed £83 million in seven years, and Jagger and Richards took out a full-page ad claiming they were nearly broke. (As it happened, Keith banked a cheque for $805,629 that same week.) 'Junkie time' now extended to the road, and there were boos and catcalls most nights as the Stones' fans awaited them. On 12 March, Keith managed to miss his train from London to a gig in Liverpool. A private jet, hurriedly chartered for him at Heathrow, broke down on the runway. A second plane was then summoned, and also broke down. Keith, Anita, Marlon and their puppy Boogie finally arrived at the theatre two hours after the band had been due on stage.

The shows themselves were sloppy at best, though not without a ragged charm. In their better moments, the Stones' ramshackle act suggested the early Faces, with much the same theatrics. The raveup came at the very end, when Richards tore into Brown Sugar and Chuck Berry's Let It Rock. Keith's chugging guitar sucked the audience out of their seats, the bedenimed crowds going into a synchronized boogie. Mick Jagger, not for the last time, took the role of a power-aerobics instructor.

The tour ended with a televised gig at the Marquee, the same venue as in 1962, the same manager uttering the same misgivings about Keith's playing. It was tactless of Harold Pendleton to insist on installing a bright neon sign, MARQUEE CLUB, directly above the Stones; more so to mutter audibly 'still shit' behind their backs. History repeated itself when Keith swung his guitar at Pendleton's head, before being dragged backwards, still seething, by Mick and Charlie. Heated discussions followed, Keith screaming some more and Jagger loudly demanding that the club be cleared before the Stones performed. Various managers and TV executives debated the wisdom of this for hours. When Perrin eventually gave the order the audience stumbled out, looking dazed and utterly exhausted.

'The Rolling Stones Farewell Special' was never aired.

Keith tried another cure shortly after that, and Anita checked into a private clinic in north London called Bowden House. Richards was considered to be in partial recovery, but he remained expressionless, as slack as a rag doll, on the day Stu arrived to move everyone across the Channel. As guitars and clothes were loaded into a van Keith stared at a spot on the wall, hardly moving except to repeatedly brush his shaggy hair from his forehead.

Around the third day in France, Keith and Anita began using again. Through a Bill Burroughs connection, two Marseilles dealers arrived at the door, 'perspiring profusely in their Daks lightweight suits and carrying identical black fibreglass executive attaché cases'. The bags contained two pounds of pure Thai heroin.

Richards and his entourage settled into Nellcôte, an exotic, mock Roman villa perched on a clifftop overlooking Cap Ferrat. The house's original owner, a British admiral, had thrown himself off the back balcony to his death. Keith loved the place, with its cool, tiled floors and frescoed ceilings. A guest would remember Nellcôte as 'a Scott Fitzgerald fantasy, ten people for lunch ... fifteen for dinner'. It was one of the best fixed mansions on the Riviera, combining pomp with surreal touches like clouds painted on walls. There were extensive gardens where palm and fig trees, and musky lavender bushes, blew about in the sea breeze. Along with his new E-type, Keith soon bought a powerful Riva speedboat and a schooner he named *Mandrax*.

6 April 1971. The Stones cruised into Cannes to formally sign their new, four-year deal with Kinney–Atlantic. There was a celebration that night at the Carlton hotel. Scantily clad guests were soon jumping on the dais where a band played, peeling their tops off, bumping and writhing against one another. One teenager strutted across stage, pumping her arms in a homage to Jagger's famous 'rooster on acid' dance, which he'd first trotted out when she was in primary school. Mick himself was mobbed by photographers, much taken by his pink satin suit and the pregnant Bianca's low-slung blouse.

Keith left early. 'I have to find my dog,' he said. 'He's my only friend at the party, man.'

Sticky Fingers. Even without the bulging crotch on the front cover, these forty-five minutes would capture the debauched essence of the Stones in all their fucked-up, Seventies glory. The album is soaked in sex, drugs and rock 'n roll. Teaming up once again with Jimmy Miller, Keith is more successful on this outing than ever before in translating the rude energy of the live act to the studio. The Stones also jump a few borders, slipping in some gentle country and soul grooves, not to mention a nod to

Carlos Santana, among the dirtier guitar slashes. Similarly, *Fingers* knows no lyrical bounds: everything is game, from social commentary to dope – 'cocaine eyes', 'speed freak jive', 'head full of snow', 'needle and a spoon' – quite apart from the harrowing Sister Morphine. The true show-stopper is Keith's Wild Horses, one of the few tracks slower than a fleeing getaway car, with a chorus that's downright smoochy.

Brown Sugar, another frothy, open-G raveup, kicks off the album, Jagger's hot riff and a staple of classic-rock radio through eternity. Sway's bluesy languor gives way to Horses and the stripper beat of Can't You Hear Me Knocking, which swerves, halfway through, into a mariachi jam session. Side two opens with the Chuck Berry stomp of Bitch, then showcases Keith's little-known gift for understatement on I Got The Blues and Dead Flowers, a Stax and Nashville pastiche respectively. Those seeking evidence of Keith's continued brio as a junkie find it in the infectious swagger and panoramic breadth that makes *Fingers* the finest slab of white blues-rock for years; since, in fact, *Let It Bleed*. Too slick for traditionalists, perhaps, but a stone masterpiece for everyone else.

By midsummer, *Sticky Fingers* was number one in Britain, America and fourteen other markets.

Some Stones insiders found it a bit odd, though. Nine of the ten tracks were credited to Jagger/Richards, with no mention of Gram Parsons (Dead Flowers) or Mick Taylor (Moonlight Mile). Marianne Faithfull would lobby for a cut of Sister Morphine for years, a campaign decided in her favour when Keith intervened. Fully quarter of a century later, Jagger would complain that 'she did a couple of lines; she always says she did everything, though'. By 'a couple of lines' he presumably meant the lyrics Marianne had written in June 1968 and the Stones then kicked around with Ry Cooder. Ry himself played slide guitar on Morphine, and generally goosed the song along. Still no credits.

In early May, through Jo Bergman, Mick notified his family and seventy-five other guests (including Paul and Ringo, who were suing each other) that he was getting married. Attempts by Keith to dissuade him from his decision failed. By now Richards and Pallenberg could barely bring themselves to speak to Bianca, who was 'stuck up', 'a drag' and – as if there could be anything worse – 'the Yoko type'. Anita theorized that Bianca had had a sex change. Bianca referred to Anita as 'that cow'.

Jagger went down the aisle on 12 May at the small, whitewashed chapel of St Anne on a hill above St Tropez. The groom wore a cream three-piece suit, his bride a floppy hat and a white St Laurent jacket splayed to the nipples. Keith was the only one of the Stones invited. He arrived late, arguing furiously with Anita, and couldn't initially get through the scrum of fans, demonstrators and *Paris Match* reporters at the door. Pallenberg could tell that a few seconds of sharing a confined space with the mob was already imposing unbearable strain on his fragile PR sense. When Keith finally squeezed in, he threw an ashtray at the verger. The bride was then given away by the Queen's cousin Lord Lichfield. At Bianca's request the organist played snatches of Bach's Wedding March and, interminably, the theme from *Love Story*.

Later, back in the Hotel Byblos, Terry Reid and some of Jagger's other guests were changing for the reception.

'By and by we could hear a clanking noise growing ever louder, coming down the corridor towards us. Clanking and rattling; very weird. All of a sudden it stopped right outside. The door swung open, and everyone did a double take. A man stood on the threshold. He was in full Nazi uniform. He seemed to be standing to attention, all SS tunic, with an Iron Cross dangling round his neck, and black jackboots. It was Keith.'

'Hi guys,' he said.

The party that night took place in a private theatre at the Café des Arts. Celebrities embraced and grew ecstatic at the sight of one another as Terry Reid sang. Keith, still in his military garb, blacked out in a corner. Bianca danced once with sixty-year-old Joe Jagger, then left alone. Years later she gave it as her opinion that her marriage had ended on her wedding day.

After that, there was little to do but spend the summer at Nellcôte with Gram Parsons and a constantly shifting cast of friends, musicians and drug dealers. The house's formal salons were decorated with antique brocade chairs, and its floors inlaid with purple and white tile. White silk curtains flowed from the french windows, which offered a commanding view of hills almost obscenely bright with bougainvillaea. Down the twisting back steps lay a private beach. Keith himself rarely went there, preferring to lie in darkened rooms, toking and listening to thunderous Chuck Berry records. A cordon bleu chef served exquisite meals at all hours of the day and night. Keith drove him mad by asking for bangers and mash, with plenty of brown sauce.

Nellcôte cost Richards some £4,000 per week: £500 each on food and drink, £1,200 on rent and £1,800 on 'cotton candy', or pure heroin.

It was Keith's idea to record an album not in Paris or Nice but, by means of the mobile unit, in the cellar of his own home. Even though some early tracks had been cut at Olympic, and the final product was mixed in LA, *Exile on Main Street* duly became the greatest and most profitable rock and roll to ever emerge from a basement.

Stu and the truck arrived in early July, followed by the Stones and their crew. Bianca, by now heavily pregnant, hated the experience. Anita: 'She was really, like, totally self-absorbed, like she'd come to my house and disappear for four hours and do makeup and then have these airs and barely talk to anybody.' Keith ran the sessions whenever the Jaggers split for Paris, which was at least weekly throughout the summer.

Exile was cut in fetid, swelteringly hot conditions that Keith, characteristically, compared to Hitler's bunker. It was perhaps a tad less formal than that. Down among Nellcôte's extensive wine collection everyone sat around, shirtless and tipsy, while Keith riffed on the guitar. There was a constant fear, with all the dope and drinking, that at some critical moment he'd flake out. But such anxieties were also a tacit acknowledgement of the band's dependence on Keith. The two-take classic Rocks Off was further proof that he was still, unquestionably, the gaffer. Keith cooked the dinner; the Stones washed the dishes.

Rolling Stone featured a dazed-looking Keith on its cover that August, a major milestone down the road to his status as rock's 'most elegantly wasted' practitioner. Painfully thin, with a purple tongue and cracked lips, he struck even Bill Burroughs as 'fairly sick'. Keith posters began to appear in bedsits and JCRs the length and breadth of Britain. Virtually every biographical scrap was swept up and recycled into variants of the legend. Words like 'ghoul' and 'zombie' went round like drunks in a revolving door. One wag who interviewed Keith at Nellcôte reported 'he looks like a million dollars – green and wrinkled'.

To the *Exile* crew, Keith was the real thing, as a mate and a musician, even if his life did take its odd turns. Mostly these were dope related, such as the time he and Anita set their bed on fire. Stu, for one, was horrified at the sight of his old friend jacking up and then nodding off in the studio, snoring. By now Keith had livid bruises on his arm from all the skin-popping, and was obviously a stranger to the dentist. 'It was a bloody tragedy, really, him falling apart like he did.'

But the monster was also a model of hard work and creativity. Most afternoons Keith sat outside with his guitar, strumming and cracking his friends up with jokes about the Jaggers – 'royalty's having a baby'. The new riffs kept coming, Richards working with a core band of Watts, Mick Taylor and Bobby Keys. Fooling around one day before the rest of the Stones showed up, Keith, Taylor and Keys ripped off a hot song called *Happy*. Jimmy Miller remembered 'many mornings after great nights of recording, coming over to Keith's for lunch, and within a few minutes of seeing him, realizing something was wrong. He'd say, "Jagger's pissed off to Paris again." I sensed resentment because he felt we were starting to get something and when Mick returned the magic might be gone.'

Trust came naturally to Keith, who surrounded himself with people who started off as employees and ended up, instead, snorting his drugs. Playing host to twenty-five or thirty stoned musicians and friends, Nellcôte soon became the Riviera's answer to Graceland. Mick Jagger: 'Everyone was so out of it. And the engineers, the producers – all the people that were supposed to be organized – were worse than anybody.' When a guest did, eventually, lose it he was dealt with according to the law of Keith Richards. Gram Parsons spent weeks at Nellcôte strung out on coke and irritating Anita. This wouldn't do; Keith threw his best work friend out and made a new one in Bobby Keys.

Relations between Keith and the wider community were also rocky. One afternoon Richards got into a minor traffic accident in the nearby town of Beaulieu. The harbourmaster, one Jacques Raymond, wandered out of his office to investigate and Keith addressed him as a 'fuckin' idiot'. From this point on, things began to deteriorate rapidly. Keith pulled out a toy gun belonging to Marlon, and M Raymond drew his own very real revolver before calling the law. The Stones' handlers saved him on that occasion, and Keith later invited the local mayor over for dinner and a few autographed albums. But given the constant parade of stoned foreigners trooping in and out of Nellcôte, it was almost inevitable that the police would put the house under surveillance. Apparently they weren't yet at their posts early one Monday morning, when thieves broke in and stole eleven of Keith's guitars.

Exile ground on, with borrowed equipment, into the hottest September in Provence history. It was the last non-air conditioned album the Stones would ever make, and the temperature in Keith's crypt reached 110°F. By now the sessions were going under the working title of Tropical Disease. For the first time since Chastilian Road, Keith was effectively living over the shop – a boon when inspiration struck, but also a distraction. Like most DIY jobs, *Exile* had its snags. Keith would typically call everyone down to the basement around midnight, after a long dinner. Much as the Stones enjoyed the hospitality, it also wore them out. Almost as soon as the band started playing, Keith would saunter back upstairs, calling over his shoulder, 'Keep swingin', guys. I'm listenin'.' When everyone was dozing over their instruments four or five hours later they'd be jerked awake again by Keith announcing he'd 'put Marlon to bed' and was ready to work.

Unsurprisingly, the music that emerged was sludgy, chaotic and often tired sounding. It was also the Stones' greatest and most enduring moment. *Exile*'s raw power reinvented the way a classic album could sound, and ushered in several decades' worth of lo-fi knockoffs. To this day, every record that shuns studio polish for a rootsy, field-project approach draws comparison to Keith's masterpiece.

In late September, the local Nice tabloid ran three imaginative scoops about *affaires* on the Riviera, obliquely mentioning an expatriate pop star. 'Monsieur X', the paper helpfully called him, busy conducting some ghastly experiment down in the grotto-blue light: a rock Boris Karloff. Keith himself didn't read the press, but word about him got round. Back in England, Keith's mate Eric Clapton, bouncing between one crash cure and another for his own addiction, went to visit Nellcôte. This was roughly the equivalent, in junkie's terms, of a phoenix chasing an arsonist. A week of debauchery followed. Eric went back to his Surrey mansion and locked the door for the next two years.

The Fréjus police contacted the narcotics bureau about Keith's reported habits in early October. Worryingly, one of the Nellcôte staff was also spilling to *les flics*. When Richards picked up his phone, he was convinced he could hear someone breathing on the line.

The gendarmes thus discovered what the West Sussex force already knew. Keith was, more or less, a sitting target. From now on, he decided, *Exile* should be recorded at top speed 'before they sling us inside and throw away the key'.

With that, everyone made for the basement.

Jagger came back for a week, and it was clear that some of the Glimmer Twins' old warmth had cooled. Friends felt that there was something brewing: the set of Keith's mouth, his silence, something. Mick had finally exchanged cheek for *chic*, dressing like a Frenchman in his beret and tight suede maxicoat. 'I didn't have a very good time,' he noted. 'It was this communal thing, where you don't know whether you're recording or living or having dinner; you don't know when you're gonna sing – very difficult.'

To expedite things, the whole band moved into Nellcôte for the final sessions. One afternoon, Keith sent a secretary up to everyone's rooms to present the Stones with bills of £100 each for bed and board. Bill Wyman got so upset that he broke his vow of silence. 'It's a joke, isn't it?' he asked over the dinner table that night.

'No,' said Keith, with more than a hint of venom. 'You're getting accommodation dirt cheap at that price, and anyone who doesn't like it can piss off.'

The Stones paid up.

A young engineer working on *Exile* remembers seeing Keith lurch down the steps into the studio, which was mouldy and strung with hurricane lamps, for the first time. The whole place fell silent as he plugged in: the black shag of hair, sickly pallor and unsteady gait all gave the crew instant visual gratification. This was what they'd come to see. For the rest of the night, while the police listened in through a bug planted amongst his wine bottles, Keith rocked the joint, remaining at his post for eight hours and laying down rhythm on Good Time Woman, aka Tumbling Dice. What the law was enjoying, in a post hidden in the woods behind a sign saying *Chiens bizarres*, was a preview of the Stones' feisty new single.

In fact, many of *Exile*'s best songs worked in close connection with Keith's lifestyle. Happy celebrated the news that Anita, after suffering several miscarriages, was pregnant again. Tumbling Dice and Casino Boogie were influenced by the band's frequent excursions down the coast to Monte Carlo. Friends could almost hear the banished Gram Parsons on Sweet Virginia, like a musical phantom limb after an amputation. Likewise, Soul Survivor seethed with subversive energy and a riff that lingered long after it was over. Around dawn, Keith sat in Stu's truck parked upstairs and listened to a playback. He grinned when he heard the night's work and said, 'Mmm!' like someone tasting a candy bar in a commercial.

*　　*　　*

According to Anita, *Exile* was recorded with power diverted from the French railway system. Mostly, though, it drew its electrical charge from an interior source, the tension between Keith and Mick.

The Jaggers' daughter was born at a nursing home in Paris on Thursday 21 October. After prolonged discussion she was named Jade, because, said her father, 'she's precious and quite, quite perfect; she looks a little like Bianca and a lot like me'. Jagger phoned Keith that night to say that he wouldn't be coming back to Nellcôte. The band were to finish up the basic tracks and he, Mick, would lay down his vocals when *Exile* was mixed in Hollywood.

The contrast between the grim reality of the Glimmer Twins and the fantasy peddled to the press was bad enough, but even more distressing was Keith's fury at being 'jilted'. That Jagger was extremely possessive of his mate was plain to all their friends; he'd only to look at another collaborator, like Gram Parsons, for Mick to freak out. Jagger wanted Richards all to himself. But Bianca had made it clear that she regarded Keith, and the whole 'Nazi state', as rivals not to be tolerated.

Richards was speechless when Jagger phoned him that night. He kept working on *Exile* for the next two weeks, edgy at the growing police presence outside Nellcôte and gloomy at Mick's defection. A good case can be made for saying that he and Jagger would never be quite as close again. It was exactly ten years since the two teenagers had met up on the platform at Dartford station.

By early November, as *Exile* wound down, Nellcôte was beset on every front. The narcs were making their surveillance more obvious by the day. Burglars walked off with Keith's replacement guitars. A stoned Anita managed to set the couple's bed on fire. Dave, the chauffeur, broke down the door to find them lying there, comatose, with the mattress in flames all around them. Keith and Anita had dabbled with a variety of new drugs since moving to the Riviera, indeed considered them one of the perks, but, as Bill confirms, 'they were on a slippery slope'. The humidity generally remained unbearable, and Keith was lubricating himself with cases of Jack Daniel's. Stu had a presentiment of disaster. He wasn't alone. During the next fortnight, increasing fears of a bust led Keith to evict a gang of Marseilles coke dealers living in

Nellcôte's gatehouse; he also started making enquiries about moving to California.

The final straw came when Fat Jack, the Nellcôte chef, learnt that Anita had given his daughter heroin. Jack tried to blackmail Keith, who told him to fuck off. The gendarmes arrived the next morning, took statements, and asked why internationally known drug couriers had been seen wandering around the premises.

While Keith pondered that, the senior officer glanced up to find Anita scowling at him. The instant their eyes met they bounced apart again like billiard balls; he reported having felt a 'sudden chill'. Anita continued staring at the police, but none of them would look at her.

On 30 November, Keith, Anita, Marlon and most of the crew flew to America. Keith made a side trip to Nashville, where a guitar broker named Ted Newman-Jones replaced the entire collection of Gibsons, Strats and open G-tuned Teles stolen from Nellcôte. Newman-Jones was impressed at the way his famous client behaved exactly the same in public as in private: 'he's always Keith Richards'. The family then settled in for the winter at a rented home in the Hollywood hills.

Some doubt exists about what happened next. In one version, the French authorities had let Keith leave the country only on condition he continue to rent Nellcôte while he was away, as proof he meant to return. In another popular account, the local force were unaware their wrecked-looking prey had moved on.

Exactly two weeks later, on 14 December, a squad of twelve policemen rammed open the gate and poured into Nellcôte through the doors and windows. According to published reports, they turned up enough heroin, coke and hash there to throw the book at Keith and Anita. A maid told them that everybody had suddenly left one night, taking their canisters full of tape with them. Not a trace of *Exile* would be left behind, nor would a forwarding address.

Keith never actually returned to Nellcôte, but in spirit he did, two years later, when a court in Nice handed him a suspended sentence and a 5,000-franc fine for 'use, supply and traffic' in heroin and pot. The judge added another provision. It was meant as a punishment, but might well have been a relief to the couple whose dream life on the Riviera had quickly turned into a nightmare. Keith and Anita were both banned from France for two years.

* * *

The band's love–hate relationship with Brian Jones found its most public voice that winter, with the release on Rolling Stones Records of his posthumous *Joujouka* LP. Ironically, this was a whole new Brian. Recorded in August 1968, the album saw Jones setting aside his fucked-up rocker persona for the role of godfather to the World Music movement: *Joujouka* covered territory from meditative spaciness to full-bore freakout, sometimes in one tune.

When they got to LA, Jo Bergman sent Keith a copy of *Joujouka*, and he's said that it deeply touched him. Jones's epitaph deflated the old Popeye buoyancy to focus, instead, on a sense of love and loss. All the Stones sat down one night in Hollywood to listen to it, and were choked up at Brian's music. They wondered why they were so moved by something they couldn't understand.

Keith, Mick and the engineers spent most of the winter of 1971–2 at Sunset Sound, goosing Tropical Disease into *Exile*. Between them they took Keith's first drafts, picked them up and shook them inside out until they were as clean and crisp – though never starchy – as a freshly laundered sheet. The effect was to give a vital boost to the songs' foot-stomping potential. Horns and washes of pop-gospel hollering would flesh out Tumbling Dice, among others. Shine A Light got the full Billy Preston organ treatment, while Dr John tended to Let It Loose. Keith himself spent days buffing his Happy to a high gloss. Wyman apparently wanted nothing to do with any overdubbing, and would be credited on only eight of *Exile*'s eighteen finished tracks.

Instead, the great Indo-jazz pioneer Bill Plummer got a call one wet Monday night to report to Sunset Sound. He walked in and met the Rolling Stones.

'The words I'd choose would be cool and professional,' he says. 'Keith knew exactly what he wanted. I did four tracks in about two hours, shook everyone's hand, went home. There was a big crowd at the back door, I remember, and people were worried it was the Hell's Angels. Keith and Mick were being hassled by them.'

Bill Plummer's bass helped make *Exile* a major hit in both Britain and America. He was paid his standard fee, 'a couple of hundred bucks', for the session.

Keith also reconciled with Gram Parsons and his avocado mafia, as Gram fondly called them, who went on to form bands like the Eagles. At one point, there was renewed talk of the two men working on an album, but the start date kept slipping back. Eventually, Richards' interest seemed to pass from the active stage, leaving Gram to brood on the mysterious train – or trains – of Keith's thought. When other friends sympathized, which they did, Parsons would shrug, as if to say he'd expected no more. Even as he related the disappointing news, his voice never rose much above the matter-of-fact.

Something similar would happen between Keith and the Mamas & the Papas' John Phillips. Phillips was then living in a Hollywood mansion with his third wife and his 12-year-old daughter, Mackenzie. The decadent squalor of the place reminded Parsons of Nellcôte crossed with a particularly tacky branch of McDonald's. Mackenzie notes that there was all the junk food and TV she could ingest, no such thing as bedtime and regular visits from Keith, Mick and Gram, 'most of whom [I] wanted to shag'. (Her little girl's dream came true when, aged eighteen, she scored with Jagger.) Keith and Mick would regularly pledge to make John's comeback LP the focus of their lives, but again, in Phillips' words, 'the drugs could always fuck things up'. The warning was as well. Over the next ten years, delay was the norm and procrastination the rule. Eventually, the original project was shelved.

John Phillips: 'Mick reminded everyone of royalty. He had the same obsession with form, the same elusive quality. People took to calling him Liz behind his back.'

Also that winter, Keith and Mick managed to get themselves thrown offstage at a Chuck Berry concert. One of Berry's managers had waved them up and Keith tore into a loud Sweet Little Sixteen, accompanied by Mick's mad, martial dancing. The audience went nuts. Richards says, 'It developed into a little ego thing ... people were paying more attention to Chuck's band than they were to him.' Berry's own version is even stranger: 'I didn't know who they were.'

While the crowd enlightened him, Keith and Mick sank into a waiting black Cadillac. Then they were gone. Fast. Berry tried to shout through his microphone to catch them, but it was too late. Once snubbed, the Stones had no intention of going back onstage.

Up in the Hollywood hills, Keith began noticing 'funny things' that convinced him he was still being wire-tapped. He just didn't know by whom.

'We rented a place next to [Richards]', reports Dale Marr, a former FBI station chief. 'There were orders from Washington [and] we snuck a young girl in there to keep watch. Her ear was literally to the wall.' Within a few weeks of arriving, Keith and his family were already growing weary of California.

Back in April 1964, Keith had made his first visit outside Britain when, to plug Not Fade Away, the Stones taped a special *Ready Steady Go!* in Montreux. Everyone but Brian had marvelled at the sight of Lake Geneva. Lush vineyards dropped sharply down to the water, which was covered with a dove-blue haze. From his bedroom window Keith looked out over the town, with its steeply angled roofs, and a rich pasture grazed by cattle. Farm-workers went by the hotel and up the road and the dust they raised coated the leaves of the apple trees.

Eight years later, Keith now returned to this alpine idyll. Anita was heavily pregnant, and still fixing three times a day. Her gynaecologist warned her the health of her baby was being jeopardized, and recommended Dr Denber's discreet private clinic in Vevey. Keith and Marlon moved into a suite in the nearby Metropole. Vladimir Nabokov, author of *Lolita*, was living just upstairs, meaning that two of the century's more colourful artists were under the same Swiss hotel roof. Over the next few weeks, the place became an unlikely Rolling Stones commune as band and crew gathered to rehearse their next tour.

The Stones never forgot how they were treated in Montreux, where they could walk around the lake with their families and no one ever hassled them. The tax break didn't hurt, either.

Dandelion Richards was born, with a cleft palate but otherwise perfectly healthy, on 17 April 1972. Doris, who took over most day-to-day responsibility for her granddaughter, renamed her Angela. Nine months later, Keith would come up with the words and music of Angie in her honour.

Meanwhile, Anita and the baby joined Keith and Marlon in the Metropole.

Spanish Tony: 'Keith and I would take the children out for walks [while] Anita languished in solitary splendour, smoking her joints, jabbing needles in her bottom ... After three weeks ... there were empty bottles everywhere, fag burns on most of the mock Louis XIV furniture and the sheets were an uninviting shade of grey. The maids stuck with the onerous task of cleaning out the suite insisted on fumigation.'

Like Anita's, Keith's body was a human blender of toxic substances. He remained chained to the razor and the syringe, enjoyed a toke and a drink, and had recently discovered the heady effects of amyl nitrates – poppers. In May he went in for a cure of his own at the Vevey clinic. Two days after admission, the doctors were able to offer some tentative conclusions. They believed he had 'epic recuperative powers', and with three or four weeks' rest could leave Switzerland and resume light work. In fact, the doctors thought he'd be almost as good as new if he watched his diet and worked on a normal schedule – not for a brief period, but for the rest of his life.

Keith left the clinic a day later and began planning a forty-gig tour of America. He and Jagger quickly hit on a manager. A former organizer of May Balls at Cambridge, the faultlessly hip Peter Rudge, twenty-five, had gone on to run the Who. Rudge, whose duties had included identifying the body of Keith Moon's driver after Moon ran him over, wasn't a man easily shocked. The Stones swiftly hired him, as well as the best publicists and photographers. 'It wasn't fun,' Jo Bergman says. 'And it wasn't supposed to be. Be efficient, make money, and don't hurt anyone; that was the given system.'

This would lead to occasional friction with Keith, not a man who liked to be tucked up in bed early with a mug of Ovaltine. But he played his full part in planning the tour, and there was no doubt about his devotion to Marlon and Angela. Doris was also a frequent presence. 'She and Keith cackled about Dartford a lot,' says one of the tour's sixty-plus former employees.

May 1972. Twenty years before grunge, there was *Exile on Main Street*. The album's legacy will loom large over the whole history of rock and roll. Admittedly, Keith did give the original Tropical Disease tapes a Hollywood makeover, but *Exile*'s bluesy clatter still sounds like life itself. With Jimmy Miller threading horns, honky-tonk pianos and upright basses through the mix – and Jagger's vocals sounding as if they'd been recorded down a well – the LP resounded with rich echoes from the band's Crawdaddy Club past.

Rocks Off announced *Exile*'s intentions – Keith's riff raced by Charlie's neck-snapping beat – and then made the point with honks of sax, juggernaut rhythm and dimly moaned vocal interjections. (With lines like 'Ten liddle nigga/Sittin' on de wall' elsewhere on *Exile*, some tactical slurring was probably wise.) Richards and Jagger flexed their tag-team skills again on Rip This Joint, sung in a raspy burr and apparently accompanied by a vacuum cleaner. Keith's intro to All Down The Line was shrill, nutty, out of tune, a noise that managed to sound both tossed off and perfectly suited to the song. The Stones perpetrated an apparent publishing scam with Robert Johnson's Stop Breaking Down, which was credited (as Johnson's Love In Vain had been) to Trad, prompting allegations of piracy. The actual tune, for all its medieval-Delta charm, fell a few yards shy of epic. Shine A Light started like some churchy piano track, then built slowly through Mick T's scorching solo to climax in a massed-voice chorus. Even better was the ominous Soul Survivor, where Jimmy Miller cleared a space around Keith, showcasing his jagged riff. As usual on a Stones album, there wasn't much melody involved, but overall *Exile* packed the biggest guitar wallop since Satisfaction. And for the lyrically minded, there was also Turd On The Run.

Exile was raw, dense and arrestingly packaged; the filmmaker Robert Frank did the double LP's artwork, which mingled shots of circus freaks with the band, the one merging with the other. A few reviewers got tetchy, making it a point of honour to show their independence by carping. Keith earned himself some of the critical yappings and shin-bitings that invariably greet true class, while the fans sat up and bayed for him. Almost everyone agreed that his 'basement album' was well timed. The consensus was that, emerging from the anaemic pack of cod-soul, glam and ditties by Max Boyce, *Exile* was both retrograde and a catalytic blast of loud, electric rock. It went straight to number one.

Keith: 'I learnt to ski and I made *Exile* when I was heaviest into heroin. I would definitely not say it affected my ability to play.'

As the album was released Keith checked himself out of detox and began rehearsals with the Stones in the Montreux Rialto. Here some discrepancy exists between what Stu saw ('It was bloody tragic, him falling apart like he did') and Keith's own take ('I only ever [got] ill when I quit dope'). Towards the end of May he gave a few interviews to promote *Exile*. In private, Keith proved a charming mix of drug casualty, with a barely intelligible speech pattern, and south London geezer. All paternal pride, he said that with the new album, he'd 'give[n] a kick up the arse to Led Zep'.

On 22 May all five Stones were issued work permits at the US Embassy in London, and all five proceeded to miss their plane to Los Angeles. Rehearsals eventually continued on a sound stage at Warner Brothers, 'very larky' (Stu) in a postmodern, it's-only-rock-'n-roll way. Jagger was dressed in a scanty rhinestone catsuit with a pink sash.

The Stones settled with Allen Klein that month for $2 million, instead of the roughly $30 million the band had claimed. Bill, for one, was fuming. Asked for his own reaction, Keith would smile calmly and call Klein 'my higher education'.

'Don't take it so fucking personally,' Keith advised Wyman. 'It's only showbiz.'

A hectic schedule now began. Jagger's and Rudge's plan had been to release *Exile* in April, then hit half a dozen selected American cities in May and June. Long before then, there were clear signs that the original itinerary was far too modest. The album flew off the racks, while both Atlantic and Pacific Bells went into crisis mode to handle the band's phone bookings. In Chicago, whole families moved on to the street, sleeping under the Loop for nights on end, all on the mere rumour of tickets. In Detroit, the local agency fielded 140,000 applications in a day, more than for King Tut. Around New York, the going black-market rate was $200 for a $13 pair of seats. Soon the Stones were being plastered over the *Wall Street Journal* and their takes and yields debated like those of a blue-chip stock, which they now were. It was 'bank time', Jagger told Richards.

Keith found most of the hype extremely depressing. Once again, he was leaving Anita and their newborn baby to barnstorm America.

To a certain generation, the Stones' 1972 tour remains the ultimate in glam rock 'n roll junketing: the one with all the sex and dope and a documentary about it called *Cocksucker Blues*. A critic has written that 'for years afterwards, every kid – male and female – in every high school lunch room wanted to look like Keith Richards'. In one spectacular period in late July, Keith played a dozen riotous gigs, got busted for assault, took in an airborne orgy involving a film crew and two groupies, and found himself being serenaded by Muddy Waters at a New York bash graced by the likes of Zsa Zsa Gabor. Keith was criticized there for his 'aloofness' and his failure to schmooze sufficiently with the Beautiful People, whose parties he relished like a root canal. 'Right now,' he told a friend, 'is when you realize you're a product.'

The national media recycled several juicy rock-biz titbits about Keith, loosing a torrent of gossip and lively anticipation wherever he played. Early on, rumours swirled that he was high on a non-stop diet of tequila, that he rarely slept and that the Stones' private DC-7 – the Lapping Tongue – was a flying *Satyricon*. All true, but when 'the creeps' at a launch party pressed the point that Keith was also a hopeless zombie, who Rudge wheeled around in a cage, they got an earful.

'They don't give a crap how I look in Kansas,' Keith snapped. 'They're only interested in how I play.'

'How can you actually know, up in your jet?' a reporter asked him. Keith stared.

'I get out once in a while,' he said.

One way or another, the creeps continued to plague Keith throughout the tour. There would be several more scenes with journalists and photographers, most of whom learnt not to cross him.

Robert Greenfield, who wrote eloquently about Keith, remembered him deplaning that first night, 'wearing a black and white striped suit made out of silvered sailcloth that glowed in the dark. Huge silver shades hid his eyes. Wound around his neck as a scarf was a bright yellow Tibetan prayer flag which used to hang on a window shade somewhere ... In his hand he carried a small black doctor's bag.'

Stevie Wonder enjoyed major crossover success as the Stones' warmup act, but felt shunned by Richards and Jagger 'because I wouldn't get high with them'. When Wonder begged off one show because his drummer had quit, Keith reacted by punching a steel dressing-room locker. From there things began to deteriorate badly, with Richards yelling, 'That bloody cunt! Fuck that Stevie cunt. He's a cunt!' and various Stones frantically trying to protect Keith's hand. Wonder would privately say that he was 'never sure where Richards was coming from'.

The setting of Keith's public performances was a vast, portable dais, painted bright white, with a 40-by-16-foot mirror hanging above to reflect the band from all angles. When Keith walked out he sometimes complained he felt like a circus freak – the whole thing was '*so* Vegas'. The stage itself was washed in a solution of warm water and 7Up to render it danceable, and from the first song Jagger was away to the races, bumping and grinding in his skimpy jumpsuit. Little silver bells on his shoes jingled in time with the beat.

Opening night, Vancouver: thirty policemen stretchered off after clashes with rioting fans. Nothing happened in Seattle. In San Francisco, the Stones played out of tune and Stu thought they sounded 'worse than bloody Status Quo'. The reviews were still terrific. As the Lapping Tongue taxied on the runway that night, a young woman in hotpants approached Rudge. Could she ask the band for their autographs? For her daughter? The Stones' vaunted aloofness notwithstanding, they rarely declined convivial meetings with female fans, wearing, as this one was, a snug *Exile* T-shirt. Led by Stu she walked down the aisle of the plane, leant over a seat and said, 'Mick?' He nodded, so she went on: 'I am hereby serving you, Michael Philip Jagger ...' and began reading off a list of charges relating to Altamont. The next thing anyone knew, said Robert Greenfield, 'this sweet lady came rocketing unsteadily down the airplane stairway screaming, "He hit me, he hit me", followed through the door by Keith, silhouetted by the light from within, swinging an armful of papers up to the sky'.

The woman, a process server named Vivian Manuel, later told a court in California that she'd been 'assaulted and manhandled'. Jagger successfully countered by petitioning for a dismissal on the grounds of 'improper service'.

In Chicago the band moved into Hugh Hefner's Playboy mansion, mingling with the Bunnies in Hef's underwater bar. The customary arrangement was that, after a little socializing, each Stone would pick the two or three girls who struck his fancy and retire to his room. An honourable exception was Charlie, who preferred playing snooker.

Onstage, Keith kept the canonical riffs coming. After a barn-burning Brown Sugar, Jagger went jogging downstage in Bitch, before Gimme Shelter and Keith's frantically gasped Happy. The centrepiece was again Rambler, which the Stones brought to a runaway freight train-climax; not for the first time, the band's raw power belied their queasy appearance. An extended medley from *Exile* evoked the album's raggedy charm, full of hip-swaying blues stylings, windmilling guitar and funky drums. Keith turned up the juice for the run-out section of Honky Tonk Women, Bye Bye Johnny and Flash, with smoking solos all round. The hell-for-leather gallop of Street Fighting closed the show in a gale of power chords. As Jagger threw rose petals, the 20,000 faithful were busy kicking the hall into matchsticks. The decibel level of screams and cracking seat fixtures rivalled that of the music. Overall, it was the definitive ninety-minute mix of big beats, tight britches and classic, chant-along choruses. By the end of the night everyone in the arena, and the millions who read about it afterwards, had indelibly imprinted on his mind Sam Cutler's line about the Stones: the greatest rock 'n roll band in the world. 1972 delivered on that boast once again.

By mid tour, unsurprisingly, Keith was flagging – 'totally fucking knackered'. Stu would remember pushing the world's greatest band out of their dressing room in towns like Akron with the phrase 'Come on, my little shower of shit – you're on.' A doctor named Larry Badgley was having to help everyone keep going. The constant round of showbiz parties and society clearly wasn't Keith's scene. In St Louis the band ran straight offstage, into five limos, and headed to a French restaurant downtown. Jagger then spent some fifteen minutes studying the wine list, before finally selecting a 1939 Mouton Rothshild. When the steward arrived, lovingly blowing the dust from the bottle, Richards asked to taste it. 'He brought it over to Keith, who started swigging it straight from the bottle,' says Gary Stromberg, the tour's PR man. 'Keith turned to the steward and casually said, "It's very good," and put the bottle down. The steward literally had tears in his eyes.'

Truman Capote and his companion Princess Lee Radziwill (Jackie Kennedy's sister) both travelled with the Stones. To Keith, unimpressed with the glitterati, they quickly became the old tart and Princess Radish. He addressed such people the same way he addressed the police. The great author turned up at a party one night in Keith's hotel suite, which he remembered as looking like a Bedouin encampment. Scarves and flags were draped over lamps, and there was a cauldron of something stewing on the floor. After deciding not to write about the tour, Capote would call the band 'complete idiots ... That unisex thing is a no-sex thing. Believe me, Mick Jagger's about as sexy as a pissing toad.'

On 12 July, in Indianapolis, Brian's old friend Stash de Rola was beaten up by the Stones' security goons in a misunderstanding about drugs. Keith, who also liked Stash, was extremely upset by this development. 'He started hollering at everyone ... He was on such a rant, he even yelled how mad Brian would have been [then] got quite choked about the old days.' It happened to be exactly ten years since Jones had first led the Stones out on stage at the Marquee club.

Keeping everyone organized was a problem, too. The Stones were well known for missing planes, running late, forgetting things. Even when they belied their devil-worshipping, dope-smoking image and behaved immaculately, events seemed to conspire against them. On 18 July, the Lapping Tongue was diverted by fog on its way into Boston and forced to land fifty miles away in Warwick, Rhode Island. The band were already late, tired and irascible when an agency photographer named Andy Dyckerman pulled up and started taking 'unauthorized' shots – as opposed to the kind usually seen in glossy magazines. There was a tense standoff as Rudge and Dyckerman loudly debated the media's First Amendment rights. Things might have gone on indefinitely had Keith not then slugged the paparazzo as he ran past him on the tarmac. The Port Authority cops arrested Keith, Jagger trotting alongside shouting, 'Look, man. What are you *doing?* We got a show tonight.' After the third or fourth 'fuck you', Mick then joined Keith in the paddy-wagon. As an afterthought, the police also arrested Marshall Chess and Robert Frank for obstruction. While the remaining musicians were bussed to Boston, Peter Rudge hired a lawyer. On stage Stevie Wonder was told to play for two hours.

A combination of the mayor of Boston, the governor of Rhode Island, Rudge and F. Lee Bailey finally sprang the Glimmer Twins at one a.m. But they weren't yet ready to call it a night. Far from it. Out on bail, Keith and Mick were driven at wild speed north to Boston, coincidentally suffering its worst outbreak of civil disorder in a decade. From the window of his screaming squad car Keith could see the glow of burning rubble. The Stones pulled up at the back of Boston Garden, ran straight onstage and played one of the killer shows of the tour.

As usual, Keith had his private crew in tow throughout: Stash, an older friend called Fred Sessler (an executive at Merck, the drug manufacturer) and Dr Larry, staff physician to him and the band. Stanley Booth also notes that 'a boy who worked for [Robert] Frank carried ounces of coke and brown Mexican heroin for Keith'. Gram Parsons showed up, huffy because he felt the Stones had burnt him. A rumour went round for years afterwards that Keith had thrown Gram out of his hotel suite, and that Parsons had threatened Richards with a knife.

Another friend went up to Keith's room in Manhattan, and found him crashed out on the bathroom floor with one hand held stiffly aloft. Twelve or fifteen people he didn't know were milling around snorting coke and calling for more booze to be added to his room service tab. Occasionally, one of the freeloaders would come in and offer Keith a toot, and his head would snap up, a big tipsy smile spreading across his face. And then slowly, almost imperceptibly, his head would begin to fall again until he was gone. An eighteen- or nineteen-year-old woman, a friend of the band's called Suck, got up and slowly peeled off her top as Keith continued to sink further into himself. Finally, he was jerked back awake. He propped himself up with the back of his head resting on the tub, lit a cigarette, and looked around at the scene. 'Go home,' Keith advised the now completely nude groupie.

The photos of Keith taken during the *Exile* tour were startling stuff. Instead of the typical mid-Sixties mug shot – bouffant hair, bright eyes, the whole face a cheeky chappie mask – here was a man who seemed to have aged thirty years, a gaunt, hollow-cheeked ghoul. Keith's skin was translucently pale, his posture that of a crone. In a word: slumped. *Rolling Stone*'s Annie Leibowitz would take a classic backstage shot of Keith nodding off, apparently dosed to the eyeballs. In his book *The Triumph of Vulgarity*, Robert Pattison calls this an example of Keith 'instinctively reproduc[ing] the death-throes seen in Henry Wallis's 1856 painting of Thomas Chatterton – eyes shut in languorous self-annihilation, one arm limply falling to the ground while the other lies across a chest exposed by an open shirt-front revealing the pale, erotic flesh of beleaguered youth.' Which has to be one of the most roundabout ways ever devised of defining a wreck, albeit an elegant one.

Last stop but one, Pennsylvania. Robert Frank wanted an orgy scene for his film and two young fans obliged on the plane. It was all done like a stag movie, wobbly cameras, woeful dialogue and groupies with giant tits. Everyone came out of their private staterooms to watch, shaking maracas and wailing away in time with the action. Bill Wyman's ten-year-old son happened to be on the flight and Bill, missing out for once, took him up to the far end of the jet to look out of the window at Pittsburgh.

New York. Mick Jagger's birthday and the final concerts came together in a rush that stretched from Madison Square Garden to the roof of the St Regis hotel. The Stones played the three climactic gigs as though their lives, and those of their fans, hung on them. Sound and lights were both exemplary, Keith cuffed the riffs, and nobody needed binoculars. These were some of the most consistently hot, yet coolest sets in Stones history.

But the rock and roll life wouldn't be all work for the lads. Mick received his birthday dues at the close of the final show, when Rudge and members of the crew stepped out, custard pies at the ready, and let fly. An hour or so later the band were partying in the elegant environs of the St Regis. *Le tout* New York was there: Capote, Tennessee Williams, Woody Allen, Bianca Jagger; Bob Dylan sat posing for pictures with Zsa Zsa Gabor. Andy Warhol took Polaroids. Somewhere in the background Muddy Waters, engaged for the evening, played Rollin' Stone. While the liggers grazed on caviar and champagne, the man who had made the whole thing possible modestly enjoyed a boxed supper.

Out on the terrace Keith stood with a few friends, raising their glasses to the moon, which went into a total eclipse that night.

During the eight-week tour the Stones played to 462,000 fans, each paying $6.50: three million bucks. Of this the group (via their holding company Promo Tours) grossed two million, minus 30 per cent withheld for tax. Each of the Stones and Rudge thus took home $233,333. Having kicked off at the beginning of June and finished in the last week of July, Keith made $3,888 a day, $27,216 a week or, for purposes of comparison, $1,419,000 pa – roughly 300 times more than Bert Richards at the Osram factory. The tour also saw *Exile* reach number one, selling more than a million copies. Keith's fortune was invested wisely, and Prince Rupert confirmed that no retirement plans were on the table.

Keith's tenancy at Nellcôte formally lapsed in the autumn of 1972. The local rental agency was reportedly shocked by the overall condition of the property. Its inventory check showed the familiar cigarette burns and breakages, as well as numerous souvenirs of Keith's pet – though not tame – mongrels. Nor had Marlon neglected to leave his mark on the premises. From mid September Keith and his family were installed first in Gyron and then in a chalet called Le Pec Varp in Villars, high in the foothills between Montreux and Lausanne. The eighty-three-year-old Charlie Chaplin was a near neighbour. While living in Switzerland Keith not only learnt to ski but, a journalist named Hervé Muller reports, bonded with Angela. 'The greatest thing was to see him playing with his daughter . . . he was obviously thrilled with her. I found him extremely bright, extremely honest, no bullshit and incredibly nice.'

Keith's alpine fastness also had its drawbacks. It proved extremely hard for him to sit down and work on an album. Visitors like Jagger would go to Villars and sit looking out at the mountains while Keith fielded phone calls. There were an awful lot of briefcase-carrying friends constantly coming and going. Mick and the other Stones became quite frustrated. They didn't have a lot of free time, and they were under pressure from Atlantic's boss, the suave Ahmet Ertegün, who wanted more product, fast. A certain tension consequently developed between Keith and Jagger, just as it had at Nellcôte.

Keith couldn't move back to France for legal reasons. There were tax and visa hassles in Britain and Stateside. Like the Duprees before him, he was living a vagrant life now.

Hitting on a compromise venue, everyone moved to Dynamic studios in Kingston, Jamaica, in November. It was a particularly significant choice for Keith, who quickly discovered not only the local skank but what he called 'marrow music', reggae, while on the island.

There was no denying Keith and Mick worked best as songwriters, just as in the old days, while locked in the same confined space. But *Exile*-type tensions were probably intensified, too. Keith would later confirm that Jagger and he had 'different attitudes', and that 'throughout the Seventies I was living in an alien world from him ... It kind of got up my nose, his jet-set shit and the flaunting of it. But he's a lonely guy, too. He's got his own problems.' Stu would witness an odd and touching instance of the alien worlds when, one day in Kingston, Jagger challenged Richards to a game of tennis. Mick appeared for the contest dressed for Wimbledon; his opponent, who'd last picked up a racket in 1958, sported ragged jeans and kept a butt end clamped to his lip throughout. Keith won the match 6–1.

On 2 December 1972, the French police issued a warrant for Keith and Anita on charges of 'use, supply and traffic' in drugs. Front page stories in Nice wrongly reported that all five Stones were wanted for interview, and remained at only 'provisional liberty'. Two days later Jagger, Watts, Wyman and Taylor flew to the Riviera to 'deny categorically we have been charged with the buying and use of heroin' and promising to sue should anyone report otherwise. Keith himself remained in Kingston, primarily to avoid arrest.

Although only Keith was charged, the bill that came in from the band's Paris lawyers (at $58,700, representing $8,000 for each month spent in France) was split six ways. Anita's was the final share.

While the rest of the Stones were closeted with Sgt Maurey of the Sûreté, Keith found himself working alone at Dynamic, finishing up what became *Goats Head Soup*. The fact that he was inconspicuous, even for a few days, was noteworthy in and of itself. Keith was well on his way to his own Interpol file and a deserved reputation as rock 'n roll's hard man. In Kingston he went around armed with a 12-inch ratchet knife. Richards had few quiet moments, and, as it turned out, 1973 wasn't to be one of them.

Jamaica affected Keith more profoundly than anything since he first pulled up at 2120 South Michigan Avenue in Chicago. He was soon talking about (derisively) 'Paris and that shit' and planning, instead, to put down roots in the Caribbean. It happened over two months, in three phases. First, Keith took a suite at the exclusive Terra Nova hotel while commuting to the studio. Then he rented a house called Casa Joya overlooking Mammee Bay on Jamaica's north coast. Finally he laid down $152,000 in cash to buy Tommy Steele's villa, Point of View, craning out over the fishing village of Ocho Rios and the sea. The property came equipped with orchards of lush fruit trees, an Olympic-grade pool and a courtyard the size of a football pitch where a dozen cars were normally parked. Visitors fondly dubbed the place Nellcôte West, with dreadlocked Rastas straggling up to the estate at all hours to smoke and hang out. Stu noticed that Keith loved being courted and fêted. 'He was really in his element [in Jamaica], a sort of Sun King. I mean, he treated those guys with respect, and they loved him for it.'

Meanwhile, Jagger was busily planning for the Stones to tour Australia, Japan and a few outstanding cities in North America. On 4 January 1973 both the Australian and Japanese authorities banned them. The US Immigration Bureau quickly followed suit. While some of the rock press were already lashing Keith for selling out on the Riviera, at least three governments continued to view him as unsafe, a fourth was about to try him and he was still, for tax purposes, officially exiled from Britain. Keith would describe himself during this period as 'on the lam', a prisoner of his own myth. On 18 January the Stones did, however, headline a Hollywood benefit concert for earthquake victims, after which Mick was formally thanked by the US Senate. Coincidentally, both American and Australian immigration services soon lifted their bans.

Early in February, Keith took the completed *Goats Head* backing tracks to LA's Village Recorder for a final polish. Jagger was writing the lyrics to a song he called Starfucker. In this tune Mick's emotional distress was revealed to moving effect. He missed his absent girlfriend, with her Polaroids and can of tasty foam. Jagger promised that, on her return, he would make her scream all night.

Amid rumours of being chronically stoned, Keith spent sixteen-hour days (admittedly without a work permit) arranging the ten songs to give each its killer punch. At least half would consequently sound like chart hits of the day, only done right. While Keith toiled, the BBC sent a producer called Jeff Griffin to LA to interview him for *The Rolling Stones Story*, which aired in April. As negotiations veered between Broadcasting House and Hollywood, there was, to Griffin, the sense of an historic encounter – rock's version of a papal audience. He eventually found Keith sitting alone in his villa one warm afternoon, toasting himself in front of a log fire.

The small, ill-clad man who met Griffin was a revelation. Keith seemed, by turns, playful and professional. He claimed that the 'difficult period' – he meant his being locked up in Wormwood Scrubs – was now over and life was getting better. Although he no longer liked giving interviews, Keith had a certain directness about him, and a way of tuning in to his guest. Wherever he was at that very moment, Keith seemed to say, was the place to be.

Jeff Griffin: 'People say, "Oh, he's a junkie." I always say he was extremely friendly, the sort of guy you could have a laugh with about cricket or football. He had a human quality.'

When opening night in Brisbane came, Keith kicked out the jams. Jagger, who appeared to have been watching David Bowie, danced around in ballet tights while holding up a rhinestone mask. You had to be there.*

6 April 1973. Keith put a temporary end to his tax exile, returning to 'good old England', as he was quoted as calling it, to see his mum and finish up *Goats Head*. Anita remained at Point of View. According to Spanish Tony, Richards seemed to go into Rod Stewart mode that spring, sitting around London clubs like Tramp wearing tight pants and a suggestive leer. Keith's respect for concepts like marriage remained on the hazy side, and at moments of tension with male rivals he wasn't above whipping out his foot-long machette from Jamaica. 'I can handle myself', he quite truthfully

---

* While in Australia, Keith, Mick, Charlie, Bill and Mick Taylor travelled under the names of, respectively, Fred Trueman, W.G. Grace, Trevor Bailey, Len Hutton and Peter May. These were the perfect cricketing aliases. Trueman was the mercurial 'bad boy' of the English game at about the time Keith was growing up in Spielman Road.

told Tony. Keith evidently thought he'd scored one night with a scantily clad blonde model who introduced herself as Chrissie, wife of the Faces' guitarist Ronnie Wood. There was some encouraging talk about a nightcap. Keith seems to have assumed that Wood himself was out of town. Doing the gentlemanly thing, he offered to drive Chrissie home in his bright yellow Ferrari. Once at her south London mansion Keith found, though, that they weren't alone. Down in the basement studio was Ron Wood, working on a hot new song with Mick Jagger.

An awkward moment followed as Keith recognized Mick, but it passed off when Ronnie poured everyone a large brandy. It turned out that Bianca (recent winner of the coveted Hat of the Year award) had been complaining that the Stones' music was nothing more than second-generation pop, with little in the way of a 'serious message'. Mick's reaction was to pen the song that he and Wood were slaving over that night, It's Only Rock 'n Roll (But I Like It).

Anita came back to London later that spring, after allegedly being thrown in the Kingston jail where she was serially raped and beaten up. The family divided their summer between Redlands and London. Early on the morning of 26 June, Luigi the caretaker opened the door of 3 Cheyne Walk to DI O'Hanlon and his drugs squad. The narcs took away armfuls of hash as well as Keith, Anita and their house guest, who were all charged with possession.

August: *Goats Head Soup*, the first stop on a funky continuum that climaxed in *Some Girls*. The album sported butt-wagging horns and clavinets (Bobby Keys and Billy Preston, respectively) and more wah-wah pedals than the theme from *Shaft*. Keith's lovesick ballad style, heavily layered with strings, also cast a long shadow. The smash hit Angie was typical of the overall feel – a classic, sultry groove with a melody that sat in the pocket just so.

Goats Head owed its bluesy tang to Mick Taylor's lead guitar, which strutted out on tracks like Heartbreaker. Silver Train again proved how hot he was, sliding up and down the frets over Stu's piano boogie. Keith's Coming Down Again was his boldest statement yet about what made his heart beat and his blood boil. The lyrics spoke of stickin' his tongue in someone else's pie, a head-bobbing salute to Keith's backup girlfriend Uschi Obermeier. Winter remains one of the great underrated Stones songs, all shimmering guitar lines and a trailing dust cloud of piano, strings and, yes, dreamy vocals. The album ended, aptly, with the last track recorded, one to which there was no answer. When he first heard Star Star (aka Starfucker) even the urbane Ahmet Ertegün paled. Not only was the one-word chorus slavered some fifty times, but the lyric sheet also made reference to pussy ('Bad', an Atlantic memo noted) and Steve McQueen (worse). Eventually one was bleeped, the other signed a waiver. It was a classic libidinous Keith track, as well as a cheerful bit of self-parody.

Goats Head went straight to the top of a chart dominated by the likes of Gilbert O'Sullivan, the Carpenters and Donny Osmond. In a natural but also debatable reaction, Mick Taylor privately questioned the paternity of certain songs (all credited Jagger–Richards), and told friends he felt diddled. The Stones didn't know, at this point, that Taylor was already planning to bail on them.

When the band toured Europe late that year, Keith was looking much like he sounded. Wasted was the word. All his guitars had capos on them so he didn't have to play barre chords, but even then Taylor had to fill in some of the key riffs. Pop critics forgave him, straining for 'elegantly wrecked' metaphors instead. Keith's claim to the Next Rock Casualty title was staked against stiff competition from Keith Moon and a host of less celebrated but formidable junkies.

His speciality was the extreme. In one coke and heroin binge Keith went for nine days without sleep. At the height of his consumption he was managing to get through an ounce a week. On the days he actually went to bed, Keith typically awoke around 4 p.m. and drank a triple tequila for breakfast while swallowing several aspirin and simultaneously chain-smoking Marlboros. A galaxy of other drugs would pump him up until it was time to go onstage or, failing that, to hit the club scene. While Anita was home in Villars, Keith did the town with both Uschi Obermeier and another friend whom he briefly installed at Cheyne Walk.

Tony Sanchez: 'Later, when Anita phoned to say she'd be back from Switzerland with Marlon and [Angela] the next day, Keith promptly turned around and threw the girl out. "Sorry, darling", he said. "But my family is very important to me."'

Everyone was together in London when the drugs squad again came calling that summer. The narcs hammered for a long time before Luigi finally opened the door. They trooped in, finding themselves in a kind of replica of the kasbah.

There was an impression of purple-painted rooms, gold lamps studded with jewels, overturned bottles and ashtrays, rotting food underfoot; the air thick with incense and cigarette smoke. Luigi, as if suffering from some painful disease in the lower half of his body, slowly led the way upstairs to the tripping room. It was Stash de Rola's bad luck to be visiting Keith overnight, just as he'd been staying with Brian Jones when Brian was busted in 1967. Stash, who sometimes uses the title prince, went on to write two scholarly books on alchemy and to campaign for saner drug laws. Keith's own plea for the decriminalization of pot proved thirty years ahead of its time.

On 26 July Keith dressed in a brown pinstripe suit, bought especially for court appearances, to do the honours at Jagger's thirtieth birthday. Five days of partying later, Richards, Pallenberg and their children were at Redlands. Some time in the early morning of 1 August, the house burnt down.

It was a desperate scene, with the dry thatch quickly going up in smoke above their heads. Keith and Anita managed to escape to the garden, where she apparently berated him while police and fire engines clanked up the lane. 'Fucking hell, Keith. Fucking hell! The only reason for coming down here was so we could get some rest, and now look at it! Go on. Look at it.'

'Not too good,' Keith was forced to concede, as the roof fell in, sending up a shower of sparks, just as Spanish Tony managed to lug the huge refectory table out onto the lawn. Everyone spent the rest of that night giving statements, and then dozing fitfully in the guest cottage.

When the smoke cleared, Keith found himself without an English home. Redlands would take three years to rebuild and Cheyne Walk was off limits due to security concerns and general paranoia. Instead, he moved into the cottage at Ron Wood's house, the Wick. The main property sits on top of Richmond Hill, less than a mile from the old Crawdaddy Club. Keith took a long look at the circular entrance hall and the elegant black-and-white marbled bar, at the comfortably furnished library and home studio, and pronounced it a 'cool scene'. On and off, he lived there for the next three years.

By now it was autumn. Keith had made little progress in resolving his romantic quandary during the summer, but when Anita went back to detox, matters fast came to a head. Friends noticed how much happiness Uschi's company seemed to give him. Beautiful, lithe and blonde, she was eerily like the Pallenberg of 1965.

As the year drew to a close, the little triangle entered its final stage. Uschi travelled with Keith on the next Stones tour, and had her photograph taken with him. 'We really loved each other more than we intended. We really fell in love,' she says. But whenever Keith tried to clarify his relationship with Anita, he wound up confessing he needed her. He went back to Switzerland in 1974, while continuing to see Uschi quietly for the next few months.

Musically, too, Keith was on the edge. He seemed to swing between bursts of creativity and total inertia. He clearly needed careful handling, particularly with Atlantic constantly demanding more product.

The Stones were understandably concerned, and missed the Good Old Days when Keith was still bright-eyed and 'clean', and writing songs that changed the culture. With the exception of Charlie, few of them bothered to speak much to him now. Jagger was miffed at the negative publicity which kept the law at everyone's heels and only again complicated matters with the US Immigration Service. Soon someone at the Wick told someone else's hairdresser who told a journalist that Ron Wood was going to join the Stones if Keith's drug hassles got any worse. This particular rumour was the biggest thing in British rock in late 1973.

Keith himself seemed to revel in his cadaverously zonked, punk incarnate image. 'If you're gonna get wasted, get wasted elegantly,' he told one reporter. A typical Keith interview dwelt lovingly on his appearance before mentioning the music. Thus we learn that his lips were bright blue, his teeth rotten, and that he staggered about under gobs of black eye liner and shaggy hair. The *NME* critic Nick Kent, who made something of a name as a Keith watcher, would call him 'the big Lord Byron figure. He was mad, bad and dangerous to know. He had immense personal charisma. He just sits there and he's the centre of attention in that room and Jagger is like a little boy running around doing things to get attention.'

Another great quote from Keith was that '[he] didn't have a problem with drugs, just with cops'. Yet many of his best friends, lacking his iron gut and powerful backup, were dropping at his feet. Anita, Mick Taylor and Marshall Chess had got themselves deep into dope trouble; Bobby Keys and Jimmy Miller were both strung out, couldn't work, and found themselves unceremoniously fired. Spanish Tony checked into rehab and went on to write his own version of *Elvis – What Happened?* Michael Cooper, the photographer who once roomed with Keith and Anita, killed himself with an overdose. Gram Parsons died alone in a Hollywood flophouse that September, aged twenty-six and still baby-faced. Keith: 'People were dropping like flies then . . . It was nothing to wake up once a week and hear so-and-so's gone – "What, the usual?" "Yeah, the usual". Nobody seemed to die of anything but ODs in those days.'

Keith himself was minded to avoid this fate. He missed Gram, he said, but was in no hurry to fulfil anyone's fantasies. 'Despite everything, I'm a survivor.'

In fact, as with so much in Keith's life, his 'shit with dope' was far more complicated than he ever let on. He had a natural compassion, and went out of his way to discourage anyone from emulating him. While finishing up *Goats Head*, he'd first taken to warning Jimmy Miller to cool it, and then to inviting him to play tennis instead of sitting behind the mixing board shooting heroin. Stu would say that he saw Keith stop fans from fixing up on several occasions, and Stash de Rola testified that Richards worried about people 'follow[ing] him down the road' to addiction. A prince of darkness, but a prince nonetheless.

1 September 1973. The Stones started a quickie European tour in Vienna. It was a compelling two hours of rock 'n roll in a street accident sort of way. Jagger's act consisted of a series of kicks, jabs and karate-inspired chops, eerily suggestive of the fading Elvis. Keith trucked out such hits as Honky Tonk Women, but the narcotic fog never really lifted. If the Stones hadn't had Charlie goosing the beat, the worst gigs would have been clinically dead. And without Mick Taylor's bluesy leads, the best nights would have been merely ramshackle. As it was, they came close.

On another soggy evening in London, Keith and Anita set off, squabbling furiously, towards their unlikely goal: a glittering *Goats Head* launch party at Blenheim Palace. Inside, the marbled ballroom was packed with models, gossip writers, nightlife habitués and several dozen of Mick's best friends. Anyone familiar with *The Island of Dr Moreau*, with its apes and dogs surgically turned into semi-human form, has only to think of these same fauna in black tie to get a bit of the flavour. Word buzzed around that the Richards party had been delayed. Hours passed. A wave of excitement went through the crowd when, around midnight, Keith ambled in. He was pale-faced, with a stubbly beard, ashing a cigarette. Anita apparently preferred to wait outside but soon joined him, screaming at Keith to get back into the fucking limo so they could leave. Jagger eagerly advised Richards to 'just grab her and split'. Keith took Anita to the back seat of the car, where they set about punching each other for most of the two-hour return drive to London.

Three weeks later, Keith subjected himself to a course of haemodialysis, the filtering out of waste and toxins by a kidney machine. This whole saga would soon become a powerful, enduring (and misquoted) rock legend. Richards arranged his quiet 'Dracula gig' with no more fuss than marks a change of government in a small country. First, Spanish Tony went to Bern to rent Keith a secluded villa, before flying in a world-renowned blood specialist from Miami and engaging a local nurse, maid, cook and secretary for the week. In time they were joined by Keith and his entourage, which included Marshall Chess and several Rasta bodyguards. The Stones' accountant Laurence Myers in turn paid everyone's final fees and expenses, and hired a car to drive the party back to southern Germany. But the ordeal wasn't quite over; Spanish Tony had to dissuade the chauffeur from taking a shortcut through France, since the authorities there had warrants out for Keith and Anita.

The Stones played one of the best shows of their lives later that night in Munich.

Great quick-draw guitar mingled with Keith's black moods. There happened to be a German air traffic controllers' strike that week. The wreckage of the band's Frankfurt hotel on 2 October would stand as a commentary on what happened when a rejuvenated Keith was forced to spend a wet Tuesday afternoon waiting for transport. (At least two paintings were trashed.) He, Charlie, Bill and Mick Taylor eventually set off for the next gig, in Hamburg, by train. Mick Jagger had already flown ahead in the Atlantic company jet.

19 October, Berlin. Keith took Uschi to the post-tour party, then briefly slipped into a back room set aside for the Stones to enjoy a lesbian floor-show. Evidently this sort of voyeurism wasn't his thing. 'I felt like a queen,' Uschi remembered. 'He made me feel really good. The [women] would tear their clothes off right in front of him, but he wouldn't even look.'

The judge in Nice handed down a suspended sentence that same week. On 24 October Keith and Anita were then on trial at Marlborough Street magistrates' court in London. They heard DI O'Hanlon describe an antique German blunderbuss found in Cheyne Walk as 'a lethal weapon' which contravened firearms regulations, before going on to list the various cannabis, Mandrax, methadone and heroin jacks seized by his squad. The police stressed that they weren't the slightest bit fazed by the general Beggars Banquet squalor of the place, nor by the way-out ambience of rooms devoid of light and furnished with mirror-balls, black candles and a bust of Jimi Hendrix. Keith's lawyer claimed that all the drugs had been left there by a previous tenant. The bench gave Pallenberg a one-year conditional discharge, and Richards a fine. Stash was acquitted.

Keith celebrated in the Londonderry House hotel that night, burning his room down.

Richards was careening between these various crises when his beloved grandfather, Gus Dupree, died. As a connoisseur of wine, women and good music, Gus had often spoken about his deep pride in Keith. He was a particular fan of the songs on *Between the Buttons*. But the guitar wasn't the only thing he'd passed down to his grandson. There was also a great legacy of 'getting fucked up and still functioning'. Both men broke all the rules and yet went on to live, in Gus's case, well past eighty.

Keith often said, 'He was the funkiest old coot you could meet.'

The Stones regrouped in Musicland, Giorgio Moroder's flash new studio in the cellar of the Arabella hotel, Munich. Uschi Obermeier's hometown. The first day back underground, Keith wiped Ron Wood's guitar from It's Only Rock 'n Roll and dubbed in his own. Wood later got a liner-note credit for 'Inspiration', but no royalties.

The rest of the sessions were a headlong assault against the passage of time. Keith's crush on Motown led him to cover chestnuts like the Temptations' Ain't Too Proud To Beg before cutting his own, reggae-tinged Luxury. Over the next month, funk, soul and even calypso would all show up for the party. Keith's playful mood was matched by a return to writing brassy, Satisfaction-style songs.

Meanwhile, as they thrashed away, the Stones were also falling apart. The old mates grunted to one another as they flitted through the Arabella's basement, but they rarely socialized and all five were busily making their own plans. By 1974 Jagger was quite seriously considering a career in film, if not in Labour politics. Bill Wyman was already quietly recording his first solo album, *Monkey Grip*, which Keith hated. Mick Taylor often didn't even show up in Munich, blaming a 'mysterious illness'.

At Christmas everyone went back to England, where Elton John stirred the rumour that Wood was about to join the Stones. This didn't exactly endear Elton to Keith. Equally unsettling were the continued hassles with the US Immigration Service, which resolved to never again issue the band work permits. Far worse, even Charlie was talking about being pissed off and threatening to go play drums in a jazz combo.

For all their mutual aggro, Keith and the band had already been together eleven years. Back in 1966, he, Pallenberg and Jones had spent Christmas tripping in a suite at the George V hotel in Paris. Somehow the subject of death came up, and Keith, not unkindly, said to Brian, 'You'll *never* get old, man.'

Brian agreed. He saw it and feared it: the great rock 'n roll slag heap, already strewn with a thousand Fabians. 'I know,' he'd said, for once speaking quite seriously. 'Neither will you.'

On 18 December 1973, Keith threw himself a party. He was thirty.

6

'We Want to Play. You Want to Play. Where Are You?'

ANOTHER GOOD THING ABOUT MUNICH WAS THAT A WAR-OBSESSED COLLECTOR LOOKING FOR SS MEMORABILIA DIDN'T HAVE TO GO FAR. Keith could buy campaign medals, helmets and other relics from a variety of characters working the Giesing district just south of the studio. He referred to Musicland itself as the Bunker. Friends thought nothing of seeing Keith loping around in shiny leather boots, dress shirt and a full-length black overcoat. He was one of the first rock stars to speak knowledgeably about the Nazi flair for spectacle, thus beating David Bowie's remarks of a year later: 'Hitler was quite as good as Jagger . . . He used politics and theatrics to hype everyone all that time . . . The world won't see his like again. He staged a country.'

Once the Stones got back to Germany in early 1974, they essentially operated as five separate groups. Jagger and his entourage would stroll around the Englischer Garten and take in a show before dropping him at the studio door at midnight. When Mick left again three or four hours later, Keith would troop in with Uschi and his crew of spliff-wielding Rastas. Bill: 'They'd do it to each other. Jagger would be on time one night and annoyed because Keith wasn't there; then Keith would feel guilty and make it early the next night [but] Mick would be so pissed off with him he wouldn't show up.' The Glimmer Twins were also fighting about when to tour again. Keith fretted about the Stones getting rusty, Mick wanted to make films and watch cricket.

When Mick Taylor finally showed up, Keith began squabbling with him too. The second Munich sessions finally killed any lingering hopes he may have had about writing Stones songs, though again, in keeping with house practice, his help was always freely given. One night when Keith and Jagger had already gone home Taylor went to work on a Brazilian track called Time Waits For No One. Although the rhythm was nearly down, the all-important melody line and coda remained elusive. Raising a finger to his lips for silence, Taylor plugged in his guitar and came up with a sound that was both sweet and catchy, and absolutely nothing like any other song ever arranged by the Stones. It was credited to Jagger–Richards.

Keith went back to the Wick one night that spring 'and stayed three months, working and playing snooker'. Repairing to the basement studio, he was soon the head of an all-star cast guesting on Wood's first solo LP *I've Got My Own Album to Do*. (The title was a dig at Rod Stewart, who was busy just then cutting *Smiler* instead of touring with the Faces.) A friend of Woody's named Bebe Buell walked into the Wick one morning to find Keith, Mick, Ron and Eric Clapton passed out at the foot of a bed, where Angela Bowie lay in splendid isolation.

That early summer was idyllic, but beyond the fantasy island where Keith lived while bonding with Woody, things were very different. The drug intake remained massive. Sometimes Keith would go AWOL for days on end and when found would be slumped in some Soho dive. Uschi dispatched friends in search of him when his coke-fuelled outings became too prolonged. He told her and others that he could kick dope any time he wanted to, but he seldom wanted to. It began to be said that Keith was actually dying, and the Woody-for-Stones rumours began again.

The band denied it, and Les Perrin still loyally churned out press releases with titles like STONES ENJOY BAVARIA HUGELY and STONES COMPLETE WORK ON 'BEST EVER ALBUM'. The cosy atmosphere was tainted only slightly by the fact that Keith and Mick weren't speaking to each other. Jagger still refused to tour that summer. When Keith finished working with Woody he kissed Uschi goodbye and went home to his family in Switzerland.

Keith's bout of domesticity allowed him ample time to contemplate the fate of *It's Only Rock 'n Roll*, the album cut in Munich. A record that would again put the band's credibility to the test after the mixed reviews of *Goats Head*. The critical consensus was that most of the Stones' mid Seventies output marked a new low in self-indulgence. Even the friends-and-family audience at one New

York listening party couldn't help but wince as the greatest rock 'n roll band in the world chugged from one *Shaft*-cum-reggae groove to another. The highest kudos the Stones would earn for years came with It's Only Rock 'n Roll (But I Like It), the single released in August. Even then, cynics felt that the bauble was bestowed largely for Mick's great title, which quickly became a catchphrase.

Friends agree that Keith appeared to be content and even mellow during his Swiss Family Richards period. As the new album loomed, he was happy to live low-key in his alpine villa, taking skiing lessons, reading history – and modelling those vintage togs. 'Keith was quite the dresser,' notes a visitor. 'Lovely sense of style.' Others felt that he was dangerously close to living out a fantasy. Indeed, as Keith loped down the stairs of Le Pec Varp with Angela in his arms and a field tunic sheathing his bony torso, it was quite tempting to agree with Mick: the Stones needed a break. The same friend insists that Keith was 'exactly the opposite' of his public image, mild mannered and witty, but was given to understand 'things in the band were at meltdown'. Mick Taylor was now planning to get out while he could, with Bill, reportedly, close behind.

Which may explain why Richards seemed 'a bit edgy' that summer. Stoned as he was, no one was more committed to the band. All five men got together in London that July for a 'clear-the-air' summit that did nothing of the sort. It was left to Keith to close the meeting with a pep talk, which he did with the aid of a few notes he'd made on the plane over. His no-nonsense, nicotine delivery was blunt, funny and straight to the point. 'This thing is bigger than all of us,' he said.

Keith and Anita had now been together seven years. There were moments of genuine empathy – as when he played her a smoochy blues called Till The Next Goodbye – and, as a friend says, 'in the right mood they could still give a great show'. Neither tolerated criticism of the other. Both adored the children. But with the booze and the coke and Uschi and various other problems with Angela, Keith and Anita now had plenty to rattle the roof with. He stormed off once or twice, but always came back. Quite often Keith preferred to simply lock himself in the bathroom with his guitar. It wasn't an easy life for Anita, the former It Girl now reduced to living in a 'wooden shack'.

Yet Keith also had the ingredients to be a major celebrity in the 1970s: power, flair, a gift for PR and, above all, a warped sense of style. Other rock stars talked about him. Even the Hollywood crowd seemed to be a bit in awe of the feisty-looking guy from ... *somewhere in Transylvania, was it?* Steve McQueen publicly called Keith the 'coolest cat in town'. The Hollies' Allan Clarke was once invited to a Stones session already awash with celebrities. On the Human Riff's arrival, Clarke says, all eyes immediately turned to him, adding: 'Keith dominates the room without doing anything.' For his part, Stu denied that his mate was ever – like a Keith Moon – committing suicide on the instalment plan. 'I worked with him, and I should know ... [Richards] came alive the second he picked up a guitar. That never changed.' It was the key to happiness and a cure for almost all ills, physical or mental.

Besides his music and his drugs, Keith's other close relationship was with Marlon. The five-year-old accompanied his father everywhere, on planes, in dressing rooms, even romping around behind the amps onstage. The younger Richards was already a veteran of the world's finest hotels, racing up and down the hallways and jabbering away in rapid-fire French, English and German. That Marlon (who called Keith Keith) was a tad wild was no news flash. But what he lacked in tact he made up for in other ways. Many gave him credit for greater insight than his father into the true motivation of Keith's various friends and hangers-on, whom Marlon often invited to fuck off.

Instead of touring with the Stones, Keith spent much of that summer exploring Montreux with his permanent sidekick, conscience, minder and best friend. He and Marlon strolled in front of the jewellers' shops on the Rue du Théâtre and patronized the Casino. One local woman remembers inviting Keith back to her place for what she thought would be a 'hot date'. Instead, he arrived with his son and entourage, all of them five years old and younger.

On 13 August, three days after dressing up as a clown to celebrate Marlon's birthday, Keith went back to the Stones.

He'd only performed in public twice in the last year. Honouring a commitment to his host at the Wick, Keith played at Ron Wood's stoned debacle titled 'A Weekend of Rhythm & Booze' at the Kilburn Gaumont in London. With their identical dark eyes and pasty skin, Keith and Ron reminded Nick Kent of 'degenerate Everly Brothers', if not quite as tuneful. Rod Stewart and various others were rumoured to be backstage in Kilburn, ready to join in. About halfway through, Himself strolled on in a white suit to deliver some raw, wizened vocals while Keith belted out the Happy riff.

There were a few jeers from the crowd and one heartless soul yelled, 'Bring on Rubber Lips'. Perhaps wisely, Mick, in the end, declined to show.

The Stones then spent a day with Michael Lindsay-Hogg, filming a chaotic promo for It's Only Rock 'n Roll. Although, for some compelling reason, the director nearly drowned Charlie in soapsuds, the clip survived to become a staple of *Top of the Pops* and something of a rock-video pioneer. Despite the hype and a graffiti campaign orchestrated by Jagger, the single sold modestly. Taylor would call it 'Keith and Mick trying to write something in the classic Stones style', implying that self-parody had stalked the Bunker.

Later that month the Stones hired a woman named Jane Rose to replace Jo Bergman. Rose, who was to be a key figure in Keith's life, started her day by checking the newspapers each morning to see if everyone was still alive.

On the surface, *It's Only Rock 'n Roll* marked a welcome return to rough-and-tumble roots with a taste for grand gestures. Guitars never chug when they can soar; songs don't end when they can extend. The cover illustration looks like something staged by MGM. *Rock 'n Roll*'s overblown seriousness led to some genuinely hilarious moments: what the Van Morrison impersonations were about was anyone's guess, but Mick crooned 'Yes, star crossed in pleasure/The stream flows on by/Yes, as we are sated in leisure/We watch it fly' with parody-worthy urgency.

Rock 'n Roll's best moments were smaller scale. The lovingly covered Ain't Too Proud proved Keith could still play a lean solo, and Goodbye brooded with quiet regret. Luxury and the other sun-baked tracks bobbed and wove engagingly. Just for old times' sake, If You Really Want To Be My Friend lifted the gospel harmony from *Exile*'s Let It Loose. The album ended with Fingerprint File, a slab of Spy v Spy melodrama with Mick cooing, over a nerve-tight riff, about being bugged by the FBI. *It's Only Rock 'n Roll* was the first in a string of productions credited to the Glimmer Twins, which in this case largely meant Jagger. Coincidentally, it was also the first on which the vocals were fully audible.

Rock 'n Roll wasn't quite as revolutionary as the music that came from Keith's basement on *Exile*, and once or twice the Stones imitated their imitators. The result was pleasantly funky and slightly innocuous – without Jimmy Miller (another drug casualty) the band lost some of their midperiod clout. As it was, tracks like If You Can't Rock Me and File sounded uneasily like the Faces and *Diamond Dogs*-era Bowie, respectively.

It's Only Rock 'n Roll sold decently, though Ron Wood learnt that 'Inspiration' didn't necessarily turn into royalties. Twenty-three years later he ruefully told a reporter, 'It's a hard nut to crack, the Stones' financial side.' Mick Taylor was on turf well beyond that, 'in a virtual coma', according to one source, at not being cut in on Goodbye and Friend, let alone Time Waits For No One. Taylor's ambitious wife reportedly flipped out when she first saw the finished album.

Keith stayed in London for a month, talking up *Rock 'n Roll* to the press. The odds were only fair that he'd get through an interview with his eyes open, though, on peak form, he remained a witty and wonderfully quotable study. He spent one evening charming Bob Harris on BBC TV's *The Old Grey Whistle Test*. After the show everyone made for Mr Chow's restaurant in Knightsbridge, where Keith, announcing he was tired, whipped out a sack of coke and graciously offered it round the table.

Harris gave it a second, then began to laugh helplessly. Keith snorted himself awake again.

In mid October, Richards formally applied for planning permission to rebuild Redlands. Nobody objected, and one of the borough council sent Keith a letter welcoming him back. 'He was a distinguished pillar of the community.'

Meanwhile, Jagger had been introduced to a high-powered attorney from Little Rock by the name of Bill Carter. Carter not only counted a hip local pol and wheeler-dealer called Bill Clinton among his friends, he was also well connected in Washington. He knew the Attorney General. He knew everyone. Carter dressed Mick in a suit and tie and had him visit the Justice Department, where he cheerfully signed autographs and posed for photos with the staff. Soon afterwards, the Stones got their provisional work visas. Everyone met back in Montreux that November and agreed to tour the following year. Keith and Mick Taylor weren't speaking.

Up against the venerable songwriting firm of Jagger–Richards, and nearly broke, Taylor was about to make a life-changing decision. Approaching a grim-faced Mick in London, he formally announced he was quitting. Immediately. Earlier that week, Taylor had rung Jagger (who happened to be visiting Nicaragua) to warn him that something was in the air. Mick apparently thought he was bluffing, and reminded him that the Stones were due back in the studio in a few days. Afterwards, a senior Atlantic executive had begged Taylor to reconsider, but he refused.

The firestorm that followed took even Keith watchers by surprise. 'Two days before a fucking album,' he seethed as he paced round waving his arms and stamping his feet. 'Two fucking days!'

At the very moment Keith's war with the Feds ended, he was faced with mutiny from behind the lines. 'No one leaves the Stones except in a fucking pine box,' he later remarked. Taylor had committed the one deadly sin in Keith's eyes, disloyalty to the group.

Keith: 'Mick was like Clapton – a lovely player, a brilliant player. But you won't have them in a band because they're not team players. They don't like being kicked up the arse ... That's why Mick Taylor is a permanent failure to me.'

'I don't really know [why he left],' Jagger told *Rolling Stone*. 'He never explained. He wanted to have a solo career. I think he found it difficult to get on with Keith.'

On 9 December, the Stones flew back to Musicland as a quartet. The day the news broke, Keith sent Taylor a telegram: 'Really enjoyed playing with you for the last five years. Thanks for the turn-ons. Best wishes and love.' Nick Kent went to Munich and remembered Keith, 'mightily pissed off', hammering a riff to death one night while Uschi watched protectively. Jagger was nowhere to be seen. Bill and Charlie sat around yawning and eating fish and chips.

Almost as soon as Taylor quit, the Stones set about getting their own sort of haemodialysis. New blood was sluiced in in the form of Billy Preston, Stevie Wonder's drummer Ollie Brown (on percussion) and a chorus line of auditioning guitarists. Alexis Korner happened to be making an album called *Get Off My Cloud* in the next room to the Stones, with Steve Marriott and Peter Frampton helping him out. Marriott spent much of his time trying to prove to Keith that he was the man for the job. Over the course of the winter Jeff Beck, Mick Ronson, Harvey Mandel, Rory Gallagher and even Geoff Bradford, briefly a friend of Brian's in 1962, all drifted in to jam at Musicland.

Eventually, Keith's eye lit on a twenty-three-year-old part-Cherokee from Texas by the name of Wayne Perkins. He came well qualified. When Keith and Uschi had a quiet night in at the Munich Hilton, their favourite song there was always Jimmy Cliff's reggae anthem The Harder They Come. Keith raved about Cliff, saying *that* was the kind of music he wanted to play from now on. A few weeks later, the Stones were recording with their mobile unit in Rotterdam. Eric Clapton put in a call telling Keith about this guy, Wayne, he was hanging with by the pool in Jamaica, who'd worked with everyone from Bob Marley to Georgie Fame. What's more, he'd actually *played* on The Harder They Come.

'Send him over,' said Keith.

Perkins arrived in Holland to be met by Stu, who drove him to the small, dark theatre where the Stones were working.

> I walked in ... It was an arresting scene; everyone was sitting around, Keith half pulling his pants down, the top of his ass showing as he examined some sore. Bill and Charlie, I think, grunted. That was my introduction. Next thing, I'm playing alone on stage while they watch. Jagger runs on from the wings without me even noticing, grabs a tambourine and starts doing this jitterbug-boogie routine right behind me. Mick's fucking with my head while Keith's sprawled down front, still ruefully prodding his ass and occasionally glancing up, checking me out ... That's my audition. Next I'm invited outside to the mobile. I did some stuff on Cherry Oh Baby, Memory Motel, Fool To Cry. Keith and I put together the song Hand Of Fate. I obviously did OK, because by now everyone's cool, there's dope bouncing up and down on top of the amps, and Keith's grinning. No problem, I thought, I'm in ...

Keith invited Perkins back to the cottage at Wood's house, where he was again staying between sessions. As well as Richards and Pallenberg, the latter offering round an antique mirror heaped with coke, in the style of a butler with a tea-tray, the Wick's guest list included various Stones and Faces, and someone recalled as a 'Jamaican ballet dancer' who amused Mick. At seven one evening, Keith and Wayne set out for a 'quick' drink, which lasted until 5 a.m. Perkins found himself in the passenger seat of the yellow Ferrari, barrelling down Richmond Hill with Keith 'doing his usual 90 mph, wearing sunglasses'. Somehow, in the dead of a London night, Richards found a musical supplier willing to sell him a £12,000 piano. There was a dark thrill to be had, too, back at Jagger's house on Cheyne Walk. Keith soon disappeared down the street with Marlon.

Mick then placed a phone call summoning the ballet dancer, and Perkins watched them bumping and grinding away to some 'disco bullshit' on the sound system, while Prince Rupert and Bryan Ferry both materialized at the door. Before long the room filled with well-groomed men in smartly cut suits. Backed into a corner, Wayne, in his T-shirt and jeans, shifted uncomfortably as Mick's guests stared a hole through him. Everything was 'very weird'. Next day, back at the Wick, Keith told him to learn the Stones catalogue. 'We're going on tour.'

Perkins was soon practising 'thirty or forty' of the old standards. Rehearsals entailed plugging in guitars around the time other people went to bed, then bashing away while Richards called out 'Faster!' or 'Cool it' and swarthy aides replenished the various bottles and tins jumping up and down on the amps. Lady Jane and Satisfaction were first in the bag. Meanwhile, as Keith and Wayne traded licks in the cottage, fifty yards away in the Wick's oval living room, Ron Wood was pondering his career options if, as seemed likely, the Faces broke up.

March 1975. Back in Munich, the 'great guitar hunt' entered the vital phase Keith called 'the Mick Taylor factor; can I live with this cat?' It extended well beyond mere musicianship. Perkins had little trouble keeping up with the continuous dope, drink and lack of sleep. 'You get used to that.' But even he was floored when Keith snorted some coke one morning and casually suggested a trip to Dachau.

Not long afterwards, Jagger summoned Perkins to his hotel suite.

> Mick was lying alone on the huge bed. He sort of patted the covers, and I sat down next to him ... There was a heavy atmosphere; Mick offered me a toot and lay there, kind of fidgeting around. Somehow he started this rap about adolescence and chicks, and before long he leant over and said, 'What was your high-school girlfriend like?' Well, I don't know. Maybe it was the drugs, but I felt sick. That's when I puked all over Mick's bathroom. He had to change suites for the night. Right after that there was a phone call between Jagger–Richards, sort of a dogfight about whether or not I was in the band. Keith was definitely voting for me.

Asked why Perkins wasn't hired, Keith would flip between 'he play[ed] too like Taylor' and 'we just had to own up that we were an English rock 'n roll band'. Others saw it as one more small victory by the man who, not without justice, now thought of himself as the Stones' head partner. Keith later told Perkins he'd been a pleasure to work with, and the two remained friendly. (Perkins calls Richards 'the greatest rhythm guitar guy on the planet'.) Bill went on to tell *Rolling Stone*, 'Wayne's very good. He's pencilled in as a potential future choice.' Perkins was never formally told otherwise, and over the next few years Keith would occasionally try and revive the idea, but it remained more fantasy and fiction than a real effort. 'Keith was great, but Mick Jagger was the guy running things,' says Perkins. 'He was fascinating company.'

On Sunday 30 March, Ron Wood was one of the guests at Eric Clapton's thirtieth birthday party. Next afternoon he woke up, found he had nothing particular to do and made a phone call to Munich. Woody flew in that evening. Later that night in the studio, he asked Keith how the search was going.

'We're looking for a Brit who looks cool, with a fucking good sense of humour, who's slightly shorter than you, plays OK, likes a pint, won't freak out on the road, isn't going to jump ship and can get on with Jagger.'

'Where are you gonna find someone like that by next Friday?'

Woody then played on a song called Hey Negrita, and was swiftly hired for the tour. Keith: 'After literally one number, we thought: That's it. It's obvious.' The arrangement was that Wood, like Taylor before him, initially join the Stones on probation rather than as a full member. As it turned out, he would be kept on salary for nineteen years. Long before then he attached himself more or less officially as Keith's mate and sidekick. With his bog-brush hair and ready laugh, Wood lightened the heavy atmosphere around the band overnight. What he lacked in musical savvy he more than made up for in other ways, contrary to the critics who called him a barely competent, bum-note merchant and, at worst, a total joke. The Keith–Ron dream ticket looked great in photos, and Woody was as willing to muck in as Taylor hadn't been. 'He's the one that kept the horse on track,' said Korner. 'To categorize [Wood] as just a tag-along guy who got lucky? No. Not true. There were other, better guitarists but none of them had his personality.' Keen-eyed observers didn't miss the point that Woody had finally joined the Stones to support Keith, not to replace him.

So began a pre-tour countdown that took Keith off first to have his teeth fixed, and then to suffer the latest indignity at the hands of the Feds. As well as charming the Justice Department, Jagger had recently had dinner with his friend Walter Annenberg, US Ambassador to the Court of St James. Annenberg advised Mick that Keith would be granted an H2 temporary work permit, provided he first pass a full medical. At this point, Sanchez says, the haematologist was again discreetly flown in from Miami. 'As soon as the cure had been effected, Keith went to London and presented himself at the American embassy for examination. The doctor pronounced his blood as pure as spring water, his passport was stamped and he was back on the road again.'

Meanwhile, Jagger was busy ordering his Giorgio Saint Angelo tour outfits, inspecting the band's customized 707 and booking the hottest possible support acts. Keith countered by inviting the great R&B singer Etta James, a favourite of his and Doris's, to open for the band. James happened to be in hospital at the time, trying to detox. Keith wrote to her saying 'he always felt like the best way to get your head together and deal with your troubles was to go out and tour'. James wrote back and told him she was too sick just then, and Keith promised that he wouldn't forget her. (He was as good as his word. Exactly three years later, James would be hired to open on the *Some Girls* tour of America.)

On the Monday night of 21 April, Keith began putting the new Stones through their paces. The band rehearsed on a remote coastal estate in Montauk, Long Island, arranged courtesy of Andy Warhol. Woody knew he'd hit the big leagues when he saw two of the band's security men fencing off the house's private beach with barbed wire. The rumour was that deranged fans wanted to kill Keith and Mick, and might try an amphibious strike.

At noon on 1 May, the Stones 'spontaneously' drove down Fifth Avenue atop a flatbed truck to announce the tour. Keith gave his first American performance in three years standing on a wooden plank, belting out Brown Sugar and bringing Lower Manhattan to a screeching halt. Half a million tickets were sold in the following week. Back in Montauk, more fratricide between the Glimmer Twins: Keith wanted Bobby Keys on the tour. Mick betrayed minimal enthusiasm. Richards repeated the demand. Jagger displayed his distaste for direct confrontation, reportedly having an aide pass the decision to Keith. 'Telling him was like tossing a match into a gas tank . . . the explosion was predictable, but massive.' Towards the end of May, Keith passed yet another physical, this one for insurance purposes. The doctor asked his age, noted his height and weight and praised his ability to read off a chart. Then he had his nurse come in and take a picture of himself with his superstar patient.

On opening night, 1 June, Jagger appeared to the strains of *Fanfare for the Common Man*, cavorting on the hydraulic, lotus-shaped stage in his silk pyjamas, straddling an inflatable phallus in Star Star, swinging on a wire and generally doing the funky strut with Billy Preston. As for the rest: stage left, Woody demonstrated his woozy good cheer, if not his acumen; there were some similar hijinks from Ollie Brown, who otherwise did little for the Stones' already vast beat. Richards was on peak form throughout, sporting a soiled white jacket and snug leather pants. According to *Rolling Stone*, he, at least, 'didn't need makeup to look bizarre or sinister'. Keith barely concealed a sneer as Jagger and Brown inflated yet more simulcra, this time a fire-breathing dragon and a frosty snowman. The show itself blew similarly hot and cold, but nobody could fault the Stones' gamut-running: in two-and-a-half hours the fans got everything from Aaron Copland to a queasily burlesque minstrel act. It seems fair to say that the $8 and $10 seats represented better value than those for John Denver, the Carpenters and Donny & Marie – America's other pop idols that summer.

The frenzy began a few days later, when the band started playing the biggest arenas in Texas. Slash-and-burn gigs, sex and drugs: the STONED headlines soon followed, along with rather full pictures of Mick's rubber cock. Keith, for his part, sometimes seemed to lose a little zing in the bigger halls. One minute he'd be centre stage, hitting the down and dirty riff of Happy, and hollering like a banshee. Next minute he'd be slumped on the amps, his mind wandering, and an entire song, possibly involving Mick duetting with Billy, would go by almost unnoticed. Keith remained a law and lawless to himself. In fighting mood he was still the total rock 'n roller. Stu: 'You had to admire him in many ways on the '75 tour because he was so single-minded. He was really the pulse, [and] without doing anything flash he ran the Stones.'

Keith travelled through America with sixteen guitars, a crate of Rebel Yell and a fiercely protective crew including his friend and alleged bag man, Fred Sessler. Sessler was something of a mystery, particularly surrounded by all the young rock 'n rollers. He was then fifty-two, and didn't look a day over seventy. He had what he insisted was a legal licence to import top-quality, pharmaceutical drugs, though his job spec went well beyond that. On tour he and Keith would soon be talking five or six times a day, in person or by phone, sometimes for hours on end. Sessler, a Pole who had fled the Nazis in 1939, seemingly never tired of discussing the war. When the rest of the band mustered to go on stage, Keith would often keep them waiting by calmly finishing his latest history lesson. Refreshingly, too, Sessler was one of the few people around (Stu was another) who favoured a more open and direct style than the 'paid arseholes'. In time, he'd come to play some of the surrogate-father role with Keith once taken by Tom Keylock. Rounding out the entourage were Marlon, Woody, Uschi Obermeier, assorted Rastas and three or four moonlighting doctors who travelled under names like Ziggenpuss and Stockfish. This gave the tour the feel of a Marx Brothers film.

5 June, San Antonio. Moved by both deep respect, and £4,000 from the *Daily Mirror*, the Stones agreed to pay homage to Davy Crockett and the American heroes who died at the Alamo. The *Mirror* photographer brought along a box of props for the shoot. Keith, by now almost concave from drugs, bulked up by the expedient of stuffing several flags down the crotch of his jeans. Back in London, the resulting full-page splash was widely considered a new low point in Anglo-American relations.

Next night the Stones played for 80,000 fans in Kansas City, the Eagles opening. Several of the crew sported T-shirts asking 'Who the fuck is Mick Jagger?' In Toronto, Richards heard about a young blind fan, Rita Bedard, who was hitching from gig to gig. This brought out Keith's humanitarian streak. He began arranging for the roadies to let the girl ride with them, anonymously paying for her to have a hot meal and a bed at night. Keith's simple act of generosity would be repaid, in nearly incredible fashion, three years later.

Six sold-out gigs in New York, with everyone from Dylan to Raquel Welch partying backstage. Somewhere in the crowd at Madison Square Garden was a pretty 19-year-old blonde, from a good Lutheran family (there much against their better judgement) named Patti Hansen. She, too, would resurface in Keith's life three years later.

The Stones then played live, if they could be called that, up and down the east coast. There were some fair shows, others that were phoned in. Keith's beefs about Jagger soon became the tour's worst guarded secret. He referred to him as royalty, specifically 'the Queen Mother'. 'If Her

Highness had her way, we'd be playing in a fuckin' panto,' he'd say, giving his gravel-pit of a laugh. Mick now travelled with his own court of stylists, hairdressers and the society makeup man Pierre LaRoche. More and more, his stage act honoured its roots in traditional British showbiz, and the world of drag queens like Danny La Rue (a man whose birthday Mick shares.) His reputation as an organizer was well earned, even Keith allowed. Jagger was famously awake at the wheel. But Richards also feared Mick was succumbing to Lead Vocalist Syndrome, a fatal weakness for toys like the trapeze and balloons that opened him up to mass ridicule.

Mick's antic performances were bad enough. But both Richards and Jagger freaked out when, on 1 July, Bianca got herself photographed with the president's son, 'Disco Jack' Ford, and then started dragging both him and his Secret Service agents backstage. A year or two later, the Glimmer Twins wrote a song about 'the rag trade girl/the queen of porn/the easiest lay on the White House lawn'.

Live, Mick sometimes concluded this ode by bawling 'Get out of my life! Don't fuck my wife! Don't come back!'

The tour was now about halfway through, with the Deep South coming up. Keith flew into Memphis through heavy turbulence and reeled off the plane to be serenaded by eighty-two-year-old Furry Lewis, the great slide guitar king who never earned enough to give up his day job as a street cleaner. (This despite having a wooden leg.) Although rattled and by now running late, Keith insisted on squatting down on a flight bag to listen. Worried handlers soon began barking into walkie-talkies, '*Stones party delayed!*' and tapping their watches. Keith's thirst for the 'real shit' and Furry's penchant for playing it helped to seal a sudden deal. Lewis was invited to open for the Stones at Memorial Stadium that night and, what's more, Richards ensured, be well paid for it. Instead of arguing against Keith's wishes, Jagger and the tour managers accommodated them: Lewis went on in front of 55,000 white rock 'n roll fans, who cheered him to the rafters.

After his set, one of the handlers asked Lewis if he wanted to stay and watch the Stones. 'No, I don't care nothin' 'bout it,' he said.

From Memphis, Keith, Wood, Freddie Sessler and a Stones heavy named Jim Callaghan decided to drive to the next gig, in Dallas. Late in the afternoon of 5 July, after the four left a burger joint in rural Fordyce, Arkansas, they were stopped on Highway 79 by a State trooper who later said he smelt dope and that there were 'enormous clouds of smoke' pouring out of the limo, which gave him his due cause.

After asking everyone's name and occupation, the officer took a crowbar to the car boot, which allegedly contained coke, the property of Fred Sessler. Keith was also relieved of his favourite hunting knife. The cops took everyone to the courthouse, variously charged with possession, carrying a concealed weapon and reckless driving.

Bill Carter, the Arkansas native now working for the Stones, flew in by chartered jet within the hour. News crews turned up from as far afield as Dallas and Atlanta. A large pro-Stones crowd also gathered in the square outside the picturesque white courthouse. A second Learjet of the evening soon hit Fordyce, carrying a man holding $50,000 in cash to be used as bail if necessary. Immediately on arrival Carter grabbed him by the arm and steered him into the judge's chambers. Outside, the 'Free Keith' crowd grew more vociferous in their demands. Carter made an impassioned case for illegal search and seizure, and at this stage, at nine on a Saturday night and the mob beginning to pelt the courthouse with stones, the judge decided it would be in the interests of public safety to set everyone free.

Richards and Sessler (described in news reports as a 'hitchhiker') posted bail of $162 and $5,000, respectively. The party then ran for their limo, which accelerated away to the airport, one occupant waving a bottle of Rebel Yell out of the car window. All charges were later dropped. Keith's knife still hangs on a plaque in the Fordyce courthouse, along with a framed photo of the judge and police chief posing with their famous prisoner.

Ten days later, Sessler arranged to fly Uschi Obermeier into San Francisco. With Anita home in London, Uschi and Keith enjoyed a week travelling back through the midwest. When they were alone, he was 'very sweet', asking what she planned to do with her life and what she thought of various rock stars. 'It was heady,' she recalled. But Uschi also chafed at the 'Nazi state' where, like others, she was forced to compete for Keith's attention. One night in California she and Richards went to bed 'and when I woke up there was a guy lying like a dog across our feet'. On 23 July, Uschi made a hurried departure from their Chicago hotel suite. Keith was in a deep sleep, so she left him a breakup note.

Heightening Keith's grumpiness that week was a gig in Denver 'ruined' by Elton John. Few guests ever got to perform in public with the Stones. But this was Elton's home turf – he was recording *Rock of the Westies* nearby – and he insisted he wanted to play on just one song, Honky Tonk Women. No problem, said Jagger. Elton got onstage, did the number, then wouldn't get off. Keith was livid, and even Stu remembered being 'surprised Elton stayed as long as he did, [considering] he didn't seem able to pick up the tunes'.

In Greensboro, Richards and Wood relaxed after hours by playing country blues in Keith's hotel suite, with Faye Dunaway, among others, crooning along. The cops tried to bust the dressing room before the final gig in Buffalo. Peter Rudge, Jim Callaghan and assorted lawyers held them off. Keith and Jagger both dropped LSD, ran on and goofed through a twenty-four-song set, Mick barking the words in the general direction of the tune. 'It's only rock 'n roll,' Keith yelled after the second encore, 'but I like it.' And there, with him slumped on his knees, it all ended.

For their sixty-nine-day, twenty-seven-city tour, each founding Stone earned $400,000 post-tax, or just less than $10,000 per two-hour show. Woody was paid $250,000 for his services. They also sold a million-plus copies of *Made in the Shade*, the latest official hits collection, and, less agreeably, of *Metamorphosis*, a ragbag of outtakes, demos and rehearsal numbers put out by Klein.

At tour's end Keith went off to LA, meeting Anita for the first time in three months. What had long been an on-off affair now swung, almost incredibly, back towards the former. Anita got pregnant again.

Keith was ecstatic at the news. Never having perfected his own father's talent for reserve, he announced himself 'fucking chuffed' at the prospect of a third child. Everyone agrees he was a loving parent. Now aged six, Marlon had Anita's blond looks but a broad streak of Keith – self-absorbed, a budding rock 'n roller who kept vampire hours, sat around on barstools and swore at his nannies. Three-year-old Angela seemed sullen and withdrawn, but no one blamed Richards for that. His friend Bebe Buell says she always looked to Keith as 'the wise owl' in the mid-Seventies. 'He was the head of the clan ... When people would get hyper, he'd say, "Don't get so fucking excited. It's ridiculous. Mick is such a drama queen. Everybody calm down" ... He was perennially laid-back and understanding.'

Physically, Keith was all over the shop: Swiss skiing parties, Hollywood boogie nights, trendy London clubs with Woody and John Phillips. Prince

Rupert would later tell a court that Keith's casual spending had totalled $175,000 in 1975, and $300,000 in 1976.

By then, Phillips was living in Chelsea with his teenage daughter Mackenzie, still trying to put together his comeback LP after losing his shirt producing a film about a boy whose ambition is to take wing and fly inside the Houston Astrodome. Richards quite often stayed with the Phillipses when he needed a safe berth in London. One day Keith and John told Mackenzie they were going out, and that they'd be back later.

By later, they meant three days. 'There was no telephone and no food. There was just cereal in the cupboard, and I remember sitting in front of a mirror with my journal, writing about how I had been abandoned. I was fifteen years old. I guess I was being dramatic, but that was how I felt. Dad and Keith came back, totally wasted on heroin. They were crawling around on the floor, looking for bits of drugs that had fallen on the carpet. I remember looking at them and thinking how ridiculous they were.'

Others thought Keith the suavest of rock stars. He was genuinely funny, charming to colleagues he liked and unwilling to tattle on those he didn't. He hated being treated as royalty ('that Prince Charles shit', he'd sneer) and was far too dignified to share his thoughts on multiculturalism, global warming or dolphins. Plus, he enjoyed red meat and beer. 'Keith was always a man,' says Fred Sessler.

Later in the autumn, Richards let it be known the next album, still 'steaming ahead' after twelve months, would be called *Black and Blue*; and that, the Faces having finally imploded, Wood could now be regarded as a fixture. The sessions resumed at the very moment Woody's predecessor was selling his Stones memorabilia (£75 a gold disc) at auction in London.

Keith wanted to keep cutting, and soon decided the Stones needed to work somewhere 'we can get a really shitty, rock 'n roll sound'. Naturally, they chose Switzerland. In October everyone set up at Mountain Studios in Montreux, where Charlie Chaplin's son Eugene was the staff engineer. From there the Stones moved back to Munich. By Christmas they had most of *Black and Blue* in the can, as well as dozens of outtakes: one called Slave, one called Start Me Up, one (working title only) called Cunt. Some of these were recycled years later, and sold in the millions.

While Keith and Woody were in Munich, the drug squad finally hit the Wick. They kicked down the door, couldn't find any stoned musicians lying around the studio, but carried on up the grand staircase carpeted in royal red to the top bedroom. They found Chrissie Wood fast asleep there with a girlfriend. By some mysterious means, the next day's press was full of the 'pink knicker raid', and how the two women had been shamelessly 'embracing' and 'cuddling'. (There was also a coke charge, which was later dismissed, thrown in.) The pink panties were a detail of such sheer perversity as to make even the Munich paper.

'Welcome to the club, son,' Keith told Woody.

In this context, the hard-drinking, drug-struck Keith was the unlikeliest of 'wise owls'. He was proudly nonpolitical, shrugged off his own run-ins with the law, and avoided the soapbox. Yet he also worked hard to make sense of his life. Keith, Bebe Buell says, 'was well versed in philosophy – brilliant, in fact. He was open to all types of spiritual [beliefs]. He could talk for hours about the Mayans and the pyramids and we discussed the mystery of Stonehenge. Keith had a theory that the Bible was really a series of fairy tales.'

Over long dinners on Welfenstrasse, friends would listen intently while Keith talked about himself, his family, his hopes and even sometimes his slightly wacky New Age beliefs. Meanwhile, the Human Riff legend was polished anew by men like Les Perrin, who told would-be interviewers that Keith was writing great, great songs but that it wasn't the right moment, in the long spin cycle of his career, for him to be 'visible'. (Earlier on, of course, Perrin practically rang doorbells to get the word out.) Through it all, Keith kept his keen sense of humour. His love for end-of-the-pier types like Max Miller gradually came to embrace a new wave of British comics. If you wanted to watch a pirated copy of Peter Cook and Dudley Moore's *Derek & Clive* skits, for instance, he was your man. Keith's beery rapport with Pete 'n Dud often surprised those who knew him only as the satanic rock star. Even Cook sometimes wondered how he handled his past, what he made of 'all the Mars bars and human sacrifice' stories?

'Jesus,' Keith would say. 'I just laugh.'

Although he was never in Jagger's class (and didn't want to be) Keith began to adopt a more rakish style in his mid-thirties. He bought a Rolex and a Ferrari, saw a dentist, and occasionally got his name in the gossip columns. He and Uschi drifted apart after her 'Dear Keith' note, but he had his moments. Unlike Mick, he was never a tabloid Romeo. Keith saw himself as a great defender of women, and enjoyed their company. The mother of his children, meanwhile, had just been deported from Jamaica for a second time.

Pallenberg continued to use coke and heroin during her new pregnancy. By early 1976, Anita seemed to be on an emotional roller-coaster that paused only for her to alight at detox clinics. Later that spring, Keith arranged to move her back into the private hospital in Switzerland. Tara JoJo Gunne Richards was born there, four weeks early but perfectly healthy, on 26 March. He was named after Keith and Brian's late friend Tara Browne, and a character in an old Chuck Berry song.

Easter 1976. The Stones went back to the Riviera, rehearsed a new tour, finally wrapped *Black and Blue*. All told, it had taken them eighteen months. Many fans still wince at an album which – what with the likes of the Sex Pistols coming up, fast – almost seemed suicidal. If you wanted the Stones who made *Exile*, with all its curt guitar, you'd have to wait for their next outing, *Some Girls*. Meanwhile, for all its funky-Ohio Players allure, this one fell a few yards shy of a *Soul Train* revue.

Whereas even a *Goats Head* strove for the old style, *Black and Blue* closed up shop and started over with reggae-and-roll jokes like Hot Stuff. (It wasn't.) The Stones milked this groove elsewhere, on Hey Negrita, faking the funk with a zeal that was touching coming from middle-aged men recording, after all, in Switzerland. Hand Of Fate, at least, was time-honoured garage-rock fare. The jazzy shuffle Melody droned on interminably, and Fool To Cry (inexplicably, the first single) made Angie sound rootsy by contrast. Keith sang a few lines on Memory Motel, his voice husking on a combination of nicotine and dental work; the result was pleasantly woozy. Elsewhere, Jagger stuck doggedly to the James Brown playbook. Hot Stuff assures us 'you're hot/you're hot/you're hot stuff'; Hey Negrita urges us to 'shake your body/hey, do it up now'; and so on.

Keith later described *Black and Blue* as 'rehearsing guitar players'. Even Jagger thought it 'not very good – certainly nowhere as good as *Let It Bleed*', flung together under similar conditions. The two albums shared another distinction. Not for the first time, the Stones' back-room staff found themselves cut out of the action. There were no songwriting credits for Ron Wood, Wayne Perkins or Billy Preston. *Black and Blue* did, however, come with lavish full-page ads that showed a bruised, scantily clad blonde, with her hands bound above her head, legs akimbo, pouting. The caption read: 'I'm black and blue from the Rolling Stones and love it.'

'I thought it was quite funny,' Keith said.

On 28 April the Stones played the first of thirty-seven European dates. By now, a familiar pattern was re-emerging: tour followed by album followed again by tour. Keith commented on this when he told a reporter, 'I like to play live, because for me it helps everything else. But I have to respect the fact that there are other members of the band who have a need for a really stable home life. They need that anchor, whereas my old lady and me are very nomadic sort of people.' Keith and Anita were enjoying one of their cyclical bouts of happiness following Tara's birth. At one point, they even contemplated a rock 'n roll wedding ceremony right on stage. Keith was beginning to feel optimistic, but Anita moved out of the tour hotel and flew back to Switzerland. Marlon stayed on the road with the Stones.

Keith was a perfect fit for the tour, which aimed for a still-crazy image in which the Stones, with their torn T-shirts and nonstop booze and fags, differed in scale but not in style from the punks thrashing away in their dives. On opening night, Keith fell down during Jumpin' Jack Flash, couldn't get up, and finished the song flat on his back. Often, the problem seemed to be the opposite extreme. Keith was so wired, he reminded Korner of a caged lion prowling from side to side. Critics began to talk about the Stones' 'narco-flop music' . . . a 'total shambles' . . . 'self-parody' . . . 'crudely exaggerated' . . . 'stylized up its own ass'. Never one to avoid giving a sly wink, Keith played in front of thousands of fans wearing a silver necklace with a snorting tube and coke spoon on it.

On 19 May, Keith was driving home from a concert in Stafford when he lost control of the Pink Lena and bounced the car off a guard rail and into a field just outside Newport Pagnell. It was four in the morning. When the police arrived they found Keith, wearing sunglasses, his pockets allegedly full of acid, wandering up the side of the M1 with six-year-old Marlon. A search of the Bentley revealed the snorting tube squeezed under the driver's seat. The cops charged Richards with possession of coke and LSD.

A month later, the Ministry of Transport sent Keith a bill for damage the Lena had done to the motorway crash barrier. Rashly, an official had decided to protest his love of the Stones by scrawling 'How about some concert tickets, then?' across the top. Keith's lawyers lost no time in formally complaining. Still seethingly angry – he was going on trial again in the new year – Keith muttered that this was typical of the 'poxy Feds' wanting it both ways.

Six sold-out gigs at Earl's Court, some of the worst Keith ever played. One night Jagger invited Princess Margaret backstage, the Stones shuffling up to be presented like a sick Cup Final team at Wembley. Mick, who adored the attention, waded toward the cameras, flashing lipstick and major jewellery, to introduce Her Highness to 'our old friend' Keith Richards. By now, Keith and Mick were hardly speaking.

When the Stones played in France, Jeff Griffin remembers 'Richards could just barely stand up'. The critics saw a pattern over and over again whereby 'Keith would reel on and somehow get through two hours', while Jagger flew around at the end of his trapeze. The French press gave the band some of the worst reviews of their career.

Tara Richards was just seventy-two days old on 6 June, when Anita found him dead in his crib. He had reportedly suffocated. Keith, who was informed by phone, played some blistering solos on his black 'skull' guitar when he went onstage in Paris a few hours later; many of the tracks on *Love You Live* were recorded that night. Tara's tiny remains were cremated in Geneva on 14 June. News of his death was released to the press a week later. Richards and Pallenberg locked up the house in Switzerland, and never set foot in it again.

Anita: 'Keith was very calm and protective and normal and loving. He just said, "Forget it." And everybody else told me the same thing. They all said, "Forget it. Look after your other children."

'I'm sure that the drugs had something to do with it. And I always felt very, very bad about the whole thing.'

Keith would probably be the one rock star ever to have nodded off on stage in front of 20,000 screaming fans, shortly after playing the solo on Fool To Cry in Munich. The Stones then did a few desultory gigs in eastern Europe, before winding up in Vienna. Richards and Wood wrecked their hotel suite there. The next time anyone saw Keith was on 21 August, when the Stones performed to 200,000 at the Knebworth festival, their first since Altamont. Richards, for once loath to rock, hadn't slept in days. The band went on around midnight, and played until 2 a.m. The concert was a shambling parody.

Keith was now thirty-two, prone to blackouts and memory gaps. He smoked and drank as if he had no wish to see thirty-three. That summer he and Anita, evicted from their suite at Claridge's, shuffled between the Montcalm hotel and John Phillips' house on Glebe Place. As was Keith's habit, all the lamps in whatever room he inhabited were draped with long Moroccan scarves. Reggae throbbed from the sound system. He never seemed to be without an entourage of leather-clad aides tagging along with attaché cases. Keith was looking hatchet-faced. Everything seemed to fall apart after Tara's death. Marlon wasn't going to school, and had little supervision. Angela was sent off to Doris in Dartford, and would never live with her parents again.

As for the Stones, their stock plummeted. They'd stunk at Earl's Court, but if merely doing that damned a band, they should have had plenty of company on the way down. Instead, they rode alone. The Knebworth gig was badly panned, and Mick was worried about seeming out of touch – being perceived as a dinosaur (at *thirty-three*). Keith, for his part, was famous for merely surviving, the pinup of the chemical generation. While gobbing on the likes of Rod and Elton, most punks made a non-aggression pact with Richards, and would often drop in on him for advice. Before long, his shag hairdo was everywhere, and a host of Keith clones ground out tunes previously heard only from factory drill-presses. Richards' nightly arrival at the Montcalm, with his court of boss-eyed cronies, was one of London's great tourist sights. With almost endearing immodesty, Keith would insist that his M1 arrest was 'nothing to do with justice or legality. It was just a trophy bust.'

Even as his latest album hit the bargain bins, Keith enjoyed adding up all the references, imitations, cops, rip-offs and grand larcenies doing the rounds – everyone from the Clash down. As Jagger said, 'He's the original punk. You can't out punk Keith. It's pointless.'

Yet deep inside, Jagger also felt that Keith was trouble. 'He fuckin' gets busted every year,' Mick later noted. Richards, in turn, laughed at Jagger for his ROCK STAR IN LOVE ROMP-type headlines. On occasion, he'd rail against Mick's pretensions. 'Jagger didn't like arguing with Keith, because Keith was always so much nastier and better at it,' says Bebe Buell. '"Oh, yes, we're so street smart, aren't we, dear! Yeah, right, Mick . . . we had to suffer as children, didn't we, Mick!"' Keith had no time for the likes of 'Princess Madge poncing around' backstage. He also thought Jagger 'never treat[ed] women right'. Richards scoffed at Mick's gladiatorial sex life, just then zeroing in on Bryan Ferry's fiancée Jerry Hall. The tabloids began splashing Jagger's breakup with Bianca, and Keith, contemptuous of this 'dumb shit', was pissed off and frustrated.

Richards' sessions with John Phillips were disappointing, and they launched a long winter of discontent. It was marked by hours spent in dark rooms, listening to concert tracks and haggling with record bosses about a new deal, the latter of which Keith loathed. Musically of no fixed abode, he was at least able to enjoy some moments of domestic stability. After a committal hearing at Newport Pagnell (for which he arrived three hours late), Keith finally moved back into Redlands in December 1976. He'd last lived there three-and-a-half years before, when he was finishing *Goats Head Soup*. Richards looked sickly to Nick Gough now. Some glossy articles that Christmas speculated on various female 'friends' of the band – Jerry Hall and Sabrina Guinness – but ignored Keith. Once again, he and Anita seemed to have reached an accommodation.

Now that things were settling down, the US Drugs Enforcement Agency wrote a formal letter to the Home Office. They wanted to be kept up to date with Keith's latest trial.

10 January 1977. Richards appeared at Aylesbury Crown Court, charged with coke and LSD possession. As TV crews gathered in the bustling market square, something like a mob orgy broke out on the courthouse steps. Monday morning shoppers jostled with busloads of Stones fans driven in from London, many of whom paraded through the streets in support of the accused. One buxom woman screamed 'I love you!' at Keith and followed him inside when he pulled up, forty minutes late, in a chauffeured black car.

Adding to the drama, Jagger arrived unexpectedly from LA, where he was enjoying a winter break with Linda Ronstadt. Half a dozen news crews perched up on the library roof opposite turned on their kleig lights to capture the scene, attracting even larger and louder crowds. By mid morning two or three hundred people had massed tightly at the courthouse door for a glimpse of their idols and, whenever they got tetchy, a Stones aide came out with a handful of glossy photos. Meanwhile, local opinion provided the flip side of the fans' shrill support. From time to time a few callous souls down in the market yelled 'Lock 'im up', and there were soon dull thuds and groans from that general area. Aylesbury had seen nothing like it since the Great Train Robbers went on trial in the same building exactly thirteen years earlier.

Keith pleaded not guilty. The prosecutor, Bruce Laughland, said that police had found about 130 milligrams of coke in a small tube, as well as

LSD in Keith's coat pocket, when they arrived on the scene at Newport Pagnell. Asked about this in the dock, Keith said that he didn't own the tube, and that the acid could have been slipped in his pocket by a fan. 'We all wear each other's stage clothes,' he added. 'It could belong to anyone. I don't even know what it is.' Laughland then produced a photograph of Keith wearing a chain and tube identical to the one seized by the police. 'I don't know anything about it,' Richards insisted.

Next, as the fans in the front row of the balcony leant forward, Keith began his defence. He was dressed in a dark suit and spoke in a level, pleasant voice; but there was no hiding the bombed-out eyes and gaunt cheeks. He'd been thin before he discovered heroin, and had lost weight since. For the record, Keith said that he'd been sharing driving duties that night with Jim Callaghan, which happened to be the then Prime Minister's name. The judge had to gavel down the laughter. 'May we proceed?' he asked gruffly.

Staring ahead, Keith stayed doggedly on message as he spoke about his career and busy work schedule until his QC, Peter Rawlinson, slipped in a 'What does being a lead guitarist mean?' question. 'It means I make the most noise,' Keith said. Everyone laughed again. It was a well rehearsed answer.

Keith later admitted he was heartened by the jury reaction when he'd described the pressures of life as a Rolling Stone. 'I'd been expecting a whole panel of housewives. But most of them were young, and one chick was crying.'

On 12 January, Richards was convicted of coke possession and acquitted on the LSD charge. The judge, Lawrence Verney, decided against a jail term, noting that Keith had had every chance to dump the evidence if he'd known it was in his possession. 'There is some support for your defence,' the judge told him. 'But under the circumstances, another conviction will certainly lead to a prison sentence.' Keith was ordered to pay a £750 fine and another £250 in court costs.

After passing sentence, the judge, at the request of the prosecution, ordered that the silver chain and tube be destroyed. 'It ain't mine,' Keith commented, 'so they can do what they like with it.'

Richards could afford the fine, 'casually disbursing' $350,000 in 1977. He spent the next month shuttling between New York, Paris and finally Redlands. It was never going to be easy for Keith to move back to the

Sussex countryside, and kick drugs with a woman who was shooting heroin. The dealers arrived nightly, and on top of that the house was being watched again. Nor was it easy for Anita: 'I suffered a bad bout of depression after the baby died and I wasn't able to cope with [Angela],' she said of that difficult year. Before long, Keith was spending more and more time locked in the Redlands bathroom with his stash and his guitar. With massive aid from his new snorter, he wrote a haunting ballad there called Beast Of Burden.

Downstairs, the American journalist Barbara Charone was busy researching Keith's authorized biography. The couple she witnessed were heartbreaking in their concern for one another. Also their fury. 'I haven't been fucked in months!' Anita screamed one night. 'Is television more important than me?

'You think you're Superman, don't you? Well, you're only Superman when you're playing the guitar! You think you can handle drugs, but you can't! I know what I am and I've been that way for seven years! You pretend! You're *afraid* ... You just go upstairs to the bathroom. You think people don't *know*? You're no different than anybody else. You can't handle drugs either!' Keith, watching TV, appeared comatose.

Richards started taking Concorde to New York, where he was soon pulling double shifts in the studio, partying with the *Saturday Night Live* crowd in their uptown lofts and scoring heroin on the streets of SoHo. He was always quite well received there. Keith Richards walking into a drug den was a bit like Oliver Reed walking into a pub, or Cary Grant into a tailor's shop. They were glad to see him, though Keith normally armed himself with a gun and a knife on his dawn forays to Washington Square. He later told Jeff Griffin that being a junkie was a dirty business and he had no illusions about it, but late at night he'd sometimes confide to friends that he didn't like what he was turning into.

Meanwhile, Jagger wanted the Stones to record some club dates for *Love You Live*, and soon fixed on Toronto. It seemed to be a surefire plan: spend a day or two rehearsing, hustle out some R&B classics, interview a few more record bosses. Take the money and run. Toronto was only an hour's flight from New York, and had the added bonus of being part of the Commonwealth – 'no visa shit'.

Keith was back at Redlands on the night of 12 February 1977. Mick and Charlie were there too, talking to neatly suited-and-tied label heads while

Brown Sugar blasted from the stereo. It happened to be ten years to the hour since the unpleasantness with Chief Inspector Dineley and his men. Keith winced as he was reminded of this. 'The fuzz are still a pain in the bum. Well, not really a pain, they're more of a habit.'

He reflected further, and added sadly, 'An expensive habit'.

Four days later, the Stones announced a new £7 million deal with EMI for all territories outside America. Everyone but Keith then caught their flight to Toronto. The band gave him a day or two, then started sending sarcastic telegrams: WE WANT TO PLAY. YOU WANT TO PLAY. WHERE ARE YOU? As the week wore on, Mick arranged for Stu and his crew to set up a round-the-clock watch at Toronto airport. Back at Redlands, Keith had taken the phone off the hook.

On Thursday 24 February, Richards, Pallenberg and Marlon finally packed their twenty-eight suitcases and boarded a BOAC flight to Canada. Midway across the Atlantic, Keith excused himself and disappeared into the first-class lavatory. He didn't come out again for three hours.

It was an inauspicious way to enter Canadian air space. Worse was to come.

Between them, Keith and Anita were carrying ten grams of hash, some heroin and coke, and what the charge sheet calls 'various drug-related paraphernalia, namely a spoon and hypodermic needle'. Mysteriously, there were no Stones representatives on hand to meet their plane when it landed at six that evening. Canadian Customs, however, were there in force; their inspection quickly turned up the hash and the burnt spoon – both in Anita's bag – but missed the white powders. Pallenberg was arrested, and immediately released on a promise-to-appear notice.

The following is Keith's version of events from a book called *The Early Stones*.

> We were just crossing into Canada – big Bentley, very comfy – especially for me, having a rest in the back seat ... And this bloody great Mountie reaches out and, very deliberate-like, picks something off [Anita's] shoulder – a bit of lint, or dandruff maybe ... picks it up, between thumb and forefinger, and then straightaway he pops it *into his gullet*! And I'm lying in the back seat, watching this come down ... and this twisted copper starts picking another bit off her shoulder. 'Flake,' he says, then tastes it –

probably a part of his kick, know what I mean? – doing it in front of people – 'Peruvian flake, if my guess is any good, and probably more where this came from! Call HQ. We're *taking 'em in!*'

The actual bust aside, this is a classic bit of Keith's knockabout humour. None of it happened.

From Toronto airport, Stu drove Richards and his family downtown, where they registered, under the name Redlands, on the thirty-second floor of the Harbour Castle hotel. On 25 and 26 February the Stones rehearsed on a soundstage at the Cinevision film studio. On Sunday 27th, Keith retired to suite 3224 for one of his deep, Rip van Winkle sleeps.

Around four that afternoon, five members of the Royal Canadian Mounted Police knocked on the door and, after some effort, having managed to slap Keith awake, served a search warrant. In his stupor, Richards thought the Mounties – 'all weeds in anoraks with droopy moustaches and bald heads' – might have been reps from EMI and, in truth, they weren't all that different. The RCMP then swiftly relieved Keith of two plastic bags containing white powder, a razor blade, flick knife, brass lighter, silver bowl, teaspoon and sheet of tinfoil all with similar traces, three purple pills, a hypodermic needle and two pouches 'believed to contain hashish and heroin'. (The transaction wasn't totally one-sided; the officers also took the opportunity to plant a listening device under the bed.) Keith, who remained calm throughout, told the law that the drugs were his and that he'd been a 'heavy user for four years' who 'purchased in bulk to reduce the risk of detection'. He begged for a gram or two back to get him through the evening. Instead, the Mounties took Keith uptown, where he was booked with possession for the purpose of trafficking. The charge carried a potential sentence of seven to life.

When Richards was bailed and got back to the Harbour Castle that night, one or two of the band dropped by to offer condolences. Bill: 'I'll never forget going to Keith's room with Woody to find him writhing on the floor, vomiting. We tried to give him pills but he threw them up. Nobody seemed to be looking after him.' Afraid that Keith might die, Wyman and Wood scored some heroin for him.

Toronto was never the ideal place for a drug user to run foul of the law. Hendrix had been busted at the airport there eight years earlier, and got off only after perjuring himself on the stand. Possession, let alone trafficking, was a particularly serious business in Ontario, which had just announced a new 'zero tolerance' policy on dope. On the very day Keith was charged, two local men were sentenced to five years in prison for conspiracy to sell coke. They'd been arrested with less than half the quantity he had.

There was frantic jockeying overnight between the police, court officials and the local media. Down in the waterfront bars, some investigative reporting – muckraking as it was called back then – turned up the first whispers about a celebrity bust. The rumours were confirmed by a source at the Brampton justice of the peace's office, who was quoted, anonymously, as saying that Keith would do time and the Stones had 'had it'.

Next, a crossfire hurricane. Keith was greeted on Monday morning by an Associated Press flash: 'Richards, lead guitarist with the Rolling Stones, has been charged ...' The Toronto *Star*: 'WILL STONE GET ANY SATISFACTION?' And the *Globe*: 'COULD *THIS* BE THE LAST TIME?' Reporters stormed the hotel and swooped in helicopters outside Keith's window while fans brawled down in the street. Jagger locked everyone in his room and read them the Riot Act about not blowing the new American record deal. An hour of peak-decibel debate followed. Keith was raging that the narcs were 'out to make rock 'n roll illegal', while admitting he'd been a twat. As with every indignity, he laughed at himself, pretended not to care.

Jagger's concerns proved sadly on target. RSO Records released a statement early the next morning. The label announced it was 'withdraw[ing] a seven-million-dollar offer to the Rolling Stones for their recording rights to the USA after protracted negotiations'. At this point, Mick slammed the door of his suite and got on the phone to Jerry Hall. Later that night, he started writing a song he called Miss You.

Compounding the problem was the presence in Toronto of Margaret Trudeau. The Canadian PM's twenty-eight-year-old wife – Madcap Maggie, to friends – had recently been hospitalized for stress, and was spending more and more time apart from her fifty-seven-year-old husband Pierre. The fourth of March happened to be their wedding anniversary. Margaret celebrated the occasion by checking into a suite on the thirty-second floor of the Harbour Castle hotel. That night the Stones played, brilliantly, at a local dive called El Mocambo. Keith's riffing was full of surprises, most of them good ones. For starters, he elected to do some of the old Crawdaddy Club chestnuts for the first time in fourteen years. Given the strong possibility that this could have been the last Stones show ever, it was strangely moving to hear him blast out the likes of Route 66 again. Jagger, too, was on top form, singing straight into the face of a pop-eyed young woman enjoying a toot in the front row. There was a playful lilt to Mick's voice as he boogied up to introduce Starfucker. At song's end he spelt it out: 'Aawrite, Margaret?'

The press exploded. Among the saner headlines were 'PREMIER'S WIFE OGLES ACCUSED', 'MRS TRUDEAU'S ROCK FOLLY' and, from the Toronto *Sun*, 'C'MON MAGGIE':

> Ever since Margaret Trudeau went to hospital with emotional problems, the country has been understanding of her periodic eccentricities. But there's a limit ... It is not only reprehensible, it is unacceptable for the wife of the Prime Minister to be cavorting with a group like the Rolling Stones.

That day every political correspondent in North America got orders to report to the Harbour Castle. They arrived in droves. Government stocks dropped, followed by the Canadian dollar, disinvestment in the oil industry, financial panic, censure motions – that was for starters. The entertainment writers were flashing their own leads about Madcap Madge and various hotel capers. There were also reports, filtered through the mists slowly, like a Brezhnev health bulletin, that Keith was taking more and more smack. He was in bad shape. Would there even be a trial?

A day or two later, a terrified Marlon knocked on Margaret Trudeau's door. Anita was out shopping and Keith was curled up on his bathroom floor, retching. Margaret and her police protection officer raced down the corridor to suite 3224. Together they picked Keith up, walked him around, and stayed with him until Anita returned. 'He's my friend. He's my friend. I reached out!' Mrs Trudeau would say in a low, halting voice when later asked about Keith. But the painful scene wasn't quite over yet. Before leaving his room that day, Margaret considerately leant down to give Marlon a hug. It was an outreach too many. 'Fuck off,' the seven-year-old told the First Lady of Canada.

On Friday 4 March, Anita appeared in court and pleaded guilty to possession of heroin and pot. She was fined $200 on each count. Three days later, Keith went to Old City Hall to be told that the police lab tests were back. As of then, he was being charged with possessing coke in addition to heroin. Several bystanders shrieked abuse and spat at him on his way into the courthouse. Richards was locked in a holding cell for an hour while the judge held a private session in camera with the lawyers. The prosecution moved, unsuccessfully, that the defendant be remanded in custody. On 8 March, Keith went back to court and was bailed for $25,000. The swarm of reporters outside had few questions about the El Mocambo gigs, or even about drugs. All they wanted to know was what Margaret Trudeau was up to. 'No comment,' Keith told them.

On 9 March, Mick and the other Stones were smuggled out of the hotel and on to separate flights to New York. The First Lady followed them there. Over the next year or two, Margaret T would become a darling of the Studio 54 crowd, whose other great star was Bianca. Once in Manhattan, Jagger then pulled off a coup in re-signing the Stones with Atlantic for North American distribution, at a reported $20 million for six albums. Mick and Ahmet Ertegün put out a mutually upbeat press release. It didn't discuss Keith.

Back in Toronto, Richards went into Sounds Interchange studio accompanied only by Stu and sang lonesome, Gram Parsons tunes all night. The five or six ballads, softly offset with a few doleful guitar strokes, expressed all the anger, the fear, the bile and frustration Keith felt while he waited to learn, the next day, whether or not he was going to jail. These were extraordinarily moving songs – stuff, said Stu, 'you wanted to listen to, not just hear' – played in rural American style. Keith also traded on his bruised voice, exploring a range of snarls, guttural moans and lower-register sighs as he gasped out lyrics about heartbreak and suicide.

Keith nodded off in court the next morning. While he slept, the Crown argued that he was a bad bail risk (residences in London, Paris and Jamaica), but the Stones' counsel prevailed. The judge ordered everyone to reappear on 27 June. Bill Carter then immediately petitioned US Immigration for emergency medical visas on behalf of Keith and Anita. Richards knew of a London-based homeopath named Meg Patterson who practised neutro-shock therapy, a kind of mild acupuncture in which a current is passed through electrodes attached to the ears. The idea was that the charge generated would affect the natural opiates of the brain – endorphins – allowing rapid if not always painless withdrawal. Patterson and her black box had had some success in treating both Eric Clapton and Pete Townshend.

On 1 April, Keith and Anita gave themselves celebratory shots of coke and heroin, then boarded a private jet out of Toronto. For the next month they were under Dr Patterson's care on a heavily fortified estate in rural Paoli, Pennsylvania. It happened to be the very house where, in 1958, Steve McQueen had starred opposite a man-eating Jello in scenes from the cult film *The Blob*.

In the event, Richards and Pallenberg were cured of the physical dependence on heroin within a week. They suffered just a day of the dreaded symptoms. Keith's cleanup, however, lasted only as long as he was under Meg Patterson's full-time care. By early May, just four weeks into the programme, he was able to check himself out of Paoli and move back to New York. It was a poor choice for anyone seeking the 'cool-out time' Keith insisted he wanted. The city was about to embark on an extended binge of murder and madness – the so-called Summer of Sam – with the psycho killer David Berkowitz on the loose and the disco scene taking off like a rocket. There was a heroin epidemic in much of Lower Manhattan. As Berkowitz himself later put it, everyone was 'seeking pleasure and finding death'. It was here that Keith chose to continue his long-term therapy. Instead of persevering with Meg Patterson, as she'd begged, he was installed in a suite at the Mayflower hotel and left to his own devices.

On 11 May Prince Rupert called the other Stones to say he was 'extremely worried' about Keith. He seemed set on a downward spiral.

With his customary professionalism, Keith actually spent much of his time that summer at Atlantic studios. He combined business and pleasure there, mixing *Love You Live* and dining with the likes of Clapton, Bruce Springsteen and Lou Reed after hours. It was noticed that Keith often had a different woman with him. He began to drink heavily now, partly in response to his anxiety over 'the Anita thing', which was clearly falling down around his ears. Even Jagger began to object to his boozing, reminding him, one night, how much they had to do and begging him not to pass out. (Several hours later, it would be Mick himself who crashed, having downed a bottle of tequila, while Keith worked diligently through the night.)

On 27 June, Richards failed to appear for a pre-trial hearing in Toronto. A bench warrant was issued for his arrest, with instructions that it not be served until a new court date scheduled for 19 July. Keith missed that one, too, instead staying put in the studio. On days when he didn't feel like working on *Love You Live*, he turned back time and again to the lovesick ballads he'd cut with Stu. Keith was obviously worried that summer by the decidedly mixed reports from Toronto. At the 27 June hearing the court refused to reduce the charges against him to simple possession. The Ontario Justice Department discussed offering Keith a plea bargain, until the police vetoed it. An unnamed official told the Toronto *Star* that the public and Crown were 'looking for the system to do what it was designed to do – offer some justice for a grave crime'.

Keith was running true to form, working hard then relaxing flat out. He actually spent a few nights at Studio 54, the disused theatre hurriedly converted by Bianca and friends into the Oz of discos. Though derided by Keith as a place 'full of faggots in shorts waving champagne bottles in your face', he enjoyed the chance to unwind in the club's private gallery. It was there that he came to know Bianca's successor, Jerry Hall, the young Texan with the peek-a-boo blonde hair modelled on the late Veronica Lake's. Keith was extremely conventional in many ways (a true son of Bert Richards), and didn't like the idea that a woman would ever mess with a man's work. Given Hall's glitzy profile, it's not surprising friends began to associate Mick and her with what one called the 'social disease', whose symptoms included an obsessive need to party: an association Keith loathed.

Les Perrin was critically ill by now, but the Stones press office ground on in his absence. As well as weekly tips for *Rolling Stone*, there were carefully scripted TV, radio and print interviews, all part of a strategic year-long blitz that would lead to a cover story ('Jagger's genius partner Richards tells how he kicked heroin . . .') in *People*. 'I'm not a junkie,' Keith informed the world on 8 August. The clean-living image was undermined when Robert Frank chose that very moment to release his documentary of the 1972 tour, titled *Cocksucker Blues*. Frank talked to the Montreal *Star* about the film, detailing some scenes that he said the public might find 'revolting'. These included Keith being injected, and Jagger snorting powder. Not long after that, the Stones slapped a writ on him.

Later that summer Keith and Anita took refuge on a farm called Frog Hollow in South Salem, about forty miles north of Manhattan. Richards began commuting down I–87 both to wrap *Love You Live*, and to try and fulfil his commitments to John Phillips. The latter soon broke down amidst heavy dope-taking. Keith went through yet another cure at the private Stevens Psychiatric Clinic in New York. Again, kicking the habit was the least of it. There was a growing feeling around that Keith would also have to split from Anita – make a clean break. This scattered chorus would become a full-blown posse, with the lawyers, too, insisting that they let it go.

Keith spent more and more time, meanwhile, taking in the punk bands downtown, gigs that recalled all the 'sweat and shit' of the old Crawdaddy Club. After a while he started to notice how many of the seventeen- and eighteen-year-olds acted like slightly muted descendants of the Human Riff: rhythm guitarists with that same shag cut and smacked-out phiz – it was like watching an entire audition for *The Keith Richards Story*. Almost every one of them knew at least the Satisfaction riff, and the solo from Happy, and the way Keith had of prowling around stage. Quite literally thousands of would-be impersonators. It wasn't a bad legacy.

September, *Love You Live*. Keith sounded on good form, but didn't get much help from his friends. Holding it all together was the sense that the Stones actually had fun dusting off the old R&B over those two nights at El Mocambo. Keith's souped-up guitar on Around And Around sounded like it was 1963 all over again.

Unfortunately, with few exceptions, the other songs on *Live* were heavy on synths and crotch-grabbing references to sex, money, dope and disco. Jagger sang as if shouting the lyrics from a passing car. At best, all you could say for *Live* was that everyone's heads had been higher than their feet when they recorded it. At worst, with its whiny keyboards and stark, boxy drum sound, the album was little more than a joke. It was, however, a singularly practical joke, a Top 10 smash on both sides of the Atlantic for the rest of the year.

When the Stones signed with EMI for all territories outside America, one of the main perks was free use of the label's famed Pathé-Marconi studios in Paris. The band arrived there on 1 October. Everyone knew they had to deliver a great album. *Goats Head*, *Rock 'n Roll* and *Black and Blue* had all sold respectably for six months or so, then been reduced to slumming it in the bargain bins. Few other companies would have been willing to risk £7 million on an enterprise as hard to quantify as hit-making, and, as EMI acknowledged, there was the question of whether 'Monsieur R' would even be around for six albums. 'Watch my tail-lights fading,' he famously advised his fans. There was a very real sense that everything depended on how things went that winter at 62 rue de Sèvres.

Keith's first order of business in the studio was to fire all the 'clever bastards' like Billy Preston. For the first time since *Let It Bleed*, the Stones would pare back. The band had originally been built around two famously interlocking guitars, blurring the lead–rhythm divide, and would be again. It was immediately apparent that the 'More Fast Numbers' sessions would be Keith-led, which meant plenty of loud, electric rock 'n roll and no interminable synth fugues. Songs like Respectable went in for a stripped-down riff over snappy drums, while Lies kept things nice and simple with a jaunty, cut-and-paste punk thrash. The album title was changed to *Some Girls*.

Keith was on an up again.

You saw him in Paris and then you didn't: walking down the Champs Elysées with Marlon trotting alongside; heading off to see *Star Wars* for the third or fourth time; slipping in and out of the back door at rue de Sèvres. Richards had most of the album in the can by 1 December. He was back in court in Toronto the next day. Keith told the Bench that he was working hard, both on his music and his therapy, and that he was 'firmly resolved' to put drugs behind him once and for all. He concluded that his life on the road could be hell, but that he was sincerely determined to kick his addiction and fully justify any clemency the court might be willing to show him.

The judge committed Richards for trial.

Keith was in a dark mood later that night when he flew, alone, to Jamaica. The debate was over: he had to split from Anita. First he tried cold turkey again, and twenty years later would vividly remember, 'The only recurring dreams I had [were] always that the dope was hidden behind the wallpaper. And in the morning, you'd wake up and see fingernail marks where you'd actually tried to do something about it.' For Richards, Point of View was also a place to make music; Jagger's 'social disease' bred its own antidote, and Keith was soon swinging less with the Studio 54 crowd than with the groups who packed the all-hours clubs around Kingston. The loose collective of bands, habitually bombed on the local herb known as Goatshit, included seminal figures like Angus Gaye, Brinsley Forde and the legendary rhythm section of Sly & Robbie. Keith apart, most rock stars still ignored or mocked reggae, whose success was a genuine populist phenomenon back when such a thing was still possible — when a Peter Tosh could excite audiences on a regional circuit before the LA or London press pronounced judgement. World music was a guilty pleasure among a few, studiously hip New York critics, but Keith was the one shouting its joys from the skyscraper tops.

Back in South Salem, Anita's own focus was shifting from drugs to alcohol. 'Jack Daniel's and ginger ale. That was my favourite. Vodka ... wine ... tequila ... anything. Keith was never there, and then I had Marlon. Marlon was like nine years, ten years old and he hadn't gone to school. So we had to find a way of like inserting ourselves into society. I didn't want to have this regular life, with Marlon going to school, but I had to. There was no other way. So I drank myself into oblivion.'

Not surprisingly, Anita began to find herself physically ill as a result: she put on weight, had flu-like symptoms, spent time in hospital. Cecil Beaton's Scott-and-Zelda shots of the couple in Morocco were like relics of a bygone age. It had been exactly ten years now since those Saharan nights.

Keith was remarkably loyal to Anita, whom he joined in New York over Christmas. 'She's everything, man,' he announced. 'It all comes from her. The lot.'

15 February 1978. Constable Bill Seward, the arresting and chief investigating officer in Keith's drug case, was killed in a car crash. Shortly after that, the Justice Department ordered that the charge of possession for the purpose of trafficking (potential life sentence) be reduced to simple possession. In a separate ruling, the RCMP – who argued strongly against the lighter charge – were formally barred from reading Keith's prior arrest history into the record. Unless they happened to be rock music fans, none of the jurors would know anything about the proceedings in Nice, London or Aylesbury. By then Keith himself was back in the studio in Paris. He again failed to appear in court on 6 March. The judge declined to revoke Keith's bail or, as prosecutors demanded, to throw him in jail. He set a trial date of Monday 23 October.

6.45 on a Saturday morning, 1 April, and the Stones called an end to *Some Girls*. The last take of the last session produced Before They Make Me Run, a cocky tune driven by a nasty electric guitar. 'I'm gonna find my way to heaven, 'cause I did my time in hell/Wasn't looking too good, but I was feelin' real well' Keith sang, as if reviewing the past seven years. The thirty or so outtakes were similarly winning; Richards left behind yet another version of Start Me Up, done reggae style, and half the songs for *Emotional Rescue*.

Now Keith wanted to go on tour. Jagger refused, telling the press he'd never take to the road 'with a geezer pushin' a heroin charge'. While agreeing that it was a terrible thing Canada was doing to Keith, Mick preferred to stay low, concentrating on his impending divorce proceedings and a child-support suit brought by Marsha Hunt.

Harsh things were said over the next month, especially by Richards about Jagger. 'Anything I do, he's got to negate,' Keith fumed. 'He's very dictatorial lately.' Richards was soon able to rally Charlie and Ron Wood to the idea of a tour (no one consulted Bill, or apparently cared), with Atlantic and EMI also on board. By early May 1978, Keith was back on heroin, fighting with Anita and facing the possible end of the road in Toronto. Mick finally agreed to go out on stage with him.

Keith got his way, too, when he signed Peter Tosh to Rolling Stones Records. Tosh was right on the edge, a spliff-toting black avenger who wrote songs like Legalize It and Equal Rights. (Mick was said to have wanted Eddy Grant, whose Walkin' On Sunshine would be a big crossover hit.) Keith dubbed guitar on Tosh's *Bush Doctor*, then hired him to open for the Stones on the summer tour. He also honoured his earlier promise to Etta James.

Some Girls. The band's finest album since its certified masterpiece, *Exile*. Even the cover provides some cheap thrills – a collage of a Frederick's of Hollywood bra ad, inspired by Jerry Hall, over which Raquel Welch threatens to sue. A week or two later, it would be Jesse Jackson's turn, railing at Jagger's fey lyrics about black girls wanting to get fucked all night. ('But they *do*,' Mick protested.) Although Keith's Beast Of Burden wedges a blues riff into a Motown-type ballad, *Girls* otherwise sticks to a sleazy itinerary down the alleys of New York. If the album's ugly travelogue, Shattered, describes a city that the Chamber of Commerce doesn't know, both Keith's riff and Mick's 'Looka me!' vocal catch the true spirit of the place. For once, the battling egos only bring out the best in one another.

Miss You, the album's opener, draws on funk, dance, spoken word, Manhattan's avant-garde scene and 4/4 disco without specifically being any one of them or even a hyphenated combo. Slow up When The Whip Comes Down and you've got Hand Of Fate with twisted lyrics. Far Away Eyes is sung for laughs, the honky tonk women gone rhinestone; Keith, among many others, found the Lyle Lovett-on-acid vocals a tad overdone. Charlie slaps out crafty-bastard cousins of the Rocks Off beat on Respectable, a parting salvo at Bianca with screaming guitar riffage that sounds uneasily like Slade.

Nearly all's forgiven, however, thanks to Keith's whiplash version of My Way, Before They Make Me Run. Supple slide and steel work from Wood, rock solid support from Watts and a vocal that almost swings make for a classic. This was Richards telling a few million friends about his music, his bust and the prospect of doing hard time. Part of his inspiration on *Some Girls* was the chaos of his home life – it's not hard to hear Anita's influence in the tough lyric of Keith's Curtis Mayfield homage, Beast Of Burden. For years now, a sure sign of Keith's mood had been his regular public love letters. For sheer romanticism, it was hard to beat You Got The Silver. The warmhearted choruses of Wild Horses and Happy signalled impending fatherhood. On Coming Down Again, Keith began taking the measure of things and fearing the worst. Now the downward spiral continued. *Some Girls* ended with Shattered, a snarled Baedeker tour of Manhattan infused with new depths of alienation and scorn, along with a booty-shaking groove.

Girls resuscitated the Stones, just as *Banquet* had ten years earlier. It sold eight million copies, and actually toppled *Saturday Night Fever* from number one. With Dylan no longer bringing it all back home, the Beatles mummified and Led Zep grounded, this was the Stones searching for – and finding – a new voice.

Keith had told the judge in Toronto that he was a creative soul racked with emotional pain, but that he was 'firmly resolved' to kick drugs. In fact he was back shooting heroin three times a day that spring. His doctors needed three to four weeks to prepare him to tour, and even then things would go wrong. On 15 May he appeared at the US embassy in Paris, where he renewed his H2 temporary work visa. A week later, Keith arrived at Todd Rundgren's estate in Woodstock, New York, where the Stones planned to rehearse. Handlers had to carry him from his car up a flight of stairs to the apartment where he and Anita would be staying. Later that night Keith hooked up the black box again. According to Jerry Hall:

> He was lying there wearing these things that looked like headphones ... Mick and I would feed him. And every time

the hooks would fall off we'd clip them back on ... We'd cover
him up with a blanket at night. It gave Mick a very good feeling
to be able to help Keith.

Hall, now living openly with Jagger for the first time, remembered Keith
as having been under their care for the best part of a month. 'You know
the feeling when you have a child, and you watch him grow? We were like
"Look, he's having a bath!" and "Oh, did you see what he was doing?"'
According to Stu, Keith stayed with Mick for a total of two days.

A week later, Anita called for a car and went back to the house in
South Salem. Ron Wood's girlfriend Jo Howard soon brought a visiting
Swedish model named Lilly Wenglass to Woodstock, where she moved in
with Keith. Lill was another hot blonde, sexy, self-assured. Friends noticed
a touch of a younger Anita in the way she held herself. Lill didn't much like
drugs. If there's such a thing as a designer padded cell, it may have been that
soundproofed suite, knee-high in electrical gear and methadone and Jack
Daniel's bottles, where Keith lazily riffed on the guitar and finally decided
to kick heroin.

Jagger, meanwhile, was throwing the tour together as best he could,
adding and dropping cities faster than the press could list them. Sometimes
only he knew where and when the Stones would be playing a day later. On
10 June, 12,000 fans in Lakeland, Florida, bought tickets to see what was
billed on the marquee as 'The Great Stoned-Out Wrestling Champions'.
The cops bust the dressing room before the show, arresting a coke dealer,
and next morning Keith bought a stolen .38 Special. Elsewhere in the south
the band were touted as the Blue Boys and the Cockroaches, among other
aliases. A day or two into the tour, one of the Stones would get ill; they
played poorly in Washington, got booed as they left the stage in Philadelphia.
It was Mick Jagger.

Generally, the ninth American tour was a modest success. The Stones
knew how the game was played, and their flair for cranked-up showmanship
was close to foolproof. But behind the scenes, simmering problems now
came to the boil. For public consumption Keith and Mick were a team,
complementary, mutually supportive when needs be. Jagger was team
captain, no doubt of that. A subordinate role was accepted by Keith, if
with some muttering. But he was rather less subordinate, far more an
equal player, than in the twilight junkie years. Keith chafed at Jagger's

'Napoleon shit' and tendency to use the Stones as a backing band. Offstage, too, there were hassles with Anita, who was doing two bottles of vodka a day. Jagger and Wood were both being divorced. Wyman talked openly about quitting while he could. Charlie, in his great quip, 'just [sat] at the back and played the fuckin' drums'.

The Stones' last three American tours had, like Russian dolls, become diminishing versions of the same good idea. This one had a few departures. For seven weeks the band played a novel mix of arenas, more intimate theatres and even clubs. Jagger camped on, wearing tight red leather pants, a white dinner jacket and – more than once – a rakishly tilted golf cap. Keith laughed out loud when he first saw the outfit. The extensive staging and set-list were both pared back. Keith and Woody parodied the punks' thrashing guitar style, revved up the beat and brought in some of the classic Stones anthems in under two minutes. They got lousy reviews.

Still, however improbably, Keith pulled it off – perhaps because, by now, people focused on him as a symbol. Widespread support didn't always spare him from some ribald terrace abuse. Chants of 'You're going down' broke out at the back of certain halls, followed by the sound of punches and oaths from that general area. COULD BE THE LAST TIME and IT'S ALL OVER NOW were only the most obvious of the Toronto-inspired headlines. The Keith legend drew strength from his looming rock 'n roll martyrdom. Here was a drama in which a great man had been persecuted and destroyed at the height of his powers. The fans weren't just getting an act that was a clever mix of the exotic and the familiar. They were also enjoying the thrill of real jailhouse rock.

Or, that's one theory. Keith himself never bought it. He just wanted to play 'as many fucking gigs' as he could. The distinctions, fetishized by the critics, between the authentic and the phony were, to Keith, 'just so much dogshit'. It was all one concert for him.

The tour drove on. At the Rupp Arena, Lexington, a fan was shot and others plunged through a sheet of plate glass in a dispute about tickets. In Chicago, Richards went backstage at the Quiet Knight club to see Muddy Waters; when he appeared, Keith promptly fell down and kissed him on the hand. A week later, in Fort Worth, the Stones' blind fan, Rita Bedard, was taken backstage to meet the band. To her, Keith wasn't a martyr at all; instead, he was avuncular, kind and almost absurdly courteous – when she came in the hospitality suite, he not only greeted her warmly but introduced her to everyone else in the room, making sure she had tickets and a lift to the next gig. In Tucson, a marquee reading 'Welcome Mick Jagger . . . and the Rolling Stones' raised Keith's hackles. Steve McQueen showed up in Anaheim, demanding dozens of free passes. (Keith: 'Tell him to get on his bike.') As in 1972, the tour ended on Mick's birthday. He and the Stones each took home three-quarters of a million bucks for forty-seven days' work.

One of the few other visitors backstage was Richards' high-powered Toronto lawyer, Austin Cooper. After discussing strategy for his trial, Keith sat down in New York and, for the first time in eleven years, wrote his father a letter. This time, Bert replied. A tentative peace began, both sides talking about meeting some time. In late July Keith symbolically restored the 's' to his surname. He also wrote to Janey Perrin when her husband, Les, died on 7 August. This was an important side to Keith: he was someone who could, and did, help a friend in need; he could be warmly human in bad times, generous, compassionate. On his way back to the limo after the tour's final show, a whacked Keith got down on his hands and knees to play with some of the crew's small children, patiently and exhaustively, as always. A blond teenager with a familiar leer was also backstage that night: Brian Jones's eldest son, Julian.

For the rest of the summer, Keith, Woody and their women rented a house in the Hollywood hills. Trying to light a flaming torch by the pool one night, Keith managed to set fire to his pants instead, and had to jump into the deep end to extinguish himself. A week later, a neighbour happened to see black smoke pouring out of the house at eight one morning and called the emergency services. With police and firemen swarming onto the grounds, Keith and Lill climbed out of an upstairs window and leapt to safety. The place was still smouldering an hour later, Keith pacing up and down wearing only a bed sheet. Everyone flinched when first his guitar and then his ammo started exploding in the bathroom. The crowd on the lawn became a small mob, and some of them yelled for everyone who wasn't there on city business to leave, and Keith himself seemed anxious to go, as a policeman tried to take a statement. One of the other house guests lay down on the grass and took a nap. At that moment a sports car pulled up, driven by a friend of Anita's who lived in the neighbourhood. Keith and Lill leapt in and, leaving officialdom behind, the three tore off down Sunset Boulevard.

On 7 October the Stones played on *Saturday Night Live*, their first US television appearance since Ed Sullivan. Keith was staying in a room at the Essex House hotel, registered under the name Thomas Crapper. A fortnight later, he and Lill flew into Toronto on a Learjet and made for a suite at the Four Seasons. Everything was booked at the last possible minute, using a new alias. Give me a break here, Keith's hat and shades seemed to say. Besides, the press should have been busy elsewhere that week. Sid Vicious had just been busted in New York, for murder.

Forty-two journalists were waiting for Keith in the lobby.

Ten years ago it would have been unimaginable, during the Montreal Olympics it would have been unthinkable. But now, for the first time, Pierre Trudeau's Liberal government was in serious trouble. Published polls showed that more than half the Canadian electorate were worried about the economy; press and TV coverage reflected the widespread concern over taxes, rising energy costs, soaring unemployment. By late 1978, Trudeau was locked in a bitter struggle to reconcile provincial and ethnic rights to the federal government. The War Measures Act had been invoked. Radical Quebec separatists personally targeted the First Family, and Trudeau and his three sons lived under tight security. There was a disaffected left wing within his own party; meanwhile, the Conservative opposition were rallying support against the state's famously generous welfare provisions and well-padded budget. A general election was only five months away.

Against this backdrop, the Justice Department came up with a plan to settle the matter of *Crown v Keith Richards*. The prosecution would accept a plea of guilty to possession of heroin, then drop both the trafficking and coke charges. All outstanding Bench warrants for Keith's arrest for non-appearance at previous hearings would be waived. The plan served several purposes. On a petty level, it would avoid a long and quite likely embarrassing trial, with testimony about the PM's wife. An international furore about jailing Keith, and thus scuttling the Stones, could also mean that, if anything, the government would be less likely, not more, to shore up plunging confidence in the Canadian dollar. In a cabinet meeting on 8 September, Trudeau also emphasized the 'vital importance' of promoting the image of a 'compassionate Canada', one that was generous towards even those 'who would abuse the hospitality of our people'.

Keith arrived at the York County courthouse on the Monday morning of

23 October. A few years later, he told *Guitar Player* that 'When I'm thrown in court, or anybody like me, the jury's got absolutely no experience in the musician's way of life, so they're not your peers – they don't know what it's like; so give me Chuck Berry and Muddy Waters on the panel.' In fact, no jury would be seated that morning. Keith's fate rested solely with Judge Lloyd Graburn, a respected Liberal barrister in earlier days, the very model of Trudeau's caring state and, what's more, a tireless campaigner on behalf of the Canadian Institute for the Blind.

Keith entered the court dressed in a three-piece tan suit, white socks and scuffed brown shoes. He was sporting an earring. There were gasps, gavelled down by Judge Graburn, when the Crown's Paul Kennedy announced the reduced charges. Kennedy then made a rambling speech in which he argued that Keith had been caught with quite a lot of drugs, and had written some songs that mentioned the stuff. The prosecutor couldn't immediately remember which ones. Nonetheless, he was sure he had. Kennedy suggested that a jail term of six months, or some lesser time, might be appropriate.

In Keith's defence, Austin Cooper said that his client had a poor self-image and problems with other people. The fifty-year-old Cooper quoted movingly from a biography of Baudelaire, saying that art is created from 'pieces of the shattered self. Witness our modern greats. Van Gogh was a schizophrenic and cut his ear off. Aldous Huxley was a drug addict.' Cooper then compared Richards to Sylvia Plath and Judy Garland. A conga line of witnesses, including *Saturday Night Live* boss Lorne Michaels, testified that the Stones in general, and Keith in particular, were the world's greatest rock 'n rollers. Cooper read out glowing reports from the Stevens clinic, insisting Richards had been off heroin since May 1977. He added that Keith would personally raise $1 million for an unspecified drug rehab programme; he still might.

'The public interest would best be served by allowing him to prop up his sagging personal life, to continue his musical work and to continue his treatment,' Cooper concluded.

The judge, agreeing that 'this is a matter of great importance to Keith Richards and Canada', announced that he would pass sentence at ten the next morning.

Keith arrived, punctually for once, that Tuesday, still wearing his tan suit and tugging nervously at his earring as Judge Graburn read out his ten-page ruling. He agreed that the defendant was a heavy drug user. But, the judge added, Keith was doing well in therapy, more of which was clearly needed. 'The crown seeks a jail term,' he concluded, 'but I will not incarcerate him for addiction and wealth.' At that, a barely perceptible twitch played over Keith's face.

The judge continued, 'Maybe the Rolling Stones have encouraged drug use in their songs. Still, his efforts have been to move firmly away from the drug culture and can only encourage those who emulate him.' Now it was the turn of the press to crack a smile.

The full sentence ran: No fine, no jail; defendant to be of good behaviour for a year; to continue treatment at the Stevens clinic; lastly, to give a benefit concert within six months on behalf of the Canadian Institute for the Blind. Quite by chance – there could have been no collusion – Keith's fan Rita Bedard had personally lobbied the judge on this final point. As soon as the verdict was in, Richards slowly raised a clenched fist above his head and left the courtroom to loud applause. Clutching a tumbler full of vodka, he then briefly stopped by a press conference held at his hotel, said he was pleased 'things [had] gone according to plan', and flew back to New York within the hour. Keith put in a raucous appearance that night with the band Rockpile, jamming on Let It Rock and Happy.

Public and press reaction to Keith's non-sentence was mixed. Several of the more cosmopolitan American papers hailed it as a model of enlightened jurisprudence. In contrast, the Canadian tabloids were extremely bitter. They didn't regard the judge's ruling as an illuminating commentary on the paradox of prosecuting a crime of which the perpetrator was also the victim. They saw it as, all too literally, blind justice. Not untypical was the Toronto *Sun*: 'If you, as a taxpaying Canadian, had been arrested with 22 grams of finest heroin and coke, what would have happened to you? Would Judge Graburn have let you off? There are Canadians sitting in jail for lesser drug offences.' Trudeau's predecessor as prime minister, John Diefenbaker, told the House of Commons in Ottawa on 25 October, 'In view of the fact that the drug problem is increasing, particularly in this country, the government should give immediate consideration to challenging the preposterous and more than lenient sentence imposed yesterday on Keith Richards.' A month later the Crown duly lodged an appeal, which came to nothing. Cynics on papers like the *Sun* were left to speculate, quite openly, that an 'expensive and major fix' was in.

Keith celebrated freedom by putting out his first solo single, a cover of

Chuck Berry's Run Rudolph Run which had actually been cut two years earlier. The song bombed. After a brief interlude in Jamaica, Richards and his family flew back to spend Christmas in London. It happened to be his thirty-fifth birthday. As Keith walked through the terminal at Heathrow, a number of reporters slapped him on the back and wished him well. None of them recognized the thickset, middle-aged woman with broken teeth and matted, greasy hair hobbling along behind him. It was Anita.

7

Soul Survivor

THE BAND KEITH RICHARDS REJOINED IN 1979 WAS A SORRY SIGHT.

Having kicked heroin, and parachuted back into an executive position, Keith feared the Stones would piss it all away in one row after another. The whole thing was a nightmare. Every session was tense, every meeting fraught. Richards left his mattress throne at the Ritz hotel that 20 January and flew to Nassau to record. Jagger was soon making sarcastic comments when Keith reasserted himself in the studio. Little digs. Rolling his eyes. Vodka was replacing smack as the drug of choice. A blotto Richards annoyed Jagger so much that on 7 February Mick refused to come to work, noting that Keith was 'so out of it nothing [had] been done'. Most of the music was being recycled from *Some Girls*. The Nassau studio appeared to be echoing not so much to great rock 'n roll as to the sound of barrels being scraped. One of the engineers told Keith that Mick wished out loud that he'd go back to being a junkie. Before long the Glimmer Twins struck a non-alignment pact, rarely working on the same days and not even speaking when they did. Meanwhile, Wood was busy taking up the slack by becoming a major freebase addict. Bill Wyman talked about quitting again. Charlie reportedly told the *Daily Mail* that rock 'n roll was a load of old cobblers, which he hated.

Keith: 'In the Seventies, when I was on dope and I'd do nothing but put the songs together and turn up and not deal with any of the business of the Stones, Mick took all of that work on his shoulders . . . When I cleaned up – "Hey I'm back, I'm clean, I'm ready; I'm back to help and take some of the weight" – immediately I got a sense of resentment ... Mick [saw] it as a power grab.'

Stu, present for most of the *Emotional Rescue* sessions, remembered them as 'either Keith or Mick with a backing band. There was less debate.' When one such debate occurred, over whether or not to record Dance as an instrumental jam, Keith fumed for an hour, then left the room. Mick insisted on lyrics.

To hear Keith tell it, the very year he reclaimed his life happened to tally with a case of collective burnout. 'We were just tired of being the Stones,' he later said. 'And since we couldn't find a way out, we started fighting and smashing it all to bits.' Jagger again refused to tour in 1979. Early that spring Keith and Woody moved to LA, putting together a pickup band to support Ron's new and best solo album *Gimme Some Neck*. They made themselves scarce with the press, favouring comedians like Peter Cook or John Belushi and the *Saturday Night Live* crowd. Belushi turned everyone on to some pharmaceutical coke and, apparently, Persian Brown heroin.

At thirty-five Keith cut a stooped, gaunt figure with hard features and greying hair. Patently, he was no drug-free zone. Thanks to Lill Wenglass and to sheer willpower, he'd actually kicked the Brown; that left only coke, pot, Marlboro Reds and 80 per cent proof vodka in Keith's chemical locker. It was now, in 1979, that he began his long and sometimes troubled relationship with Stolichnaya Gold. Like so many recovering junkies before and after him, booze became a constant factor in his life. And while Keith would never call himself an alcoholic, he didn't go for extended periods without a belt of some kind. A man who suffered regular bouts of boredom and depression, he turned to drink as a mood-altering substance: a way of digging himself out of a hole that, it seemed, only lowered him in deeper as soon as the high wore off.

Mick Taylor's first solo album, *Leather Jacket*, was out that summer. The title track rolled out a veritable panzer division of hot-wired guitars and nasty lyrics. (A year or two later, Taylor chose to sue the Stones for some back royalties.) That same month, just as the Crown's John Scollin appealed Keith's guilty-but-free verdict in Toronto, Tony Sanchez published *Up and Down With the Rolling Stones*, a lurid account of his boss's junk years. Sanchez portrayed Keith and Anita as mean and pathetic, smack-addled derelicts. 'Corruption of innocents was one of their favourite pastimes ...

Sick ... Cold, hardhearted bastards.' Not the sort of testimonial to impress DA Scollin and his team.

Keith: 'I couldn't plough through it all because my eyes were watering from laughter. But the basic laying out of the story – "He did this, he did that" – is true ... Tony was a great guy. I always considered him a friend of mine. I mean, not any more.'

Keith happened to run into Sanchez in New York, a month or two after the book came out. 'I showed him a new shooter I'd gotten. Haven't seen him since.'

Although Keith kidded around about the book, in the months ahead he needed all the favourable press he could get. At one stage the lawyers warned him that the Canadian Justice Department could serve him a writ the moment he next set foot in the country, then seize his passport.

'The Stones are kind of selfish bastards,' Keith later admitted. Aside from their LA smoker of six years earlier, which raised not only money but their own profile, the band had studiously avoided most or all charity work. That Easter, however, Keith, who had never taken orders in his life, had orders to play in Toronto. In March, he announced he'd execute his sentence at two shows in the dormitory town of Oshawa, thirty miles east of the city, on 22 April. Keith's performances for the blind beat the court-imposed deadline by just twenty-four hours.

Oshawa's 5,000-seat Civic Auditorium had seen nothing like it. Particularly on a Sunday night. The small lakeside town filled up quickly that weekend with the Stones' entire tour apparatus: fleets of limos and equipment trucks; phalanxes of cops, both uniformed and plainclothes, mingling with the band's sumo-sized protection squad; various managers, lawyers, roadies and the all-important fluffers and puffers; reporters and photographers flown in from LA and London; coked-out groupies wearing flimsy Keef T-shirts and screaming that Mick was the father of their children; even, on this occasion, several hundred visually impaired fans (though only a fraction of the audience was legally blind). Ticket prices ranged from $10, face value, to $500 scalped for a chance to see justice served.

Keith and Woody's road band, the New Barbarians, opened the show, doing most of *Gimme Some Neck* along with Keith's Happy. The Stones then took over, racing through their 1978 *Some Girls* set. Jagger, still in his tour outfit of red pants and pink FUNKY BUTT T-shirt, was on top form. Along with the calculated circus-sideshow charm of a massed Stones/Barbarians Jack Flash, Keith slipped in some slower ones, bending his nicotine-stained croon into the folksy Prodigal Son. Both stompers and ballads had the place dancing or swooning, every song as thrilling as rock should be. The Stones, who paid their own expenses, lost a great deal of money by voluntarily accompanying Keith. They raised $50,000 on behalf of the Canadian blind.

Two nights later, the Barbarians opened a month-long tour in Ann Arbor, Michigan. Keith, travelling on a diet of Stoli and coke, was accompanied by Lill Wenglass. Anita remained on the farm in South Salem. Marlon commuted between the two camps. The seventh of May was the date Keith had originally been ordered to report to his probation officer in Toronto. Instead he was onstage that night with the Barbs at Madison Square Garden. The band made a great entrance, a spotlight punching up Keith and Woody looking like twin crows, rasping out Sam Cooke and Elvis classics along with a few originals, all powered by Ziggy Modeliste on drums. Richards himself performed the parts ordinarily taken by horns, double bass and organ, as well as extraordinary parts that existed only in Keith's brain. In all, those eighteen North American gigs were some of his finest moments. The Barbarians wrapped their tour on 21 May, with a sold-out TV special at the LA Forum. Unfortunately, the customized Learjet and individual limos, not to mention all the drugs and room service, did for the tour's profits. Keith, whose recent legal fees had cost him a reported $3 million, was badly disappointed. *Gimme Some Neck* stiffed as well.

Richards started talking about putting out his own album, using some of the ballads he'd recorded with Stu while waiting to find out whether or not he'd be sent down. He gave it the working title of *Bad Luck*.

On 27 June, back in Toronto, Keith's lawyer read out an affidavit on his behalf to the Court of Appeals. 'I have grimly determined to change my life and abstain from any drug use,' he stated. 'I can truthfully say that the prospect of ever using any drugs again in the future is totally alien to my thinking.'

Keith evidently couldn't live up to this promise. He spent the early part of that summer blasted on coke at Fred Sessler's house in Florida. In July he was back in Paris, rowing with Mick Jagger. Every time they worked on a song, things seemed to take a turn for the worse. 'For me an argument doesn't impinge, intrude, on my personal feelings,' Keith said. 'But it got to the point that every argument that started to come along was taken as a personal attack. And then it becomes difficult to talk about anything . . . By now [Jagger] should know my style and he shouldn't take it so hard.'

Friday 20 July. Keith was in Paris, kicking around the thirtieth take of a reggae-style Start Me Up. At ten that night, Anita was lying on the couple's bed 3,000 miles away in South Salem, watching TV with a seventeen-year-old friend called Scott Cantrell. Marlon and Fred Sessler's son Jeffrey were downstairs. In what may have been a disastrous game of Russian roulette, Cantrell blew his brains out with Keith's stolen .38 Special while Anita was 'tidying up' a few feet away. 'He was lying on his back and I turned him over,' she said. 'I heard a gurgling sound. He was choking on his blood. I picked up the revolver and put it on a chest of drawers. I don't like guns.'

Detective Douglas Lamanna, who responded to Marlon's emergency call, said that when he arrived Cantrell was breathing but unconscious. He died ninety minutes later at a nearby hospital. Lamanna said Cantrell was lying on top of the soiled bed covers, barefoot, wearing a shirt and jeans. One corner of the massive oak bed was broken and propped up with a chair. The New York *Post* would report that the first ambulance crew to arrive on the scene was staggered by the sheer squalor and air of decay: 'There was a powerful, unpleasant stench, as if there was a dead cat somewhere.' Anita, in bloodstained clothes, spent the next seven hours at Lewisboro, New York, police headquarters, where Detective Lamanna questioned her and confiscated her Italian passport. She was charged with possession of a stolen weapon.

The headlines made much of the old Stones associations with sex, drugs and death. It didn't go unnoticed that Keith and Anita's house was in a part of America historically linked with witchcraft. Over the next month, the *Post* pressed the case with excitable front page scoops about 'ritualistic' orgies involving Anita and various teenage friends and neighbours. On 16 August the paper quoted fifteen-year-old Steve Levoie, calling her 'a sick person . . . The house was filthy and she was dirty herself.' The paper added that a policeman had been attacked by 'a flock of black-hooded, caped people' a mile from Frog Hollow. The same officer had apparently found cats and dogs 'sacrificed' nearby. Nuns at a local convent told authorities of hearing 'strange chants, gun shots and loud music'.

The police later cleared Anita of involvement with Scott Cantrell's death, which was ruled a suicide, but pressed ahead with the possession charge. She was fined $1,000. The publicity came at the worst possible time for Keith, who worried, not without cause, that the Toronto DA would use it when appealing his probated sentence. According to Anita, Keith rang from Paris on the morning of 21 July and was understandably shaken, if not at Cantrell's death. 'He didn't say anything about the guy, he just got annoyed with my negligence, being so sloppy and flopped out. He just said, "Oh, you managed to lose a piece, didn't you?"' A few hours later, a large van arrived to remove all Keith's guitars from the house for 'cleaning'. Pallenberg knew then and there that it was the end of their twelve-year relationship.

Keith: 'I cleaned myself up. But [Anita] didn't. And I realized that I couldn't sleep with someone who had a needle beside the bed. I was too fragile at that point. I loved her, but I had to leave.'

In and out of hospital for the next five years, Anita would now hit bottom. Bloated and depressed, she went on a binge that, at its sorry nadir, included swigging horse tranquilliser from out of a bottle. In 1983, she was raided for drugs in London's Grosvenor House hotel. At around the same time, she spent eight weeks on an alcoholic ward. One night, a drunken Anita tore her hip out of its socket by falling out of bed. Keith was extremely supportive. His line, throughout, was that he loved Anita and that he meant to look after her whether or not they were actually together.

'Then my son started to intervene,' Anita said. 'Hide the bottles, hide the money; things a child shouldn't have to do. No friends over, lots of arguments. I was accident-prone – crashing out, emergency room, straitjackets . . . Oh, man.'

Eventually, Pallenberg was able to detox and move to a halfway house in Notting Hill, around the corner from the pop star's lair she'd so bewitched in *Performance*. No longer the wasted Stones concubine, Anita re-emerged in her forties a much-loved penitent – 'I did a lot of service'. She worked on a telephone help line, rode a ten-speed bike, went to the gym. By the late 1980s Anita was sober and back living in a flat in Chelsea. Although long admired for her design skills, and contributing to the way Keith looked on stage, she became even more focused, studying art formally at St Martin's College.

Anita transformed others, and she also transformed herself. She and Keith became friendly again, spending New Year's together and putting

Toronto and Salem and 'all that shit' behind them. Neither party has ever been busted since.

On 11 August 1979, Keith and the Barbarians played to an audience of nearly quarter of a million at Knebworth. Backstage the talk turned, as it often did, to mutual friends. Richards good-naturedly dubbed Bob Dylan, then entering his born-again phase, the 'prophet of profit'. He got off a few Queen Mick jokes. Keith was rocking to and fro in his chair, puffing contentedly. Despite the lurid press coverage in New York, and some anxious calls from the lawyers, he seemed surprisingly tranquil. He loved the Barbarians – '[I] needed a break. It's easy to go a little crazy inside the Rolling Stones bubble if that's all you do.'

On 17 September the five judges of the Ontario Court of Appeal finally rejected the Crown's case. They cited an 'extremely positive' report from Keith's doctors in reaching their decision. For the first time in two and a half years, he was now free of the threat of being jailed. The press was rife with speculation about Keith's good luck, contrasting it to Chuck Berry's fate just then at the hands of a US tax court. Berry got four months for a minor case of evasion.

Keith spent part of the autumn in Paris, part with Lill Wenglass in Florida. Stu couldn't remember any more 'specific crap' going down in the studio. He only remembered the heaviness that had replaced the fizz. When Keith returned to New York to mix *Emotional Rescue*, he and Lill continued to see each other. She was so stuck on him that she bravely kept the dealers away, and 'didn't take shit' even from Mick. But the relationship cooled. Before long, Keith would be making his way back down to Washington Square, heavily armed, to score coke. Quite apart from that, he was downing ever greater amounts of Stoli. For him life as a boozer was unpredictable, a life on the wagon impossible. Vodka, whisky and beer had become his constant companions, his most loyal friends. Sometimes, late at night, he'd take his bottles and flasks out of his bag, line them up and *beam*. As well as the pleasure, there was a certain amount of grief involved. Keith flaked out one day after seven or eight nights on the grog, bounced off the side of a speaker cabinet and shattered his nose.

Keith celebrated his thirty-sixth birthday that December with a party at the Roxy roller rink in New York. Guests noticed that he was wearing a striking silver ring, in the shape of a skull, the gift of a jeweller friend named David Courts. Due to some confusion with the arrangements, both Anita and Lill were also present. Compounding the scene was the arrival of assorted hookers, strippers and a famed New York groupie, who waltzed in stark naked but for a red ribbon tied round her neck and promptly hauled Keith into a back room.

At the end of a long night beset by rival camps, Richards met a tall, fresh-faced blonde, a friend of Jerry Hall's, named Patti Hansen. Smart, hip, with perfect features and fierce ambition, at twenty-three she was already a veteran of several *Vogue* cover shoots. She was also about to appear in her first major movie, Peter Bogdanovich's chick-detective romp *They All Laughed*. Before reporting on set, Patti spent five days and nights cruising around New York with Keith and an entourage of large, silent bodyguards, Marlon, Fred Sessler and sundry Rastas. On the sixth day, Patti found herself at a Christmas party in Mick Jagger's apartment on Central Park West. Not surprisingly, all eyes turned to the willowy blonde and her dark-eyed companion with a bottle of Stoli in his hand. They made for a striking couple. When an exhausted Patti decided to leave, Keith turned to Jagger and said, 'I'm outta here, too. I'm going with this lady.'

Patti Hansen's world on Staten Island, New York, was hardly a hotbed of rock 'n roll. She was the youngest of six children of a bus-driver father and a woman who saw *The Sound of Music* five times. The Hansens were hardworking, modest, devoutly Lutheran; Patti came from a background of early nights and clean habits, and parents who expected her in church on Sunday, and somehow managed to move in a world where such things weren't spoken of. With a doting mother who lavished praise and encouragement on her, she began modelling while still at school. Patti was at her summer job, selling hot dogs on the beach, when she was discovered by a vacationing manager from the Wilhelmina agency. Three months later, she was on the cover of *Seventeen*.

'Patti was completely uninhibited,' says the photographer Francesco Scavullo. 'She was always running around naked on location shoots. Nothing fazed her.' Even as a supermodel Hansen went for the laugh, didn't seem to take herself too seriously. Along with the apple-pie looks, her bubbling humour and unspoilt sense of decency made her 'the real thing', a star who charmed not only agents and photographers but big-time directors like Bogdanovich (with whom she had an affair). Patti enjoyed a beer and a pizza, and came across as a cheerful, well-adjusted adult. An anomaly in the profession.

Even other models speak about a woman with her priorities straight and a permanent twinkle in her eye. Patti 'never changed'. For all her raw sex appeal, 'she was a home-town girl'. A day or two after Christmas, Patti brought her new date across on the ferry to meet her family. An awkward moment occurred when Keith arrived carrying his own bottle of vodka, but it passed off when he cracked everyone up with some great jokes about Dartford. They loved him on Staten Island.

Patti Hansen: 'When I first met Keith all I could think was, "This is a guy who really needs [someone]." I gave him the keys to my apartment. There was no sexual thing going on. I knew he just needed a secret place where he could get away from the madding crowd. But he is the most romantic man. So romantic. I remember New Year's Eve '79, com[ing] back from Staten Island because I knew somehow I was going to see him. I just knew it. When I got to my apartment, there was Keith sitting on the stairs looking for me.'

It had been a tough decade for Keith, but it ended on a high: sitting on the stoop, alone for once, waiting on a friend.

Keith both aged and matured dramatically in 1980. Grey-haired and hoarse, he was fast becoming the Dean Martin of rock 'n roll. *Rolling Stone*'s Chet Flippo interviewed him in New York that spring.

'I'm ready for my bacon and eggs,' Keith announced as he marched into the offices of Rolling Stones Records at six p.m., waving a fifth of Jack Daniel's, among other things. He had just awoken and wanted breakfast – pure sour mash. Richards was having trouble breaking the seal on the bottle. 'I've got a key we could use,' I offered, but Keith interrupted me by whipping out an enormous knife and – *kachunk!* – snapping it open. He poured us both hefty tumblers.

In late March the Stones met back in the same office to talk about *Emotional Rescue*. The discussion consisted largely of Keith and Mick yelling at each other. Jagger wanted to funk the album up with more dance grooves. Many more. Next day Richards went back to the studio to put the finishing touches to *Rescue*. The last song was his breakup ballad,

All About You, Keith crooning some lines about dogs and bitches in a voice now refined by twenty years of nicotine. Anita happened to come across Patti and him one night that spring at the Ritz in New York. Stealing up behind their table, she greeted Keith by jumping on his lap, wrapping her legs round his head and squeezing it hard between her thighs.

'*Please* let me go,' he gasped.

Keith saw Lill once or twice more, but it was clear that he'd finally found the woman who satisfied both his hard and soft sides. He cut back on the drugs, even starting a gentle exercise regime. Within a few months, Keith no longer suffered from the early-morning hots for Patti. Now he had them all day long. Soon he began drafting a love song, honouring Patti and hinting, for the first time, to the Hansens and the world, that – yes – he'd have and hold her, comfort, cherish and keep her, in sickness and health, according to God's holy ordinance.

'She's my little rock 'n roll mama/My tits 'n ass with soul, uh huh' Keith sang.

The photographer Lynn Goldsmith took some striking pictures of Patti and Keith that summer. 'Things went really well. Though he drank a couple of bottles of booze and smoked some of the biggest joints I'd ever seen, he didn't appear the least bit drunk or stoned ... Obviously he was quite a hard guy to get to know, but I'd say he was happy. Shit, he was *beaming*.'

That month, Keith moved into Patti's Greenwich Village apartment.

Richards and Jagger were at it again when *Emotional Rescue* came around. Keith told *Rolling Stone* that rock was as healthy as ever. 'We all tend to forget that it's ninety per cent crap anyway. But the ten per cent is *good*. The younger kids have sort of got the right idea on how to play it; they have the right attitude. And that's what rock is, an *attitude*.'

'Rock and roll has no future,' Jagger said. 'It's only recycled past.'

That summer, Mick went off on holiday with Jerry Hall in Morocco. Richards got a 'Dear Keith' telegram from Marrakesh, once again scuppering plans for a tour. He was livid. 'Mick waits until he's three thousand miles away and then he just sends a letter,' Richards fumed to the author Stanley Booth. Unlike Jagger, Keith seemed compelled to air his grievances as openly as possible. 'The old *cunt*,' he added, among friends.

Compounding the problem, Ron Wood, Keith's crazy-kid brother figure, was now overdoing it with the booze and freebase. Before long he blew his septum, started missing sessions, got busted. All of this might sound familiar, because it was the road first Jones and then Richards had taken. As the sorcerer's apprentice, Woody had learnt to out-Keith Keith. Meanwhile, Wyman was promising to quit the band in 1982. (In a later correction, Bill said he'd been misquoted.) Given the chance, Charlie liked to stay home and raise sheepdogs.

Keith's solo album had fallen on hard times as well. *Bad Luck* was postponed and would resurface, in radically different form, eight years later. For all the great tracks he'd cut, alone or with Stu, Keith's top priority was to get the Stones back on the road.

Following a press party for *Emotional Rescue* at New York's Danceteria in late June, a sullen-looking group headed uptown by limo to Trax, where Keith joined the poet-singer Jim Carroll on a tune called People Who Died. The two men had met up at the Stones' office earlier that morning to rehearse. When Carroll arrived Keith was sitting with his feet up on the desk, snorting coke, while Patti rested on a couch.

'Maybe we should take it easy tonight,' Carroll suggested, passing Keith two capfuls of methadone.

'Right,' he agreed. 'Do you have any more? I mean, no point being too cautious about this.'

Carroll silently handed over the bottle. Keith spent the rest of the day doing methadone, pharmaceutical coke and Stoli while Patti dozed behind him. The actual gig sounded great, everyone agreed.

A week later, Allen Klein surrendered to authorities just a few streets away from Keith and Patti's at Manhattan's downtown Correction Center. A jury had found him innocent of tax evasion, but guilty of filing a false return, in charges that dated back to 1969–70. US District Court Judge Vincent Broderick concluded that Klein had 'lied during the trial' and gave him a two-year sentence, all but two months of it suspended.

Emotional Rescue. Even on *Black and Blue*, the Stones had avoided the ploddingly obvious riffs and glam posturing of most of their peers. Their own spandex debacle came only now, in 1980. Much of the album was filled with spare parts and lazy throwaways from the *Some Girls* sessions. Like its forebear, the record was a richly eclectic, unpigeonholable mishmash – the old farts meet punk and disco, with blues and jazz and even a stray mariachi trumpet thrown in. Unhappily there were few real songs this time around, just some raunch-by-rote guitar hooks and Keith's great All About You.

Compared to the rest of the album, this was an incongruous and genuinely moving bit of music. Even more amazing for a record several miles shy of sublime, All About You was nearly dumped in favour of Sam Cooke's Let's Go Steady.

The LP opened with Dance, a vague, mid-paced loosener whose dire, Englishman-in-New York lyrics only underscored the flat, monotonous rapping. Jagger did another of his parodic high-camp country skits on Indian Girl; happily, Richards framed the vocal in a firmly picked melody. Time and again on *Rescue*, Mick's insightful metaphors and lofty puns would be anchored by Keith's solid riffing. The result was shrill, faintly derivative competence. On Where The Boys Go, an outtake from the Respectable session, Keith nails a vintage Chuck Berry solo, while Down In The Hole cops the blues. The title cut is a smoothly syncopated, Bee Gees-type romp where Mick Jagger gets protective, obsesses about his girlfriend, dons his shining armour, jumps on a fine Arab charger and rides to Jerry Hall's rescue. You could almost hear Brian Jones creasing himself.

After the tossed-off pop of She's So Cold, Keith closed the album with All About You, a potent variation on *Rescue*'s standard fare. This was mood music raised to high art. At the time, everyone assumed the lyric was a parting swipe at Anita. Keith later clarified, 'It's about Jagger ... I'd just come off junk and went back to work; in the meantime, Mick had got used to being in charge. I was made to feel like an intruder.'

Keith's bittersweet song, both pissed off and conciliatory, ends in a slew of croaks, whispers and deeply personal ruminations. In the final fade, he puts his lips to the mike and growls, 'So how come/I'm still in *love* with you?'

The critics hated *Emotional Rescue*, using terms like dumb, spiritless, tinny and flat-out awful. It spent seven weeks at number one.

That summer Keith took Patti to Redlands for the first time, then flew to Paris to record. It was another standoff. In effect, the Stones never really did do a new album after *Rescue*. Rather, *Some Girls'* engineer Chris Kimsey came up with a novel idea for everyone to make a fortune without actually going to the hassle of sitting around the studio all winter. This involved dusting off outtakes like *Black and Blue*'s Slave and several relics (Tops, Waiting On A Friend) from *Goats Head Soup*. Kimsey's major coup was to persuade Keith to give Start Me Up the open-G treatment, turning a forgotten reggae jam into a razor-edged rocker.

On 1 December, Jerry Hall informed the press, 'I can't believe how weird and dirty Mick Jagger is. When I have to be sexy in front of the camera, I think of him and it always does the trick. Mick is one of the sexiest men in the world and the best lover I've ever had. He's a genius.' Somehow this thesis found itself cut out and taped to the side of Keith's amp.

Jagger then took off to film *Fitzcarraldo* in Peru, a project immediately beset by malaria, cost overruns and hostile extras. Keith was extremely pissed off. Just as in 1969, he wanted to tour, Jagger wanted to fly halfway round the world and 'play fuckin' cowboys and Indians'. In January, Patti and Keith's neighbours, unimpressed by his habit of blasting Tutti Frutti from his stereo at all hours, managed to get them evicted. They spent the rest of the winter in a hotel.

In March, the Stones put out *Sucking in the Seventies*, a limp retread of *Black and Blue*, *Some Girls* and *Rescue*. ('A ripoff' was the *Sounds* verdict.) That same month, Keith and Mick held a summit in Barbados. Jagger finally agreed to tour again. Prince Rupert swiftly signed up the promoter Bill Graham, who projected gross box-office receipts of $50 million. As a sweetener, the prince then did a quick side deal with Jovan Perfumes, who ponied up four million to print their name on the concert tickets: rock's first such sponsorship. Opening night was scheduled for 25 September, in Philadelphia.

Much had changed since the band's last outing.

By 1981 pop stars were working half-naked on custom-built stages that exploded during the encore. Jagger's friend David Bowie pushed the sense of theatre with a set straight out of the Albert Speer drama school, lit by 700 white neon tubes. The Who owned more lasers than the British government. Rock and roll had gone mad for spectacle, and Mick wanted a part of it. He ordered up a tour of the biggest arenas, and indulged his love of props with a mechanical cherry picker that let him sing while hovering over the front of the stalls. Keith was appalled. To him, the whole thing was hopelessly vulgar – 'like poxy Vegas'. Mick reportedly offered Keith a choice: stay off all drugs on the tour, or live with the cherry picker.

Live with the cherry picker.

While Jagger huddled with the designers, Richards kept a friendly eye on his protégé Peter Tosh. The *Bush Doctor* album had done well for Atlantic, and for Keith's own vanity label. But handling the ganja-mad Tosh was becoming a problem. By 1981 he'd taken to waving a cutlass around onstage, while ranting about South Africa and nuclear war, and loudly blaming the Stones for 'fucking' his career. Keith, who regularly allowed Tosh to use his Jamaican house, generously ignored such slander, apparently chalking it up to an artistic temperament.

A year or two later, Keith and Patti landed at Kingston airport, only to find that Tosh had ignored all prior notice of their arrival and was refusing to leave the villa. As he observed on the phone, 'If you come anywhere near here, I'll shoot you.'

Keith: 'Then you better load the fucking gun, Peter, because I'll be there in an hour.'

Meanwhile, Start Me Up had had its great makeover. Chris Kimsey took the other dross and, with an alchemist's touch, turned lead into golden greats. All that remained now was to pare down the twenty-odd tracks to give the new album balance. Technical EQ-ing came, in turn, from Bob Clearmountain, a sleight-of-hand guru whose forte was buffing the voice and drums in a jewel-hard mix. In an earlier life, Clearmountain had happened to be a prize-winning maths whiz. Much of the work that went on that spring was similarly number-crunching drills in adding and subtracting mere fractions of sound. At times, it was more a lab than a studio, with white-coated men speaking in hushed tones about clean-ups and DIs while Keith mumbled his layman's 'yep' or 'nope'. By early June, *Tattoo You* was ready to explode onto the chart.

Later that month, Keith and Patti happened to bump into Chuck Berry backstage at a New York club. The fact that Berry punched Keith in the nose, and Keith laughed it off, somehow adds to both their myths. 'Fucker didn't *recognize* me,' Richards explained. Berry later apologized to Wood (whom, compounding the problem, he kept calling 'Jack'), thinking he was Keith.

Resting in Barbados, Richards took a phone call from eighty-one-year-old Hoagy Carmichael. The Jazz Age bandleader liked the job Keith had done on his Nearness Of You (a ballad he'd cut, though never released, with Bobby Keys), and wanted to 'try to turn me on to like 250 other songs he'd written'. After hanging up, Keith turned to Patti and said, 'Fuck me! That was like getting a call from Beethoven.' Hoagy Carmichael died just a few weeks later.

In August, everyone settled into six weeks' rehearsal at Longview Farm, a luxurious studio-resort in the rolling hills west of Boston. Just getting the Stones there had been a hassle. Keith went AWOL at Fred Sessler's house in Florida, prompting a pissed-off Wyman to fly home to England. Charlie rang him there a few days later, the worse for booze and muttering that the band were 'finished'. Both he and Bill were raging about all the delays. Keith's timing had always been limited to his guitar. He was chronically late just about everywhere else, now flying off to Rome to get a new US work visa. All five Stones eventually straggled back to the farm, where Keith and Mick rowed about whom to hire to play piano. (Woody swung the job for his old Faces mate Ian McLagan.) Bill notes that, even as rehearsals finally got under way, 'There were frequent arguments and many absences from the guitar section.'

Keith and Mick had little to say to one another. Apart from the twenty or so songs, the old friends seemed to have nothing in common. While Jagger padded around with a calculator, Keith's preferred props were a joint and a constantly replenished tumbler of Stoli over ice. With his salt and pepper shag hairdo, pixie boots and ratty scarf looped round his neck, Richards struck the visiting *Life* stringer as a 'true blue rock 'n roll outlaw'. The jaded pop chic didn't preclude a steely professionalism. Keith typically woke at dusk, wolfed some breakfast and a vodka fix, shot pool with Woody, and then put the band through their paces for eight hours. Some warm summer nights he took to directing the open-air rehearsals on horseback, galloping up in a cloud of dust. Along with his black leather pants and skull ring, Keith now sported T-shirts bearing the legend OBERGRUPPEN-K, or plain FÜHRER.

Keith also put himself in charge of Woody, telling him bluntly not to fuck up on tour. For the next two or three years, there were constant rumours that the Stones would hire yet another guitarist. Behind the scenes, Richards and Jagger quietly made arrangements to audition George Thorogood, the young American blues virtuoso and, like Keith, a major Bo Diddley fan.

When Wood discovered this, he locked himself in his apartment over the barn with his girlfriend and his freebase kit. There were plenty more coke and booze problems ahead, but, thanks in large part to Keith's loyalty, Ron kept his job.

Richards was the only man who could have both railed against dope and imported it, and he did. At Longview, he had a consignment of coke, pot and HP sauce flown in on a private jet once a week. Jagger took care of business, doing the interviews and helping design the huge blue and red, Japanese-mural set. Between times, he ran ten miles daily through the Massachusetts woods – 'I have to stay sober, in training,' he told *Life*. Keith, who wasn't in training, crashed off a porch early one morning and sprained his ankle. Sharp-eyed reporters didn't miss the ever mounting crates of dead Stoli bottles piled up at the farm's back gate. Whenever Patti asked him why he was lighting another cigarette, Keith's invariable reply was, 'Because the last one wasn't long enough.' Even so, he passed all of the pre-tour medicals.

The Stones made their move on the morning of Wednesday 26 August. Richards and Jagger announced the tour, the group released *Tattoo You*. Within twenty-four hours, two and a half million applications had been received for tickets. The US Postal Service was forced to hire 165 part-time employees to deal with the barrage. Mick used the occasion to plug the new album, declaring it 'great', 'a gas' and 'the best thing we've done in years'.

He was right. Between them, Richards and the engineers had sprayed stardust on 'old crap' and forged a modern classic. Start Me Up flaunts the unique Keith open-G riff, turning itself around twice in the first ten seconds and featuring plenty of strategically positioned dramatic pauses. His four-note bolt, instantly plunging the song home, gives way to a catchy vamp led by Charlie's precision swing. *Tattoo You* kept building from there. Slave, once thought duff even for *Black and Blue*, re-emerged as a vacuum-packed tune with a soaring Sonny Rollins sax break. Keith retooled half-a-dozen other mid-Seventies rejects to 1981 specifications. His Little T&A managed to be both lewd and tender, with some great hell-for-leather soloing and a flying sod-you to Spanish Tony.

Keith took his past to the bank again with Black Limousine, borrowing an old Jimmy Reed blues lick and scuzzing it up into a Stones anthem. The album's one new song, Neighbours, rocked like crazy while giving the finger to the residents' committee who'd bound together to evict Keith and Patti – just as you'd expect if you had the Human Riff living next door. Mick Taylor balked when he heard himself playing on Tops, a *Goats Head* outtake whose camp-falsetto vocal ruined a decent pop chorus. Never just a riff factory, Keith strummed through Waiting On A Friend, a deft guitar-and-sax ballad which showed the melody under the mayhem.

At ten o'clock on the night *Tattoo You* was released, the Stones sent out a roadie to buy a dozen copies of the *New York Times* which contained a rave review of the album. By the time he got back some of the band couldn't read – Keith was off on a horse somewhere – but it was a great party. *Tattoo You* sold over a million copies in America that week, and would do better business than *Sticky Fingers*.

On 14 September the Stones gave their first performance of the Eighties in a 300-seat dive called Sir Morgan's Cove, a few miles from Longview Farm. It was a riot. Outside, the ticketless brawled with mounted police, prompting the mayor of Boston to ban any future such public rehearsals. Both Keith and Mick had fretted whether the band still had much to offer, apart from an obvious death-watch curiosity. With one or two notable exceptions, they seemed to have been coasting for ten years. But the whole paradox of the Stones was that, as the music got worse, the personal mythologies, mainly Keith's, got bigger and better. Those two and a half million ticket requests became four million; Bill Graham added a dozen extra shows.

The same day the Stones played Sir Morgan's Cove, Furry Lewis died in Memphis. He'd long since blown his 1975 concert fee, easily the biggest of his career, and lived his last six years in a one-room ghetto flat. Furry always had the greatest respect for Keith, if not for other rock 'n roll stars. To him, they had about as much pizzazz as a set of stuffed owls in bell-jars.

25 September 1981. The Stones' stock triennial tour of America opened in Philly. They played on a vast, sloping stage in front of glitzy pop art cartoons of pink planes and purple race cars. Much of the decor was apt to cause temporary damage to the retina, and the whole project trod a thin line between vivid and trashy. Jagger's cherry picker was cranked up for him to sing Jack Flash, while blowing kisses and pelting the fans below with red roses. The band performed thus in thirty cities in just under three months. (By contrast, the mid-Sixties tours had typically run three to four weeks.) In doing so, they embedded themselves anew into the soul of a generation now willing to enjoy them from the far bleachers of football stadia. All the old standards were there, from Satisfaction to the balloon-and-firework finale. Keith was on top form throughout.

Some people think that his career really began with *Tattoo You*, others that he never quite recovered from going off his head in the mid-Seventies.

Either way, 'compelling' wasn't an adequate word for him. Keith was a global icon of debauchery, survival and glamour.

Part of the appeal was nostalgic, or morbid; Lennon and Moon and Bonham had died, and Richards was the big fish who'd wriggled out of the net. Part was visual: Keith's tour look consisted of mouldy jeans tucked into tatty suede boots, a torn T-shirt, manacles and the skull ring. A butt-end was clamped in his mouth when he wasn't actually singing, and once or twice even then. Better yet, it sounded as if Keith was less buzzed by the image than by the music. Here, too, he scored highly, balancing his raucous, rockin' yin with his sensitive yang. Even the sparse, three- and four-note fills had half the audience jumping up and down along with them.

The curtains parted, to reveal Keith lashing out the chords to Under My Thumb, capturing everything the song had to offer but its humour. (In Philadelphia, Jagger sang while a plane buzzed the stage trailing a banner, 'ROLLING STONES UNFAIR TO WOMEN'.) Then Let's Spend The Night Together . . . Neighbours . . . Shattered. Generous chunks of *Tattoo You*, and the great run-out section: Start Me Up, Honky Tonk, Brown Sugar, Jack Flash, Satisfaction. Mick came on in sporty, gay-quarterback gear and put on a slick show. There were hydraulics, platforms that went up and down, dramatic lighting effects. He sang the encore while dressed in tights and a cape fashioned out of the American and British flags. Keith's own voice was a gravel pit. His guitar playing still had that coiled spring quality, constantly being released and rewound. While Jagger romped, Keith laid back, allowing songs to build, pausing to let Charlie and Bill solo for a moment. For all the punkish garb and death's head regalia, there was a serenity about him which made the riffs all the more thrilling.

In spite of this, or perhaps because of it, some bad blood flowed. For one, there was the great Richards v Wood set-to just a week into the tour, in San Diego. 'There was too much stuff going on in his room,' Keith recalled. 'He had some dodgy people in there.'

'He came at me with a broken bottle,' says Woody. The two mates bawled each other out, Keith accusing Ron of freebasing again, then had a brief but spectacular punch-up. Several roadies had to pull them apart. Keith dropped the bottle, called Wood a cunt, and kicked the dope dealers out of the room.

Sixteen years later, a journalist asked Wood if he thought Keith could have bottled him. 'Yeah,' he nodded.

After playing the left coast the Stones headed to the notoriously mellow Pacific Northwest. The Seattle trek wasn't without incident, however. At the afternoon show, on 15 October, a sixteen-year-old girl named Pamela Melville died of massive head injuries after falling from an outside balcony at the stadium; Keith and Mick sent flowers. A second woman was arrested for informing the crowd she intended to kill 'that evil cocksucker Richards'. Through the south, then a three-night stand at New Jersey's Meadowlands, with Tina Turner also on the slate. Backstage, Keith sat toking through an interminable version of Proud Mary with Vitas Gerulatis and John McEnroe. The tennis stars were reportedly stunned at how their host 'could get fucked up and still play'. Hot topics of conversation: the best pain relievers, lesbianism in sport.

Sunday 22 November, Chicago. Keith's first order of business was to call at the 200-seat Checkerboard Lounge, where he jammed with Muddy Waters till dawn. As usual when the Stones were involved, there was a small riot outside. It was also Muddy's last ever recorded concert. Like Lewis, he championed Keith to the end. Strained bonhomie and dubious guest spots dominated the next two nights. Phoenix was a dream come true for Jerry Hall, who at last got to perform with the Stones: 'I danced around and Mick hit me on the bottom. It was thrilling.' Next up, in Kansas, Mick Taylor appeared. The reunion overexcited him – according to Wood, 'He shocked us with how loud he was blasting it . . . bulldozing through parts of songs that should have been subtle, ignoring breaks and taking uninvited solos.' Reviewing the show in later years, Keith's smoky voice turned to steel. 'That *fucker.*'

As the tour ended, *Rolling Stone* gave Keith the cover and a 5,000-word 'No Regrets' interview. It was another landmark, buoying his reputation for being both tough and tender. Keith pulled no punches. The music business had 'always put out mostly shit'. Jagger was 'pretty good at business. He's not as good as people think. He's not as good as *he* thinks.' Brian Jones 'in many ways, was a right cunt. A bastard.'

On Patti, by contrast:

It's a big one, it's a big one. Yeah. It doesn't matter, I'll tell ya – yeah, I'm in love . . . Those are the things that turn you on, you know? I mean, it's the greatest feeling in the world right? Love wears a white stetson.

18 December, Hampton, Virginia. Richards' birthday and a nationally

televised show. Doris, Marlon and Angela were all in the audience. Keith celebrated by braining a stage-crasher who evaded security and rushed Jagger during Satisfaction. For some compelling reason, hundreds of bright red balloons were raining down at the time. Those pictures of Keith calmly unstrapping his guitar, clubbing the fan and resuming the song – all without missing a beat – redoubled the legend overnight.

'Anyone's on my turf, I'm gonna chop the mother down.'

Twenty-four hours after thrilling American television, Richards brought the fifty-first and last show to a close. Thus ended what *Rolling Stone* called a tour that 'wrapped up 1981 like a silk ribbon on a sack of spuds'. When the final curtain came down, it was Keith who accepted the bouquet of roses. He was $3.5 million richer, and even more famous for all the right reasons. After six busts of various kinds and a decade of screaming headlines, friends had begun to see a new Keith emerging from the old. He spent that Christmas in England, dressing up as a merry if rather gaunt Santa Claus for his mum and young daughter.

For seven years, Jane Rose had been the Stones' interface with the world, travelling around with them carrying a bundle of passports, visas and bail money in her handbag. When Jagger fired her at the end of 1981, Keith immediately took her on as his personal manager. Mick freaked out at the perceived snub. The Glimmer Twins would play thirty-five European shows that summer without speaking to one another.

Richards spent part of the spring editing a live album and watching footage shot by Hal Ashby (*Shampoo*, *Being There*) of the American tour. He and Charlie also arranged a private New York gig for the blues maverick Stevie Ray Vaughan, the latest hot favourite to replace Wood. Vaughan, twenty-six, could alternately channel a *Band of Gypsies*-era Hendrix or a more rootsy folk balladeer. Keith reportedly liked what he heard, but loyally refused to sack Woody. He also refused to have much to do with him. Despite their public hijinks, goosing each other around the world's stages, the two addressed each other like an elderly married couple, rarely managing more than a 'yep' or 'nope'.

On 1 June, the Stones released their concert album *Still Life*. It was a good title for a record as dull as a waxed-fruit display. The overall sound conjured joyless midwestern domes where riffs echoed among the drink cans and soggy programmes. It hit number three on the chart.

That spring, after twenty years, Keith and his father met up again in London. The storybook reunion took place, at Bert's suggestion, in the saloon bar of a pub. Keith reportedly ordered his driver to stop off at a nearby off-licence, where he bought a bottle of Stoli and extra cigarettes. He's said to have then smoked three or four while pacing up and down on the pavement. Carrying a full load – family snaps, Marlboros, a complete set of Stones albums – he then opened the door of the pub, crossed over the threadbare rug and stuck out a hand.

'Wotcher, cock,' said Bert.

At sixty-eight, the one-time 'Adolf' had mellowed into a merry, bewhiskered old man with a briar pipe. Bert's rounded, guzzler's belly hung over his jeans, a ragged scarf was tied round his neck, his cloth cap covered a mass of unruly hair, and his frizzy white beard was neither full nor neat. Father and son hit it off instantly. In the months and years ahead, Keith and Bert bonded over vodka and dominoes; the older Richards' 'fierce, skyrocket' temper had vanished, along with his resentment of rock 'n roll. He became a fixture at the summer's Stones tour.

That night, Keith invited his father up to the band's Knightsbridge hotel. After a few drinks, Bert sat down on the floor of the suite, between some bodyguards and chauffeurs. Soon seven or eight of them were in a semicircle facing a large antique desk. Keith himself sat behind it, strumming a beautifully polished Martin guitar. The entourage stared up at him.

Keith cleared his throat softly. 'Welcome back,' he rasped, and serenaded Bert with Danny Boy.

A year later, Keith settled his father in the house at Sands Point, Long Island, where he also kept Anita, Marlon and assorted mates. In 1984, while Pallenberg went through rehab, Bert moved back to England along with his grandson. After that, all three generations would spend most of their time at Redlands. Meanwhile, Keith and Anita's daughter Angela remained with Doris (now remarried to a man also named Richards) in Dartford.

Anita: 'To a certain extent, Keith had gotten very much like his father. He's very narrow-minded, very sheltered and shuttered, and that helps to keep him going. He doesn't want anything from the world. Everybody knows what he wants and what he likes and what he needs. Whether he's in Berlin or Tokyo, if you look in the fridge there's always a shepherd's pie.'

*   *   *

Late that spring of 1982, the Stones rehearsed on a stage at Shepperton studios. Long faces all around. Keith had loyally brought back Bobby Keys from the cold, much to Mick's chagrin. Ron Wood was there on probation. Bill and Charlie pottered around looking out-of-sorts in their bandanas and tracksuits. Gered Mankowitz, who'd travelled with the Stones in the Sixties, was invited back to photograph them for the first time since *Satanic Majesties*. After a series of phone calls from the band's office ('Mick's just got up, and he's in the bath – we'll call you right back' . . . 'Mick's still in the bath, but Keith's up now, and says he's looking forward to seeing you' . . . 'Mick's out of the bath now, it's definitely on for tonight') he arrived to meet a 'really friendly' Keith who suggested a second session two nights later. Mankowitz returned to a noticeably cooler reception.

'They told me to hop it,' he says. 'Apparently everyone was going through a rough time. Bill was ill and wasn't even coming. After some haggling, I finally did a roll of black and white, gave the film to them and left.'

Opening night was 26 May, in Aberdeen. These new shows were full of catchy blues-rock riffs and Jagger's raps about the concerns of the average British youth: sex, the Falklands War and getting high. At a gig in France, Keith finally managed to hijack the cherry picker, taking a lengthy airborne solo while Mick seethed below. 'Get him *down*,' Jagger kept yelling at Wood. In Sweden, by contrast, Keith stretched out and performed Beast Of Burden while flat on his back. Even or especially when enjoying a breather, he was still great copy. After a hot show in Munich, the *Morgenpost* raved about the 'veteran and no little historic' man, Herr Riffhard, who remained 'uniquely true to the Sixties'. That same night, by chance, Anita and Andrew Oldham were on hand to hear Marianne Faithfull sing to a few dozen fans in New York.

By the time they flew back to England in late June, Keith and Mick's combativeness towards the outside world was matched by similar feelings towards one another. They stayed in different West End hotels while playing two homecoming gigs at Wembley. Stevie Ray Vaughan and George Thorogood were both in town, still on standby to replace Wood. Meanwhile, Jagger had a clause inserted in the band's tour contract that read, 'If anyone is found in possession of drugs in any area, that person will be immediately banished from the vicinity, whatever his capacity.' He had a few sharp words for the singer Peter Wolf, who liked to relax with Richards after a show.

'A fair example of the kind of cunt I've had to deal with for twenty years,' Keith commented, in a room full of journalists.

At the second Wembley gig, when he forgot the riff of She's So Cold, Keith was so angry with Wood for failing to cover him that he charged over and, once again, punched him in the face. This got a Cup final-sized cheer from the crowd. A few nights later, Keith corked off at Charlie on the tarmac at Naples airport. The two bandmates had a farcical row about who was going to take which seats on a chartered jet back to London. Keith was a hard man to argue with. Charlie, in the end, muttered 'Fuck it' and walked off into the night.

The tour ended in Leeds on 25 July. Mick Jagger turned thirty-nine the next day. Again, as they had every closing night since 1966, the press brought out the IT'S ALL OVER NOW and COULD BE THE LAST TIME headlines. For once, they were nearly right.

In late summer, Keith and Patti flew to Cabo San Lucas, Mexico, a resort favoured by American swingers like Hugh Hefner, where they rented a villa on the beach. Friends and relatives came and went. The Hansen family – particularly her elder brother Harry – liked the fiancé Patti had chosen. Elsewhere, the secret engagement was welcomed as a sign that Keith might be willing to settle down after a hard decade.

Early that September, Redlands was razed to the ground again.

Nobody was hurt, and Richards was thousands of miles away at the time. The story got splashed around the world because of the house's lively past and also because the words 'Keith' and 'fire' were somehow irresistibly linked. It would be another year before Bert and Marlon could move into Redlands, where Keith ruled like a benevolent despot. In that particular, Nick Gough recalls that 'the feeling in the village was that you didn't want to go down that lane without an invitation. Ever.'

November 1982. The Stones began recording again in Paris. Jagger was reading William Burroughs' *Cities of the Red Night*, writing lyrics about rape and cannibalism while fooling around behind Jerry Hall's back. Not for the last time, the press hustled out the 'Love Rat' stories, then took to chasing Mick and his friends up and down the Champs Elysées. There was soon a reconciliation, Jerry telling the world that 'I've gotten him back and we're going to have babies'.

The story that *People* magazine and Nigel Dempster and the rest of the celebrity media ran in December was that Mick was finishing the band's sixth and final album for EMI, *Undercover*, and would then settle down with Hall. Actually it was Keith who was doing most of the work and he, not Mick, who was planning to marry. If the facts were sketchy, the story was sturdy, and found its way into the world's gossip columns that Christmas.

Up in his suite at New York's Plaza hotel in January, Keith was blasting old Everly Brothers hits from the stereo while entertaining Bert, Marlon and the man from *Guitar Player*. The management had somehow squeezed a piano into the service lift and up to his seventh-floor rooms. Charlie or Ron Wood would sometimes drop by to jam.

Keith and Patti's plans were abruptly derailed, in tragic fashion, when her father died in the second week of January. Alfred Hansen had been particularly fond of his intending son-in-law. In the last weeks of his life, he'd let it be known among his churchgoing friends that 'the guy [was] nothing like what you'd think from the press'. Keith was duly on hand at the wake, and a pallbearer at the funeral the next morning. It was a cold New York day, the ground coated by a sleet that had frozen so that it seemed that the hearse, and the whole cortège, had been glazed with ice. Pink roses covered the dark pine coffin as the Hansen brothers and Keith, dressed in a black suit and cape, shuffled in out of the snow. He was clearly part of the family now. That same night Richards joined Jagger, Watts and Wood at the première of Hal Ashby's concert movie, *Let's Spend the Night Together*: loud and hip, but sadly lacking the snap of the shows.

Back in Paris, in February, Keith made a habit of coming to the studio wearing his cape and a fedora. He soon started waving a swordstick for emphasis. Jagger's tendency to hop everything up with violent lyrics and tribal riffs was a complete rejection of Keith's musical philosophy of never pandering to fashion. The result was an all-out war between the full-throated and the meditative. There were enough styles being kicked around, in fact, to support virtually any review of *Undercover* – that it was a good album, that it was a dire album, that it was closely related to the 'old' Stones, that it wasn't.

One difference between the two creators, however, was painfully obvious: Keith aimed for timelessness, and Mick for timeliness. In Paris, Jagger kept telling Richards and Wood that he wanted more 'modern guitar' on

Undercover, 'something like Andy Summers'. Keith's roadie Jim Barber duly obliged with some African riffing on Too Much Blood, Mick's ode to one Issei Sagawa, a Japanese student at the Sorbonne who murdered his girlfriend and ate her.

A month after slamming the door at Pathé-Marconi studios for the last time, Richards and Jagger were back mixing *Undercover* at the Hit Factory, New York. Keith took the opportunity to buy Patti and himself three floors of an apartment building on East 4th Street, a block or two away from his old drug den in Washington Square. (He never set foot there now.) When they bothered to speak to each other, the Glimmer Twins fought nonstop about how much, if at all, to polish *Undercover*. Mick was busily soaking up the whole range of modern production techniques, like sampling and phasing. Which Keith hated. There were other minor skirmishes over tempos, keys, lyrics and the album's artwork. Keith left New York before the job was finished and joined Patti in San Francisco, on the set of her new film *Hard to Hold*. In June, they were in Jamaica; in July Hollywood, where Keith appeared on a TV special honouring Jerry Lee Lewis. Chuck Berry happened to run into him at the airport and somehow dropped a lit cigarette down the front of Keith's shirt.

As Richards put it, 'Every time him and me get in contact, I end up wounded.'

In August, Keith went to Marlon's fourteenth birthday party held at Anita's house on Long Island. A day later he was back in Paris, where the Stones inked an American distribution deal with CBS Records. The contract gave them $6 million apiece for four new albums. It was the sweetest in rock music history.

CBS was represented for the occasion by its president Walter Yetnikoff, a cigar-chomping fast talker, shaped like a church bell, who put some in mind of Allen Klein. Yetnikoff was the man who introduced Michael Jackson's *Thriller* to posterity. He met the band at the Paris Ritz late on the evening of 20 August, beaming and stroking the vast contours of his chins. Yetnikoff not only wanted the Stones, he wanted to make Jagger's solo albums.

Everyone at CBS, Yetnikoff confided, was convinced that Mick could be as big as Jacko. Mick joined the consensus.

A furious debate would rage in years ahead over whether Keith fully understood that Mick had made any such commitment. If not, he must have missed *Rolling Stone* of 24 November, which reported

The heart of the new deal is that CBS will release the next four Rolling Stones albums. In addition, it will also release, for the first time ever, a solo album by Mick Jagger himself. Maybe two or three. This is an unexpected breach in Jagger and Richards' long-standing no solos tradition, and Mick seems excited by it.

After signing the deal Keith spent the weekend with Peter Cook in London. Later that month, Cook would tell *After Midnight* that the Stones were 'proper stars: Brian Jones did the right thing for a rock 'n roll person, drowned in his own swimming pool. And Keith Richards, he's a proper star, because although he's alive, he's nearly dead. I don't like the kids today who don't smoke, don't drink, don't do drugs and don't screw. I mean, what kind of a rock star is that?'

Imperiously, Keith drew a line. He told Cook that he didn't sleep around.

The BBC sent Jeff Griffin to interview Richards back in Paris. Jane Rose warned him beforehand to talk only about the new album and not, under any circumstances, about drugs. But that hope soon faded. Keith himself raised the subject, recalling in hair-raising detail how he'd regularly armed himself to the teeth to go and score in Washington Square. Certain close calls, too, in the back streets of London and Paris. Griffin thought Keith a much changed character – 'the guy was beaming'. To all appearances, this was the most alive he'd been in the twelve years since *Exile*.

Next up to the suite was Julien Temple, *enfant terrible* of the National Film School, whom Mick had hired to shoot the videos for *Undercover*. Keith greeted Temple by holding the swordstick to his throat and telling him not to fuck up. The two men then shook hands and went out to scout locations. On the way downstairs the twenty-nine-year-old director kept promising that their movies would 'really shake up' the old farts at *Top of the Pops*. Instead it was he himself who was jolted as Keith swiftly took his Ferrari up to top speed, barrelling down the Quai de Bercy at 120 mph until Temple could only cower, open-mouthed, in his seat. (He passed the initiation test.) From Paris, Keith and Patti flew with Temple and Jagger to Mexico City, where they finished the shoot. In one suggestive setup, Mick would be seen being dragged out of his hotel room by three wild-eyed gunmen. The leader of the gang, who then blew Jagger's brains out, was played by Keith.

Mick's solo career got off to a head start on *Undercover*, out that November. He retooled the Stones for the Me Decade with a string of danceable romps and violent, fuck-you lyrics. Among the key reference points: Wall Street, money, murder, *The Texas Chainsaw Massacre*, flagellation, knives, razors and battered babies. Keith's clanging guitar stoked such tracks as Pretty Beat Up, but generally the album settled for easy club grooves – Too Much Blood, which had kids boogying along to Mick's cannibalism rap – that showcased the production more than the tunes. *Undercover* never got beyond an icy professionalism. It was flawless, facile and completely forgettable.

The title track, a funky brew of rapid-fire drums and guitars that sound like an angry swarm of wasps, is Mick's lament for political *disparus* in Argentina (where the song was banned in perpetuity). Keith's signature riff is paced by Stu's loping piano on She Was Hot; the melody sings, the rhythm swings and even the voice is shot through with character. Wanna Hold You is a straight reworking of Happy, and a rare moment of abandon. Keith would raid the Stones playbook again on Too Tough and It Must Be Hell, which channel the *Bleed* outtake I'm Going Down and *Exile*'s Soul Survivor, respectively. There are a few good rubbery bass lines. Charlie rocks. Generally, however, *Undercover*'s a smörgasbord of tired remakes, slamming hip-hop beats and shrill guitar – all propelled by Mick's sweet, understated lilts.

The consensus was poor fare, pretentiously wrapped. *Undercover* came in a trashy blue sleeve that showed a naked, sectioned woman. Lots of inserts and accessories. Of Temple's three videos, two were banned, while a third, in which Keith buzzed Mick with a chainsaw, graced MTV for a week or two. Immediately after that, *Undercover* was largely forgotten. It got to number eleven in Britain, number five in the US; a first commercial flop, relatively speaking, in fifteen years.

By the time the reviews were in, Keith and Patti were already back in Cabo San Lucas. His presence there excited so much comment that the police soon called at the couple's whitewashed house on Cabo Bello Drive. Sergeant Diaz and his men had apparently noticed a familiar pattern emerging. Occasionally Keith would get involved in a little music or business, but his most compelling activity was receiving late-night visitors who would invariably arrive wearing shades and carrying identical black briefcases chained to their wrists.

The authorities allegedly took Keith aside, showed him some surveillance photographs and advised him of the difficulty of pursuing his career from a Mexican jail cell. He and Patti made plans to leave Cabo San Lucas when their lease expired early in the new year.

But first there was the question of the rearranged wedding, which Keith had promised for a spare weekend that winter. Shortly after wrapping the sorry *Hard to Hold*, Patti had taken a long look at her acting career and found that her doubts about it were shared by more people than she'd hoped. The new role she settled on was at once stranger and more ordinary than anything Hollywood could have scripted, that of 'plain Mrs Richards'.

On 13 December, Patti returned to New York briefly to collect her family and a wedding gown. By the 17th a party including the Hansens, Keith's two children and Mick Jagger had gathered in Cabo San Lucas. Anita was back in London, in detox, and couldn't make it. None of the other three Stones was invited.

Both Bert and Doris Richards attended, shaking hands in their son's tropical mansion and exchanging a few pleasantries for the first time in twenty-one years. There was an awkward moment as each looked the other's partner up and down, but for the most part it was a happy and quite poignant reunion. The 17th of December would have been Bert and Doris's forty-fifth wedding anniversary.

At the bachelor party that night, Keith and Mick entertained the crowd by strumming a selection of Elvis and Buddy Holly hits. For that hour or so, everything again seemed closer to an early-Sixties singalong than to the jaded wrangling of recent years. A beaming Keith told his guests, 'I know I couldn't have beaten heroin without Patti. She's a wonderful girl. And besides, shit, I'm gonna try anything. And if I'm gonna try anything like marriage, I'm only gonna try it once. 'Cause I'm not about to try it twice. And if I try it once, it's gonna be with her. I ain't letting the bitch go!'

The wedding took place the next afternoon, Sunday 18 December, a mile or so away from Keith and Patti's villa, at the luxurious Hotel Finisterra. Their thirty guests gathered on the terrace, under a double row of palm trees and overlooking the sheer white beach. Patti wore lace, Keith a formal black suit, white shirt, and blue suede shoes. It was a shockingly normal affair for the most part. Religion wasn't Keith's bag, and particularly not Christianity with its 'logo of a guy nailed to a piece of wood'. However, in deference to his in-laws he agreed to 'the full Lutheran gig', conducted in

Spanish. Keith added an ecumenical touch of his own by performing the Jewish wedding ritual of smashing a wine glass underfoot. As the service ended the party turned to watch the winter sun setting over the Pacific.

At the reception that night, Keith knelt at Patti's feet and serenaded her with Hoagy Carmichael's The Nearness Of You. That photo, and the events of the 18th generally, won him more 'straight' press coverage than at any time since Toronto. Then, of course, he'd been the rock star most likely to drop dead of an overdose. This time round, the tone was bracingly upbeat and dealt with themes like survival, making the Human Riff an icon of self-recovery and a living refutation of his old self.

That same day, Keith turned forty.

8

One Hit (To The Body)

EARLY IN 1984, THE RICHARDSES LEFT THE HOUSE ON CABO BELLO DRIVE AND NEVER WENT BACK. What with bouncing around New York rock clubs, commuting to Jamaica and sponsoring British teams for the Olympics, Keith always seemed able to keep a number of balls in the air. On 25 February, he flew back to Paris and began scouting out a new studio. The Stones, so he hoped, would record in the spring and tour again in the summer.

While Keith did the advance work, the other four ground away at their own pet projects. Jagger and Walter Yetnikoff were busily launching Mick's solo career, driving Keith mad in the process. Ron Wood was lost to coke and spent part of that winter in an English detox facility, at Jagger's insistence. Bill grudgingly extended his deadline for leaving the band and started dating Mandy Smith, aged thirteen, thus handing the press a satirical gift for the next seven years. Charlie, hitherto the cool and quiet one, was blasting himself on pills and heroin.

Jagger finally came clean to Richards that April, explaining that he was breaking the no-solos rule, as reported, as well as the twenty-year-old writing partnership for the first time. Keith: 'My attitude when he said that was "Fine! Since I'm not going to have anything to do with it, I don't really want my name coming into it, anyway. Since I'm not going to be involved, maybe I won't like it. I don't want my name anywhere near those songs. If it's your album, you stick your name on 'em."'

In May, Mick went off to Nassau to record. Keith told the press that if Jagger toured with another band, 'I'll slit his fuckin' throat.'

With that, Keith and Patti took off to Jamaica for the summer. It was now, calling ahead from Kingston airport, that Richards had his set-to with Peter Tosh. An hour later, Keith and Patti's car was barely within sight of home when they began to see evidence of their hurriedly departed guest. Point of View had, at first glance, the air of a dilapidated farm rather than a luxury villa. A large pig, tethered by one hind trotter to the front railings, lay squarely across the driveway. Assorted sheep and goats roamed the once elegant garden. There was also a three-legged dog, which snarled rabidly at Keith and Patti as they edged past. Other pets and friends of Tosh's sprawled around the house itself in varying degrees of stupor. Keith's living room, library and studio had all been thoroughly trashed.

Tosh left Rolling Stones Records shortly after that by mutual agreement. Three years later, on 11 September 1987, he was shot dead in the course of a burglary at his home down the hill.

Having evicted the squatters and fumigated the house, the newlyweds settled in for the summer. Before long Patti fell pregnant.

Keith left the island once, to meet Jagger, Watts and Wyman at the band's new office in Munro Terrace, Chelsea, down the road from Cheyne Walk. Ron Wood either couldn't come, or wasn't invited. Mick announced that he was really, really committed to the Stones but that he needed a few months to record and promote his solo album, now going under the title *She's the Boss*.

'What you mean,' interjected Keith affably, with that flair for graceful and laconic expression people admired, 'is your shit takes priority.'

'I don't mean that at all.' There was reasonableness in Mick's voice, as always, but a stolid refusal to give ground. 'Look, man, can't we get along?'

'You tell me.'

Mick shrugged.

Eventually the four of them agreed to start work again in Paris the next winter. Meanwhile, they put out a stopgap hits collection called *Rewind*, and a video of the same name featuring two relentlessly chirpy presenters for the price of one. Jagger and Wyman duly hammered their way through sixty minutes of disjointed patter, sight gags and boffo Fawlty Towers humour. About the only watchable moment came when, asked to explain the band's longevity, Keith and Mick answered as one: 'Charlie Watts.'

In New York that October, three of the Stones got together to chat about the new album. According to Bill, 'Keith was still annoyed with Mick for working on solo material. It almost came to blows.' The band's next meeting, in Amsterdam, actually did so. A drunk Jagger phoned Charlie's hotel room at five in the morning and rashly referred to him as 'my drummer'. Charlie got up, showered, shaved, dressed in a Turnbull and Asser shirt, silk tie and three-piece suit, went downstairs, grabbed Jagger and punched his lights out.

Charlie: 'Don't ever call me your drummer again. You're *my* fucking singer.'

There were other such scenes that grew into legend among the Stones' inner circle. Not long after this, Keith leant over a boardroom table in front of Prince Rupert and assorted bankers and lawyers, shoved his face next to Mick's and warned him: 'Don't make a shit album.' There were rows in private, stony silence at press calls. Keith again found a friend in the partly detoxed Ron Wood, whom he dubbed the 'holy host'. Jagger was spending his days mixing She's the Boss in New York, and his nights at the nearby Kamikaze Klub. The bartender there was Bruce Willis.

On 2 January 1985 Wood married his long-time girlfriend Jo Howard at St Mary's Church, Denham. Keith was best man. Charlie, Bill and just about every other British rock star were present. Mick was on holiday in Mustique, installing a new sewage pump at his home there, and so couldn't come. Only fragmentary recollections of what was said have survived. The vicar had a go at the Stones, noting that 'these proceedings are the antithesis of wealth and decadence'. Peter Cook attempted to seduce the bride, then climbed into a black limo marked 'Musicians' in the car park. An awkward scene occurred at the reception, when Keith caught sight of the journalist John Blake, Spanish Tony's ghost on *Up and Down with the Rolling Stones*. The thrust of his remarks was that the book had been something of a stitch-up – if not a fucking hatchet job – in his opinion. Blake quickly left the room.

Back to Paris. The old Pathé-Marconi studio had been bulldozed, but the Stones set up in its successor on rue de Sèvres. Mick brought no new material to speak of, having just finished She's the Boss. Keith then arrived with twenty-seven songs, which went under titles like Fight, Had It With You and Knock Your Teeth Out. Nobody was speaking. Jagger took to recording his vocals in a different building from the band.

Keith and Anita were given, respectively, a ne and a one-year conditional discharge at yet nother dope rial in London 1973. Keith elebrated at a otel that ight, burning own his room.

The Stones ith Ronnie Wood (second rom right) pay omage at he Alamo, une 1975.

Above left: Keith on his way to face more drugs charges at Aylesbury Crown Court. Found guilty of cocaine possession, the judge ordered him to pay a £750 fine and another £250 in court costs.

Above right: Backstage at the Knebworth festival, August 1979.

A rare relaxed moment with Chuck Berry. As Keith once put it, 'Every time him and me get in contact, I end up wounded.'

Jagger came on for the *Tattoo You* tour in sporty, gay-quarterback tights and a cape fashioned out of the British and American flags. Ian Stewart is on the piano, far left.

Keith leaving London with his future wife Patti Hansen, the youngest daughter of a hardworking Lutheran family from New York.

Marlon, Keith, Angela and Doris Richards.

Ron Wood married his long-time girlfriend Jo Howard in January 1985, witnessed by most of the British rock elite. The couple are flanked here by Charlie Watts and Keith. Mick Jagger couldn't make it.

Live Aid. Keith and Ron busked it while Bob Dylan ran through a few barely recognizable songs.

After seven years' near total silence, the Stones plugged themselves back in like a neon sign in 1989. Their *Steel Wheels* tour set the pattern for the glitzy and hugely successful Vegas-like shows that continue today.

Although Keith professed himself bored by business, he would enjoy the best advice from the Stones' suave moneyman Prince Rupert Loewenstein.

Keith under 'the Cobra' on the 1995 *Voodoo Lounge* tour of Europe.

Keith, a long-time tennis fan, with John McEnroe at the US Open, September 1999.

Hitting the Satisfaction riff to
kick off *Bridges to Babylon*, 1997.

The Human Riff, still bringing his unique touch of warmth and humour to an otherwise tightly scripted *Forty Licks* tour.

When the press caught up with him later in the spring, Keith was in an ugly mood. Jagger had been spending 'more time doing his solo stuff instead of doing *Dirty Work*, which really pissed me off. He shouldn't have been making the album if he wasn't into it. I very nearly stiffed him at the time. But there's no joy in punching a wimp. He was around so infrequently ... it was just Charlie, Ronnie and me trying to make a record. It was very unprofessional of Mick, very stupid.'

Ironically, things only got worse, not better, when the Twins did work together.

Jagger had recorded *She's the Boss* in the same way he liked to cut with the Stones. Everything had to be written down, lyrically and musically, before a note was played. He allowed for a few embellishments by the band, but generally a steely discipline ruled. Whereas early Stones sessions had darted about, frantically aiming for a 'vibe' rather than bravura musicianship, nowadays Mick wanted a slick end-product, crafted with conservatory care.

Keith, of course, had no use for any of this shit. He liked to throw an idea at the band, recording their workups, playing them back, then recording them again – perhaps fifteen or twenty times – until a definitive version emerged. The tape would then be handed to the engineer Dave Jordan with the terse instruction, 'Don't ponce it up.' A good feel, for Keith, was better than any 'clever bastard' frills.

On 4 March, Jagger put out *She's the Boss*. It was a perfectly good album on its own terms, buffed up by a busy funk production. Over a month it sold a respectable million-plus copies. Three years later, he successfully defended one of the songs in a plagiarism suit. Nobody seriously thought it in the same league as the Stones. The fuss passed.

Keith went back to New York, where Patti was now eight months pregnant. As the spouse of a US citizen, he was no longer obliged to line up for visas (though he still needed a work permit) and was finally given his green card – permission to stay – that spring. On 17 March 1985, Patti turned twenty-nine. Early the next day she gave birth to the couple's daughter, Theodora Dupree (in honour of Gus) Richards. For the first time, Keith was present to watch a child of his born.

'What kids do is grow you up, make you think,' he said. In years ahead Keith proved to be a friend and playmate to his second family, a protective big brother more than a Victorian authority figure, someone who arranged tour dates as best he could around school outings and breaks. He was a model father.

Keith went back to Paris in mid April, recording *Dirty Work* while Jagger flogged *She's the Boss*. Mick cried off touring in the summer, then agreed to perform at Live Aid, in mid July, with a pickup band. Ron Wood: 'There were times we felt like killing people, but we got out our guitars and wrote songs instead.' After a row with Jagger on the phone late one night, Keith punched out the chords to a tune he called One Hit (To The Body).

Dirty Work was now about halfway finished, with an all-star cast including Jimmy Page, Tom Waits and Patti Scialfa (later Mrs Bruce Springsteen) filling in for the band's absentees. Stu was playing piano. In a rare moment of creative harmony, Keith persuaded Mick to sing the '69 soul standard Harlem Shuffle. Not long after that, the Stones shut up the studio in Paris and moved the entire operation back to New York.

Bill Graham, who was running the Philadelphia end of Live Aid, offered Jagger a prime 9 p.m. slot just before the night's headliner Bob Dylan – the one figure ranked above him in the rock pantheon. The worldwide TV audience at that hour would be 1.5 billion. Jagger booked a band, and invited Tina Turner to do two numbers with him. It was a major coup not only for Bill Graham, but for Mick. Everyone looked forward to a night of sex, slapstick and rock 'n roll.

A day before the event, Dylan ran into his friend Ron Wood in New York. The two of them took a car down to the Lone Star café for a drink. Bob told Ron that he was playing in Philadelphia, 'Bill Graham's got a band for me and I have to go along with it.' As an afterthought, he wondered if Woody and Keith wanted, instead, to back him. Dylan remarked that it would be a pretty big gig, and that he could really use their help as he was going on right after Mick and Tina ... When he looked up, Bob found that, for once, he was talking to himself. Wood was already speeding back uptown to find Keith.

Mick Jagger gave a stunning performance in Philadelphia. Despite being interminably rehearsed, songs like Honky Tonk Women managed to sound both fresh and raw. Ninety thousand sunbaked fans – from beer-gutted geezers to those actually concerned with the famine in Ethiopia – moshed along amid a storm of noise and strobe lights. Jagger wore a bright lemon suit. It was his first official performance outside the Stones. Mick's brand of campy, well-choreographed pop was perfect for the occasion. Somehow, he even managed to rip Tina's dress off.

Dylan and his hastily assembled band were, it has to be said, a sorry letdown. The three of them spent that long, humid afternoon drinking and jamming in a small trailer. They were allotted only a few minutes on stage. Keith and Woody couldn't hear a thing through their monitors. Dylan's first song, The Ballad Of Hollis Brown, was new to them.

Grinning sheepishly, the two guitarists stood there and busked it; in Philip Norman's great phrase, 'unsteady on old-fashioned boot heels, raddled faces confused, skinny forearms clumsily pumping, less like rock immortals than a pair of disreputable charwomen half-heartedly washing some socks'. By the time the gig ended, Jagger had clearly scored several points in the solo-career stakes and would soon begin planning to tour on his own.

Not surprisingly, the Stones were in Defcon 2 mode for the final *Dirty Work* sessions that autumn. Keith ran the show. Mick would often come and go without seeing the rest of the band. A fed-up Charlie flew back to England, where he managed to fall down a flight of stairs in his cellar and break a leg. Bill played on only half the finished tracks. Keith put together an assortment of roadies and guests, the so-called Biff Hitler Trio, to cover for the not-happening band. Ian Stewart, who had been at every session for twenty-two years, thought it an almighty mess.

Late in the year, Stu and Charlie started playing a few jazz gigs around London. Some of those present at places like Ronnie Scott's or Fulham Town Hall thought they were watching the Stones finally break up. On 10 December, Keith flew in to see for himself.

Two nights later, on a dismally wet Thursday, he was in his West End hotel waiting for Stu. Around one in the morning, Charlie, instead, phoned with the news: 'He ain't coming, Keith.'

Stewart, who was complaining of respiratory trouble during the final *Dirty Work* session, had been to see a west London specialist that afternoon. The doctor was running late, and his nurse, to whom Stu seemed cheerful enough, asked him to take a seat. During the wait he suffered a cardiac arrest and died within seconds. He was forty-seven.

A year that had begun with a wedding now ended with a funeral. All the Stones were at Stu's service on 20 December, Jagger in tears. Keith reached over and embraced Mick, and then turned to Woody: '*Now* who's gonna tell us off when we fuck up?'

Long before Satisfaction and the rest, when the Stones had been scuffling around suburban pubs, their sound was minimalist, gimmickless and rootsy. Stu's bluesy piano added a sheen of distinction to what could have been standard-issue covers of American hits. Musically, he was the unsung hero. He was also, and remained, the band's common denominator – the one man they all liked, all the time. Keith later recalled Stu's death as the moment 'the glue holding the Stones together came unstuck'.

'Why'd you have to leave us like that, you sod?'

Early in the new year, the Richardses moved into a large house in the well-heeled town of Weston, Connecticut, sixty miles north-east of New York. The distance would allow for more privacy and unimpeded views of shimmering lakes and rivers, but still be close enough for Keith to take nightly trips down I-95 to Manhattan. Weston, a town of 6,000 souls and a single stop-light, seemed straight out of a Norman Rockwell painting. Rich in ivy-clad houses and apple-cheeked tots, it had no apartment blocks, offices or public transport. There was one small market, and even that trafficked solely in string, toffee apples and *Farmer's Almanac*. Keith would now spend much of his time either here or in West Wittering.

The actual home was a rambling, two-storey affair, surrounded by neatly manicured lawns, a vegetable patch and split-rail fences. A room overlooking the back terrace would become Keith's library, with oak-panelled walls, leather armchairs and a growing collection of well-thumbed history books. The views were idyllic. This part of Connecticut had hardly changed in 200 years. Down the hill from Keith's was a country churchyard where three of the Founding Fathers were buried.

In very real ways, the Weston house changed Keith's life. It gave him a base, not just another hotel room, and lent an air of greater permanence to his American exile. From now on, even time spent in London would be time away from home.

Having bought the place and talked the matter out fully with Patti, who was pregnant again, Keith still wanted to tour that summer. He was more comfortable onstage than in the studio, which he'd recently taken to calling 'the office'. There was something about it, that faint hint of routine, that he didn't like.

In January 1986 Keith inducted Chuck Berry, whom he once dubbed 'the most charming cunt I've ever met', into the Rock and Roll Hall of Fame in New York. He got a big laugh by telling the crowd, 'I lifted every lick he ever played, man.' The two then tore through a set peppered with both old-school blues and classic rock, for once without anyone getting hurt.

A week later, the Stones met for a video shoot at the Kool Kat Club in Manhattan, miming amid a cast of animated cartoon cut-outs. *Dirty Work* was finally ready to ship. Keith was 'extremely stoked' by the album. He told Jane Rose he planned to visit CBS, schmooze their distributors and do all the interviews. In spring he would get the fucking show on the road.

Keith's commitment to a new tour was total. When not chivvying CBS, he would summon his favourite journalists, prodding Jagger through their pages. 'If Mick was to go out without the Stones,' he told *Musician*, 'I'd slit his throat ... That's the way it is. This is the first album in a new contract. We'd be *idiots*; it'd be the dumbest move in the world to not get behind it. We've got a good album here! He knows that. Spent a year making it and putting our backs to the wall. Why toss it away?'

Jagger was, in fact, enraged to read about his proposed tracheotomy and distinctly cool about *Dirty Work*, which he described as 'not special'. He had one of his staff contact Charlie and Bill to ask them to be by their phones at a certain hour. When Mick came on the line, he talked to them about Keith and what he saw as his problems.

'We all do other things on the side. Except Keith,' he complained. Mick didn't want to tour and, as he somewhat immodestly recalled in *Rolling Stone*, 'I was a hundred per cent right. It would have been the worst. Probably would have been the end of the band.'

Jagger told Watts and Wyman the Stones needed a break and, despite the lost income, both agreed. Charlie was now doing speed and heroin. His wife was in rehab. Bill talked about the day when he'd be too old to be pumping out Satisfaction – a day, he thought at forty-nine, fast approaching.

At the end of February everyone did, however, gather at London's 100 Club to pay tribute to Ian Stewart. For an hour the band hustled out the sort of R&B chestnuts Stu loved and they started their career playing. Gered Mankowitz was there and remembers Keith and Mick, 'despite what you read in the press, barely acknowledging each other'.

Two nights later, the Stones picked up a lifetime achievement Grammy in a ceremony at the Kensington Roof Gardens. Jagger scoffed at an award putting them in a 'museum', but said Richards wanted it. Immediately the cameras were turned off, Keith and Ron Wood took a limo over to Eric Clapton's and, in Woody's account, trashed the place. The Richardses then went down to Redlands for Easter. 'Keith happened to call [Jagger] in Barbados right after he'd put the phone down on Bill Graham,' says a friend. 'I don't think he had any idea he was catching Mick just as he'd kissed the tour off.'

A week later, Jagger sent Keith a telegram telling him he was recording a second solo album, this one called *Primitive Cool*. There would be no summer Stones shows.

On 1 May, the band met back at Elstree studios to cut a video for *Dirty Work*'s One Hit (To The Body). Nobody was speaking. Richards and Jagger spent much of the shoot taking flying kicks at one another. Keith called it a 'fairly good portrayal of things at the time'.

Dirty Work. On their eighteenth studio album, the Stones would manage to sound both bored and overwrought. The tossed-off filler is matched by shoutalongs like Hold Back and something-for-everyone fare that aims low and falls short. There are tunes for mum, dad, nan, the kids, and for pretty much anyone else with a disposable income. Instead of great songwriting, the band give the whole thing a kind of glazed dullness, with some untypically stiff, Led Zep-style drums. In the hideous cover photo, out of a taxidermist's nightmare, the others peer up lifelessly while Charlie, alone, gazes down at his feet. Richards' left knee appears to be poking Jagger in the crutch. Mick's right foot is cocked behind Keith's back.

The album opens with One Hit and Fight, thus returning to *Undercover*'s gory turf: we get lyrics about flesh, blood, pulp, bruises, holes and putting the boot in. From the grungy tub-thumping, through the soul and reggae covers and the rave-up Winning Ugly, *Dirty Work*'s all over the shop, loud and rambunctuous and in your face. Jagger's Back To Zero is the voice of reason, and a riff uncomfortably like David Bowie's Fashion. Keith's Had It With You sets a great rockabilly tune against a sod-you lyric. Such sentiments are, of course, nothing new for the Stones, who've been regularly slipping in a little vitriol, like ice in one of Jagger's dry Martinis, since Play With Fire. What's different is that instead of slagging someone else, here Mick is singing about himself.

Keith gives *Dirty Work* a much needed lift with the sign-off, a throaty country-rock confection backed by an endearingly tinny piano. There's not much melody, but Sleep Tonight is hands down the best Stones ballad since Wild Horses. It's the sort of thing a Johnny Cash or even a Furry Lewis would have sung, and Keith's cig-tinged wheeze rises to the occasion.

Old and new. New and old. That's the coupling that, yet again, is *Dirty Work*'s selling point, a marriage of Jagger's dance-hall grooves and Keith's bluesy shuffles. The album hit number three in Britain, number four in America. It was dedicated to Ian Stewart.

Patti was heavily pregnant, and she and Keith took the *QE2* back to New York in June. The Stones seemed to be on their last legs. There were more meetings, this time with all five and the lawyers present. Charlie kept nodding off from the heroin and booze. Then Wyman had to move back to his gated villa in Provence amid talk of being slapped with child-sex charges involving Mandy Smith. Soon after that, the headlines started up in the *News of the World* saying that Bill was, in so many words, an old perv. None of the Stones would talk to him about it.

As things went sour, Keith headed to Detroit to cut a cover of Jack Flash with Aretha Franklin. He said he wanted 'normalcy' again – to go on stage with a bunch of mates, have a few pints, even play golf. The old Stu days. Failing that, the Flash session would prove to be a turning point. 'Before the Aretha thing,' Keith said, 'I was terrified of doing something for myself. Now I know I can.'

On 28 July, Patti gave birth to their second daughter, Alexandra Nicole. By now everyone who worked with him knew Keith to be volatile. He was edgy, impatient and given to letting rip, in choice terms, at anyone crossing him. But he could also be outrageously generous. When a long-time Stones employee needed a five-figure loan, 'Keith immediately came across. No problem. He didn't give a shit about writing anything down, or even being paid back. "I've got my health and my kids," he told me. "Why sweat it?"'

Keith: 'Having babies roaming around your house is one of the most beautiful things in the world. You get a little girl coming up to you and saying, "Daddy, I love you." They keep reminding you of things you can't remember, those first two or three years. It's always fascinating.' For him, fatherhood was better than any drug.

Realistically, Keith also knew he had to do something more than spend the rest of his life in Connecticut. Jane Rose had been negotiating for him to work as music director on an all-star tribute to Robert Johnson. When the project folded Keith offered to collaborate, instead, with his boyhood hero Chuck Berry. It seemed a logical next step, given the three-part report in *USA Today* aptly titled 'The Stones at a Standoff'. Not long after begging off a summer tour, Jagger had started planning shows of his own – 'a supposedly solo act,' notes Bill, 'totally dominated by Stones songs.'

Keith wasn't happy. 'If you're going to do something different, do it,' he said. 'Don't pretend you're a solo artist and have two chicks prancing around singing Tumbling Dice, know what I mean? The Stones spent a lot of time building up integrity, as much as you can get in the music industry. And he jeopardized it ... That severely pissed me off.'

Nowadays, he and Mick never actually fought. They also never saw one another. The whole thing became a variant of their old school-playground squabbles, on a higher budget. A case could be made that Mick was, by now, the apex predator of rock stars, perhaps our greatest living trouper. He was undoubtedly the best organized. Keith, by contrast, didn't seem to give a toss. All he wanted was to get up there and play.

To no one's surprise, Richards' labour of love with Chuck Berry was fraught from the start. Late in July, Keith went down to Berry Park in Wentzville, Missouri, to talk about hiring a band for some filmed concerts in the autumn. The first hint of trouble came when Chuck greeted Keith by once again calling him Jack. After three spells in federal prison, Berry was, in his own words, 'moody and very schizophrenic', less concerned with artistic fulfilment than with the financial side. Even as Keith ploughed dutifully through the figures, he must have known that he was actually there not to 'escape shit', but to take it. By and by, the two rock idols made their way up to the projection room, where Berry played everyone some porno movies of white girls rubbing food on each other. He soon tired of it, and slipped in a feature-length film about himself. There was more than a slight air of the unreal to Berry Park, with its paying funfair, its family diner next to its lesbian floor-show, all overseen by Chuck's ninety-year-old father. Some years later, police would raid the place and seize hidden-camera footage taken from inside the women's lavatory. A somewhat dazed Keith went home, uneasily aware that Chuck would 'manoeuvre and manipulate anything ... It was very like working with Mick.'

The Richardses, complete with their newborn daughter, then played host to Berry in Jamaica. Keith kept waiting for Chuck, who seemed more interested in other matters, to come downstairs to talk about the concerts. When he did, a dialogue ensued that had virtually everyone in Ocho Rios flocking onto their porches and balconies to share the drama. For all who witnessed events that day, no subsequent Richards–Jagger tiff involving slammed doors and hissed threats would pack any real punch at all. After what Chuck remembered as hours of delicate negotiations but was probably only a few minutes of peak-decibel debate, the two had a deal. Keith would put together a band including Berry's old pianist Johnnie Johnson for two shows in St Louis timed around Chuck's sixtieth birthday. The director Taylor Hackford, hot off *An Officer and a Gentleman*, would film the whole project for a movie called *Hail! Hail! Rock 'n' Roll*.

Berry then spent the rest of the visit flipping between raucous high spirits and stony silence. Activities included a little music, and consulting a notebook and a calculator. Keith was drawing perceptive parallels between Chuck and Mick Jagger.

Back in Wentzville, Richards began putting the band through its paces. Berry had never rehearsed in his life. He kept cutting Keith off in mid-riff, telling him he didn't know his stuff. At one particularly tense pass the two ended up standing toe to toe, apparently close to blows, debating the matter. For the next ten days, Chuck showered Keith with a mixture of praise and scorn, all the while making bizarre demands about the tempos and keys of his classic songs. Between times, Berry would frequently quit the stage in disgust and bolt back up to his private cinema. The band would hear a groan, then the thunder of stairs being taken two at a time, climaxing in Chuck yelling 'Yeahhhh, baby!' from somewhere above. Johnnie Johnson later said that everyone had been 'driven half nuts just [getting] the show on the road'.

Keith: 'I'm biting bullets because I'm trying to show the band that, in order to get the gig together, I'm going to take some shit that I wouldn't take from anybody. In the film you can see me chewin'. I'm on the edge. At any moment I could have turned around and downed the motherfucker. But Chuck doesn't understand because he doesn't deal with people. He's the only guy who's hit me and I haven't done anything about it. Far worse things have happened to me in my life than Chuck Berry trying to fuck with me.'

Immediately he got to the Fox theatre in St Louis, Richards had the roadies bury a slave amp three floors below the stage and feed Berry's guitar, instead, through a dummy. That way Chuck could blast out anything he wanted without it spoiling the film soundtrack. Keith had no intention of letting him ruin his own party.

The two shows on 16 October went well enough, punched up by Johnson and Chuck Leavell on keyboards and Bobby Keys on sax. A ticklish moment occurred when Chuck boogied over during the first number and said that, for a lark, he wanted to change the key to B-flat. Keith told him to fuck off. The result, watched by a full house including Anita and Marlon, was by far the best performance of Berry's long career. And it got even better. *Hail! Hail! Rock 'n' Roll*, including footage of the many rehearsal skirmishes, was a popular and critical hit on its release in 1987. Keith had repaid a debt that began, almost incredibly, when he'd queued up fourteen times to watch Berry in *Jazz on a Summer's Day* at the Dartford Odeon. A circle was closed.

Just as he had thirty years earlier, in Spielman Road, Keith again found himself in a largely female family. He was forty-three, the age at which Gus Dupree had been settling down in London with his wife and seven daughters. The older Keith got, the more he seemed to resemble his grandfather. It was an oddly familiar scene up in the Connecticut house, surrounded, as Keith was, by his wife and blonde baby girls. According to one Weston visitor, 'Patti was a saint there. While Keith moped around, she took care of business. You've got to remember he came from that background ... Women spoilt him. Men weren't as much fun, and you didn't see them during the day. They were more for night, a rude reminder of work.'

Patti would have no regrets about her life with a lovable male chauvinist. 'Keith's so good to me. He'd fill my house with servants if I wanted them, but I've got to keep to my roots ... I have my mom come in and help with the kids. My niece comes in to help me clean. Jerry Hall says, "Why don't you get someone to cook for you? Why don't you get somebody to do your shopping?" But that's not me. I'm happy being a wife and mother.'

Meanwhile, Jagger was in Holland, running around with a laptop and a filofax planning his tour. Nowadays the gap between how he and Keith saw the Stones wasn't just wide, it was yawningly so. With the factions locked in battle like fighting beetles in a jar, Richards began to seriously think about an album of his own. The Chuck Berry gigs had proved that, if nothing else, 'I had the balls to go out and do solo stuff.' Keith admitted to mixed feelings about the whole project: 'The deal to me was – I failed to keep my band together. I felt guilty.'

The Stones were, in fact, completely academic throughout 1986–7. Mick was clearly devoted to recording and touring *Primitive Cool*. Charlie was only slowly putting himself back together after his drug-addled break. Bill Wyman remained in the south of France, being doorstepped by the tabloids.

On New Year's Eve, Jagger happened to ring Richards in Jamaica to wish him season's greetings. Keith later described their conversation as 'very polite – very formal. He said that we must have a drink when we were back in New York.'

Spokesmen for both sides loudly insisted that the Stones were still a unit. All questions about the band's alleged breakup were parried with angry jabs of a lawyer's hand. However, even as Keith threatened to sue anyone who wrote them off, he ruefully acknowledged the outbreak, that spring, of 'World War 3'. The feud went public on 2 March, with a blast by Jagger in the *Daily Mirror*. Complaining that Richards wanted to run the band 'single-handedly', Mick said, 'I love Keith, I admire him … but I don't feel we can really work together anymore.'

Keith responded twenty-four hours later in the *Sun*. He said that Jagger 'should stop trying to be like Peter Pan and grow up … I don't see the point of pretending to be twenty-five when you're not.'

When asked if he could foresee any end to 'the bitching going on' between Jagger and himself, Keith replied, 'You'd better ask the bitch.'

Furious that Mick would 'ponce about' doing Stones songs without the Stones, Keith stopped bothering to go to meetings at all, hung up whenever Jagger called, and, the sharpest slap, apparently tried to replace him with Roger Daltrey. He kept telling the press about Mick being a sad case: 'You can't sit down with a bottle of whisky with him and talk it over. He just changes the subject.' Wyman was then quoted as calling Jagger 'the guilty one. He's decided he wants to do his own thing … be famous in his own right.' This led to another kung-fu round of recriminations. Bill's New York attorney sent a threatening letter describing the interview as 'misquotes, off-the-cuff remarks taken out of context and blown out of proportion'. Later that spring, Jagger wrote a song about Richards called Shoot Off Your Mouth. Keith called Mick a back-stabbing wimp.

The war was getting worse, but Keith kept his sense of humour. He summoned another journalist that spring to talk about the Stones. 'Really,' he said, 'the only thing Mick and I fight about is the band, the music and what we do.' Keith gave that short, sharp laugh of his, like change tossed onto a counter. The general feeling was that he was winning the PR campaign.

On 7 April 1987, the *Wall Street Journal* went into print talking about a legal dissolution. It happened to be the twenty-fifth anniversary of Richards and Jagger having met Brian Jones.

Two days later, Keith began auditioning a band at the Hit Factory in New York. The drummer Steve Jordan returned from the Chuck Berry gigs, along with Waddy Wachtel, an LA guitarslinger who'd funked up the Everlys, and assorted Neville brothers. (Only Ivan actually joined the band.) Jagger was across Broadway at Right Track studios, mixing *Primitive Cool* and dress-rehearsing his tour. Mick particularly wanted to take Jeff Beck on the road with him, but it wasn't to be. 'I quit because he offered me peanuts,' Beck told the *Sun*. 'It was laughable ... an insult. I'd love to play with the old geezer, but I can't believe how tight he is.'

Late in June, Richards signed a contract with Virgin Records for two solo albums. According to a well-placed source at the company, 'He didn't seem to give a stuff about the money.' Keith's only proviso was that nobody from head office bother him while he was in the studio.

At the first full session, a grinning Richards told the band, 'Well, it's either going to be a big success or a turkey. That's the way I do everything.' He seemed to have, as one party puts it, 'a real relaxed outlook on life'.

Keith's deal with Virgin went into effect on 17 July 1987. He spent most of that summer writing, rehearsing and listening to the same sort of Zulu street music that had inspired Paul Simon's *Graceland*. The first completed song on the album, You Don't Move Me, was both ethnic and a well-aimed swipe at Jagger. Keith, Steve Jordan and the rest began recording in earnest at Montreal's Le Studio (home of the Police's *Synchronicity*) in mid August. The dreadlocked Jordan was co-producing. By then Richards was calling the band the X-Pensive Winos after he caught the rhythm section swigging a bottle of Château Lafite behind the drum kit. Keith proudly told them that they reminded him of the early Stones, 'before the shit came'.

Back in London, Mick Jagger was confiding to *You* magazine that 'we've had a very rocky time these last few years'. In the same interview he described Keith as seeing the Stones 'very much as a conservative rock and roll band with strong traditions ... and as he gets older his ideas have become more conservative. I like to be a bit more open-minded about things.'

Keith volleyed back by telling a reporter, 'I wanted to keep the Stones together and he didn't.' Based on a conversation with 'one of his closest confidants', *Today* revealed that 'Mick is very bitter ... He's had a real go at Keith [on *Primitive Cool*] and hopes that he listens to the record and realizes the significance.'

It was becoming a remarkably public spat, which caused even *Rolling Stone* to begin paying attention. Keith told the magazine that summer, 'Mick and I are incredibly diverse people. We've known each other forty years – ever since we were three or four years old. But while a certain part of our personalities is incredibly close, there's an awful lot which is very, very different ... [Jagger's] a lonely guy, too. He's got his own problems, you know?'

Even as Keith fondly christened his own group, he was tetchily calling the funk-pop quintet still rehearsing in New York 'Jagger's little jerk-off band'. *Primitive Cool*, out that September, reached only number forty-one in America, number twenty-six in Britain. Mick's US tour was reportedly cancelled as a result of poor sales – though he would still do composite Stones-solo gigs in the Far East. Most critics never took to *Cool*, which got a lot of play in wine bars, nor to Yetnikoff's boast about making Mick as big as Jacko. 'Perhaps I expected too much of Let's Work, the ballyhooed single, which is about as hip as Geoffrey Howe,' *Today* wrote. 'At least, it's not the Big Deal everyone was waiting for.'

Mick was undaunted. Worse was to come.

On 19 October – Black Monday – the Dow-Jones industrial average lost 508 points, nearly a quarter of its total value. As shares dropped vertically with no one buying, traders were sold out as they failed to respond to margin calls, mobs gathered on Broad Street outside the New York stock exchange, and by the end of the day, even some of the best managed investors – including a number of rock stars – had lost millions.

Three days later, *Primitive Cool* disappeared from the chart. One of the

Rolling Stones began calling the others to talk about putting the band back together. It was Mick Jagger.

While wrapping up his album, titled *Talk is Cheap*, Richards decided to tour with the Winos in 1988. But he also kept an eye firmly on his main brand. After one particularly prolific day in the studio, Keith turned to Steve Jordan and laughed, 'Well, *this* should wake the motherfuckers up.' Jordan, like everyone in Montreal, was both fond and respectful of 'the guvnor', but also keenly aware of the Stones connection. That spring he and Richards wrote a song called Almost Hear You Sigh, with a swooning melody pinwheeling out of Keith's classical guitar fills. It was held over from *Talk is Cheap* and left, instead, for Jagger to sing.

In Japan, Mick was playing seven sold-out shows to impassive but apparently well-satisfied customers. While in Tokyo he was joined on stage by Tina Turner. As at Live Aid they duetted on It's Only Rock 'n Roll, he, again, deftly removing her skirt. Ron Wood also happened to be in town, and on the night of 20 March the two Stones sat down for a *sake*. Several hours later, it was agreed that Ron would pass on a friendly message to Keith.

In mid-May, Jagger and Prince Rupert invited Richards to a clear-the-air meeting in London. It was the very month Keith was finishing *Talk is Cheap* in New York: 'I've got everybody in town at one time, mixing and doing that shit and editing. Bless their hearts, the Winos, they turned me around. I said, "I ain't going." They said, "Yes, you are." I'm saying, "No way." And they're saying, "You are." Of course, for the Stones, I can't say no. It's like, "Reschedule. I'm gonna go to London for a week."'

On 18 May, the five Stones met in a well-guarded suite at the Savoy hotel. There was the sense of a momentous encounter that bright spring morning, a rock 'n roll version of the Allied leaders converging at Yalta. Jagger said he wanted the band to get together in the autumn but Keith, in a notable *volte-face*, refused. He had no intention of breaking his commitment to take the Winos out on the road. However, after 'row[ing] like crazy for a day' (during which Keith took to calling Mick 'Brenda') all parties agreed to a full-scale comeback in 1989. Jagger was extremely confident, he said in conclusion, that the demographics were right for a tour.

Then came Keith's own summation.

'Listen, darling,' he chortled. 'This thing is bigger than both of us. *Capisce?*'

At that, Richards went back to New York, wrapped the album, posed for the cover and did the press. The accusations and counter-accusations of the past year gave way to a more civil tone. 'I love Mick ... I respect him,' Keith told *Option*. 'There's also animosity, but that's par for the course. You can't tread the boards every night like he did, acting like you're semi-divine, without something rubbing off.' The reconciliation took another leap forward when the two men met again, in Manhattan, with their families. Eighteen months earlier, Jerry Hall had gotten headlines after being arrested at Barbados airport allegedly carrying twenty pounds of ganja. The subsequent trial – with its parade of tropical self-indulgence – caused a scandal in England at the height of a recession. Patti Richards had been among her 'most supportive friend[s]' during the ordeal. (Hall was found innocent of all charges against her, after a customs official admitted lying under oath.)

That New York summit now triggered a very Jaggeresque piece of play-acting. While at the Hit Factory, Keith took the opportunity to blast his guests with a tape of *Talk is Cheap*. Returning from the bathroom, he happened to glimpse Mick, with his back to him, dancing away to the opening track. Keith retraced his steps, coughed, and walked in to find Jagger sitting demurely on a sofa, reading the *Financial Times*.

The spillover effects of the feud were all over the press and promotion Keith did that summer. *Talk is Cheap*, for all its scaled-down values, wasn't exactly released in a vacuum. There were no fewer than six cover stories, including *Rolling Stone*, along with promo CDs, T-shirts and the like. By late August, the PR machinery was running at full bore on both sides of the Atlantic. Keith was a famously sharp interviewee, with a habit of enlivening proceedings by waving a switchblade around the room. In a celebrity culture venerating mutual respect at best, luvviedom at worst, he was also strikingly honest. Particularly about Jagger.

'Ninety-nine per cent of the male population would give a *limb* to live like him,' Keith allowed. 'To be *Mick Jagger*. And he's not happy ... I'm trying to grow the thing up, and I'm saying we don't need the lemon-yellow tights and the cherry picker to make a good Stones show. There's a more mature way of doing it.'

Inevitably, the press devoted plenty of space to Keith's own appearance. His skin, nicked with lines, had an embalmed colour, and looked like it was about to peel off in leathery strips. Both shoulders revealed deep bruises from his years of shooting up. Keith's shiny new teeth made for a stark contrast with his ashen cheeks and kohl-ringed eyes. *The Times'* David Sinclair was one of those who met him that autumn, and remembers being shocked at his deathly pallor. Sinclair happened to run into the paper's obituary editor a few days later. 'Got anything on the stocks for Keith Richards?' he asked him.

Keith was completely unfazed by any of this. Despite or because of the decay, there was something very human about him. Even his press photos were stark, unprettified – crude and vigorous; no creamy lines, no glossy airbrushed effects, no touch of that dreary prefabrication that passed for hip elsewhere. Keith 'utterly charmed' the BBC's Jeff Griffin, who also interviewed him that month for a 'My Top Ten' programme. ('He was like Bob Hope, you know?' says another BBC hand. 'Keith had fantastic timing. You'd wait and think, "What's going on here?", and then he'd floor you with the punch line.') Keith duly supplied a list long on Otis Redding and Little Walter, though not excluding the likes of Dire Straits, Tina Turner – and Ron Wood.

Between interviews in New York, Paris and Rome, Keith would headline the Smile Jamaica gala in London to benefit hurricane victims. He took the opportunity to gripe about Jagger's then current tour of Australia. Mick replied that Keith had been slagging him 'just to get publicity for his record. It was the only way he could get any. He takes things more personally. He's had a more problematic life.'

Talk is Cheap. Keith's long-awaited solo throttles back on the Midnight Rambler guitar. There are few classic rockers or party tunes, and not much riffage. If anything, the voice is more startling: nowadays, Keith sounds as if he's always either just waking up or nodding off at the end of a vodka binge. (One wag compares him to a fag-smoking choirboy.) Generally, *Talk* is as gritty as a half-completed road. At worst, it sounds like a collection of demos that Jagger just might, conceivably, have sharpened (a view Mick himself shares). One or two of the lesser songs are little more than a chorus and a lick. On top form, the work's improvisational fervour makes it the ultimate Keith album, a harder, more rootsy counterpoint to the sleekness of *Primitive Cool*. The most frequently heard criticisms remain that it isn't long enough, and that Keith's legendary Toronto tapes don't make the cut.

The album opens with the touch-of-funk Big Enough and the dodgy chant of Take It So Hard; Struggle boasts a classic yet constantly surprising *Exile*-type riff. Make No Mistake is a jumble of soulful rhythms, honking saxes and those nicotine vocals. Accusing Jagger of greed and selfishness, the lyrics of You Don't Move Me touch on the bargain-bin fate of *She's the Boss* and *Primitive Cool*: 'Now you want to throw the dice/You already crapped out twice', and go on from there to get personal. Although hopscotching around, from the bluesy How I Wish to the cajun groove of Locked Away, *Talk* ultimately forges a niche all its own. Keith's voice projects a winning, romantic vulnerability and the Winos rock throughout. This is heavy music that moves.

Talk is Cheap was released on 4 October 1988. It stayed in the charts for six months.

On 24 November, Keith and the band embarked on a fifteen-date American tour at the Fox theatre, Atlanta. In a well-drilled set (with only Happy and Connection from the back catalogue) there was plenty of power guitar, funk-style grooves and a voice that would have scared away commuters if heard on a Tube station tannoy. (Wyman: 'He's not Pavarotti, is he?') On certain nights, Keith seemed to be doing stand-up more than performing, joshing with the crowd and tapping a fag into the ashtray welded to his mike stand. There were a lot of mutual toasts drunk. More generally, Keith used *Talk* and the spirit of the songs for an evening of rock and soul tunes mingled with raps that were heartfelt, funny and often very odd indeed. He was supported by one of the best bands in the business.

When Richards came through Memphis, he made a point of looking up his old near-colleague Wayne Perkins. Dressed in his stage gear of black jacket and white frilly shirt, Keith was 'real sweet' when the two reminisced over some coke. Another friend thought him 'a weird contrast between the high-kicking guy on stage and the quiet man back home. He really folded into himself.' Keith's was the role of detached observer, and his comments, when they came, were unexpected and always wry, followed by a quick retreat into a cloud of Marlboro smoke.

On 15 December, Richards and the band brought down the house at the Hollywood Palladium. Not one to be swayed by the fickle tides of pop culture, Keith turned the last few shows of the tour into bona fide Events, with enough passion and snap and sassing around to make Madonna look like Norman Tebbit. In short, classic rock 'n roll. Everything finished three nights later, which happened to be Keith's forty-fifth birthday. Patti and the girls were there, along with Bert, Anita, Marlon and some 200 other friends. Mick Jagger was in Mustique, so sent his regrets.

Friday 13 January 1989. Keith kissed Patti goodbye, then took a Learjet to Grantley Adams airport (scene of Jerry Hall's erroneous ganja bust) in Barbados. The plan was to meet Jagger, write some songs, put together a record and a tour. Keith was thrilled to bits, but also wary both about working with 'Brenda', and relaunching the Stones in the era of Guns n' Roses and Nirvana. He told his family that he'd be back in either two weeks or two days.

In the event, Richards and Jagger wasted no time on recriminations. Both had songs left over from their solo albums, and the juices flowed under the tropical sun. In the space of a weekend they had three tracks, including the full-throated chorus of Mixed Emotions, blocked out for the band. Prince Rupert then flew in for a business summit. Mick: 'We were in a hotel with the sea crashing outside and the sun shining and drinks, talking about all the money we're gonna get and how great it was gonna be.' By cutting out Bill Graham and going instead with the Toronto promoter Michael Cohl, who in turn oversaw a sponsorship deal with Budweiser and assorted TV and merchandising rights, the prince guaranteed the Stones a staggering $70 million profit for a fifteen-week tour.

When Keith came back to Connecticut, it was merely to pack.

On the 18th Ron Wood was summoned to New York, where he joined Richards and Jagger, and a sheepish Mick Taylor, for their induction into the Rock and Roll Hall of Fame. Mick quoted Cocteau while Keith studied his nails. After the laughter had died down the three Stones and their ex jumped on stage and played Satisfaction. Suddenly the dysfunctional, wheezing geezers were transformed back into the greatest band in the world. Charlie and Bill arrived in New York the next day.

Early in February, Keith went back to Barbados to run the first proper Stones sessions in four years. He 'heard Charlie in there as I was out in the parking lot, driving up to the joint, and I just sat there for five minutes. I was smiling like, *no problem*. He was so crisp, so tight. I thought, we've got the songs; now we've got the drummer.' For six weeks, the Stones plugged in and let her rip. Fast work. They took some of the final songs up to George Martin's Air studios in Montserrat, booting Bill off the island after his gymslip lover proposed to him and he accepted. Keith and Mick had no intention of breaking off their most productive sessions since *Aftermath* to deal with a posse of journalists flying in from London.

The siren that lured Wyman onto the rocks was eighteen-year-old Mandy Smith, whom the Stones had known about as long ago as *Dirty Work* days. Their affair, which the band followed as avidly as they did *Dallas*, had sent Keith into paroxysms. Presciently, he'd seen only 'major aggro' ahead. Bill had assured him it would be all right. Keith: 'Don't be so fucking naive!' Inevitably, the *News of the World* had got hold of the story, and reporters started smuggling themselves into the band's London headquarters disguised as delivery men; the sort of icebreaker that often led to merry laughter all around the office.

Keith in 1989: 'Love has no boundaries, and I wish Bill and Mandy every happiness for their future together.'

In May the Stones moved shop back to Olympic, their first use of the old *Beggars Banquet* studio in twenty years. Jagger called the new album *Steel Wheels*, apparently a pun on the antiques roadshow, old giblet lips-type press he was getting. He and Keith set to work on a long, spacey song called Speed Of Light, which turned into Continental Drift. They hammered away at the track, trying to capture the right voodoo rhythms, until, around eleven one night, with Concorde to catch in the morning, Jagger called for a take. 'No cock-ups!' he added. Just when a quiet passage arrived Woody knocked over a cast-iron ashtray, which fell to the floor. Mick stopped singing, and the band came to a halt. 'That's nice,' Keith said at length. 'It's different. It's unusual.' He took a nip of vodka. 'Keep it,' he said, putting down the mug, 'but make it sound like an accident.'

On 31 May, Richards was inducted as a Living Legend at the first International Rock Awards in New York. Eric Clapton did the honours. The various speeches seemed to tout Keith as the haggard relic and Nineties man – prepping the biggest tour in history – all at once.

Keith: 'We're playing at an incredible level. Why shouldn't we compete with the kids? If anybody can do it, it's the Stones.'

Two days later, Bill Wyman married Mandy Smith at a civil ceremony in Bury St Edmunds. The Stones were livid with Bill for all the tabloid aggro, as well as for opening a burger restaurant named Sticky Fingers without checking with anyone. They did, however, turn up for the wedding reception at London's Grosvenor House. Late in the proceedings some of the bride's young family approached Jagger for his autograph. Mick told them to sod off.

June 1989. The Rolling Stones plugged themselves back in like a neon sign. Keith and Mick finished up *Steel Wheels*, taking a day trip to Morocco to record some last-minute tribal pipes 'n drums for Continental Drift. (The local Jajouka musicians were still waiting to be paid for their work on Brian's album, twenty-one years earlier.) By early July everyone was housed in a disused girls' school in Washington, Connecticut, an hour's drive north of Keith's place, surrounded by sleepy New England hamlets with names like Dartford and Kent. For the next six weeks, music alternated with business. Keith loyally brought back Bobby Keys from his years of playing clubs and even a few bar gigs as 'Mr Brown Sugar'. Jagger in turn introduced Matt Clifford, a former cathedral chorister brought in to twiddle the Korg knobs and give everything a modern, electronic wash. Mick was particularly sold on Clifford, who, he told everyone, would 'punch up' the old Stones sound. Alas, Keith wasn't willing to give him that much control.

Although a holiday mood prevailed in Connecticut, Keith admitted to a few nerves. The rocket flight of Prince Rupert's graphs and charts would be disrupted by a rasped 'What if nobody *shows?*' from the far end of the table. At moments of stress Keith sometimes echoed Stu's portrayal of the Stones as a 'shower of shit', and worried that the wheels would fall off. Plenty of lesser Sixties acts had come back, knock-kneed and laughing, to give it yet another go. Few had succeeded. Thus was born a six-days a week, twelve-hours a day rehearsal regime.

Keith: 'I'd get up in the morning [sic] and feel I'd just done fifteen rounds with Mike Tyson. But we were on a roll.'

Meanwhile, the Stones organization – now with 370 employees – was putting together a year-long piece of rock theatre to be pumped out on vast, *Blade Runner*-like stages. The whole thing was so big that some American sports domes were too small to house it. On the outdoor gigs the tower from which Mick sang Sympathy needed flashing red lights on top to wave jets away.

The Stones also took unprecedented steps to maximize their profit. Among the new twists Prince Rupert added to the business of touring were record-high ticket surcharges, lucrative TV, film and live album deals, and an aggressive merchandising programme that sold everything from socks and T-shirts to $500 leather jackets. If you could wear it, the band and their logo were on it.

On 11 July, the Stones pulled in to Track 42 of New York's Grand Central Station and announced the tour. One of the 400 reporters present asked if they were doing it for the money. Mick assured her that nothing was further from his mind. 'What about love?' he asked. Keith took the mike and cackled, 'It's for the glory, darlin'. The *glory.*'

Soon the Stones were on the cover of *Time, Life* and even *Forbes.* As the press acknowledged, rumours had flown around for years that Keith and Mick weren't even talking. So when tickets went on sale, it was hallelujah time. *They're back. It's really happening.*

From the start, business was brisk: four concerts at Shea Stadium sold out overnight, two in Toronto in six hours. One block of 200,000 seats went at the phone-melting rate of 2,000 per minute. The prince also quietly signed up with Event Transportation Systems (ETS), a Canadian firm that, quite legally, resold tickets at up to three times face value as part of a package. ETS guaranteed Michael Cohl and the band $500,000, and they received more than half the profits.

'Every time I see a Brink's truck,' said ETS's president Don McVie, 'I think of the Stones.'

Back in Connecticut, Keith was fast turning his 'shower of shit' into a well-drilled, fifteen-piece showband complete with a horn section and three backing singers. When everyone was assembled he told them that he wanted not only a big sound, but also a raw one. Here some friction existed with Jagger's vision. Mick let it be known that, this time round, the Stones couldn't afford to give one bad concert. 'Everything's gotta be perfect.' The insight was followed by Mick announcing that he was 'worried about the drums coming across', and telling Keith that they needed a click-in track to get the tempos right.

Keith: 'I'll handle the tempos, mate.'

Jagger was soon jogging seven miles a day with a professional coach, while Keith trained on vodka and cigarettes. He was fast acquiring a W.H. Auden face and a voice that sounded stoned even when he wasn't. Jerry Hall came up to the Richardses' house at eleven one morning, to find Patti fixing a Bloody Mary breakfast. Jerry told her Mick was concerned about Keith, and wanted him to get in shape for the road.

'He's *in* shape,' said Patti.

In late July, Keith took the pre-tour physical. 'The bugger stuck electrodes all over my body, hooked up more monitors to me than the Stones use on stage, and told me I was "normal". Fuck! Can you imagine telling Keith Richards he's *normal?*'

On 12 August the Stones gave their first American concert in eight years at the 200-seat Toad's Place, down on the Connecticut shore. The first anyone knew about it was when a twenty-man crew pulled up in a fleet of vans and began wheeling massive Fender Twin amps through the back door. At nine that night, Keith walked on and flogged the opening chords of Start Me Up. The Stones were back to work.

Steel Wheels followed a week later. Their Big Statement doesn't exactly shoot the lights out, but proves a winning formula. Once again, Keith embroiders turgid stomps (Rock And A Hard Place) and teary ballads (Slipping Away) with his serviceably choppy guitar. The hangover from 'World War 3' is all over the record, which breaks down along party lines: Keith's songs (warm and lazy) and Mick's songs (impeccably hip), with Charlie the constant factor.

It's already eighteen years since the sounds of *Exile* first seeped out of the cellar, but, at its best, *Wheels* recaptures some of the old glory. Sad Sad Sad isn't quite Rocks Off, but the song barrels ahead like a night train out of Memphis. Mixed Emotions and Break The Spell both somehow tick the box marked 'commercial' and the one marked 'bluesy'. Mick's Blinded By Love, as well as flaunting some edgy lyrics about the Duke of Windsor, is a throwback to Blue Turns To Grey from *December's Children*. Keith, in turn, reworks the Beast Of Burden riff to good effect on Almost Hear You Sigh. The song runs through well-worn tales of faded love, made fresh again by Richards' classical-guitar work and Jagger's soulful hooting. Keith closes the album, as he did *Dirty Work*, with an end-of-the-rope ballad. Slipping Away boasts not only that gravelly voice, but one of the sweetest chord progressions in recent memory.

Both Keith and Mick would talk about *Steel Wheels* having been made at wild speed. There was clearly no time for any proper artwork, which, in the event, had all the allure of a Soviet department store display. In all, this was one of the most perverse – and catchiest – albums of the band's career. It hit number two in Britain and number one in America, their best showing since *Tattoo You*.

For twenty years, Stones tours had been famous for their excesses, for egos run amok in one-night stands hazed over by trashed rooms, dope, strange faces in packed halls, sex, and enough hero-worship for anyone. With *Steel Wheels* the drug-and-chug vibe gave way to one of icy professionalism, the groupies were replaced by wives and kids, and the operation ran like a mobile company. The old charm was lost for ever.

Keith often put it about that he was 'suspect of visuals; the eyes are the whores of the senses'. Even so, the new shows enjoyed a full set of mega-tour accessories, including giant video screens, 60-foot-high inflatable floozies and plenty of fireworks. The stage itself was a massive industrial park dressed with boilers, girders, trusses, chutes, hoses and flame-throwing pipes, inspired by the sci-fi author William Gibson (*Neuromancer*), with a touch of *Batman*. For those high up in the bleachers, the band looked like a distant Punch and Judy show, with Keith and Mick circling each other and bopping up and down.

31 August 1989. The Stones drove up to Philadelphia's Veterans Stadium in a royal progress, with flashing lights and a sixty-strong police motorcycle escort. It was the band's first paying gig in just over seven years. As fireworks exploded and turrets shot out flames, Keith ran on, alone for a second, and lit the fuse to Start Me Up. Apart from a few loopy, unanchored moments during Sympathy, he was on song throughout, with fierce, no-frills readings of Midnight Rambler, Gimme Shelter, Satisfaction. The music was rougher and less clipped; Mick shimmied around in his breeches and tails, and Charlie had, gloriously, rejoined the band.

Years ago, Keith was content to stand in one spot – right leg slightly crossed in front of the left, about shin-high – and hustle out the riffs. Nowadays, as you watched him on the big screen, he prowled around more, suddenly pivoting or launching into a histrionic twist, as if he'd been prodded with a defibrilator just out of camera shot. Jagger's own cherry picker moment would come in Sympathy, when he introduced himself from atop a hundred-foot-high scaffold. There was a section Mick then spent offstage, as Keith led the band through Slipping Away and Happy. In an operation serviced by at least twelve accountants, part of a travelling brain trust of 300, this was the set's starkly intimate climax. Some nights Keith substituted Little T&A, evincing all the self-confidence of a man with a pair of his wife's panties allegedly stuffed in his pocket.

From Philadelphia – where a recovering and again foxy Anita appeared backstage – it was on to Toronto. In familiar vein, Canadian customs were waiting for Keith at the airport, relieving him, after an intensive search, of a small knife. Meanwhile, the Toronto *Star* columnist Rita Zekas reported that a woman who identified herself as Margaret Trudeau banged on the door of the El Mocambo club, scene of the Stones' 1977 revels, and sped off again when told the band weren't on the premises.

When the limo pulled away from the stadium later that night, Keith cheered.

'Really, I love Canada,' he said.

Back in the midwest, even as Jagger danced up a storm, it was Richards who got the biggest roar from up in the steep concrete stands. At some shows, people actually gasped at his appearance. But *raddled*. At forty-five, Keith was no longer merely a great guitar player or writer. He was a synonym for nostalgia, a stalwart loved not just for himself but for having made it. It was enough that he survived. People came to the gigs out of residual affection, larded with respect and awe, just as they might visit a listed monument, whatever its current state of ruin. Steel Wheels, the company, owed much to its creative director. Just then, back in England, Keith was being voted the 'greatest living musician' by a jury of his peers on *NME*.

When they came out of that Barbados meeting, Keith and Mick had assured everyone that the blood feud was over. They painted a rosy picture for the press. Most Stones insiders, on the other hand, knew that things could unravel just as quickly as they'd come together. On tour, the 'love–hate vibe' only intensified. The sheer scale of the enterprise guaranteed not just money, but backbiting. Keith, who wasn't keen on the idea of being sponsored, fumed at having to line up backstage to shake hands with beer executives, dubbing the wheeling-dealing Jagger 'a smart little motherfucker'. Some of their differing views on high finance weren't so much aired as shouted out. The usual factions formed. 'Mick and Keith's obsession with one another went off the chart,' says a Stones manager. 'Whatever Keith said to Wood, Mick had to know. Whatever Mick said to Clifford, Keith had to know.' Meanwhile, Jagger was playing more and more guitar onstage. Richards told friends that Mick was OK on acoustic, but wasn't to be trusted anywhere near electricity. Jagger's private little tuning room was quickly christened 'the house of God'.

The tour ended, as in 1981, on 19 December. Three and a half million customers saw the Stones in sixty shows, with tickets and merchandising grossing $98 million and $40 million respectively. Keith: 'We asked ourselves, "Why are we doing this? Do we really want to?" And the answer was that we *have* to. Not from the money viewpoint as from the fact that none of us was about to let the band drift away. We're still looking for the ultimate Rolling Stones. It's like the Holy Grail.'

For all the Stones-crazy worship in towns like New York and Los Angeles, neither was the highlight of Keith's tour. The highlight of Keith's tour occurred in Atlantic City, New Jersey, in the squat barn of the Convention Center, when an elderly black man came on stage dressed to the nines and jammed with the band for twenty minutes: John Lee Hooker, who, in a simple and eloquent tribute, smiled at Keith at the end of their time together, bowed, and doffed his hat to him.

9

'String Us Up and We Still Won't Die'

DOWN A CONNECTICUT BACK ROAD, NEXT TO ROLLING FIELDS AND JUST OFF THE MERRITT PARKWAY, WAS A PLACE SO EXCLUSIVE THAT SOME OF ROCK 'N ROLL'S BIGGEST NAMES WERE TURNED AWAY AT THE GATE. It wasn't a fancy resort, but a private house: Keith began the new decade here, sitting in an oak-panelled library that belonged as much in a Noël Coward play as it did in a home where electric guitars clanged in the night. He was forty-six, bone-thin and dark about the eyes, with a shock of frizzy grey hair, and frequently dragging on a cigarette. Nowadays Keith's speech pattern, much like his guitar playing, went in not for long lines but for jagged riffing. The phrasing was laconic and gap-ridden, but it was also strangely expressive. No one ever doubted what it was Keith Richards was saying to them.

On 5 February 1990, the Stones flew into Tokyo, watched the Tyson–Buster Douglas title fight, then played ten sold-out *Steel Wheels* shows. The crowds, a mixture of dour salarymen, mothers and small kids, applauded warmly before lapsing – as if by prearranged signal – into total silence. Even Jagger, who'd done solo gigs in Japan, looked uncomfortable in the reverential hush between songs. For Keith the greatest shock may have been the 6 p.m. showtime, an hour when he'd been known to be starting breakfast. While Richards partied, Jagger dutifully did the rounds of the press and local CBS sales reps. The same ferocious discipline would be brought to his stagecraft, where Mick disliked nothing more than to be thought of as wildly spontaneous.

In late April, Keith and the Stones settled in to rehearse at Château de Dangu in Normandy. Street Fighting Man got a snazzy, Nineties makeover and would be a highlight of the European gigs that summer. Keith and Mick took to arriving separately, then holding court in different salons. A sulky Wyman was rightly concerned about his young wife. Mandy was now in a London clinic suffering from 'multiple allergy problems [that] caused stress to our marriage', Bill wrote in his memoirs, a wild understatement. (Compounding his misery, after three years in the RAF and thirty on the road, Bill had now developed a fear of flying.) Meanwhile the designer Mark Fisher came up with a pared-down set for the new shows, which Jagger named the Urban Jungle tour. He was still given plenty of toys to work with: a staircase he ran up and down, girders to swing from, and big balloons to prod with a stick. The only thing Mick didn't do was bungee-jump. Yet although he set a benchmark for spectacle, he was also hip enough to ensure that, for the most part, the props supported the music, not vice versa. Opening night, in Rotterdam, was a killer. The Stones miraculously turned the Olympic Stadium into a dark and sweaty rock club, with a whirling mosh pit and even the occasional flannel-clad stage diver.

Anita reappeared in Berlin. She found Keith happily slumped backstage eating shepherd's pie and reading a book about the Nazis. A German masseuse named Dot Stein worked on some of the Stones, at Charlie's request. (Richards, she insists, talked up a storm about health foods and breastfeeding.) Mick rashly told Keith that the crowd that night was the largest the Stones had ever played to. Keith turned the amps up to bazooka level, and Jagger would soon start working with an earplug on his left side.

Some time that month, Dick Taylor had a talk with the Stones office. Keith and Mick's old Dartford mate was giving it yet another go with the Pretty Things, and wondered if his band could support them at Wembley. As Taylor waited for a reply, Jagger was giving a series of interviews that dwelt on what he called the 'constant shit' of reliving the past (he was against it). Shortly after that, a young band named Gun was announced as the Stones' London warmup.

4 July: Keith Richards materialized on the Wembley stage through a blast of flame. The Stones' homecoming stand featured some of their more satisfying, and musical, gigs in a decade. So strong was the material, it could

sustain even pranks such as a pack of giant blowup dogs, one of which Mick poked in the arse with his long pole. The result was organized chaos – what one critic called 'an elegant din' – as Keith's amped-up guitar on Honky Tonk and Flash was seized on by the crowd's headbangers. Those dozing in the park's far reaches were rudely awoken by a 70,000-strong roar as news came in of an England goal in that night's World Cup tie in Turin. By Satisfaction the fists shaken aloft stretched up to the highest stands, and off-key audience participation nearly drowned out the band. England lost their match in Italy.

A few nights later, in the tune-up room in Glasgow, Richards carelessly nicked his left hand on a guitar string. The show went on. Afterwards, Keith complained that he was having difficulty shaping chords – one of his fingers went blue, then swelled up like a saveloy – and things started to get cancelled. Two more Wembley gigs were put back to the end of August, and the insurers reportedly made a seven-figure payment to cover the losses.

The Stones went through some hard times that summer. There was a recession on, as well as a monsoon, which led to a steep decline in business. In Rome, Mick celebrated his forty-seventh birthday in front of an audience of three or four thousand dotted around the Stadio Flamino. There were conflicting reports about the rate of trade in Spain and France. The band did, however, perform to 110,000 rock 'n roll-starved fans in Prague, at the personal request of the new Czech president Václav Havel. A ticket to the 19 August show also acted as a one-day visa for the crowds travelling west from Poland and Hungary. The Czech government pulled out all the stops. Their official poster advertising the concert proclaimed, 'Tanks are rolling out, Stones are rolling in!' Havel sent his personal jet to pick up the band. Even as they flew in, workmen were erecting a giant tongue logo in the Břevnov hills overlooking town, on a spot recently occupied by a statue of Stalin.

Keith: 'That was an amazing gig. A lot of the reason you've got major shifts in superpower situations in the past few years had to do with music. In the long term, the most important thing that rock 'n roll's done, it's opened up people's minds ... It was rock 'n roll and blue jeans that tore down that wall.'

The tour ended at the end of the month, exactly a year since opening night in Philadelphia. Julien Temple broke off from shooting *Earth Girls*

Are Easy to film the final London shows with 'rolling loop' Imax cameras. Nobody but Bill himself knew that they would be his last-ever Stones gigs. Twenty-eight years before, he and the band had caught a bus to the Methodist youth hall in Putney, having a row with the conductor who didn't want them coming on board with their guitar cases and amps. The club eventually paid them £3 (filched by Brian) for their services. Now Wyman went away in a limousine, with the press still on his case about Mandy and all her allergies.

The band tossed themselves an end-of-tour do at the Kensington Roof Gardens, where everyone wolfed kilos of caviar. They could afford it: for the year August 1989–August 1990, Keith and Mick made a conservatively estimated $12 million apiece. Anita came again, this time arm in arm with Marianne Faithfull. One of the lesser guests remembers Richards good-naturedly waving his sword around – 'a much-loved ritual'. And, as he recalls, 'Keith was the life and soul of the party.'

Aristocratic idleness was abhorrent to Mick Jagger, who toiled away on the tapes for a new live album. Keith, by contrast, spent most of that autumn with his family in Jamaica. Tasks included lying prone in his hammock overlooking the Caribbean, reading, toking, listening to Rasta drum music and strumming 'Guts', his Velasquez classical guitar.

The Stones were back in the news that November: while Mick went through a Balinese wedding ritual with Jerry Hall, Keith and Woody turned up in London to celebrate the release of Pete and Dud's latest (and last) video. Charlie began recording a new jazz album, dedicated to Charlie Parker. Bill Wyman published his memoirs, which made it clear that he'd gotten less money but more sex than anybody else in the band.

Keith: 'I could never understand his thing about counting women. What are you gonna do with a chick in ten minutes, for Chrissake? It takes them half that long to get their drawers down.' Bill and Mandy (whose weight was down to five stone) split up soon afterwards. Richards told the other Stones that he wanted to take the next year to work with some outside musicians.

In all, there was a mere three days' slog for the band in 1991. On 16 January, just as Allied bombers opened the first Gulf War, the Stones recorded Keith's Highwire. Jagger's biting critique on arms dealing (allowing him to rhyme 'tank' with 'bank') was given the open-G treatment by Richards and released as a single. Bill refused to appear on the video. The Stones knocked off a James Brown riff for the B-side, which they called Sex Drive.

In April they put out a live album, *Flashpoint*. It was the Stones' fourth and final offering under their old contract. Walter Yetnikoff had had an explosive row with Amnesty International, apparently convinced they were anti-Semitic, and then left CBS. The label itself was soon put on the block and sold to Sony. Richard Branson immediately began courting the Stones for Virgin Music, reportedly offering them $40 million. While he was pondering that Jagger hired some lingerie models for a quick Sex Drive video which was part Freud, part Benny Hill. The core ripped-panties theme got it banned in America.

Keith, meanwhile, was all over the place. He played on John Lee Hooker's *Mr Lucky*, co-produced Johnnie Johnson's best work in twenty years, wrote with Tom Waits. He and Jagger (then based in Atlanta, starring in Geoff Murphy's sci-fi romp *Freejack*) rarely spoke. The only confrontation, according to a knowledgeable source, came when Mick flew to New York and casually asked whether he could listen to any of the early tracks for Keith's next solo album. For Richards – the Human Riff, victor of 'World War 3' – this was too much. He allegedly stood up and said, 'I've been doing this shit thirty years, and I'm not going to have my stuff "evaluated" by Mr Jagger.'

Mick didn't ask again.

One terrible morning, Eric Clapton's four-year-old son Conor fell to his death from the fifty-third floor of Manhattan's Galleria Building. He had been playing alone there, by an unlocked window. At a time when many other rock stars kept silent, Keith went out of his way to support Clapton. Typically, says the same source, there was a 'steady flow' of notes and calls. 'Keith never just blew you off with the usual "Ring me" crap. He'd tell you his house and car were available, money, whatever you needed. In a crisis, you saw the very best of the guy.'

Later that spring, the Stones accepted $4 million to let Satisfaction be turned into an advertising jingle for Snickers candy. Keith's gross income for the year 1991–2 would come to more than $7 million. In years ahead, it would top $15 million.

17 October: Dartford station plus thirty. Keith was in Seville as part of the Guitar Legend show that launched Expo 91. He and assorted Winos agreed to perform with Bob Dylan. The short set that followed was greeted

by a range of reactions (mainly shock) that had in common one underlying article of faith: that Dylan was a talented nutcase. Famous for playing his hits in unrecognizable format, often in different keys, he chose Seville to rehearse some completely fresh arrangements – during the concert. Later that night, a reporter asked Richards why Dylan would have done such a thing.

Keith (good naturedly): 'Because he's a cunt.'

On 23 October, the Stones' old promoter Bill Graham died in a helicopter accident. Keith, whose appreciation for lost friends often went far beyond the stock showbiz pieties, could manage but a brief eulogy. 'That's the end of nighttime chopper flights for me, baby.' Some of his family believed that Graham never fully got over being dropped by the band in 1989.

Back in London, Virgin's Richard Branson had been agonizing about whether to sell his independent record company (whose accounts recorded post-tax earnings of £500,000 and assets of some £3 million), for around £500 million. On 20 November 1991, he fulfilled a long-held ambition and signed the Rolling Stones. The deal gave the band a reported $45 million, with an upfront payment of $8 million per album. Virgin got the distribution rights to the back catalogue since *Sticky Fingers*. That night Branson took Keith, Mick and Woody for a celebration dinner at Mosimann's. Stories praising this triumph of British entrepreneurship were splashed all over the morning's press. Those who questioned Virgin's finances, or Branson's well-advanced plans for the label, were silenced by the threat of a writ.

Just over three months later, Virgin Music was sold to Thorn EMI for $1 billion, the most ever paid for an independent company in England. The Stones deal (which Bill refused to sign) would reap a quick dividend with *Jump Back*, the latest in a golden-greats continuum that began as long ago as *Big Hits (High Tide & Green Grass)* in 1966.

In December, Virgin put out *Keith Richards & The X-Pensive Winos at the Hollywood Palladium*, a sixty-seven-minute shot of the *Talk is Cheap* tour. After *Flashpoint*, it restores the live album's good name. The guitars grab you by the throat and slap you round the face; there's a salvo of oldies that climaxes in Happy; and some not-to-be-missed interplay between Sarah Dash (one of Patti LaBelle's Blue Belles) and Richards' burnt-to-a-crisp vocals. Incendiary proof that Keith continues to set the pace in the Stones solo-LP stakes, with Jagger and Wood to the rear.

Richards was back at the Rock and Roll Hall of Fame in New York that

January, posthumously inducting the guitar pioneer Leo Fender. Andrew Oldham also happened to be in town, invited along by Allen Klein. For years Andy had waited, on and off, for signs of a thaw in the chill from the Stones – a phone call, backstage passes, a message through friends. There had been some sulphurously bitchy remarks in the late Sixties. But when Keith met his old manager coming through the lobby that night he strode over, held out a hand and welcomed him to the party. Oldham joined Patti, Marlon and Jane Rose at the head table for the ceremonies.

'Shit' was how John Lennon, for one, always characterized such affairs. The spirit of rock 'n roll, he felt, couldn't reside in the Waldorf-Astoria, or in lachrymose speeches from men wearing tuxedos. But Keith made a bold stab at it, working the stage like a seasoned comic and getting off some dry one-liners.

'Leo gave us the weapon,' he concluded. 'Caress it. Don't squeeze it.'

With that he set to rehearsing his new solo album, to be called *Main Offender*. Keith and Steve Jordan sat down in the Richardses' East 4th Street apartment with their guitars, some drums and a case of Stoli, and let inspiration strike. One night the phone in the music room rang three or four times, each of them a wrong number. When Jordan answered it, a male voice muttered the word, 'Eileen?' Where other men might have fumed, Keith started chanting the name and soon set it to a lurching, Stonesy tune. Simple – and stunning, just as rock should be.

In February, Mick Jagger got pulled over at Narita airport, Tokyo, where he'd flown to promote *Freejack*. He was detained there, to much tabloid mirth, as a 'convicted drug felon'. The last time Jagger had been in dope trouble, *Let It Bleed* was climbing the chart, and England were still World Cup soccer champions. Even so, he was subjected to a five-hour grilling. While investigators took Mick step by step over his entire life, justice ministry officials began debating his twenty-two-year-old pot conviction, for which he was fined £200. (They must have missed him when he slipped through to perform sold-out concerts in both 1988 and 1990.) After two days Japan finally declared Mick no threat to public morals, and allowed him to enter. *Freejack* died at the box office.

Keith, meanwhile, moved the Winos to San Rafael, California, and cut *Main Offender*. He had nothing public to say about Jagger's hassles.

Those who met the Glimmer Twins were always struck by how tough Keith was on Mick. He was scathing about *Primitive Cool* and the film projects, for instance. 'But the more you see them,' notes a former friend, 'the more you get why [Richards] withholds the approval Mick seems to need, at times desperately.' That's what the act had now become, a scrap between all the vanity projects and movies and sideshows and the main brand. 'There'll be no tour next year,' Mick, reportedly, again told Keith. 'It's too soon. Jesus! Everybody knows you can have too much of a good thing.'

'Everybody *doesn't* know that,' Keith snapped.

An hour after giving Mick his slap on the wrist, Keith – warm and friendly now – strolled into the Hit Factory in New York. The cops in the precinct house immediately across West 54th Street lined up to cheer him. None of them hassled him any more. By all accounts, Keith was at his most charming during these final weeks of mixing *Main Offender*. The ice wall thawed as soon as he was back with Jordan and the gang. Wags endlessly speculated on whether the Stones would survive once Keith took the Winos out on the road. What he still had in common with Jagger was anyone's guess. While Jerry Hall was once again being humiliated by Mick's fling with Carla Bruni, Keith went home every night to his wife and kids in Connecticut.

'I hope the man comes to his senses,' Richards told *Vanity Fair*. 'He should stop that now, the old black-book bit. Kicking fifty, it's a bit much, a bit manic.'

That same summer, Mick became a grandfather when Jade Jagger had a baby girl, named Assisi.

Bill Wyman, meanwhile, now fifty-five and a tabloid fun-figure, was yet again promising to quit. Keith theorized that he was off his rocker. 'If we did go out on tour without him, I'm sure he'd be very pissed off and that's what I'm counting on. But then, Bill's from a different generation. For him success is going on *The Michael Aspel Show*. I think he's on his third menopause.'

Later in the year, Keith went to London to 'sit down, eyeball to eyeball' with his bass player. Wyman avoided him. 'I did everything but hold him at gunpoint,' Richards muttered, but Bill, tired of flying around the world and playing in football domes, wanted out.

Wyman knew that he wouldn't be leaving empty-handed. Cash continued to rain down into the Stones' offshore companies. Even at his grumpiest Bill had joined Keith and Mick in speaking up for Prince Rupert's shelters and against British tax rates, an uncontroversial subject.* The four original band members had shared a reported $60 million from the *Steel Wheels* tour alone. Keith soon started appearing in the *Sunday Times* Rich List, with a fortune estimated around £120 million. One of the tax accountants on the Stones' payroll remembers 'a ragged-looking character, ash grey, with a face like cat litter, but an absolute charmer. [Keith] kept telling us he didn't know what all the fuss was about. I'm sure he does know what all the fuss is about, but he didn't have boats or mansions. I don't know what he did with the money, but he didn't spend it on himself.'

20 October 1992, *Main Offender*. Keith (who'd talked about being more into the roll than the rock) does just about anything here to keep things moving. His second solo is a chugging party album that ditches big-beat bravado for reggae grooves and garage-band workouts. With its warped soul breaks and horn punches, Hate It When You Leave sounds like a grungy Otis Redding. Words Of Wonder goes in for a Jamaican lope over snapping drums, while Runnin' Too Deep keeps things nice and simple with a husky, cut-and-paste romp.

Eileen is the stand-out track, exuding both punky grit and soulful cool. Although Mick, Charlie and Ron don't actually play on it, this is the best Stones single since Start Me Up.

Holding the whole album together is the sense that Keith and the Winos had fun making it. Where other superstar outings seem motivated less by adventure than by weary careerism, *Main Offender* combines moments of wiggy abstraction with a gift for kick-ass rock 'n roll. (One recurrent moan: there are still none of the great busted-heart country songs from Toronto.) Keith may not make much of a breakthrough this time around – stalling at number ninety-nine in the *Billboard* Hot One Hundred – but *Offender* is as vital as any record he's done.

In Lower Manhattan that week, Richards sat self-consciously behind a long wooden schoolroom desk set in a corner of Tower Records. It was a torrentially wet Tuesday night. Any doubts about the Human Riff's pulling power in 1992 were dispelled when 3,000 fans lined up around the block for autographs. Keith was there several hours, fortified by a tumbler of Stoli

---

* Keith's directorship of Mirage Music was dissolved on 22 September 1992, leaving him with, among others, Nanker-Phelge Music, Rolling Stones Limited and Promopub BV, the company handling his publishing rights.

and flanked by posters of himself wearing a T-shirt that read WHO THE FUCK IS MICK JAGGER?

From there, Keith flew to LA to film the album's promos. For *Talk is Cheap*, these had tended to the old standby post-nuclear rubble setup, with plenty of dust and ashes. Four years on, there was a subtle shift in the 'vision thing'. *Main Offender*'s sleeve photos, coupled with Keith's accessory-heavy new videos, created a phenomenon in which a skull ring became, in and of itself, a cultural icon. People who knew Keith best would say that the 'old devil shtick' gave a highly idealized view of a warm and witty family man. It rang of truth, though. It might not be realistic, but it felt real, and it felt right – if this wasn't what Keith was like, the line went, it's what he *should* be like.

In late October, Richards flew to Paris for a week of European media. He came back to New York, rehearsed the Winos ('Three niggers and a Jew' he called them fondly; 'I got it covered'), played to 40,000 fans in Buenos Aires. Somehow he found time to sit for an interview with Hunter S. Thompson (*Fear and Loathing*), a post-junkie version of a Thatcher–Reagan summit. On 27 November, Keith started a European tour in Copenhagen.

His press profile, which had been strong before recent events, now took off to Jaggeresque heights. Keith was on the cover of twenty-two magazines that winter, everything from *Guitar Player* to *Punch*. Some eighty print hits in all. 'Most artists in our business lose their magic,' Phil Quartararo, the president of Virgin, put it. 'Keith's gotten better. He was the first purist, and he's one of the only remaining purists.'

Keith: 'I love my kids and my wife most of the time. Music I love *all* the time. It's the only constant joy in my life. You're never alone with a guitar. It's the one thing you can count on.'

Now Richards went back on the road, playing four weeks of theatre dates in Germany, France, Spain and Britain. All sold out. As Keith ran on, his grey hair corralled by a thin red headband, his appearance brought roars as loud as the percussive blast of the music. The various TV and film cameras zoomed in, as did tens of millions of continentals.

What Europe saw was a show of unaccustomed simplicity, standing at the farthest remove from the Superdome-sized, flashy pomp rock of *Steel Wheels* days. Playing material mostly from his two solos, Keith threw in some Eddie Cochran covers and a run-out section including Happy and snatches of Brown Sugar. The familiar formulae were made fresh again by the spare arrangements, with an absence of gospel choirs and, for that matter, of sixty-foot-high blowup dolls and flamethrowers. Old chestnuts like Gimme Shelter sounded as strong as ever, all the better in fact for being given the lean treatment rather than the stadium glitz. These were what all gigs should hope to be; Keith laughed a lot between numbers, and nobody needed binoculars.

Richards and the Winos played London on 18 December, his forty-ninth birthday. Jagger came but got hassled by the press, leaving early. Bill Wyman couldn't make it.

Keith spent Christmas in Connecticut, with his family and Anita. On New Year's Eve he played the 2,000-seat New York Academy. Pearl Jam were the warmup. Bert Richards wandered around backstage in a cloth cap, challenging one and all to a game of dominoes. It was another great raveup. Keith reached back into the pop archive, where he found some Elvis and Frankie Paul hits to goose the set. The effect was as invigorating as a cold shower.

While in London, Keith had told the Stones office he wanted to record and tour with the band in 1993. He had a headful of great, stripped-down new songs, he said. Many were in rockabilly key, with some swinging drum and bass parts. It didn't matter, because when Wyman heard of the plan, he reportedly rang the office in a huff.

'A record *and* a bloody tour?' he asked.

'That's right. Both.'

'I'm not going out on the road.'

'Then we'll have to get somebody else.'

'Start looking.'

Bill publicly left the Stones on 6 January, by announcing it live on *London Tonight*. Keith was fuming. Over eighteen years, he hadn't given up his core belief in loyalty to the band.

Bill told Charlie Watts he reckoned he had only twenty years left, and didn't want to waste them playing oldies for screaming kids.

While Wyman pulled the plug, Keith went back on the road. He and the Winos started another American tour on 17 January, in Seattle. In all they played fifteen cities, twenty-two sold-out shows, over five weeks. The whole project tied together the creative strands of Keith's life: music, theatre and vaudeville. Carefully polished jokes filled out the gaps between songs. Keith roamed around as he played, sometimes crouching down, spinning, then shooting sideways like a demented crab. His singing voice was well tuned to the material, if somewhat on the raw side. Even the forty-year-old covers like Cochran's Something Else were made to sound fresh and rootsy again. The purveyor of this embalming fluid was on sparkling form, zinging out the three- and four-note riffs and bringing the house down with Happy. By that point he was leaning over the front of the stage, slapping hands with the first two rows. Richards took an obvious delight in dressing up, putting on a show. His ensemble of ruby-red jacket, black suit pants and chunky jewellery seemed just right for the occasion. Keith acknowledged rock 'n roll's frivolity but played it for real, and those little jigs and lopsided smiles got him over even the weaker material.

'Richards', the *Times* said, 'stepped out on almost every song, from the opening classic rock of Something Else to the bluesy finale. Not stingy with the solos, he played with the guitar slung low and using a pick in his bony fingers. There was an added attraction – the Winos, having the kind of good time that only comes when everybody's in a groove.'

Mick Jagger, meanwhile, put out his third solo album *Wandering Spirit*. Keith told friends that this one, with its old soul covers and Irish sea shanty, wasn't too bad. Leading the Winos around had also given him new insight into what 'Brenda' went through with the Stones. The Glimmer Twins got together at Mick's West 81st brownstone in Manhattan late that February. It was now nearly four years since *Steel Wheels*.

Keith: 'We sat around . . . I said, "I got stuff." He says, "Yeah, I got stuff." I came out with one word – focus. We're looking down the same scope this time, we've got all the other ingredients, what we need to do is *focus*.'

There was only one problem. Wyman's defection had left the band a man light. Keith put out feelers, got Bill on the phone, told him he was making a big mistake. Still no joy: Bill announced he was getting married again, thinking about starting a blues band and maybe writing another tell-all book. There would be no more calls. The Stones had to deal with only their third team change in thirty-one years.

Keith and Mick went back to Barbados, kicked some songs around and auditioned bass players. ('I was ready to kill Bill Wyman,' Keith confirmed. 'How *dare* he?') To help things along, they added a good-luck charm. One night Richards was loping through a tropical rainstorm on his way from his villa to the studio, when he spotted a tiny and half-drowned kitten under a tree. Characteristically, he picked the runt up and brought it inside. 'Meet Voodoo,' he announced. Friends at the session recall vividly how Keith mothered the cat, how, clearing a room in the studio, he gave it its own living space, how he nursed and fed it, then arranged for it to be flown, by Learjet, to the States. A year later, the stray was living happily in Connecticut, a guest of the Richards family. The new Stones album became *Voodoo Lounge*.

In June, the band gathered in New York and auditioned more hopefuls. Keith gave each of the thirty applicants a warm handshake, a drink and the chance to play Brown Sugar. Nobody meshed. Instead, the Stones started rehearsing as a quartet at Ron Wood's pile in County Wicklow. Woody had his own, fully stocked pub on the premises.

On 9 July the Stones went to work in earnest, recording at Windmill Lane down by the Dublin docks. Keith came up with a great guitar-and-fiddle homage to Gus Dupree, called The Worst. There were some rockin' *Exile*-type songs, with a few forays (Blinded By Rainbows) into social comment. And for the romantically inclined there was Mick's crooning on Sparks Will Fly. Lyric: 'Gonna fuck your sweet ass!' The band worked at top speed throughout, Keith living, just as he had twenty years ago in Richmond, in Woody's staff cottage. Later in July, everyone broke for a day to celebrate Mick's fiftieth at a French Revolutionary ball, complete with guillotine.

Autumn 1993. More *Voodoo Lounge* sessions, more cattle-calls. Doug Wimbish of Living Colour reprised the Wayne Perkins role on *Black and Blue*, not quite getting the job. Taking advantage of the delay, Richards played most of the bass parts himself. He was also up for some piano and vocals. The result of all the extra work was a beaming Keith and a production that was wrapped three weeks ahead of schedule. In mid November Jagger formally announced that Bill had left the Stones, should anyone have missed Bill himself having said so on live TV.

Later that month, Darryl Jones walked through the door. He was Miles Davis's old bass player, who'd gone on to work with Sting in his bebop phase before touring with Eric Clapton, Peter Gabriel and Madonna. Charlie, thrilled at the hep connection, soon voted him in. Jones was thirty, black and American. He'd never even seen the Stones play. Their first single came out before he was born. However, Keith and Mick hatched a plan that satisfied everybody: Jones was put on salary for some added *Voodoo Lounge* tracks and the tour.

His wasn't the only new face back in Dublin. At Jagger's invitation the writer-producer Don Was (Walk The Dinosaur) came to the sessions. Keith went ballistic, treating Was to an extended speech on why, nothing personal, he wasn't needed. Was walked out thinking, 'At least I've got something to tell my grandchildren.'

Two days later, Keith phoned him back as though nothing had happened. Was co-produced *Voodoo Lounge*.

Working with the Stones, Was agreed, was very cool. It was also quite strange. So much so that you tended to find yourself in situations where hero-worship met with utter bemusement at the band's mood swings. Jagger announced he wanted a faultlessly hip new album of 'groove songs, African licks and stuff'. Was had more of an *Exile* in mind. Some technical chitchat ensued, Charlie noting that, for once, he wanted his drums turned up louder. This brought a fresh round of debate and muttered asides, until somebody mentioned *Freejack*. Then there was the noise of slammed doors, and soon Was found himself sitting alone with the guitar section.

Keith: 'Don't sweat it, man. Have a drink.'

The Stones finished the *Voodoo Lounge* sessions on 11 December. Richards celebrated by going to another Pete and Dud party, this one held on the top floor of the Cobden Working Men's Club in west London. Kensal Road had seen nothing like it since the coronation. Keith arrived in a handbuilt white 1920s coach, surrounded by three enormous bouncers. People were struck, even so, by how together he was, how unassuming. Once upstairs he sank several pints then moved on to the Stoli, impressing even his well-oiled hosts. Peter Cook suggested adding a splash of tonic, but Keith refused, laughing, 'No thanks, mate. I don't want to rust.'

Waitresses in stilettos, fishnets and mink knickers did the honours.

Seven days later Keith Richards, the man death forgot, turned fifty. There was a party at the Metropolis restaurant in New York, attended by 250 of his best friends including Eric Clapton, Bobby Keys and Phil Spector. Mick Jagger couldn't come. Keith's hair was going, and there was the matter of his leathery tan. Still, for all his grizzled air, he seemed miraculously unchanged by hard living and the passage of time. When meeting strangers Keith tended to an impenetrable scowl, half hidden behind a fog of smoke, a face as stony as any of those on Easter Island.

Although mellowed, he could still erupt with blowpipe suddenness. He'd been known to menace a roadie at gunpoint for no worse crime than helping himself to some of the guv's personal meat pie. Then there was the time he throttled Woody when the latter chose to watch television against Keith's wishes. He was also the most self-aware of rock stars, telling the writer Bryan Appleyard, 'I can be the cat on stage any time I want. I like to stay in touch with him … But I'm a very placid, nice guy – most people will tell you that. It's mainly to placate this other creature that I work.'

14 January 1994. Keith, Mick and Don Was began mixing *Voodoo Lounge* at A&M Studios, formerly Charlie Chaplin's place, in Hollywood. The cheers that had gone up when recording ended turned to groans five weeks later, as all three men bickered about what constituted the world's greatest rock 'n roll band in the mid-Nineties. Mick favoured the slick approach, Don Was pined for *Exile*, Keith – no details man – just wanted authenticity. 'Not like the other times where we're trying to sound like the Stones. We got to get over that. We already *are* the Stones.'

Somehow they patched together an album.

On 21 February, Richards took time out to help legendary country singer George Jones (back on his feet after bankruptcy and rehab) record some duets. Thirty years earlier, Jones had turned Keith on to the high-strung Nashville tuning later refined by Gram Parsons. Impatience would have been the natural reaction of most people kept waiting all day for a take while their own record badly needed them. But Jones would remember only 'a real gent', the rock 'n roller who still longed to be a cowboy.

In pre-tour manoeuvring that spring, Keith's directorship of Rolling Stones Limited was dissolved. After nineteen years Wood was finally cut in on the action, with points instead of a salary. And work began on a new, industrial-sized stage, with 300-foot-long walls of light and a fire-spewing steel arch known as the Cobra. This delightfully wacky concept was part of a travelling company that would operate for thirteen months in twenty-five countries, selling eight million seats. In 1989 Michael Cohl had packaged an all-in deal that guaranteed the Stones around $70 million. He promised them even more this time.

In mid April, Keith put the finishing touches to *Voodoo Lounge*. It was apparently a bloodbath to the last. A Virgin rep reports that 'working with those guys was tough. They all came in with barrels loaded, they all came in to fight. I couldn't believe the way they operated.' Mick griped that a lot of the album got 'lost' while being bounced between Dublin and Hollywood. He and Richards couldn't decide whether Don Was was a genius or not. Then the producer won a Grammy, so they let him get on with it.

Keith went back to Connecticut, slept for a week, and read all six volumes of Gibbon's *Decline and Fall of the Roman Empire*.

On 3 May, the Stones chugged in to New York to announce their new megatour. It was one of the slickest press events since the days of Colonel Parker, if not P.T. Barnum. In the past the band had sparked riots at the airport, snarled up downtown traffic, and, in 1989, brought Grand Central Station to a halt. Twenty years before that, Sam Cutler gave them the world heavyweight rock 'n roll title every night as they hit the stage. This time around, the Stones commandeered the Kennedys' old yacht *Honey Fitz* and bore down on Battery Park like some latter-day British Invasion. When Jagger said to Richards, 'How are we gonna top *this*?', Keith just smiled. It was a hell of an entrance.

Keith had plenty to say to the press, both then and over the summer. Famously quick-witted, he was only modestly equipped in the tact department. He took a typically hard line, for instance, on the Kurt Cobain Test. The prince of grunge and mouthpiece for a generation had committed suicide in early April. Elder-statesman reaction was near unanimous. McCartney, Clapton and Sting all sympathized, and Neil Young wrote a moving tribute. Bowie called 'Kurt's loss one of [the] really crushing blows in my life'.

Keith wasn't impressed. As far as he was concerned, 'the guy had a death wish'.

By contrast, Keith himself nowadays was a wild optimist. His reading of Gibbon, he said, had given him new perspective on the Stones' comparatively small but long-running empire. 'We're out on this limb all on our own,' he told the journalist David Fricke. 'Nobody's kept it together this far ... We have no road maps, no way of knowing how to deal with it. Still, it's the old story – who's gonna get off the bus while you're still feeling good about it?'

In harsher vein:

'Go screw the press and their slagging about the Geritol Tour. You assholes. Wait till you get our age and see how you run. I got news for you, we're still a bunch of tough bastards. String us up and we still won't die.'

*   *   *

Keith spent that summer in, of all places, Toronto. Rehearsals began there, in a converted school gym just five miles from the scene of the crime in 1977, on 16 June. The band chose Canada because it happened to be Michael Cohl's home turf, and also because they had only six-month US work visas.

Keith had no problem being back in town. 'If I held grudges against every place I've been busted, there wouldn't be much left.' He stayed clear of the Harbour Castle hotel.

'Don't bother about copying Wyman,' Richards told Darryl Jones. Jones took that as a vote of confidence, and soon jazzed things up with some new bass licks. Keith then put the Stones through their paces for six weeks, nine hours a night. Nobody buffed up a band quite like he did. Prowling around in a voodoo top hat, his sheer physical presence was massive: his shadow fell over you before he even entered the room. The routine rarely varied. In a corner of the gym, a roadie would sort through a stack of CDs and, on Keith's command, cue up a track – Rocks Off, say, from *Exile*. As the classic basement riff boomed over the p.a., Keith stood there, guitar in hand. He sank deeper and deeper into himself as he listened, frowning once or twice, whooping at a high spot. Soon he was playing along, tracing the original recording. Charlie picked up the beat and Mick, reading from a lyric book, crooned the verse about his orgasmic dancer friend. Within a minute or two, the old Stones were letting it rip like the young ones. They had the full showband sound, too, with Chuck Leavell, Bobby Keys, two singers and a horn section. Matt Clifford wasn't invited back.

Elsewhere, in a Toronto aircraft hangar, Mark Fisher and his crew were at work on the latest $3 million stage. This one said something about the twenty-first century, 'with the future as clean and cool and very upbeat'. As well as the Cobra there were 1,200 lights, a 90-ton sound system and more giant rubber dolls. The set travelled around in fifty trucks, the band in a customized 727 with four staterooms.

As a gesture to the whole spectacle, Keith agreed to dye his hair.

Out that July, *Voodoo Lounge*. What's a band to do when one of its songs is used in a Snickers commercial? Get down and dirty, from all indications. The Stones' twentieth studio album finally earns them a Parental Advisory sticker for some choice lyrics about fur, juice and 'alcoholic cunts', as well as a rubbery sex-toy logo and generally hideous artwork. The music is surprisingly accomplished. At first *Lounge*'s loose, grungy structure makes it sound as if it was knocked up overnight, but after repeated listens, songs such as New Faces and I Go Wild roll over and reveal their charms. Keith croaks a George Jones-like blues, mixes melody and harmonies with some wonderfully sozzled riffs and, in all, retains his crush on the 1950s.

The album opens with Love Is Strong, a good rockin' confection of booming drums, harp breaks and strategic guitar bursts. Keith's latest helping of country comfort is an amiably sloppy dirge, titled The Worst, that flies squarely in the face of his Godfather of Punk persona; with its soul-searching lyrics and mellow, folky riff, it's the antithesis of feral Seventies cock rock. Next up, some ballads by Jagger. Most are bereft of pain, warmth or vitality, though New Faces is notable both for its harpsichord and Mick's use of the word 'indolent' in a Stones song. The cha-cha Sweethearts Together signals one of Jagger–Richards' bouts of personal and creative harmony. Rainbows, by contrast, presumes on a liking for *Wandering Spirit*. Keith's Thru And Thru is a slow-burn blues that wobbles about, barely scaling the ladder to songhood, but eventually turns out highly musical, poetic and sad.

Elsewhere, most of the chord progressions are familiar – not derivative but pleasantly expected, even archetypal, most obviously on You Got Me Rocking. Their power comes from their inevitability. The quiet beauty of Keith's Nashville fare, like The Worst, breathes with strange reserve.

The Stones spent the early summer plugging *Lounge* on anything with a tube. VH1 ran an entire week of videos. Pictures of Keith in his voodoo top hat, and Mick in devil's horns, loomed out from billboards and newsstands. Two of *Lounge*'s singles duly grazed the chart, then cratered. The album went to number one in Britain, number three in America, selling five million, figures that would have sent modern pop gods into ecstasies. Keith was stoked by the record, and especially generous about Jagger's harp playing. 'That was one of our original instruments,' he told *Rolling Stone*. 'And his phrasing is so uncanny. If that can roll over onto the vocals . . .

'After all,' Keith rasped, 'it's just pushing air out of your mouth.'

Late July: the Stones started runthroughs amid *Antiques Roadshow* mockery and sneers about milking the teats of nostalgia. Over the next year they would play 125 shows, grossing half a billion dollars, thus making the *Wheels* tour look like a whelk stall. Opening night, instantly sold out, was 1 August in Washington D.C.

By now backstage at a Stones concert had come to resemble the royal palace of a small country. There are potted palms, Persian rugs, a pool table, wives, children, manservants, strolling musicians and an audience chamber for guests. Keith spends much of the afternoon here, with a sound check before each show. Then it's back to the family pen, where Patti reads her Bible and Bert chortles over the dominoes. Technical aides come and go, delivering set lists and discussing acoustics. Nowadays Keith's interested not in scoring dope but in consulting with the band's video director about camera angles. An hour before the gig there's a meet and greet with Budweiser reps and a few lucky VIPs – a Tom Cruise, say, or Bob Dylan. It's all over in sixty seconds. Then a sacred half-hour when Keith and Woody shut themselves away in the tuning room. Eventually they're ready. Three of the Stones come out draped in foppish floor-length hunting coats, tight pants and boots, and stride off confidently towards the stage. Charlie (dressed for church) sits down at his kit. The crowd has no idea that the show is about to start: they're all too busy screaming at the flame-belching Cobra. The lights dim and there's an almighty roar.

'*I'm gonna tell ya,*' Mick crows, '*how it's gonna be.*'

It's the old, potent spell, big magic. That one phrase sets the night up. Omigod! They're *right there*! Jagger struts out, and does a wiggle or two. The band punch up the grainy chords of Not Fade Away. Intercut with this is a bank of flashing lights, screens and various explosions. Everything is amped up to the pain threshold. The Rolling Stones are back to work.

After the opening stomp Keith comes on full tilt with Shattered and Rocks Off. The first half hour is irresistible, Mick yelling optimistically '*Yeahh!*' and '*It's a gas!*' before things slump in mid-set. Live, there are various hoops the Stones feel obliged to jump through, presumably in the name of sales and marketing. Jagger screams, he spins, he does the mashed potato – but Sparks Will Fly remains stubbornly earthbound. Rows of light bulbs ripple behind him like the facade on a Vegas casino. The song ends to polite applause. 'Everything OK?' asks Mick, still clinging to vestiges of his optimism. A low groan goes up as, yet again, he then announces 'one off the new album'. Some of the *Voodoo Lounge* ballads are tolerated rather than seized on. There's another kleenex moment in Angie. Richards, Jagger and Wood manage a bit of Status Quo-like shtick, riffing in unison, during I Go Wild. The Stones then kick in with a bazooka-rock finale. Honky Tonk Women goes down a storm. After the last verse, Keith sidles up behind Chuck Leavell and, gently nudging him to keep playing at the low end of the keyboard, reaches in to pick out a wickedly funky right-handed solo. Sympathy erupts against a backdrop of giant dolls, among them Elvis and the Thug goddess Kali. There are fast-changes, lashings of smoke and mirrors, and the great call-and-response raveup in Brown Sugar. The night ends in a choric Jack Flash.

Friends remarked how Richards was only truly himself during those two hours. It was incredible to see how they fed him, it was like blood, he came alive.

Keith: 'I look around and say, "There's Mick, there's Charlie, and here's me, and we're the Stones, and God knows [how] that happened." It's just you and your mates from way back. And then you start playing, and it feels the same as it did in the beginning. You might feel like dogshit two minutes before a show, but the minute you hit the crowd, you feel great. It's a cure for everything.'

As the tour progressed, Keith dressed for the part as Captain Blood's debauched son, with red bandana, red jacket with sash, boots filed to red rapier points, and red eyes. His body language relied on a small but restless vocabulary: the spider crouch, the scuttle. Most nights, he came down into the crowd during Jack Flash to slap some palms. That was the image you went home with. A hip fifty-year-old, radiant all over, playing the greatest riff of the past half century one-handed.

The Stones were in Boston, on 6 September, when they heard that their old piano player Nicky Hopkins (*Beggars Banquet, Exile*) had died aged fifty. Six weeks later Jimmy Miller, their producer of the same period, succumbed to liver failure. He was fifty-two.

On 8 October, Marlon Richards married supermodel Lucy de la Falaise in Italy. Keith was en route to a date in New Orleans, so was unable to attend.

Seven days later, for the first time, the Stones played Las Vegas. On 25 November their Miami show was broadcast nationally on pay-per-view TV. Later that week they announced European gigs for 1995. On 4 December Richards met up with his blind fan Rita Bedard, backstage in Toronto. Everything ended a fortnight later in Vancouver, where the crowd sang Happy Birthday to Keith.

Some three million fans had bought tickets for the North American tour, which grossed more than it costs to make a Steven Spielberg film. Each of the Stones, already Croesus rich, took home around $18 million. The year-long marketing blitz was relentless, and there was some chaffing at the line of 'top accessories' – everything from silk ties to golf balls. Stand-up comedians had a field day at the band's, and Keith's expense. And yet most Americans loved the shameless codgers who weren't, in the end, that old. They just knew their way around.

The Stones also defied imitation. Though universal in terms of the music, the band's brain trust was unique. No one but Charlie could possibly look as bored as he did while hustling out the beat; no one but Woody would sink quite as many pints of Guinness both before and during a gig; no one but Mick could do such a creditable strip-tease at his age. And, at the calm centre, no one but Keith would spend nearly all his waking hours with these three.

On 14 January 1995 riots broke out around the Rodriguez stadium in Mexico City. Some 15,000 ticketless fans wanted to get inside and watch the Stones. It was the same in Brazil, Argentina, Chile and South Africa. All sell-outs. On stage, Jagger was still the main visual event. Off it, Keith's agenda prevailed. Once in Tokyo, he had the band check into Toshiba/EMI, where they gave classics like Wild Horses and *Exile*'s Shine A Light the *Unplugged* treatment. Added to some club gigs recorded in Europe, the result would be the best live Stones album since *Ya-Ya's*. Keith had the last say on everything, from songs and studios to production. He may have coolly pulled off the largest rock 'n roll tour in history, which most people saw by aiming binoculars at a Jumbotron screen. But he also dug the intimate, 'record the room' vibe of a band, a stage and two or three hundred fans. 'Right at the start, I realized that if we didn't watch out, we'd end up with *Voodoo Lounge Live at the Stadium*,' he said. 'I wanted something more relaxed, more *fluid*.'

In April, the Stones played Australia and New Zealand. On May Day, a planned gig in Beijing was called off because of visa hassles.

Keith: 'I got a long letter from the Chinese government saying why I can't come. Number one on the list is "Cultural Pollution" and about number thirty is "Will cause traffic jams". And in between is a whole load of other crap.'

Four weeks later the Stones, billed as the Toe-tappers & Wheel Shunters band, recorded some more acoustic gigs in Amsterdam's Paradiso club. The full *Voodoo Lounge* express got under way again in Stockholm. Volkswagen put up a reported $10 million to sponsor the summer's thirty-nine sold-out gigs. The historic car firm took the opportunity to launch the 'Fabulous VW Golf Rolling Stones-Mobile', a limited-edition saloon with the tongue logo stitched into the seat fabric. It was a rather dire addition to an otherwise stunning tour.

By and large the Stones stuck to the well-rehearsed set, but with a few novelties. Back from the archive: Connection, I'm Free, Let It Bleed. An acoustic medley dotted the wastes of the stadium din. In a self-referential nod, they started doing Dylan's Like A Rolling Stone. There was a gig in Sheffield – the band's first on home turf in five years – then three at Wembley. Richards threw a small backstage party there an hour before curtain-up. Everyone from Bert to George Harrison to Jimmy Phelge (an Edith Grove flatmate in '62) stood in a lavishly furnished tent and waited for Keith to change out of his street clothes into his nearly identical stage togs. They dimmed the lights to create atmosphere, and Jane Rose offered up some aged brandy. Muddy Waters records played out of the sound system. When Keith arrived he was in high spirits. 'This is like the *Sixties*,' he beamed, throwing an arm around the Hollies' Allan Clarke. (Clarke calls him the 'nicest guy in showbusiness'.) Someone good-naturedly mentioned Marianne Faithfull's new book, in which she described her night with Keith as 'the best of my life'. He was justifiably proud at the tribute. 'I'm a *lover*,' Keith announced, for once throwing modesty to the winds. 'I've been trying to tell people for years.'

The final rites of *Voodoo Lounge* came at the end of August 1995. Keith declared himself 'tired but chuffed', insisting that all hatchets were buried. 'The Stones have never been better. I've never seen Charlie so happy on the road; he's brought his old lady with him more, and I think he's enjoying playing with Darryl. And Mick's extremely charming these days, even to me. We're getting along great.'

Keith spent early September with Patti and the girls at Redlands. He did a quick video shoot for Like A Rolling Stone, then went on holiday with Marlon and his new wife to Rome. Sometime that week, Keith learnt that he would become a grandfather in the spring.

'I'm joinin' the crowd,' he cackled. 'Designing my little grandpa suit. I'll get a bag of candy in the pocket and grow a beard or something.'

At just that moment the German weekly *Der Spiegel* rashly claimed that the Stones had been in the habit of miming certain *Lounge* shows to backing tapes. This was the signal for one of those sudden mood swings Keith's friends knew and feared. He went berserk. *Fucking jam-rags. Shits. Hacks.* 'Call me whatever you want – junkie, crook, culture-pollutant, but don't tell me I don't play live.

'First, I want an apology from them, and then, no matter how much we get, it'll be sent to the kids of Bosnia. I don't even want to see their fuckin' money.'

Der Spiegel would soon admit they had made a ghastly mistake.

The tour album *Stripped* followed in November. Keith's vision of the Stones live wasn't exactly unplugged; more an amplified acoustic affair with moments of real musical electricity. The band shone with an anthemic, singalong Like A Rolling Stone, the nostalgic twang of Wild Horses and the fluid honky-tonk of Let It Bleed. Keith's singing on Slipping Away was as raw as ever, but tempered by jaunty cadences, some melodic gasps and groans and deft guitar fills. At times like these, he somehow reminded you of the Clint Eastwood character in *Unforgiven*, a dusty mixture of craft and guts. Toss in some bonus CD-ROM tracks and Anton Corbijn photography, and you had the best Stones concert album in twenty-five years.

Keith and Mick spent weeks promoting *Stripped* that Christmas. In a tribute to the staying power of classic rock, it went gold at the same time as the latest Elvis release and the Beatles' *Anthology*.

Keith went back to Jamaica and started recording some instrumental, scorched blues tunes and reggae chants. The studio was his living room. Instead of the usual non-view he worked to a foreground of tropical plants and vines. Just beyond them a raw green mountain cut across the sky, its slope plunging straight from the heights down into the valley where the ocean began. Keith would spend the next two years developing the album, eventually called *Wingless Angels*, with some Rasta friends. He took the master tape back to Connecticut at Christmas, and it followed him from there to New York, Barbados and Hollywood. In 1997 he released it on his own label, Mindless Records.

Meanwhile, Microsoft paid $5 million to use Start Me Up in their advertising campaign. Keith turned down an offer to write music for the new Bond film.

10

Performance

EVERYTHING AT KEITH'S HOUSE IN CONNECTICUT HAD A BRIGHT SHINE BUT HIS WELL-SCUFFED BOOTS. The lucky guest was greeted by two young girls with happy faces who turned him over to a stunning woman near forty with straight blonde hair and a smoky laugh, who led him at length to Keith's father, a florid eighty-year-old who won everyone's heart with his Pickwickian jowls and bone-crushing handshake. Everything around gleamed with a polished intensity. The watered silk curtains gave on to green fields; a sunny outlook, with plenty of bright sea sky. Even in winter, Keith could work well into evening without turning the light on.

He spent much of 1996 here, producing *Wingless Angels* (for which he did the artwork), walking, reading a lot. Keith was a popular figure in Weston, if not as visible as his wife and children. Patti had become more religious as she got older, attending a weekly Bible study group. She favoured a healthy diet, early nights, affirming the sanctity of marriage. Swearing around the house was frowned on. Later that year, she voted for Bob Dole for President.

Keith became a grandfather in May, with the arrival of Ella Rose Richards. In July, he, Patti and Marlon took the two-month-old to see Charlie Watts' jazz band at the Supper Club in Manhattan. Everyone said how well Keith looked. He was wearing a bright red waistcoat over a ruffled shirt and black pants, with fuzzy blue ankle boots and white socks. His grey and brown hair stood in short, stiff points, like a cornfield after a frost, and his cigarette lolled into the corner of his mouth as he spoke. He signed scores of autographs.

In October, the Stones and Allen Klein released *Rock 'n' Roll Circus* twenty-eight years after the event. On the 15th, there was a gala première in London. None of the band attended.

A week later, *Der Spiegel* dropped its claim that anyone connected with the Stones had ever mimed on stage. Jagger was seeing the actress Uma Thurman in LA and getting HEART OF STONE headlines back home, where Jerry Hall consulted a lawyer. The Charlie Watts Quintet finished a tour of Japan. Woody was resting between projects. Keith took the opportunity to call an early November band meeting in New York.

Right away, tension. Mick advised everyone to take a year off, they'd earned it. The Virgin reps balked, talking instead about market share and reworking the proven album–tour–video formula. For once, Keith and the suits were as one. He had no formal plans for the Stones, but he knew a good thing when he saw it. 'Nobody should get off this bus while it's still going,' he told the room. 'It's dangerous. You hurt yourself that way.'

In late November, the Stones started working in a Greenwich Village rehearsal studio. Keith had the riffs for Low Down and Too Tight, while Mick wrote Already Over Me and Always Suffering. Invention began after dark, around the time others turned in. At fifty-two, Keith was still on the permanent late shift, going ten or twelve hours without a break. At dawn he'd drive home to Connecticut. During the day, Don Was sat at the desk and interpreted the work of the night before. By Christmas there was an album taking shape, and the band's publicist announced they would tour again in 1997.

Early February. Richards and Jagger were back in Barbados, at the start of the old cycle. Mick was writing more and more songs about his love life. He wanted a sharp, digital sound for the new record and hired hipsters like Danny Saber and the Dust Bros to co-produce. Along with Don Was and the engineers, that added up to a dozen experts on what made a Stones album. No wonder, then, Keith lost his rag. For him, recording wasn't a matter of tape loops and drum machines. It was 'four or five guys letting rip', preferably in the same room.

In March the Stones moved to Hollywood's Ocean Way studio, home of sunny Sixties classics like Don't Worry Baby and California Dreamin', among many others. All the good vibes went once Keith and Mick hit town, the latter fresh from dinner with Tony Blair. Jagger was soon driving down Sunset to deliver the rough tapes of Anybody Seen My Baby? and Saint Of

Me to the Dusts, whom he apparently thought 'very today guys'. Keith said that to the extent he considered them at all, it was as techno-geeks. To him they were self-styled knob-twiddlers who, ideally, should never have been let near the Stones. 'You say Dust Brothers,' he growled, 'I say ashes to ashes.' He didn't play on Saint Of Me, a song two other composers later claimed as their own.

One night Keith met Kenny 'Babyface' Edmunds on his way into the studio. Jagger had invited the thirty-seven-year-old prodigy behind Paula Abdul and Toni Braxton to lend yet another ear to the proceedings. 'You cut with Mick,' Keith told him, 'your face is gonna look like *mine*. You may be Babyface now, but you're gonna be *Fuckface* after you're done with that guy.'

Keith did sprinkle around some words of praise that spring. He loved playing on sessions with B.B. King and Elvis' old guitarist Scotty Moore. And he enjoyed the steady income flow from Klein's office in New York; as well as the back catalogue and the $4 million Snickers deal, he now made a fortune without actually going to the hassle of doing anything. The Verve's comeback single that year, Bitter Sweet Symphony, was a huge hit, but they paid dearly for using a small sample of The Last Time from Andrew Oldham's 1966 masterpiece, *Today's Pop Symphony*. Klein went to work. The song was legally removed from the Verve and credited to Jagger–Richards–Oldham.

By late June, Keith and Mick had taken to recording their contributions in a different room, and often a different town to one another. They were artistic rivals, each with his own crew of Stones irregulars: Jagger worked in one studio with Danny Saber and Doug Wimbish, Keith in another with Blondie Chaplin (ex-Beach Boys) and Waddy Wachtel from the Winos. It was the *Dirty Work* sessions all over again. Keith polished off the last two tracks without Jagger's help. One of them, titled Thief In The Night, allegedly referred to problems at home with Patti. At the last minute Richards hired Jeff Sarli (Bluesiana, Marshall Crenshaw) to add the rockabilly-bass stomp as done by Bill Plummer on *Exile*. By then Jagger was back in London with Jerry Hall, who was pregnant. After discussing it on the phone he and Keith changed the album's title from *Blessed Poison* to *Bridges to Babylon*, with, aptly, a smoking tower of Babel in the artwork. Don Was called an end to the whole thing late on 30 June. Next morning, Keith flew back to England to watch Wimbledon and launch Mindless Records.

A fortnight later Richards was listening to the *Babylon* tapes at Redlands when, in a Verve moment, his daughter Angela told him there was 'something funny' about one of the tracks. Jagger had quite unconsciously used the tune of k.d. lang's Constant Craving for Anybody Seen My Baby? Keith got on the phone to Mick right away. There were some long faces at Virgin that week, with certain parties frantic about a lawsuit. When k.d. herself heard of it, she couldn't have been nicer. In a solution that satisfied everybody, the Stones gave her and her partner a writing credit and royalties. The money came out of Mick's share.

18 August 1997. The Stones rolled into Manhattan on a Monday morning, tying up the rush-hour Brooklyn Bridge by cruising across it in a red '55 Cadillac. It was another inspired bit of street-drama. Keith and Mick jumped out of the car, told the waiting press about the album and a tour. There were a few snide questions about their age, and someone asked Keith whether it wasn't too soon after *Lounge* to be hitting the road. Keith pursed his lips, promising to be 'real candid' in his answer, which turned out to be no. At that the band and entourage went back to Toronto for five weeks' rehearsals. Any doubts about the terms of trade being in their favour were allayed on 27 August, when a million fans tried to buy tickets for the opening gigs in Chicago.

Ironically, probably the one person who wasn't overjoyed about it all was Keith himself. He seemed in a somewhat tetchy mood that autumn. There were muttered reports about his drug use, and of issues with the church-going Patti. Then her elder sister died, and Keith flew back to New York to carry the coffin. It was about then that he throttled Woody, when the latter wandered off from rehearsal one night to watch a boxing match on television. 'I made a mistake,' Keith told *Rolling Stone*. 'I was pissed off at being there, and I was left alone.'

When not drilling the band, Keith sat up all hours in his Toronto apartment, dubbed Doom Villa, listening to gloomy Portuguese music and toasting a framed photo of Gus Dupree. The handlers came to him one day and asked if he'd mind dyeing his hair black again. Keith told them to fuck off.

Entertainment Weekly then talked to Keith about Princess Diana, which gave him an opportunity to share some thoughts on Elton John. Elton's great gift, he said, was writing 'songs for dead blondes ... I'd find it difficult to ride on the back of something like that myself, but Reg is showbiz.'

'He's so pathetic, poor thing,' Elton retorted. 'It's like a monkey with arthritis, trying to go onstage and look young. I think if the Stones had thrown Keith Richards out of the band years ago they would have made better records. He's held them back.' Keith actually had no interest in looking young, but the monkey tag stuck. Proving he could take a joke, he named his backstage suite the Baboon Cage.

When the tour got under way, Keith noted that he particularly enjoyed doing All About You, with its lines about bitches and getting laid. He dedicated the song to Elton.

Late September, *Babylon*: the Stones juggernaut rolls on, embracing explosive rock 'n roll, hard-edged funk, slow-boiling reggae, maudlin pop and even a torchy spiritual. The bullet-train beat of Flip The Switch gives way to the looping riff of Low Down and the gonna-kill-my-old lady *noir* (see Hey Joe) of Mick's Gunface. Elsewhere, *Babylon* cuts the testosterone level: a jazzy, mariachi flavour permeates You Don't Have To Mean It; Saint Of Me's the product of a rare face-to-face collaboration, followed by a tiff, and brings Billy Preston in from the cold after twenty years. Always Suffering likewise doffs a stetson to Gram Parsons. In all, *Babylon* is a rich, mercurial work full of soul, sung with campfire sincerity. And the best's yet to come.

The album winds up with three of Keith's: Thief follows Too Tight in a hopscotch between floppy blues-rock and speed-addled punk. It's a carefully balanced finale, run out by How Can I Stop. This is Keith in sentimental-gangster vein. The stark riff and lyric make it a rare unguarded moment on a slick record, sung in that familiar raspy burr. Like All About You, it's catchy but disquieting, and enough to make the entire set worthwhile. Despite or because of all the aggro, the fires burn hotter than ever.

Bridges to Babylon was the best Stones album since *Exile*. It sold some six million copies during the two years the band were on tour.

As obsessive, lifelong troupers go, few could hold a candle to Keith at fifty-three. He seemed to settle down, then grow positively happy as the road approached. By late September, even Jagger and he were on the same wavelength, if not quite as harmonious as a Seventies Coke commercial. 'Mick's my mate,' Keith said. 'There's no chance of divorce; we gotta take care of the baby.'

Several interviewers asked him if the Stones weren't getting a tad past it. He didn't think so. Keith loped around with his Stoli and ratchet knife, assuring everyone that the band and he had never been fitter. 'I still do what I do,' he told *Rolling Stone*. 'I'd hate to have to go round thinking about [derisively] health and shit. There's only one really fatal disease, I've concluded. That's hypochondria.'

Keith put out his Rasta album, *Wingless Angels*. It was defiantly ethnic. Basically a collage of drums and traditional Jamaican hymns, it showed strong *Joujouka*-type possibilities. The effect was like eavesdropping on some exotic tribal rite. When a soulful guitar and bass wove in, they created a pan-cultural disco Keith called 'marrow music'. The overall result, he said, wasn't just cool; it was good for you. It was also a vehicle for Keith's little-known organizational skills. *Angels* featured reed and horn players, assorted percussionists, numerous guest musicians and the singer Justin Hines, all of whom he co-ordinated. The project suggested that if Keith so chose, there might be a stage for him somewhere other than an American football dome.

Meanwhile, several million fans were lining up at box offices to see the Stones. The good seats were $80 and, later in the tour, $300. For skinflints, there were a few 'restricted view' bargains at fifty bucks.

The Stones united America like nothing else. Along the dark miles of desert highway, the reassuring points of light were huge *Babylon* billboards and tour ads. There was wall-to-wall press coverage. TV and radio became a giant band playing one tune. Curiously, this whole blitz flew in the face of the fresh-air-and-fruit mania seizing much of the country. The more people were nannied, it seemed, the more exciting Keith and co. became. By now America was a land where you weren't allowed to smoke a cigarette in a rock concert, unless you were the ones actually giving it.

23 September, Chicago. The Babylon tour got off to an explosive start. Fans screamed as the Stones began Satisfaction, hitting its riff simultaneously with a zap of quasar-bright light on the Jumbotron. Keith loped up in shades and a ratty tiger-fur coat, planting himself stage right. Once again he was the calm eye of the storm. Elsewhere, cartoon characters raced by on urgent missions. Jagger waved as he sped past in tight black breeches and a white opera scarf. Woody scampered about on high heels, nose aquiver, cranking at his guitar. Darryl Jones chicken-strutted across the boards before coming to a skidding halt in front of the trumpet player, who waved his horn around like a fly-swatter. The choral section bopped

from foot to foot. About the only composed figures were Keith and Charlie, who both sounded better than ever.

The show itself was Variety, with plenty of quick changes. Jagger owed a lot to the set designer and the props department. And they in turn owed everything to a dazzling crew that included Warhol, Dali, U2's Pop Mart, *Arabian Nights*, Cecil B. de Mille and, chiefly, Fritz Todt. The stage was a hi-tech marvel that resembled something out of a biblical epic shot in Las Vegas. Pineapple-shaped clusters of speakers sat atop giant columns. Busty inflatable nudes crouched, in chains, next to the world's biggest video screen. Halfway through the gig, a bridge rose out of the main stage and, swelling like a fireman's ladder, arched onto a small dais in mid-dome, which itself rose up to meet it. The Stones trotted down for a quick blast of R&B classics like Little Queenie. Then it was back for the Big Three, Honky Tonk, Start Me Up and Jack Flash, echoing out from between the gold Roman pillars. (You somehow remembered that the band had spent weeks rehearsing in a Masonic temple.) More eruptions, confetti, fireworks. The applause went on so long that the Stones came back and, seemingly as an afterthought, did Brown Sugar.

After Chicago the whole spectacle settled into a groove. Jagger's ad-libbed remarks were smoothly done, as was the moment in Honky Tonk when Keith casually boogied up to play a piano solo. Since 1989 the Stones had become known as a sure bet, and now the tour inquests also ran on familiar lines. They followed down one of two tracks. On one hand, the tabloids and most reviewers touted the shows' scale and enterprise, noting how the runways of certain far-flung airports – like Miami – couldn't handle the band's fully laden 747. The other view was taken by those who measured the Stones against a *Stripped*. To them, the much-hyped props were the product of narcissism and vanity, the playthings of a rich kid transported into middle age. At worst the combination of a thirteen-piece band, giant sparklers and blow-up dolls was thought risibly naff, like *Spinal Tap* had never happened.

Afterwards, everyone would agree on one thing. It's the best sounding rock 'n roll show yet.

Amid all the commotion, Keith stands stock still back by the horns, doing his 'na-na-na' vocals with a dull, faintly peeved expression while nailing the riff. Visually, he and Jagger are a mesmerizingly odd couple. While Mick pogos around, careening into Gimme Shelter and Miss You,

Keith's apparent boredom intensifies. During Under My Thumb, Jagger's a dervish of crotch-thrusting action, performing what looks like a fertility rite dance – to Richards' stony indifference. He's a statue during Saint Of Me. But when the tempo shifts to ballad pace Keith suddenly blossoms, taking the spotlight, literally, to gravel through All About You. After some more in this vein he actually cracks a grin, bowing down and giving a little tap to his head, heart and crotch. The energy centres. He's even better on the satellite stage, doing much the stuff he and the band used to strut around thirty-five years ago. (Nowadays the mums fling bras and knickers when the Stones play the blues.) As for the finale, hot as it is, nothing competes with Keith's aura. In Jack Flash he even dances a bit, tugging up his pant legs to reveal his blue suede shoes and happy feet.

As winter approached, the Stones migrated south and west. Keith was steeling himself for the outdoor gigs with Stoli and cranberry juice. Sheryl Crow was the warmup, sometimes joining the band for a duet or two onstage. Telecomms giant Sprint had replaced Budweiser, and was pumping millions into the tour. Every night an emissary knocked on the tuning-room door to ask Richards and Wood if they minded coming out to greet the sponsor.

'Fuck off,' said Keith. 'Can I do it by phone?'

In mid-October the Stones doubled back for two shows at Veterans Stadium, Philadelphia, grossing $7 million. Mick came down with flu. He and Keith, enjoying yet another major renaissance, landed on the cover of *Rolling Stone*. In late November the band played Vegas, packing 'em in for a glittering night at the MGM Grand, where much of the audience bussed in from an Avon convention across town.

As for the gibes: 'I can only put it down to jealousy,' Keith said. 'They can't understand why I can do what I do "at my age". What is it with these guys? Because they can't do it? Just because chicks throw their panties at me and I'm fifty-four? Well, stuff you.'

In off-duty hours, Keith was defiantly fashion-backward, a throwback to the age of Aquarius. Women were 'chicks' or the 'old lady'. He sported serious chunky jewellery. Keith's choice of music tended to Otis Redding and various soul stars of the 1960s. For relaxation he was reading the Beats, *Erotica Universalis* and a book called *Hashish* – 'excellent; a whole education in chemistry and folklore'.

18 December, New York. If you were Keith, you regularly got to hear

40 or 50,000 people wishing you Happy Birthday. This time around, some local gigs had been rearranged and he spent the day, instead, with Patti, Bert and the girls in his Manhattan duplex. The first leg of the tour wound up with a hot show in St Louis. While preening hairdresser rock continued its US comeback, Keith's gruff minimalism, as seen in Bruce Gowers' concert film, was an invigorating breath of stale air. Age hadn't slowed him. On Sympathy, he very nearly hit the heights of the *Ya-Ya's* version. The chorus of Jack Flash met with a sea of shaken fists. Richards rounded off proceedings dressed in a purple shirt, cut to the waist, dragging on a cigarette while cuffing the riff to Brown Sugar. When Woody seemingly forgot his part, Keith stepped up to play that too.

The first thirty-three *Babylon* shows would gross around $89 million, with $200 million more to come. In January '98 the Stones upped the price of a good seat to $300. On 15 February they played the Hard Rock casino in Vegas, where tickets were $500. 'It's only money,' Jagger observed. 'I'm sure the people who go and pay $500 don't worry about it. Any more than I would.'

That winter, Keith and Mick licensed Paint It, Black for use in some Steinlager commercials, reportedly in exchange for free beer. When Pepsi-Cola came calling, they weren't as flexible. After Prince Rupert concluded the deal, the band flew to Hawaii, where they played at a beach resort for 3,000 lucky bottlers in celebration of the company's hundredth anniversary. Pepsi also bought the rights to Brown Sugar (original working title: Black Pussy) to sell their product. They paid $3 million for the show and $1 million for the song.

Babylon went back on the road for more pricey, instantly sold-out concerts that spring. Keith was travelling with Bert, Patti and his dog Doobie. He told journalists, 'There's an addictiveness that comes into play. The creak of the boards ... It's what I do.' Then that wheezy Keef laugh. 'If nobody turns up, I'll sit on top of the stairs, where I started, and play to myself.'

Not long after that, things began to go wrong. The tour suffered a spate of postponements and breakdowns due to a bewildering variety of problems. There were blizzards and floods, broken ribs for Keith, laryngitis for Jagger, and hassles with the Inland Revenue. A yacht with Charlie and Woody aboard enigmatically caught fire on a day off in Brazil. Mick settled into a momentary lull of domestic contentment with Jerry, who gave birth to their fourth child, until a Rio thong model announced that she, too, was carrying his baby.

The American *Babylon* eventually wound up where it began, in Chicago. Twenty-five thousand tickets sold out in forty minutes. President Clinton noted that there were only two acts around whose mere announced arrival guaranteed pandemonium on the streets: the Pope, and Richards–Jagger.

In April, the Stones played South America. Five nights in Brazil scored them another $15 million, coincidentally the same amount Mick reportedly settled on Jerry after Luciana Morad, twenty-one, had his son. Keith then went back to Redlands, where he opened a letter appealing for funds to save the village memorial hall. The council wondered whether local residents might be willing to donate £30. No problem, said Keith, and wrote out a cheque for £30,000. One Saturday night a week or two later he fell off a ladder in his Connecticut library, handing a gift to stand-up comedians (Keith Richards? A *book*?) and derailing some European gigs. As a result, the seven-month tour announced in August 1997 would run three times as long.

Thirty-five more shows that wet summer, including a great night in Paris. The drummer Carlo Little, last seen thirty-six years earlier, went over on Eurostar to watch the gig. The way Alexis Korner told it, Carlo – who taught Keith Moon everything he knew – could have easily been in the Stones instead of Charlie. The band heard he was in town, and from then on

> It was like a dream ... First of all I'm travelling in to the gig with the band's families. Someone gives me a pass. Next thing I'm under the stage, chatting to Johnny Depp, at a private bar larger than most pubs. Keith comes out of his tuning room, lurches up against Depp, throws his arm around me and says, 'Wotcher, mate. Want a drink?' He hands us a pint of wine. Smashing bloke, very down to earth. The rest of the Stones sort of grunted.

It was Jagger's birthday. They flew in a blues band from Chicago to entertain two or three hundred guests, including Carlo, at the post-gig party. Keith was still going strong at dawn.

By August the Stones were moving through eastern Europe like a hip army. On the 11th they played Moscow, where the audience once again chanted *Icantgetno! Icantgetno!* for Satisfaction, and Keith told them, 'Great to be here. Great to be *any*where.' The good vibes didn't, however, extend to London. Two Wembley shows got blown off by tax problems. Mick claimed that, under new laws, it would have cost the band £12 million merely to set foot there before April '99.

'A downer,' Keith agreed.

Meanwhile, Jagger and Hall continued to put up a good front for another couple of months, holidaying on the Turkish Riviera. But by then the gossip hounds were onto them. Keith was galled by the 'whole soap opera', and unimpressed by Mick's role as a faded drag queen in the film *Bent*. (While at his French château, Jagger enjoyed his Saturday night cross-dressing parties.) The Richards family, though nomadic, seemed positively quaint by comparison.

In September, Keith walked his daughter Angela, now twenty-six, down the aisle of a London church. An attractive woman who loved horses, she married a carpenter. Anita, Marlon and Keith's two younger children were there. Everyone was very polite. The kids had firm handshakes. No one seemed like demon spawn. People saw Keith chugging away on stage and imagined that was the whole story. But, more and more, his strength lay in roots and domesticity.

The Stones put out another live album in November. With its cheesy effects and intros mired in endless takes on 'How you doin', America?', *No Security* opted for musical tourism rather than a sense of place. It sank overnight.

On 17 December, Keith got up onstage at the Life Club, New York, to jam on Run Rudolph with Ronnie Spector. 'The way he tucked in to the overall sound was unique,' says the guitarist Lenny Kaye, who was on the bill. 'That rhythm was just so singular and playful – something you don't get from Nineties music.' The next day, Keith turned fifty-five.

A month later, the Stones were back on the road. Tommy Hilfiger put up the cash to sponsor a so-called *No Security* leg of the never-ending tour. The band took the whole show indoors, stripped the stage, and shed some of the old evergreens. Out went warhorses like Satisfaction and Miss You, replaced by Jagger's poignant commentary on his marriage. Some Girls became a pissed-off snarl, while sharp-eared critics noted the ad-libbed 'Get outta my life/go fuck my wife/don't look back' in Respectable. For the first time in thirty years, Keith did the timeless You Got The Silver, his love ode to Anita.

No Security boasted one or two other changes. The gaunt, sloe-eyed Keith had dyed what remained of his hair blue, then dressed it with baubles and ribbons. It made for a late-seasonal effect, like a badly moulting Christmas tree. Conversely, he'd never sounded better. Instead of rehashing the stadium set yet again, Keith came up with something riskier and more surprising, not just rock's Old Devil doing his bit. Moonlight Mile (*Sticky Fingers*) and Shine A Light (*Exile*) both came out of the closet, and a long bluesy set, including Route 66, made even Madison Square Garden feel like the Marquee club.

Rolling Stone called the new tour 'leaner and more musical, [played] on a stage uncluttered with inflatables or cherry pickers'. Keith was in 'all his ragged glory', mixing the little-heard ballads with carefully preserved crown jewels like Happy.

While Keith had been home with his wife and teenage daughters, the multi-timing Mick was in the divorce court. Early in 1999 Jerry Hall filed for a separation and reportedly demanded £30 million. Jagger contested the action on the grounds that they were never formally married, thus in the tabloids' view bastardizing his two youngest children. The twenty-two-year relationship was legally wound up that July.

Meanwhile, Jerry rang her friend Patti Hansen to warn her to keep an eye on the Stones' money. Keith told Patti he didn't give a shit about it, but there always seemed enough of the stuff to go round.

Keith added that he didn't talk to Jagger about his love life. 'I'm always sorry for Mick's women, because they end up crying on my shoulder. And I'm like, How do you think I feel? I'm *stuck* with him.'

Babylon/No Security officially ended on 20 April 1999, in San Jose. A brief Euro tour was bolted on from late May to mid-June. As well as gigs in Spain, Italy and Germany, the Stones finally remembered their London fans. The two Wembley shows were rescheduled. A year earlier, they'd upset everyone – the taxman, the critics and the audience – and, for the first time in decades, there were rows of empty seats on the band's homecoming.

Tuesday 8 June. The Stones fired up with a gig at the Shepherd's Bush Empire, where the balcony included Anita and Marianne Faithfull. Meanwhile, huge billboards proclaimed *Bridges to Babylon* as THE CLASSIC

NEW ALBUM. And, as a more realistic slogan: 'First UK appearances in four years!' Hairy and bedraggled, thin smiles pasted over their craggy features, Keith, Mick, Charlie and Ron squinted out from every possible cranny. Friendly critics called the two shows that weekend (with tickets around £40) the band's biggest ever, but this was a stretch, as was a banner hanging off Wembley's doomed terrace reading 'Jagger for PM', which merely confirmed the low standing of politics in modern Britain. Patti and Anita were both backstage with Bert Richards, now confined to a wheelchair after suffering a stroke. Keith proudly spoke of the steel bond – he tapped the bracelet on his left wrist – he and his father enjoyed. Ten days later, the tour wound down in Cologne. Keith's two younger daughters joined Leah Wood and Lizzy Jagger for some backing vocals. Patti surprised her husband by coming out to hand him his guitar.

The late Nineties belonged to the Stones. They'd now grossed $300 million since the day they drove into New York to announce 'a few quiet' gigs.

Keith went home to Connecticut and made a determined effort to kick the road. He started getting up at seven in the morning, an hour at which he'd normally be enjoying a nightcap. After a few weeks, he was driving his two girls to school.

Back to London in November for the *Q* awards. Keith, who was getting a 'special merit' gong, ate nothing at the formal lunch. He did, however, turn up with his own supply of Stoli. *The Times'* David Sinclair happened to be in the next seat, struggling to wrench the top off a bottle of beer. Richards reached over and smacked it open on the edge of the table. Froth spewed out into people's laps. 'That should do it,' Keith said calmly.

All was good cheer. Everyone laughed a bit. Keith told them it was an old trick he'd learnt from 'forty years of hanging around in dressing rooms'.

Later in the meal, he accidentally stubbed his cigarette out on Patti's arm. She smiled evenly, apparently dismissing it as the kind of petty mishap bound to occur from time to time when you're sitting next to Keith Richards. His actual acceptance speech was superb, everyone agreed.

That same month, *Pulse* magazine asked Keith to list his ten desert-island discs. People who only saw him punching out the riffs had a shock coming. As well as the usual suspects like Otis Redding, there were picks from Louis Armstrong and Nat King Cole. At the very top of the list, Little Richard vied with Beethoven's third symphony.

At fifty-six Keith was constantly on the move, and constantly talking and laughing, too, saying so much you were amazed by how much he also heard. When listening to music, he reacted by sighing with pleasure or dismay, punching happily with his fist in the air or, in dire cases, yanking the disc out of the player. The general view was that Keith was blossoming. He responded to everything he saw and felt, and no one was ever in any doubt about what he wanted. Early in 2000, Keith was already lobbying Jagger for another tour. Unlike Mick, he felt the Stones were only really alive if they were onstage.

On 18 May, Eva Jagger died of heart failure at eighty-seven. Keith flew in from Connecticut for the London funeral, where he joined Mick, Joe and Chris Jagger, Jerry Hall and the other Stones. It was the first time in a year the band had been in the same room, and would be the last for two more. The next day, Mick was back on location producing the film *Enigma*. There would be no Stones tour in 2000. Keith slumped down in his hotel chair and said, 'Tick tock, tick tock' – the sound of another year passing by.

The strain of trying to mobilize the world's greatest and longest-running act, while at the same time keeping pace with two school-age children, proved too much. Keith closed his eyes and took a nap.

Later that month, a husband-and-wife team by the name of Mark Gaillard and Mary Anderson sued Jagger, Richards and the Dust Brothers over Mick's song Saint Of Me, which they claimed was lifted from their own 1979 tune Oh Yeah. Three weeks later, the US 9th Court of Appeals opened the way for Stephen LaVere, owner of the Robert Johnson copyright, to sue for royalties on Love In Vain and Stop Breaking Down, which had long been credited to 'Trad'. Both cases were defended by the Stones, and would continue. Woody, meanwhile, having extended his tour regimen back home in London, now checked into the Priory to dry out. Charlie Watts was incommunicado on his Devon farm, where he liked to play with his twenty-nine dogs or sit, in motoring cap and goggles, behind the wheel of his 1937 Lagonda Rapide. (Since Charlie hadn't learnt to drive, the car never left the garage.) He had no intention of going back on tour anytime soon.

Keith himself spent a month at Redlands, where he seemed to fly lower than in New York or Jamaica. Both hip and nostalgic, his taste was Middle British: he loved books, dogs, horses and, above all, the Sussex countryside. 'Get kicked out of England. Why the fuck should I be?' he railed. Marlon and his wife presented Keith with his first grandson, named

Orson. Later in the summer he left West Wittering for a rental home on Martha's Vineyard, Bill Clinton's pet resort, off the Massachusetts coast. Keith took his daughters into town to see the teen band 'N Sync. A few days later, he managed to slip back in himself and jam with the blues legend Hubert Sumlin.

On 22 September, Bert Richards died. He was eighty-five. Bert had lain peacefully asleep until, right at the end, he suddenly opened his eyes, looked round for Keith, smiled, and winked at him.

The 'steel bond' had held for eighteen years.

Two weeks later, Keith was up on stage in New York playing with Chuck Berry's old pianist Johnnie Johnson. He wouldn't stop working. The back catalogue was busy too, with Satisfaction enjoying a boom year; VH1 voted Keith's dream the 'best rock song ever', and there were fresh covers by everyone from Cat Power to Britney Spears. The Richards family lived quietly but well whether in Sussex, New England or the Caribbean. According to the *Sunday Times*, Keith was now worth £130 million.

He still wanted to work.

One night that winter, Keith hailed a cab outside a Lower Manhattan studio. Lit up on the car roof was an advertisement: 'The Hard Rock Café, Proud to feature fried items – chicken, onions, Keith Richards.' He fired off a letter, saying he'd worked hard to build up his reputation and would they remove the ads. They did.

Altogether, 2000 was a big year for Keith. He may not have toured, but he'd played with some of his childhood heroes, and was backstage at a clutch of shows. Many smaller clubs made their names merely by having him on the premises.

One such venue, Village Underground, had just been opened by Keith's friend Steve Weitzeman. Like most rock clubs, it banned smoking. 'I couldn't get Keith,' Weitzeman lamented. 'I wanted him for New Year's Eve. I told him I'd let him light up onstage, but he wouldn't come.' It was the principle of the thing. Nobody, not even a mate, was going to tell Keith what he could or couldn't do at a party.

January 2001. By now it was eighteen months, nearly nineteen, and the old war resumed. Keith was hot to trot, but Mick and his Jagged Films were busy elsewhere. *Enigma* was in post-production and there was more to come: internet cricket, apparently, as well as *The Man from Elysian Fields* and *Map of Love*. Talk of a new solo album. So Keith read history in Connecticut, casually playing on a few tribute CDs, and drolly inducting James Burton and Johnnie Johnson into the Hall of Fame. In the press room backstage, the three men were asked if, in retrospect, they'd do anything differently in their careers.

Keith: 'We'd shoot the lead singer.'

That spring, Keith and Jagger were in the odd position of having one of their songs adopted by the folks slashing funds and programmes from the new federal budget. The US Treasury department took You Can't Always Get What You Want (written about Marianne Faithfull, and smack use) as its theme tune while preparing George Bush's new spending plan. The Stones themselves, who some thought as much a brand as a band, were said to be worth £400 million. They got a special citation from the British Council for their part in the arts export boom. Mick let it be known that he wouldn't be averse to a knighthood. Some of his friends, including Prince Charles, expressed surprise he didn't have one already.

John Phillips' album Pay, Pack and Follow, with help from Keith and Mick, was finally out in May. Sadly Phillips himself had died, aged sixty-five, six weeks earlier.

One night that summer, Keith and Patti enjoyed dinner in Manhattan followed by a concert at Carnegie Hall. When they left through the stage door, a fan reportedly pushed out of the crowd, gave Keith a beautifully polished Fender and asked him to sign it. Clearly the street noise intruded, because Keith merely grunted, apparently assuming the guitar was a gift, grabbed it and made for his Cadillac. The car walloped the pavement, swerved from some pedestrians, and headed downtown.

The bewildered fan gave it a moment, then took off down Sixth Avenue in hot pursuit. He caught up with Keith's limo at a light and hammered on the front door. 'Piss off,' the driver invited him.

There was a brief pause, and the fan's eye tracked to the smoky rear window and back again. A goodly crowd had gathered to watch.

'I just want my guitar back.'

'Fuck you,' the driver answered. 'Buy another one.'

Some weeks later, Jagger got up on stage as part of the Concert for New York, following the 9/11 terrorist attacks. When Keith joined him, fresh from schmoozing backstage with Hillary Clinton, there was bedlam in the hall. It stopped dead for a brief eulogy to the fallen; but as soon as this ended the yelling started again. With the opening duh-duh-duddle-duh bass notes of Miss You, the two slowly began to morph into something larger than the bickering old couple they'd been in rehearsal just an hour before. Keith got a groove going in Salt Of The Earth, and the transformation was complete – they were the *greatest rock band in the world*! And the crowd went crazy.

The buildup to Jagger's fourth solo album, *Goddess in the Doorway*, his first in eight years, was reverential. There was a vanity TV documentary called *Being Mick*, giant billboards and commercials, with every media outlet bar al-Jazeera celebrating the Thanksgiving-day release. But the record itself drew a surprisingly mixed response. Writing in the *Sunday Times*, Dan Cairns called the film 'nightmarish, [as] the lambswool-sweatered grandad jived around his drawing room', and the album plain 'dismal'. Jagger had better luck in America. Many of the critics there noted that he came over as a far more solid citizen, with his antiques and oil paintings, than his Romeo image suggested. Some of the dailies called *Goddess* a gutsy Big Statement, showcasing Mick's ever-deepening interpretative skills and use of subtle phrasing techniques to broaden the scope of even the simplest lyrics.

Keith called it dogshit.

'I listened to three tracks,' he revealed, 'and gave up on it.' A reporter later asked him what, in particular, he didn't like about Jagger's solo albums. 'Wimpy songs, wimpy performance, bad recording,' Keith said. 'That's about it.' Keith had kinder words when George Harrison died, aged fifty-eight, later that month. 'Let's hope he's jamming with John.' Harrison had been the one to urge the Stones on Decca's Dick Rowe back in May 1963.

Goddess dashed some of the high hopes that Mick had for it. On its first day, it sold fewer than 1,000 copies in the UK, compared with the 80,000 Robbie Williams' latest managed. Not long after that, a Stones spokesman announced that the band would tour again in 2002.

Going to a New York film première that Christmas, Keith now found his car surrounded by six armed US marshals who had apparently mistaken him for a crazed drug lord. After a bit the feds all backed off, red-faced, and started asking for his autograph. Keith was extremely gracious about it.

In the new year, Richards provided a brief but deft foreword to Robert Gordon's biography of Muddy Waters. Keith's essay wasn't just moving; it was rich, droll and crisply phrased. His prose style was fabulously lucid. Once again, it showed the gap between the man and the image he lugged round with him. He and Jagger soon enjoyed the accolade of appearing on *The Simpsons*. Keith balked only when *Fortune* magazine called Mick the 'sole business brain' behind the Stones. 'We're a mom and pop operation,' he corrected them. 'He's mom, I'm pop.'

Later in the spring, the talk turned back to solo projects.

Keith: 'I think that everybody – with the possible exception of Mick himself – has learnt the lesson that he's really good when he's with the Stones. But when he ain't, I don't think anybody gives a fuckin' toss.'

Thus it was that Keith, Mick, Charlie and Ron met up, for the first time in two years, aboard a bright yellow Zeppelin hovering above the Bronx. It was 7 May 2002. Presently the Stones' blimp landed in Van Cortlandt park, where its famous passengers strolled across the lawn and took the usual questions. Yes, they were touring. No, you wouldn't have thought it – not forty years ago, anyway, when it all began. As the band stood there in their shades and bandanas, with Charlie looking bereaved, even their crumpled faces seemed endearing: they were like Merrie Melody cartoon heroes – no matter how often shot, vaporized, tossed off cliffs, they always bounce back and get on with the show. They were doing it, as Keith said so succinctly, because 'it's fun'.

After negotiating with Klein for a day and a night, the Stones agreed to put out a definitive greatest-hits album, the first to include songs from the band's pomp as well as from the three decades that followed.

Keith and Jagger flew to Paris to cut four new tracks and assorted outtakes, of which there were dozens, for the package. Don Was produced. Mick was, by consensus, the driving force at the sessions. What he wanted to happen tended to happen, and what he didn't tended not to. Things moved at top speed. Six days later, Keith concluded proceedings with his usual busted-heart ballad, this one called Losing My Touch.

Jagger, who'd been seeing various models and starlets including Sophie Dahl, Amanda de Cadenet and the 'cracker from Caracas' Vanessa Neumann, now sued his ex-chauffeur Keith Badgery. Badgery had written a book revealing that Mick wasn't the shy, retiring type. Jagger and his solicitor characterized the lurid accounts of his love life as 'baloney'. Much of their specific legal complaint against Badgery remained under wraps. When announcing some *Babylon*-era gigs, Mick had capered up to the mike to face yet more bonk-related jibes. 'Maybe groupies don't fancy me any more,' he'd said, thus tucking the press neatly into his pocket. When he came on stage nowadays people roared with glee, and he gave them just enough – a crotch poke, a mike stuffed down his pants – to signal that, while it was only rock 'n roll, the randy old goat was lurking just behind the performance. Sex succeeded where every other image, sooner or later, had failed. Mick was in the tabloids almost every day now.

In early June rock's elder statesmen, including Sirs Paul, Cliff and Elton, lined up to play at the Queen's jubilee concert. Keith, the former royal chorister, wasn't interested.

The entire Stones apparatus nearly ground to a halt a week later, when Jagger rang Richards with his news. The one-time Prisoner 7856 at Brixton Prison was being knighted. Keith, who saw it as rank hypocrisy, was foam-flecked. He vowed to pull out of the tour – a move that would have left some 300 people jobless and millions gobsmacked – while Mick kept repeating, 'But Tony Blair *insists* I take it.' The triumph of graft and perseverance that had, almost incredibly, led to this scene had begun fifty years earlier, when Eva Jagger took her elder son in hand. Now the supposed hellraiser was filling his houses with Old Masters and fine wine. Mick had embarked on a Late Period, and it was she who took him there.

A month later, Keith still wasn't happy. 'I went berserk and bananas,' he told *Mojo*, 'at [Jagger's] blind stupidity.' Keith particularly objected to his always being told such news on the phone, not face to face. He denied it was just knighthood envy on his part. 'I doubt they thought of offering me one, because they know what I would've said ... They knew I'd tell 'em where they could put it.'

Keith's good humour gradually returned, along with the carefully sharpened jokes. By August he was laughing it off as 'a paltry honour. I told him, "Hold out for the lordship, mate."' In private, Richards reportedly referred to Jagger by the slightly extended title of 'His Royal Fuckin' Highness'.

On that note the Stones and crew began six weeks of rehearsals in Toronto. They put in six nights a week at the Masonic Temple, paring 140 songs down to a working set of twenty-five. Prince Rupert, Michael Cohl and various lawyers, accountants and publicists came and went. The band's gatekeepers, sleek young women with mobiles, now allowed the press to glimpse their stars only at Halley's Comet-like intervals. And in return for access they insisted on certain strict preconditions: never, for instance, ask Keith about drugs or Mick about women. If everyone behaved, the

PRs were chatty and affable, and many of their phone conversations closed with a toot of optimism: 'Super! Lovely! Fan*tastic!*' Whole planeloads of stylists were also landing in Toronto. Jagger now had his own travelling fashion guru, one Maryam Malakpour. Even Richards, we learn, allowed his hair to be dressed with 'Bumble & Bumble Tonic, Grooming Creme and Lotion, available from selected salons'. There were large photo spreads in everything from *Fortune* to *Vanity Fair*. Some two months later, Keith was back on the cover of *Rolling Stone*. Although bare-chested and bleary, as if only just staggering from his bed to the shoot, the fine print credits three lines of helpers. The actual photographs were terrific, all agreed.

The story that 16 August had a familiar ring: Stones to play secret club gig in Toronto. While much of the rock world was honouring the twenty-fifth anniversary of Elvis' death, the band gave their first show of the new century at the tiny Palais Royale. One key difference from 1977: afterwards, Richards went back to a rented estate with split-rail fences and high walls, rather than to the Harbour Castle hotel.

Re security, Keith now lodged a motion with West Sussex council to move an ancient public footpath away from Redlands. He complained that the path, within ten yards of his back door, left him at risk of a 'George Harrison-type nutter attack'. Keith won his case.

The Stones took their past back to the bank with the new anthology, *Forty Licks*. The first of the two CDs was sublime. You marvelled again at how Keith could swing out or keep it short and sharp as a ransom note. Although the second half sagged in parts, the album duly rose as though fuelled by Viagra. It was a critical and popular smash.

3 September, Boston. The curving hallways of the Fleet Center this Tuesday night are lined with walkie-talkie aides squawking 'Stones party en route!' As the handlers bark commentary there's a roar from out of the dark arena and a nearby, softer sound, echoed from man to man on the backstage ramp: 'Aawrite? Aawrite? Aawrite?' The Stones are three twitchy figures in black, and Charlie. On the other side of the scrim there's now an abbatoir-like lowing. Loud tribal drums play on the p.a. On a nod Keith steps forward, Mick following, and hits the riff of Street Fighting Man. The audience goes nuts.

The next two hours would be a glorious rebellion against the march of time. There were generous helpings of *Banquet* and *Exile*, a sexy, transcendent Gimme Shelter and Keith's playful version of Soul Train. Midnight Rambler ranked up there with the original. Working on their smallest stage in thirty years, the band put the premium back on music rather than showbiz glitz. (The sole props: a $5 million screen, and the B-stage.) Everything sounded digitally sharp, but *loud*. Howls of 'Keef!' and 'Mick!' rang from the rafters. This first-night audience had come to be pleasured, and you could feel them willing the show on. Some of them had paid $400 to be there. No wonder Keith seemed to bow in thanks to those in the premium seats down front.

He looked fairly scary. While one or two of the satellite Stones, like Darryl Jones, had gone to pot, the band themselves roared on like well-preserved vintage hot-rods. Old, but cool. With his tanned, leathery face and makeup Keith himself bore more than a slight resemblance to a Red Indian. His playing, too, managed to sound both elegant and raw. Charlie and the rejuvenated Wood funked up even the newer numbers. Jagger's anxious cockerel strut came out on Brown Sugar. He changed clothes six times during the performance. The big finale: Mick in a Joseph-style 'fantasy coat'. This item had begun quite sensibly, with just a tongue logo stitched to the shoulder, but had evolved beyond all common sense: scraps of denim and leather, silk squares printed with design motifs from previous tours, a Jeff Koons swirl, splashes of red and blue, multiple pockets and zips and shiny brass buttons all went into the mix. It got a special little gasp.

Later that night, Keith went into a backstage room and posed for *Rolling Stone* sporting just his pants, a guitar and a ratchet knife. That one shot, looming out of the cover on 17 October, headed all the annual readers' favourites polls. Various critics spoke of it as 'classic', 'timeless', a 'welcome reminder that not everyone cops out'. It was as if rock 'n roll had decided it was through with all this wholesome crap and gloriously gone back to basics.

For the next three months the Stones mixed it up in a variety of domes, arenas and clubs, sometimes all in the same town. As a result they sold fewer tickets, but at a higher price – in some cases $500 for a ringside seat. After *Babylon*, it seemed it couldn't have got any bigger, and yet it did. They now grossed some $90 million before Christmas.

The band's main competition in 2002 were men like Elton, McCartney and Neil Diamond. Even the Eagles sold millions of tickets. A few cynics asked how such characters would have felt if in 1967, the year of *Satanic*

Majesties and drug busts, the big draws had been Rudy Vallee and other Jazz Age crooners who sang through a megaphone. The Stones didn't care. They continued to favour their old repertoire, and they also continued to do it better than anybody.

Nowadays, too, they could handle any format. The Stones moved between the largest shed and the smallest dive, with a few unscheduled stops along the way. After an Altamont, Chicago's 4,000-seat Aragon Ballroom must have seemed like someone's living room. Wild Horses got an outing at the fringe gigs, with Sheryl Crow stepping up to duet with Jagger. Keith's touch-of-twang rendition of Thru And Thru stole the show at the downtown mega-concerts. As the Toronto critic wrote, 'His performance brought a moment of real contingency and punch to an otherwise tightly scripted recollection of youthful rebellion.' In one west coast gig, Keith unstrapped his guitar and sang Slipping Away in a low, husky voice, turning what could have been merely sappy into a confession – a catalogue of all that he'd tried and failed to be. By the time the lights came up, and Mick reappeared, even the most gnarled fan was sitting forward in a state of rapt attention. You don't get many moments like that in the Tacoma Dome.

On 16 November the Stones played in Vegas, at what was billed as the world's most expensive birthday party. The hippy turned lawyer David Bonderman paid them $6 million to entertain him and his 1,500 guests. Part one of the *Licks* tour ended in Nashville.

Despite the bleak Connecticut weather, Christmas and New Year's were palmy days for Keith. The press came calling, and he got to rag on Sir Mick again. Meanwhile, both album and tour were busily selling each other. The US recession, which did for several other music and sports events, never showed its teeth at the Stones' door. They went back on the road from early January, in Montreal. By now some of the northern audiences had taken to smuggling in not dope but hot chocolate, and sat watching the show in their coats and hats. Yet they, too, responded as people everywhere responded to Keith, by cheering and stomping and howling for more.

Five years earlier, Mick Jagger had talked about licensing Start Me Up to Microsoft. 'I fucking hated it,' he said. 'The rest of the band loved it. I just don't wanna be involved with this stuff. I don't want my songs to be used in television ads.'

Keith just shrugged, then reminded Mick of what he might have preferred to forget, the time the two of them had written a catchy jingle for Rice Krispies. In early 2003, the Stones allowed Ford to use Start Me Up to promote their new cars.

It teemed millions. Keith, of course, didn't bother to stop and count the stuff. He was too busy performing, with little heed for geography, in Chicago, LA and Manhattan. On 18 January the Stones' return to Madison Square Garden set a live-TV record. The mayor of New York, Michael Bloomberg, was supposedly livid when Keith calmly smoked his way through the concert, in defiance of a new city-wide ban. Ever huger grosses and history-making deals. The whole franchise, from high-end publishing rights, down to the fifty different pieces of official merchandise, was well tended on Keith and Mick's behalf. Later that month, Allen Klein chanced on a rogue video about the band's early days, and was moved to mark his displeasure with litigation. Keith had been the one to speak up loudest for Klein right from the start. He'd told the band that the guy was sharp, sure, but that he also had the clout to turn cheap singles and one-nighters into well-promoted albums, tours and – who knew? – even films. The strategy was known in the trade as 'going Elvis'. Over time, it worked better than anyone had expected.

By mid February, when the American tour ended, the Stones were basking in the best reviews of their career. They still set the standard for remorselessly honest rock 'n roll, with no gratuitous solos or 'clever bastard' frills. In an era of pre-packaged, computer pop they were strutting out gloriously ragged tunes like Rocks Off. Keith's rumpled face was in itself an affront to the scrubbed, aerobicized figures bouncing around on MTV. He was enormous fun to watch.

On 6 February, for the first time since Altamont, the Stones played a freebie; done partly as a favour to Mick's friend Steve Bing (the father of Liz Hurley's son), it touted the Resources Defense Council, an environmental group. The American gigs then wound up on a Saturday night in Vegas. A few days later, Keith and the band were flying around Australia and the Far East.

They smashed records there, too.

After that, there was little to report on but Keith's looks. In a business that considers neutral a style and bland a statement, he may have been the most colourful living rock star. Like Austin Powers, Richards was brazenly old-fashioned, a throwback to the age of clanking chains and skull rings.

Silk shirts splayed open to the navel. Keith's hair, which he claimed he cut himself, again enjoyed cult status. Some thought his face reptilian, while to others it was earthy, sixty years old but looking good at any age. The very idea of Keef-the-geezer is a joke we never seem tired of. A standard gag was that, after a nuclear holocaust, only cockroaches and him would be left alive.

Keith: 'Poor old cockroaches.'

That spring, the seemingly unstoppable tour roved up the Pacific to the Yellow Sea, until recently virgin turf for rock 'n roll of the sort ancient map-makers used to label 'here be dragons'. The more operatic show the Stones brought with them went down well, and Keith learnt that he had fans on five continents, as well as his friends in North Africa. The band played in Bangalore and Mumbai, though long-awaited concerts in China were cancelled because of the SARS panic. Even in Indian press conferences, the questions would always be the same: drugs for Richards, sex for Jagger, and age for them both.

Keith himself had responded to Mick's resurgent love life by telling *Rolling Stone*, 'Chicks see the other side of me, which guys don't. I have a good empathy with women. Nobody ever divorced *me*.'

Three weeks passed without a word from the Stones. Then came the European gigs: Vienna (where the government issued a stamp in their honour), Paris, London. 'The sound of the Sixties', as in Keith and Mick's age, now replaced earlier gags about antiques roadshows. The band finally played Twickenham, after cancelling the night before when Mick felt ill, just forty years after a gig down the B361 at Eel Pie Island. In the interim, their fee had risen from £60 to a reported £4 million. They'd also seen off eight British prime ministers, nine US presidents. Watching Keith backstage with his family, clutching a small dog, told you almost everything about the man. In private he wasn't the thug beloved of men's-magazine fiction but, instead, warm, smart and almost absurdly mild-mannered.

Keith drank mineral water most of that hot Sunday afternoon. Then just before showtime, he filled a pint mug of Stoli and added a few drops of orange juice. The band met up in a backstage marquee, shook hands, and walked down a tunnel to the arena. This time, Twickenham roared.

At the end, Keith came out for a final bow and stood between Mick and Charlie. The three of them held their fists aloft and shouted something back into the din.

But no one heard. Their words were drowned by cheers.

Keith went back to Connecticut, where he did some recording in his basement, walked and sailed, read his usual quota of books. 'I have no fixed routine,' he said. 'I wander about the house, wait for the maid to clean the kitchen, then fuck it all up again and do some frying.'

When Keith was home, he exuded everything that had made him an institution and, increasingly, an anachronism: his intelligence, his elegance, his spontaneity, his wit – and an air of brute determination enhanced by his classic punched-in boxer's nose. A charmer, rough and smooth at once. Well aware of his legend. 'People should say, Isn't it amazing ... Here's hope for you all,' he announced. 'Just don't use my diet.' Most nights Keith still enjoyed a hefty shot or two. Besides vodka, there was cognac, rum, wine and a drink of dynamite strength a guest describes simply as 'spirits'. Keith, who had no use for doctors, claimed he was never sick.

Patti Richards ate mainly fruits and salads, and drank only water. Her idea of extravagance was a day out at the local Health & Wellness spa. She and Keith made a striking couple. He described their two teenage girls, Theodora and Alexandra, as his best mates. 'If they got a problem, they come and talk to me. They've grown up with people whose idea of me ... who knows what they've been told at school? But they know who I am.'

Anita was back from the brink in London, where she enjoyed fame as a designer and an occasional model of swastika-emblazoned shoes. Marlon and Angela were both happily married. Keith and Mick Jagger still regularly exchanged tapes and song ideas, even on the days they had nothing else in common. Brian Jones was in Cheltenham, on a green hill overlooking the church where he'd sung as a choirboy. The old flat at Edith Grove had been turned into a battered-women's refuge.

Keith told anyone who asked that he was still around because he'd taken the trouble 'to find out who I am'. And who he wasn't. 'I ain't gonna live in the box people want to put me in,' he'd say. 'That's their trip; it's not mine.'

Keith would talk a lot about the box. The box was the reverse of keeping it real. It was phony, corrupt and exclusive. Instead, he wanted truth, spontaneity ('Mick has to dictate to life,' Keith said; 'to me, life's a wild animal'), and harmony for all. 'Music's the best communicator ... And I doubt anybody would disagree, if they think about it, that a lot of the reason you've got some sort of – whether you wanta call it "togetherness" – anyway, some major shifts in superpower situations in the last few years has an awful lot to do with the last twenty years of music, or just music in general. It's like the walls of Jericho again.'

It wasn't just the freewheeling and good vibes, though, that earned Keith the respect of his peers. He could be 'fucking heavy', too, a colleague recalls. 'I mean, the guy goes around armed.' Still, Keith's rages, if dark, tended to be brief. He also had a quiet and long-standing habit of helping others less lucky than himself. Bad debts would be forgiven, old foes rung up and invited for a drink. Wayne Perkins, who had nearly joined the Stones instead of Woody, suffered some serious health problems years later. 'Keith was great,' he says. 'I thought it was a cool thing for him to do, something he didn't have to do, to rally round. And I'm sure I'm only one of the people he's helped out.' Keith gave his time and money generously, and, rare in his world, always anonymously.

As Stu said, 'I saw the old devil do good deeds on the sly.'

In the end, some people wondered whether the strangest thing about Keith Richards might be that, beneath a veneer of total self-indulgence, he was a kind and deeply moral man.

When the Stones got started, even the two guitar players had thought they might last eighteen months. Now Keith could look back on a forty-year career that had cost him at least five court appearances, a miserable night in jail, frenzied assaults by fans, cracked ribs, blackened eyes and a near-electrocution, assorted car crashes, mountainous legal and medical bills, and a permanent place on the Customs watch-list. And it was worth it.

Bibliography

Berry, Chuck, *Chuck Berry: The Autobiography*, New York: Harmony, 1987

Bockris, Victor, *Keith Richards*, New York: Poseidon, 1992

Bonanno, Massimo, *The Rolling Stones Chronicle*, London: Plexus, 1990

Booth, Stanley, *Keith*, New York: St Martin's Press, 1995
  The True Adventures of the Rolling Stones, New York: Random House, 1984

Carr, Roy, *The Rolling Stones, An Illustrated Record*, London: New English Library, 1976

Charone, Barbara, *Keith Richards*, London: Futura Publications, 1979

Cooper, Michael, with Terry Southern and Keith Richards, *The Early Stones*, New York: Hyperion, 1992

Dalton, David, *The Rolling Stones*, New York: Knopf, 1981

Davis, Stephen, *Old Gods Almost Dead*, New York: Broadway Books, 2001

Elliott, Martin, *The Rolling Stones: Complete Recording Sessions 1963–1989*, London: Blandford, 1990

Faithfull, Marianne, and David Dalton, *Faithfull*, Boston: Little, Brown, 1994

Flippo, Chet, *On the Road with the Rolling Stones*, New York: Doubleday, 1985

Greenfield, Robert, *A Journey Through America with the Rolling Stones*, New York: Dutton, 1974

Hall, Jerry with Christopher Hemphill, *Tall Tales*, London: Elm Tree Books, 1981

Hector, James, *The Complete Guide to the Music of the Rolling Stones*, London: Omnibus Press, 1995

Hotchner, A.E., *Blown Away: The Rolling Stones and the Death of the Sixties*, New York: Simon & Schuster, 1990

Jasper, Tony, *The Rolling Stones*, London: Octopus Books, 1976

McLagan, Ian, *All the Rage*, London: Sidgwick & Jackson, 1998

Mankowitz, Gered, *Satisfaction: The Rolling Stones Photographs*, London: Sidgwick & Jackson, 1984

Norman, Philip, *The Stones*, London: Elm Tree Books, 1984

Rawlings, Terry, Keith Badman and Andrew Neill, *Good Times Bad Times*, London: Complete Music Publications, 1997

Rolling Stones, The, *A Life on the Road*, New York: The Penguin Group, 1998

Sanchez, Tony, *Up and Down with the Rolling Stones*, New York: William Morrow, 1979

Sandford, Christopher, *Mick Jagger: Primitive Cool*, London: Gollancz, 1993

Scaduto, Anthony, *Mick Jagger*, London: W.H. Allen, 1974

Trudeau, Margaret, *Beyond Reason*, New York: Paddington Press, 1979

Warhol, Andy, *The Andy Warhol Diaries*, New York: Warner Books, 1989

Wood, Ron, with Bill German, *The Works*, London: Fontana, 1988

Wyman, Bill, with Ray Coleman, *Stone Alone*, London: Viking, 1990

Sources and Chapter Notes

SOURCE ONE FOR THE LIFE OF KEITH RICHARDS IS THE ROUGHLY 350 SONGS WRITTEN AND PERFORMED OVER THE COURSE OF FORTY YEARS. If nothing else, *Satisfaction* aims to pay due credit to the music as well as the man.

The following notes show at least the formal interviews, conversations and/or other material mined from around the world. I should particularly thank Tom Keylock and the late Frank Thorogood, both of whom shed light on Keith and the Stones during the 1960s. As well as those listed, I also spoke to a number of people who prefer not to be named. Where sources asked for anonymity – usually citing a healthy respect for Keith Richards' lawyers – every effort was made to get them to go on the record. Where this wasn't possible, I've used the words 'a friend' or 'a colleague', as usual. Once or twice, I've resorted to the formula of an alias. No acknowledgement thus appears of the help, encouragement and kindness I got from a number of quarters, some of them, as they say, household names.

Chapter 1

First up, I should admit that it's not clear whether Keith Richards in fact sang for the Queen at her coronation, or on a later date; both versions have appeared in print. It's the first question I would have asked him had he felt able to speak to me. I hope the reader will bear with the treatment I've given here, which is both plausible and has the added advantage of being topical.

If Keith didn't sing *Zadok* in Westminster Abbey on 2 June 1953, it's certain that he did so sometime that summer or early autumn. Moving forward, I should stress that I wasn't, personally, party to Keith's backstage routine in June 1999; the events here are a composite of published reports, a journalist friend admitted to the fabled Baboon Cage, and my own observation from Wembley's far reaches. I should also acknowledge reports in the *Los Angeles Times*, the *New York Times*, *People*, *Q*, the *Seattle Post-Intelligencer* and *The Times*. Tony Sanchez's *Up and Down with the Rolling Stones*, albeit labouring under its author's note of simulated moral outrage, is as good an account of 1973 as any.

Chapter 2

For events from 1943 until fame struck, exactly twenty years later, I'm grateful to a Dupree relative, an old source at Livingstone Hospital, Dartford, and the dozens of those who spoke to me either in 2002 or at the time of my Mick Jagger biography in 1993, notably Bob Beckwith, Alan Etherington, Eileen Giles, Charlie Gillett, Dick Heckstall-Smith, Peter Holland, Joe and the late Eva Jagger, Paul Jones, Carlo Little, Robin Medley, the late Yehudi Menuhin, David Pracy, Chris Rea, Clive Robson, Walter Stern, Dick Taylor. The last declined a formal interview this time around, but spoke to me at length, about both Richards and Jagger, in 1992–93. The Dartford *Chronicle* was a mine of information, as was Companies House and the UK Family Records Centre. I visited the scene of Keith Richards' youth. Secondary sources included Stanley Booth's *Keith* (New York: St Martin's Press, 1995), Stephen Davis' *Old Gods Almost Dead* (New York: Broadway Books, 2001), Philip Norman's *The Stones* (London: Elm Tree Books, 1984), my own *Primitive Cool* (London: Gollancz, 1993) and Bill Wyman's *Stone Alone* (London: Viking, 1990). A number of the Mick Jagger quotes, both here and elsewhere in *Satisfaction*, came from his *Rolling Stone* interview of 14 December 1995.

Anita Pallenberg's 'Brian broke up . . .' quote first appeared in Victor Bockris' *Keith Richards* (New York: Poseidon, 1992). There is no suggestion whatever that Keith and Mick Jagger ever shared a bed for anything but warmth, and that only in the coldest winter in over 200 years.

'Happy' (Jagger–Richards)
© EMI Music Publishing Ltd.

Chapter 3

Interviews and/or taped conversations, some conducted at the time of my Jagger biography, took place with Allan Clarke, Adam Faith, Chris Farlowe, Nick Gough, Ryan Grice, Jeff Griffin, the late Al Hendrix, David Jacobs, Edith Keep, Tom Keylock, Carlo Little, Gered Mankowitz, Mike Oldfield, Andy Peebles, Anthony Phillips, Mike Richards, Don Short, Chrissie Shrimpton, Robert Stigwood, Carol Ward, Walton Wilkinson. I should particularly credit *Melody Maker*, the *New York Times, Nova, Queen, Rolling Stone, The Times, Variety, Vogue*. It's also a pleasure to acknowledge, as any Stones author should, Victor Bockris' *Keith Richards*, Stanley Booth's *Keith* and, more especially, his *The True Adventures of the Rolling Stones* (New York: Random House, 1984), Barbara Charone's *Keith Richards* (London: Futura Publications, 1979), Stephen Davis' *Old Gods Almost Dead*, Philip Norman's *The Stones*, Anthony Scaduto's *Mick Jagger* (London: W.H. Allen, 1974) and Bill Wyman's *Stone Alone*. The Rolling Stones' *A Life on the Road* (New York: The Penguin Group, 1998) and their *25 x 5: The Continuing Adventures of the Rolling Stones* (CMV Video, 1989) were both useful; a number of short quotes by Keith Richards, included here, first appeared in one or both of them. I should thank the Gulf Beach Motel, Clearwater, Florida, and Companies House, London. I visited Redlands.

Keith Richards has often spoken of his first, paint-soaked meeting with Muddy Waters. It's only fair to point out that a number of those who knew Waters best, including Marshall Chess, aren't sure of the specifics but don't doubt the broad truth of the story. Chess remembers Keith, perhaps significantly, downing a large amount of sour mash on the historic day in question.

The Keith Altham quote, included here, first appeared in *Fabulous*; Keith Richards' 'takeaway chicken' and 'drinking Coke' quotes both appear in Stanley Booth's *The True Adventures of the Rolling Stones*; the two quotes from Linda Keith are both from Victor Bockris' *Keith Richards*; the Gered Mankowitz quote appears in *Satisfaction: The Rolling Stones Photographs of Gered Mankowitz* (London: Sidgwick & Jackson, 1984) – I also spoke to him at the time of my Jagger biography.

Keith Richards, in my and many people's opinion, acted with commendable restraint when Brian Jones began to self-destruct, and there's no suggestion Keith in any way accelerated the process. Just the opposite.

Chapter 4

Keith's purple patch was recalled by, among others, John Birt, the late James Coburn, Judy Flanders, Jeff Griffin, Joan Keylock, Tom Keylock, the late Alexis Korner, Terry Reid, Don Taylor, the late Frank Thorogood. On an institutional note, I'm grateful to the American Clinic, Tarn, HM Prison Service and the RN Officers Club, Portsmouth. I should also thank both Noel Chelberg for his always canny deconstruction of Keith Richards' songs, and David Waldman, formerly HM Coroner for East Sussex. I visited Cotchford Farm.

Secondary sources included *Life*, *Melody Maker*, *Metro*, the *News of the World* (5 February 1967), *Rolling Stone*, *Sounds*, *The Times*, *Vogue* and, particularly, both Stanley Booth's *The True Adventures of the Rolling Stones* and Albert & David Maysles' *Gimme Shelter* (Home Vision Cinema).

Keith Richards' 'We never actually *played* ...' quote first appeared in *Guitar Player* of December 1989. His 'We had to go down ...' quote is from *25 x 5*. Ian Stewart's 'Alitalia' quote appears in *The True Adventures of the Rolling Stones*.

As stated in the text, there's no suggestion that Allen Klein acted in any way illegally or improperly in his management of the Stones. By far their largest objection was that funds weren't always wired from New York as quickly as they might have liked.

Nor is there any suggestion in *Satisfaction* that Keith Richards or Mick Jagger ever expropriated any other musician's work, even if from time to time, and in keeping with standard songwriting practice, they accepted the help freely given them. Their guests' session fees were always paid in full.

'Street Fighting Man' (Jagger–Richards)
© ABKCO Music, Inc

Chapter 5

Comment on Keith's *Exile* and later period came from, among others, Dick Allen, Paul Bibire, Jeff Griffin, the late Eva Jagger, Joe Jagger, Tom Keylock, the late Alice Ormsby-Gore, Bill Plummer, Terry Reid, Don Short, Winston Stagers, the late Frank Thorogood, Lisbeth Vogl. I should particularly acknowledge Victor Bockris' *Keith Richards*, Stephen Davis' *Old Gods Almost Dead*, Robert Greenfield's *A Journey Through America with the Rolling Stones* (New York: Dutton, 1974) and, notably, Tony Sanchez's *Up and Down with the Rolling Stones*. I'm also grateful to the Edgwater Inn, Seattle.

Nick Kent's 'Lord Byron' quote and Marshall Chess' 'If the Stones finish tomorrow . . .' quote first appeared in Victor Bockris' *Keith Richards*. Keith Richards' 'I think Bianca . . .' quote and Jimmy Miller's 'Many mornings . . .' quote first appeared in Barbara Charone's *Keith Richards*. Tony Sanchez's 'Keith and I would take the children . . .', 'Later, when Anita phoned . . .' and 'perspiring profusely . . .' quotes are from his *Up and Down with the Rolling Stones*.

'(I Can't Get No) Satisfaction' (Jagger–Richards)
© ABKCO Music, Inc
'Can't You Hear Me Knocking?'/'Moonlight Mile'/'Dead Flowers' (Jagger–Richards)
© ABKCO Music, Inc
'Sweet Black Angel' (Jagger–Richards)
© EMI Music Publishing Ltd.
'Coming Down Again' (Jagger–Richards)
© EMI Music Publishing Ltd.
'Star Star' (Jagger–Richards)
© EMI Music Publishing Ltd.

Chapter 6

Keith's personal and creative highs – and the nadir of *Black and Blue* – were crisply brought home by Ross Benson, Geoff Bradford, the late Peter Cook, the late John Diefenbaker, Jeff Griffin, Bob Harris, the late Furry Lewis, Chris Page, Graham Parker, Don Peltz, Wayne Perkins. I'm particularly grateful to the last.

Secondary sources included the *New York Times*, *Rolling Stone*, *The Times*, the *Toronto Star* and virtually every UK and Canadian tabloid for the period 24 February–1 April 1977. I happened to meet Keith Richards myself the week before his ill-fated trip to the El Mocambo.

Other published sources included Bebe Buell with Victor Bockris, *Rebel Heart* (New York: St Martin's Press, 2001), Stephen Davis' *Old Gods Almost Dead* and Chet Flippo's *On the Road with the Rolling Stones* (New York: Doubleday, 1985).

The Mackenzie Phillips ('There was no telephone ...') quote first appeared in *Night and Day* of 7 October 2001; Anita Pallenberg's 'Keith was very calm ...' quote first appeared in Victor Bockris' *Keith Richards*; the majority of the Bebe Buell quotes are from her *Rebel Heart*; some of the brief quotes relating to January and February 1977 first appeared in Barbara Charone's *Keith Richards*. Richards' 'Mick was like Clapton ...' quote appears in *A Life On The Road*. I should credit, finally, *The Early Stones* by Michael Cooper, with text by Terry Southern and comments by Keith Richards (New York: Hyperion, 1992).

There is no suggestion, whatsoever, that Keith Richards' interest in militaria was ever anything more than a visual style appreciation – one shared by many people around the world.

'Time Waits For No One' (Jagger–Richards)
© EMI Music Publishing Ltd.
'Hey Negrita' (Jagger–Richards)
© EMI Music Publishing Ltd.
'Hot Stuff' (Jagger–Richards)
© EMI Music Publishing Ltd.
'Respectable' (Jagger–Richards)
© EMI Music Publishing Ltd.
'Before They Make Me Run' (Jagger–Richards)
© EMI Music Publishing Ltd.

Chapter 7

Keith's first great comeback was vividly recalled by, among others, the late Hal Ashby, Pete Brown, the late Peter Cook, Jeff Griffin, Lenny Kaye, Chris Page, Andy Peebles, Tim Rice, Don Short. I'm grateful to the source at the Hotel Finisterra, and to the Lewisboro, New York, Police Department.

Published sources included *Billboard*, *Life*, *Melody Maker*, *New Musical*

Express, the *New York Times*, the *Seattle Post-Intelligencer*, *Seattle Times*, *The Times*, *Variety*, *Vogue*. I should again particularly mention Chet Flippo's *On the Road with the Rolling Stones*.

Keith Richards' 'I'm ready for my bacon and eggs ...' quote first appeared in *Rolling Stone* of 21 August 1980; Anita Pallenberg's 'To a certain extent ...' quote appears in Victor Bockris' *Keith Richards*.

'All About You' (Jagger–Richards)
© EMI Music Publishing Ltd.
'Little T&A' (Jagger–Richards)
© EMI Music Publishing Ltd.

Chapter 8

Primary sources included the late William Burroughs (16 February 1995), Ryan Grice, Jeff Griffin, Edith Keep, Gered Mankowitz, Nick Miles, Andy Peebles, Terry Reid, Tim Rice, David Sinclair, Tony Smith, Don Taylor, Carol Ward, Adele Warlow. The Richards-Jagger feud of c. 1984–89 was well detailed in *Rolling Stone* and *USA Today*. I also read the *Daily Mirror*, the *New York Times*, the *Seattle Times*, the *Sun*, *The Times*, the *Toronto Star* and the *Washington Post*. I'm grateful to the source, who preferred anonymity, on the *Steel Wheels* tour.

Keith Richards' 'I've got everybody in town ...' quote first appeared in Stanley Booth's *Keith*.

'You Don't Move Me' (Richards–Jordan)
© Promopub B.V.

Chapter 9

Help in recalling the *Voodoo Lounge* era came from Allan Clarke, the late Peter Cook, Nick Gough, Jeff Griffin, Roger Hayes, Lenny Kaye, Edith Keep, Carlo Little, Tim Rice, David Sinclair, Don Taylor, Carol Ward. I enjoyed a VIP pass to the Rolling Stones shows in Seattle and Vancouver in December '94. I'm grateful to Mick Jagger's then secretary Janice Crotch, and to A&M Studios, Companies House and the Hollywood Roosevelt hotel.

Secondary sources included *Billboard*, *Guitar Player*, *Musician*, *People*, *Q*, *Rolling Stone*, the *Sunday Times*, *Vanity Fair*, *Variety*.

The 'Richards stepped out ...' quote first appeared in the *Seattle Times* of 19 January 1993; Keith Richards' 'I look around ...' quote first appeared in *Rolling Stone*, 25 August 1994.

'Sparks Will Fly' (Jagger–Richards)
© Promopub B.V.
'Not Fade Away' (Petty–Hardin)
© MPL Communications, Inc.

Chapter 10

Parting comment from: Tom Keylock, Chris Page, Wayne Perkins, Bill Plummer, Terry Reid, David Sinclair, Carol Ward; I'm grateful, too, to Terry Lambert, Vince Lorimer and the Villars. The backstage reports are a composite of eyewitness and published accounts. Secondary and/or printed sources included *Mojo*, the *New Yorker*, the *New York Times*, *People*, *Pulse*, *Q*, *Rolling Stone* and the *Sunday Times*.

Keith Richards' 'Music's the best communicator . . .' quote first appeared in Stanley Booth's *Keith*.

'Respectable' (Jagger–Richards)
© EMI Music Publishing Ltd.

Index

Note: MJ stands for Mick Jagger; BJ for Brian Jones; AP for Anita Pallenberg; KR for Keith Richards; RS for the Rolling Stones. Song titles are given 'in quotes'; titles of record albums, films and books are in *italics*.